MW00714892

YANKEE
DOODLE
DANDY

YANKEE DOODLE DANDY

BRIAN MULRONEY and the AMERICAN AGENDA

MARCI McDONALD

Copyright © 1995 by Marci McDonald

All rights reserved. No part of this publication may be
reproduced or transmitted in any form or by any means,
electronic or mechanical, including photocopying, recording,
or any information storage and retrieval system,
without permission in writing from the publisher.

Published in 1995 by
Stoddart Publishing Co. Limited
34 Lesmill Road
Toronto, Canada
M3B 2T6
Tel. (416) 445-3333
Fax (416) 445-5967

Stoddart Books are available for bulk purchase for
sales promotions, premiums, fundraising, and seminars. For details,
contact the Special Sales Department at the above address.

Canadian Cataloguing in Publication Data

McDonald, Marci
Yankee Doodle Dandy: Brian Mulroney and the American agenda

Includes index.
ISBN 0-7737-2880-5

1. Mulroney, Brian, 1939–   . 2. Canada –
Politics and government – 1984–1993.* 3. Canada –
Relations – United States. 4. United States –
Relations – Canada. I. Title.

FC630.M33 1995   971.064'7   C95-930052-X
F1034.2.M33 1995

Cover Design: the boy 100 and
Tannice Goddard, S.O. Networking
Printed and bound in Canada

Stoddart Publishing gratefully acknowledges the support of the
Canada Council, the Ontario Ministry of Culture, Tourism,
and Recreation, Ontario Arts Council, and Ontario Publishing Centre
in the development of writing and publishing in Canada.

To my mother, Sherry Young,
who gave me my spirit
and my American roots

The merchant has no country.
— Thomas Jefferson

Contents

Acknowledgments

*Y*ANKEE DOODLE DANDY was made possible by the 1992 Atkinson Fellowship in Public Policy, and portions of several chapters, plus additional research, were first printed in the *Toronto Star* in October 1993. As part of that process, I'm immensely grateful for the support of John Honderich, the patience of Dr. Abraham Rotstein, and the editing of John Ferri. Enormous thanks as well to Jack Stoddart, who persuaded me to turn that research into a book and who had already demonstrated that, even if Mulroney or the Conservatives remained in power, he had the courage to publish it. His patient and encouraging managing editor, Don Bastian, kept his belief in the project even when mine flagged. Charis Wahl offered a helpful first reading. And Sandy Farran, my indefatigable Toronto researcher, astonished me with her kindness, good spirits, and enterprising intelligence. To Rosemary Shipton, who bore with me through the final edit, offering inspiration, wise counsel, and, most cherished of all, laughter when it was sorely needed, I can only say thank you for restoring my faith in the gifts that an extraordinary, insightful editor can bring to the all-too-solitary process of book writing.

Of course, this exercise would never have been possible without *Maclean's*, particularly its former editor Kevin Doyle, who gave me a nine-year ringside seat on Washington even when I was not sure I wanted one. His successor, Bob Lewis, and senior editor Ann Dowsett Johnston have both showed forbearance over the past eighteen months while I finished writing a book whose perceptions in no way reflect the views of the magazine or the corporation that now owns it. And a special thanks to Charlie Peters, the legendary Washington windmill-tilter, who took me under his wing, gave me faith in my voice at a time when I had lost it, and first published a version of "Partying to Win" in his *Washington Monthly* magazine.

But most of those who sustained me throughout a difficult move back to Canada after seventeen years have no official connection to this book at all. Two who deserve the most credit are my parents, Jim and Sherry Young, who offered constant cheerleading and who never complained when they saw almost as little of me as when I lived in Paris and Washington. Of the many journalistic colleagues who shared their time and experiences with me, I'd like to single out Stevie Cameron, Bob Collison, E. Kaye Fulton, Robert Fife, Lawrence Martin, Peter Moon, and Allan Robinson, as well as my former *Maclean's* bureau-mate Ian Austen. Among those friends who never ceased to astonish with their support are Elaine and Stephen Dewar, who offered hospitality on my trips from Washington, and, throughout their own professional ordeals, demonstrated an awesome capacity for both editorial acuity and friendship; Diana Crosbie, who brought flowers and her lifelong gift for making me laugh in my most cheerless hours; and Jeanne Laux, whose incisive perceptions and tireless fax give a new meaning to the notion of thoughtfulness. Norma Greenaway, my respected Southam News Service colleague from Washington, always knew when it was time to call in from Cyprus or Cairo with a reminder that, at its best, journalism can be a magnanimous profession. And never will I be able to repay the generosity of spirit of Norma Geddes, with her equally uncanny ability to reach out from Richmond, Virginia. Finally, to the gang at Prem, thank you for the gift of Courage.

Prologue

IT WAS MY FIRST WEEK ON THE JOB, and, in a sense, it was his as well. On September 24, 1984, a week after being sworn in as prime minister, Brian Mulroney flew into Washington to cement his ties to Ronald Reagan, who had already realigned the American political landscape. Now pundits were crediting Mulroney with extending that neoconservative gospel north of the border, predicting he would refashion Canada in the image of Reagan's America. But would he? Could he? And how would Canadians react to such a repudiation of their institutions and values? Those questions still hung in the air on the steamy afternoon that I presented myself to the Secret Service guardhouse at the White House gate — the beginning of a nine-year odyssey charting Mulroney's increasingly ardent embrace of the American way.

For a reporter who had just arrived from Paris to take over *Maclean's* Washington bureau, the assignment provided an instant immersion in bilateral relations at the very moment they were being reborn. The pomp, the caricatural U.S. patriotism, and the constant reminders of the inequity of Canada's clout as a continental room-mate — all were on vivid display as I joined the White House press corps for a privileged insider's glimpse of that first official visit to the U.S. capital. For a brief, heady moment I found myself swept along on a jostling tide of reporters and cameramen pouring into the sacrosanct confines of the Oval Office, where the two leaders sat in their ivory brocade armchairs, posing for what had become the high art of the Reagan administration — the staged photo op. At the time, I marvelled at the showbiz quality of the public ritual, more meticulously articulated than any extravaganza I had ever covered in Hollywood. But six months later I was back on the set, this time perched uncertainly across from Reagan in one of those brocade chairs — a designated photo op myself.

Before his Shamrock Summit with Mulroney in Quebec City, *Maclean's* had been chosen by the White House for an exclusive interview with the president. There was only one hitch: not only would written questions have to be submitted in advance but the answers would come back in the same form. While the magazine finally acquiesced to that decidedly unusual journalistic practice, the editor, Kevin Doyle, insisted that I be given at least a few minutes with Reagan and an opportunity to lob some impromptu queries his way. Preparing for that encounter, I had stopped by the State Department for a briefing by Jim Medas, the personable Reaganaut who had been rewarded for his campaign services in California by being named to head the Canada desk. "Did you get the answers to those questions back yet?" he inquired. When I assured him I had not, he scratched his head. "That's funny," he puzzled. "I sent them over the other day."

With that gaffe, Medas had acknowledged the administration's open secret — the depth of which I would see played out a day later when I showed up for my presidential rendezvous. For once, I was instructed to avoid the cramped White House press room. Instead, I was directed to an official doorway through which I had watched countless dignitaries disappear. Ushered past a rifle-toting Marine guard and minor columns, I found myself in a vestibule whose décor offered a disconcerting sight: a taxidermist's glass-walled heaven of stuffed wildlife. But soon the vestibule began to fill up: Thursday, it turned out, was Photo Op Afternoon at the White House when the president did his political gladhanding — occasionally, it was later revealed, in return for secret donations to his cherished Contras. On this particular afternoon, however, no Republican sugar daddies were in evidence. My session had been scheduled between a ninety-nine-year-old man and the Easter Seal Child.

For a reporter, it was a nightmare of an interview situation. But

for Reagan's handlers the prospect clearly held its own perils. For
days, right until an hour before I left for the White House, deputy
press secretary Bob Sims had been calling, nervously checking on
what I planned to ask. The more evasive I was, the more frequently
he phoned. Then, before he ushered me into the Oval Office, he
himself disappeared inside to give the president a twenty-minute
briefing on Canadian issues. Sitting opposite Reagan in what felt
like a sound stage banked by blinding photo lights, listening to his
mellifluous radio-announcer's tones, it became clear that every
sentence was delivered as if pre-scripted. When the conversation
risked veering towards touchy issues like acid rain, which Reagan
still stoutly insisted was provoked by trees, Sims swiftly jumped in
to announce my time was up. Scarcely ten minutes had passed. The
commander-in-chief had once more played out his public role, but
by then it was obvious that the real work of wielding global power
was going on elsewhere. Only later would the reason for all the ner-
vousness become clear: the administration had an enormous stake
riding on Mulroney as he prodded his recalcitrant citizenry towards
an economic vision made in the USA — one that held scant benefit
for Canadians.

Over the next nine years, as I tracked his successive pilgrimages
to Reagan's court, whose imperial style he would so enthusiastically
attempt to ape, that encounter would provide a cautionary
reminder. Not only were things seldom as they seemed, but the
press, too, played its part in accommodating the charades of power.
Among Canadian journalists in Washington, there was often a reluctance to report on how scornful U.S. officials could be when
discussing the country's concerns; at times, we even came to take it
for granted. In the rush of events, scrambling to stay abreast of the
overwhelming flood-tide of news, reporters realized only later the
extent to which we had been manipulated by both nations' spin
doctors — glimpsing a truth at odds with what we were encouraged
to report. Almost invariably, the view from Washington offered a
markedly different perspective from that being fed to the mainstream media back home. This book is an attempt to further plumb
that perspective, a second glance over a continental vista where so
many questions remained unanswered while their consequences
were becoming ominously clear.

In the spring of 1992, as the Americanization of Canada was
proceeding apace, I leaped at the opportunity to revisit some of

the issues and events that had coloured that process, leaving a kaleidoscopic impression, dazzling and sometimes disturbing, but an indistinct and occasionally misleading design. Just as my Washington posting was drawing to a close, a fellowship in public policy from the Joseph S. Atkinson Foundation offered me the chance to retrace some of the relationships, both personal and political, that had shaped Mulroney's defining continental dreams. What I found was occasionally surprising and frequently alarming, but it may help explain a decade that has left Canada irrevocably transformed.

1 Hail and Farewell

ABOVE THE ROLLING HILLS OF SIMI VALLEY, north of Los Angeles, the view from the hacienda-style terrace of the Ronald Reagan Presidential Library unrolls for miles, unsullied by inconvenient monuments to daily living. No house or unsightly strip mall mars the vista of serene, undulating greens, leaving a sense of endless possibilities.

A distinctly unreal sense. Only a year earlier, a jury from Simi Valley, the unseen white suburb of split-level bungalows below, had acquitted three white LA police officers of savagely beating a black drunk driver named Rodney King, despite an amateur's video footage of the incident. That verdict had set off three days of rioting in the ghettos of south-central Los Angeles, leaving the poorest neighbourhoods charred and gutted, black turning upon black in a frenzy of frustration and impotent rage. Now, as the trio's retrial on civil charges wound up, LA was braced for another round of violence.

But that unpleasantness seemed worlds away as Brian Mulroney's limousine wound its way up the mountainside to the library on a balmy spring morning in early April 1993. The occasion was billed as Reagan's farewell tribute to Mulroney, who had announced his resignation only weeks earlier. But it was also something more: a ceremony of self-congratulation on the triumph of a free market economic credo once ridiculed as Reaganomics, for which Mulroney had served as the chief steward north of the border.

Even as they met, one manifestation of that faith, the North American Free Trade Agreement (NAFTA), was beginning its tumultuous struggle for passage in the United States Congress — another step towards a free trade zone planned for the entire hemisphere. On the library terrace, a small crowd had been hastily assembled on folding chairs to pay homage to that victory.

It was not perhaps the crowd that Mulroney would have liked — no glitz, no big names or movie stars, even of the Canadian variety. In fact, despite the tiny maple leaf flags that organizers had sprinkled through the crowd, hardly anyone from LA's Canadian expatriate contingent had made the hour's drive to the remote mountaintop. One dapper gentleman in the back row who sported a flag in his seersucker pocket was pounced on by reporters eager for Canadian content, but he turned out to be Reagan's makeup man, Webster Phillips, who had been wielding the pancake stick for the Gipper since his 1950s' stint as General Electric's TV pitchman. A class had been bussed in from nearby Cal Lutheran University to pad out the crowd, and, as it settled into place, the Fifteenth Air Force Band of the Golden West struck up "America the Beautiful."

A disembodied voice borrowed from the Academy Awards intoned "Ladies and Gentlemen, the fortieth President of the United States and Mrs. Reagan." To the strains of "Hail to the Chief," Brian and Mila Mulroney marched onto the stage behind the Reagans in practised lockstep. In unison, they settled on little gilt ballroom chairs of the kind usually found at *haute couture* shows.

"Welcome to another Shamrock Summit," joked master of ceremonies John Gavin, an aging former Hollywood B-player best known as Janet Leigh's boyfriend in *Psycho*. But hardly anyone got the joke. The Shamrock Summit had, after all, been in another country, long ago and far away, when Mulroney had been in power barely six months and even his enemies were still dazzled by his attempts to mimic the glittering showbiz style of the Reagan White House.

Back then, Gavin was Reagan's ambassador to Mexico, an appointment that had appalled the Mexicans, on whom he pushed what many regarded as one of his boss's wackiest schemes: a free market from the Yukon to the Yucatan. Most Mexicans had dismissed it merely as an update on old-fashioned Yankee imperialism, but now, more than a decade later, Gavin could boast of his role as "a pioneer in the NAFTA."

Indeed, as he and Mulroney flanked Reagan like bookends, the supporting players in some larger drama that would carry on without them, there was a sense of anticlimax in the air, a sense of mission accomplished. Certainly, no one had done more than Mulroney to integrate that recalcitrant chunk of northern geography known as Canada into Reagan's continental dream. And now, ignored by the mainstream American press he had so assiduously courted, this was his thanks.

Milky-eyed and reading every word of his speech, even the jokes, from a TelePrompTer, Reagan hailed him in terms few Canadians would have recognized back home — a leader whose "tax cuts and deregulation in the 1980s spurred seven years of economic growth and unprecedented job creation in Canada." In his reassuring TV host's voice, only slightly dimmed by Alzheimer's disease, Reagan intoned his tribute: "As you near the end of your term as prime minister, Canada is stronger, more confident and more secure than when you began your stewardship."

In the back row, members of the Canadian press corps rolled their eyes at the enormity of that whopper. After nine years in power, Mulroney was leaving Canada both economically and psychologically devastated. His popularity was almost even with the unemployment rate — a record 11.6 percent. Ontario's manufacturing base had been decimated by a haemorrhage of industries flowing south. And despite Mulroney's hated Goods and Services Tax — which had spawned a thriving underground economy — the national treasury still staggered under a multibillion-dollar deficit that would provide a convenient excuse for slashing the country's historic social safety net.

Regional enmities had never raged so fiercely, nor so threatened the national fabric. Even one of Mulroney's former friends and lieutenants, Lucien Bouchard, now stood poised to catapult his separatist Bloc Québécois into parliament's official opposition, dedicated to the breakup of Canada. From coast to coast, a cynicism and uncertainty gripped the land — a sense that the nation had irretrievably lost its way.

But no matter. Here on this dreamlike mountaintop where the library's gift shop contained only a picture history of the Reagan presidency, upbeat rhetoric was the order of the day.

Not since the Second World War, when William Lyon Mackenzie King had met with Franklin Roosevelt on the banks of the St. Lawrence to scribble their continental defence pact, had a Canadian prime minister steered the country so firmly into America's orbit. But with one eye already on the history books, Mulroney took his turn at the microphone, defensive about portrayals of him as Washington's lapdog.

"As prime minister, I have placed a premium on good relations between Canada and the United States," he said. "I have been criticized for this in some quarters in Canada by people who tend to equate civility with subservience in foreign affairs. Their view seems to be that independence in foreign policy is principally measured by the extent to which we can disagree with the United States. The more churlish, the more different."

But if, as he noted, Canadians hadn't cared for his particular brand of cosiness, Republicans like Reagan and George Bush had been rapturous in their praise of him — unlike the Democrat who had succeeded them. In fact, Mulroney had just flown in from playing host to Bill Clinton's first summit with Russian president Boris Yeltsin in Vancouver, where the White House press office had been furious with him. Despite an agreement that he would drop out of a staged shot of the strolling duo, he had stuck to them with such tenacity that one of Clinton's press handlers dubbed him "Velcro Man."

In contrast, Reagan and Bush had always treated Mulroney like some favourite nephew, with affection and protective indulgence, never stinting on the media events he gloried in. He was, after all, a member of the global conservative team, fulfilling the agenda of the one constituency that counted in the post–Cold War world taking shape: the forces of Big Business and Big Oil, most of them U.S.–based multinationals who had found Reagan's obsession with minimalist government a handy rationale in their rush towards globalization. Inside the lofty marble foyer of the library, their names were etched in gilt upon the walls: the Adolph Coors Foundation, American Express, Amway Corp., Dwayne Andreas, Walter Annenberg, Chase Manhattan Bank, Chevron, and Paramount Communications, Inc.

A visitor did not have to read far down the list of hundreds of library donors to see the American interests that had chafed at the nationalistic policies of Pierre Trudeau and found their concerns assuaged under Mulroney. Three months after arriving in power, he had proclaimed the country open for business, and U.S. corporations had taken up his invitation with alacrity. Nine years later, his government had approved foreign takeovers of 6,000 Canadian companies worth $140 billion, further cementing the country's distinction as the leading foreign-controlled economy among industrialized nations.

Not that Mulroney had received any public gratitude for his efforts. In fact, some analysts had been unkind enough to question just what his personal chemistry with two U.S. presidents had won the nation. In an unprecedented wave of trade harassments, many of those U.S. conglomerates had launched beer wars and wheat wars and salvos over Ottawa's cultural policies, costing Canadian industries millions in lawyers' and lobbyists' fees. Some of those fees, in turn, had enriched Mulroney's cronies who had signed on to represent the multinationals' interests in a system of access-for-hire that increasingly resembled the one in Washington.

But not all the corporate donors to the Reagan library were American. The Saudi Arabian government, Britain's arch-conservative billionaire Sir James Goldsmith, the Japan Entrepreneurs and Presidents Association, and even Vancouver's own one-man conglomerate, Jimmy Pattison, had also coughed up for this tribute to an economic mindset that had gone global. American, Canadian, Japanese — what difference did it make? In the new world order of commerce, where capital roamed the world unfettered, constantly seeking out the cheapest labour and the highest profit margins, the niceties of national allegiance were increasingly irrelevant.

Multinational corporations, known on the think tank circuit as transnationals, were fast replacing nation states as the powers that decided the fate of populations. Governments no longer dared make policies that might incur the money markets' wrath, no matter what fury they risked provoking in their own voters. National sovereignty had become a quaint sentimental notion trotted out for election campaigns and ceremonial occasions. And no one understood that drift better than Mulroney, a corporate lawyer who, once out of office, would promptly return to the continent's boardrooms.

As Mulroney's speech wound down, clouds began rolling in, casting an ominous pall over the gathering. A chill wind skittered across the courtyard, and Nancy Reagan hugged her thin arms sheathed in their Galanos white. The audience accorded Mulroney only polite applause before a canned orchestral overture cued the Pepperdine University Choir's rendition of "God Bless America." Then it was over.

A lacklustre buffet with coffee in styrofoam cups had been set up by the door, but within minutes the crowd had dispersed and the press bus had pulled out. As the library's ticket sellers opened for business, the Mulroneys and Reagans repaired upstairs for a private lunch. But hours later, the Secret Service cleared a path for them among the tourists drifting through the exhibits. Nancy Reagan insisted on showing them one last thing. Not the baby-simple historical displays that glossed over world events with facile summations and memorabilia, nor the exact replica of the Oval Office where, before the ceremony, Reagan and Mulroney had relived their old glories in exact copies of the cream brocade chairs they once occupied in the White House.

No, what she wanted them to see was the museum gift shop, which featured among its wares a postcard immortalizing one of those Reagan-Mulroney summits. Amid the Ronald Reagan key chains and jars of jelly beans and boxed sets of champagne glasses etched with the presidential signature, there were also Canadian flags. Even communism's collapse had been neatly packaged for the souvenir trade: tiny chunks of the Berlin Wall were being peddled in elaborate cardboard boxes marked "Certified," in red letters, and "An Actual Piece of History."

Here, everything had its price.

2

The Colonel's Boy

"**S**IR." The word wafted out from the South Portico of the White House and hung in the swampy September afternoon air. It was only a little word, an innocuous nicety really, slipped into Brian Mulroney's wrap-up speech after a two-hour luncheon visit to Ronald Reagan just eight days after he was sworn in as Canada's eighteenth prime minister in September 1984. But as it drifted across the south lawn where the press corps had been herded onto a hastily erected set of risers behind a rope, it fell with the weight of dread — and prophecy.

"Sir." Along the risers, Canadian journalists winced. After Mulroney's repeated campaign promises to recreate a "superb relationship" with Washington following the tensions under Pierre Trudeau — after all his rhetoric about giving Americans the benefit of the doubt — was this then the form it was to take: the fawning deference of a nervous upstart to his powerful benefactor?

Most Canadian journalists were so uneasy at the reference that they left it out of their reports entirely. After all, hadn't Mulroney insisted only two hours earlier, within the apricot silk walls of the Roosevelt Room, that his new cross-border cosiness "implies no subservience"? That made a more reassuring clip on the nightly newscast back home. And who, after all, could deny that the visit had gone well?

In the White House Family Dining Room, the pair had traded Irish priest stories with the rapid-fire gusto of two gunfighters who had finally met their match. "They had this whole repertoire of Irish jokes they just kept shooting at each other," recalls Mulroney's foreign policy guru, Charley McMillan. "The whole table was in stitches. Out of a two-hour lunch, the business of what we were going to say to the press later was done in maybe eight minutes."

Shaking off the chill of the Trudeau years, Ambassador Allan Gotlieb was both incredulous and ecstatic at their kibitzing. "Just a couple of North American Irishmen," was the White House line scripted by spinmaster Michael Deaver, who was relieved that Reagan could finally indulge in his favourite ethnic stories with impunity. During the presidential campaign, one ill-advised Polish joke had nearly cost him the New Hampshire primary, prompting him to promise he would stick to lampooning his own ancestry. Now Mulroney's shared Irish roots would provide the chief public relations plotline for their summits over the next four years — and a subtext of continental family ties.

But Reagan's handlers also had their own reasons for playing up the camaraderie. In less than two months, the president was up for re-election, and, despite the fact that pollsters were giving him a sure lead over his uncharismatic Democratic challenger, Walter Mondale, they also revealed that his support was increasingly soft. The public was no longer laughing at the late-night talk-show routines on his hazy grasp of facts or his hyperbolic crusade against the Kremlin's Evil Empire. Surveys showed that the American public's greatest terror was a nuclear showdown with Moscow — a confrontation that Reagan's provocative rhetoric seemed to risk enflaming. As the press catalogued his catnaps during cabinet meetings and his inability to function without cue cards, doubts were seeping into the mainstream media about the competence of the seventy-three-year-old who was already the oldest president in American history.

Accordingly, not a moment of Reagan's meeting with Mulroney had been left to chance — not even the possibility that the president might forget he had entertained his guest as Canadian opposition leader only three months earlier. "It is a pleasure for me to welcome you back to Washington so soon," Reagan's briefing notes read, "this time as prime minister."

For the president's handlers, Mulroney's visit was a dress-rehearsal of sorts. In only three days Reagan was to meet Soviet foreign minister Andrei Gromyko — his first encounter with a top Kremlin official since taking office nearly four years earlier — and his aides were eager to squelch any questions about his diplomatic prowess or his ability to hold together the fractious Atlantic alliance. They leaped at the chance to show "the Old Man," as they routinely referred to the president, palling around with a youthful new NATO leader who had just swept into office carrying the conservative colours of the Reagan Revolution to America's liberal attic.

Not that some in the White House harboured any misconceptions about the ideological distance between them. In his briefing notes for Reagan, the State Department's Richard Burt had hailed Mulroney as "the frankest advocate of pro–U.S. positions to run Canada in thirty years," a leader who supported the American investment agenda and "the free market mechanism." But, Burt had cautioned, "his positions are by no means identical with Washington's; a distinctive Canadian 'spin' goes on each."

In those briefing notes, Burt sketched out the bilateral relationship that the administration already saw taking shape. He counselled continuing U.S. pressure on Mulroney to make good on his campaign promise of increasing Canadian defence spending, while acknowledging that "increased funds will be hard to find." On the other military front that had become Reagan's obsession, his guerrilla war against the Sandinistas in Nicaragua, Burt suggested that, with the congressional cutoff of aid to the Contras, the Canadian government ought to be nudged towards helping Washington's Central American efforts.

As for the two countries' standoff on acid rain, the administration clearly had no intention of budging on the issue. "Mulroney will feel obliged to mention acid rain," Secretary of State George Shultz had advised Reagan before the meeting. "You could hold to our established policy, but phrased in a manner that avoids embarrassing Mulroney with his public." On the White House steps, Reagan took that advice so much to heart that he refrained from even uttering the dread phrase "acid rain," vaguely referring instead to the prime minister's "environmental concerns."

But one key item on their agenda would rate no mention whatsoever on the public stage. Over the next six months, it was a topic that Canadian officials would pretend had barely caught their attention. Despite that elaborate charade, as Reagan's luncheon briefing notes show, the two leaders were already laying the groundwork for free trade talks. That news might have startled more than a few Canadian voters. Throughout Mulroney's leadership campaign, whenever suspicions arose that his romance with Washington might lead to a contentious trade agreement, he had recoiled in melodramatic horror. But by the time he showed up at the White House, U.S. officials were confident of forging a deal with him, even if they were not yet clear what form it would take. "Politically," Burt warned Reagan and Shultz, "Mulroney will want to put his own stamp on any talks."

Still, as the Honor Guard lined the White House drive and the resident fife and drum corps struck up a brisk patriotic medley, White House officials had every reason to beam. At the very moment he and Reagan were trading Paddy jokes, his international trade minister, James Kelleher, was in Toronto assuring the Canadian Chamber of Commerce that Ottawa was in the process of emasculating the two Trudeau measures that had most infuriated Reagan and his corporate allies on both sides of the border: the Foreign Investment Review Agency (FIRA) and the National Energy Policy.

Eight days after taking power, Mulroney had already delivered everything Washington might ask for — without demanding a thing in return. McMillan argued that he made those gestures not for the White House, but for Canadians, particularly those in the oil patch who were furious that U.S. exploration and drilling had dried up. "You just have to look at the investment figures," he bristled. But as political economist Stephen Clarkson noted at the time, it was "like signing a blank cheque very quickly — not a very effective negotiating technique."

Now Mulroney stood in front of the news cameras, addressing a fellow leader as "sir." What made matters worse was how nervous he looked, his fists clenching and unclenching, darting in and out of his pockets as he perspired in the noonday humidity through Reagan's affable farewell. Even ABC correspondent Sam Donaldson, who had achieved stardom for barging through the White House bafflegab with his nervy nasal tenor, interrupted a briefing by Reagan's spokesman Larry Speakes to demand what had happened to make Mulroney so ill at ease. "He doesn't seem to know what to do with his hands!" Donaldson exclaimed.

In fact, it was the first glimpse that the press would get of Mulroney's struggle with an inner ear problem that had left him with a terror of losing his balance — an affliction that top logistics experts of both governments would go to enormous lengths to hide over the coming years. But at the time, the Prime Minister's Office had explained it away as a sudden case of the flu.

Still, Mulroney might have been forgiven for his awkwardness. Here he was at last at centre stage — at least, in the centre of the only stage that had ever really mattered to him: in the spotlight of the U.S. capital. For other Canadian leaders, a visit to the White House might have been a necessary adjunct of the job, even an ordeal to be gotten through. But for Mulroney, it was the apotheosis of everything he had dreamed of since his boyhood in the Quebec milltown of Baie Comeau, where he first glimpsed power in a man who was to help shape both his political outlook and his life: Colonel Robert Rutherford McCormick.

HE was tall, elegant, and aristocratic — and one of the most influential men in the United States. Presidents courted his favour and trembled at his pronouncements, and when he swooped down on the tiny isolated town he had ordered carved out of the wilderness on the banks of the St. Lawrence, *his* town, it was as if God himself had deigned to drop by in a private, luxury-refitted B–17 bomber.

In Baie Comeau, which he had raised from scratch around the pulpmill he built to feed his *Chicago Tribune* presses, Colonel McCormick was not only regarded as the creator; he was also the source from whom all blessings flowed. The weekly paycheques, the plant, the roads, the wharf, the hospital, the three schools, and the workers' houses, even the skating rink, were all owed to the colonel. So, too, were the vast forests that stretched as far as the eye could see. The timber limits granted to the *Tribune*'s Canadian newsprint subsidiary, the Ontario Paper Company, sprawled over 32,500 square kilometres. When the colonel came to town, he was indeed lord of all he surveyed.

By the early 1930s, McCormick had already built one plant 120 kilometres east of Baie Comeau at the mouth of the Rocky River. But despite his knack for euphemism, which had inspired him to christen it Shelter Bay, his fleet of freighters needed a less hazardous year-round port to ship his logging harvests south for processing into the 100,000 tonnes of newsprint that the *Tribune* and its sister

New York Daily News consumed each year.

By 1936, when the new town was still a glimmer in his eye, the colonel was so outraged over Franklin Roosevelt's New Deal that he had started off the year with an editorial bellowing "Turn the Rascals Out." His tirade was only one sign that he was growing increasingly impatient with the plodding pace of history. Baie Comeau was another, his personal riposte to the New Deal: a planned model town that would be conservative, family oriented, and, above all, paternalistic. As his own social experiment, it was designed to serve his corporate needs and to exist under his exclusive control — a town, in short, created entirely in the colonel's own image.

A glossy black-and-white promotional brochure, "Baie Comeau: A Modern Model City," detailed its prospective charms. Seven years into the Great Depression, the colonel was offering workers "an opportunity to build their own homes in delightful surroundings." As ever, his copywriters had attempted to put a happy face on the wilderness, depicting the St. Lawrence's savage north shore, which Jacques Cartier once christened "the land God gave to Cain," as a "healthy climate in picturesque surroundings."

When a taciturn Irishman named Benedict Mulroney saw the ads, he left his wife and daughter behind in Quebec City and headed for a labourers' tent city on the hillside where Baie Comeau would rise. After Christmas in 1937, when the mill's No. 1 paper machine, as big as a football field, rumbled into operation, he finally moved his young family to the hamlet of mud streets and fresh plyboard he had helped hack out of the bush. Two years later, on the day before the spring solstice, with ice still choking the river below, Brian Mulroney arrived in the world — a child of the colonel's imperial vision.

For the first fourteen years of his life, Mulroney scarcely strayed from the isolated milltown that was bound by an umbilical cord, not to Ottawa or Quebec City, but to the *Tribune*'s gleaming neo-Gothic towers in Chicago. He came of age in a universe whose unquestioned *raison d'être* was to service the needs of its distant American seigneur who, once a year, swept into his fiefdom, trailing intimations of glory — wealth and grandeur of mythic proportions to a daydreaming north shore electrician's son.

Colonel McCormick traditionally flew in for a July fishing trip to celebrate his birthday, settling into Le Manoir, the luxury hotel he had built for himself and other *Tribune* executives on the hill above town. By then, few in Baie Comeau were not up to date on his latest exploits — his prowess at polo, his taste for South Seas' dancers on the paper's front page, and the armoured car that protected him from Al Capone's wrath after his crusade against the mobster's henchmen in Chicago.

The colonel's appetites, like his opinions, were the stuff of daily gossip. In the rare well-thumbed copies of the *Tribune* that circulated around town, Baie Comeau's residents could track his political pronouncements, which were seldom constrained by the need for consistency. Like Charles Lindbergh and other conservative America Firsters, the colonel had vociferously opposed Washington's entry into the Second World War — all the more strenuously after the Canadian government had commandeered part of the *Tribune*'s fleet. One ship was attacked off Cuba, another lost in the English Channel. "How can the U.S. hope to intervene in Europe," an editorial worried, "when it lacks the power to enforce the Monroe Doctrine?"

Yet once the United States was in the fight, no one became more infatuated by General Douglas MacArthur than the colonel, who flew off with his new wife to visit the commander in his Tokyo stronghold. After the war, McCormick threw himself into the battle against communism with equal fervour, never wavering in his support for the ideological witch-hunts of Senator Joseph McCarthy. Even the *Tribune*'s humiliation in the 1948 presidential race, when its infamously misguided headline "Dewey Defeats Truman" became a national joke, failed to diminish McCormick's clout.

In 1947, when the paper marked its one hundredth anniversary — complete with a fireworks replica of the U.S. atomic blast over Hiroshima — *Time* magazine put McCormick on its cover, hailing the *Tribune* as "easily the loudest and perhaps the most widely feared and hated" of America's 1,700 dailies. Chronicling that influence, the magazine inquired whether the colonel had designs on the presidency of the United States. "Out of the question," he snapped. "As any fool could see," *Time* concluded, "if a man had a commanding view from the Tribune Tower, what would he want with the White House?"

No wonder, then, that Colonel McCormick provided the defining mythology for Mulroney — and for his political enemies. Time after time, oblivious to the fodder it served up for armchair psychologists,

Mulroney would retell the tale of his boyhood triumph: the knock at the family's modest door summoning the workman's son to come sing for the master of Baie Comeau. No matter how often friends warned him against it, Mulroney loved to recount how McCormick's aides had boosted him atop Le Manoir's grand piano to warble the colonel's favourite, "Dearie," for which he was rewarded with a crisp new US$50 bill. From his earliest days, the United States — and indeed the American press — had symbolized the big time, the height of aspiration.

Nor could the colonel have been far from his mind as he stood in the White House Rose Garden in September 1984. Only three weeks earlier, he had sat in Colonel McCormick's guest house at Le Manoir, the command post for his parliamentary riding, watching the election results roll in. There, where the colonel himself had often pondered his nation's fate, Mulroney had received a congratulatory phone call from Reagan and an invitation to this rendezvous with history: the dawning of an era in Canadian-American relations when, as Charley McMillan would later lament, personal chemistry would obscure — and even sabotage — policy.

It would be another three years before McMillan, an architect of the country's new continental tilt, would dispatch a blistering memo to Mulroney berating him for a style of bilateral chumminess that "went way overboard." But already he had a foreboding of the costs that the politics of personality would exact. "If the public image of Canada–U.S. relations is tied to an image of Reagan and Mulroney — and almost an obsequiousness on Mulroney's part to get the photo shot — the substance drops by the wayside," he said. "It just undercuts the whole thing."

3

The Candidate from Big Steel

FOR MONTHS, his face had stared out of the newspapers and nightly newscasts as they chronicled each new sensation in a riveting provincial thriller: teenage boys beaten to a pulp when union thugs failed to locate their fathers, and corpses unearthed with their lips sewn together by baling wire. The daily litany of gruesomeness and gore emerging from the Cliche royal commission into violence in the Quebec construction industry rivalled the lurid twists of some Hollywood horror plot. As the most media savvy of the commission triumvirate, Brian Mulroney swiftly emerged as the hearings' chief spokesman — and, not incidentally, a celebrity.

Other aspirants to the nation's highest public office might toil on the back benches for years hoping to rate a mention in the press. But in 1974, when Robert Bourassa asked Mulroney to join his former law professor, Judge Robert Cliche, in a probe of the province's construction unions, the wily Liberal premier had handed Mulroney the launching pad for his political career.

Not that the gesture was without calculation. For Bourassa, the hearings represented a gamble — one that would ultimately cost him re-election. But when a union bulldozer rampage set off a massive fire at Hydro-Québec's $12 billion James Bay hydroelectric project, the premier who had campaigned on the slogan "James Bay

— *c'est moi"* had no choice but to call an inquiry. As a Conservative, Mulroney reinforced the panel's gloss of nonpartisanship, but as a close personal friend, he would also prove loyal: it was he who would later dissuade his fellow commissioners from forcing Bourassa to testify.

Retaining his plump salary as a partner in Montreal's prestigious law firm Ogilvy Cope, Mulroney filled a key gap on his own political curriculum vitae. Before the hearings, his Tory cronies had been nudging him to throw his hat into the ring to succeed Robert Stanfield, the plodding, principled longjohns heir who was stepping down as party leader. But even Mulroney was aware he remained a longshot, known mainly in Conservative backrooms. Overnight, the televised hearings transformed him into a respected public figure — a metamorphosis that carried the added cachet of a civic duty which required two armed escorts and a black guard dog named Gucci.

But if Mulroney's performance made his name a household word in Quebec, it also caught the attention of another constituency that was to prove equally vital to his political prospects. Bourassa, after all, had named him to the commission as management's man, the role he had played throughout his career as a labour lawyer. And with James Bay, management interests involved not only the Quebec government but also some of the most powerful figures in corporate America.

For many of them, Canada had long represented a vast natural resources depot to which Washington enjoyed *droits de seigneur*. Indeed, in a province littered with U.S. investments in mining and lumber, it was hardly surprising that the construction of the world's largest hydroelectric scheme — routinely referred to in the Quebec press as the "project of the century" — had attracted the barons of the Fortune 500.

The most illustrious among them was David Rockefeller, chairman of the Chase Manhattan Bank, whose family had kept close tabs on Canada since the dawn of the century when his father had called on another Canadian labour relations expert to rescue him from one of industrial America's worst crises. On April 20, 1914, in Ludlow, Colorado, the militia had fired on coal miners striking against the Rockefellers' Colorado Fuel and Iron Company, in the process setting their tent city ablaze and killing nearly one hundred women and children. Even the *New York Times*, no friend of the United Mine

Workers, had denounced "such horrible means." Seven weeks later, still struggling with damage control, John D. Rockefeller Jr. had turned for help to Mackenzie King, the former Canadian labour minister who was then between engagements.

King's mission had been considered so sensitive that he was paid through the family's philanthropic arm, the Rockefeller Foundation, on whose books he was listed for the next four years as director of research. An advocate of softball tactics with a smooth public relations spin, he had come up with the notion of forming a company union — a concept that later put him under the scrutiny of a congressional committee, but made him the darling of U.S. industrialists.

So deftly had King dispatched his assignment that he became a lifelong Rockefeller confidant, even after he left the family's services to win the Liberal leadership in 1919. And so enduring was Rockefeller's gratitude that, after King left public life in 1948, the family provided him with a birthday gift of $100,000 in company shares for his retirement. Whether that token of appreciation was partly for services rendered while in office never became clear; but long after King had returned home to become prime minister, Rockefeller sent his youngest son, David, then fresh from Harvard, to Ottawa for an inspirational talking-to from the former family retainer.

In 1971, when Robert Bourassa unveiled the James Bay project as the centrepiece of his new regime, then promptly pilgrimaged to Wall Street to raise the money for it, his first stop was David Rockefeller's princely seventeenth-floor headquarters at One Chase Manhattan Plaza. There, he was received with more than the usual elaborate courtesies accorded foreign statesmen: not only did Chase rank as a substantial lender to his government, but it stood to make millions from its power sales to New York state, whose four-term governor happened to be David Rockefeller's brother Nelson. For Rockefeller, a ponderous amateur entymologist who spent his spare time in search of order in the universe — collecting, organizing, and classifying rare beatles — the prospect that union violence or pay-offs might threaten such a monumental energy scheme must have seemed intolerable.

Equally wary of the Cliche commission testimony was another scion of the American Establishment: Stephen Bechtel Jr., chairman of the privately held and highly secretive construction conglomerate founded by his grandfather in San Francisco. The Bechtel Group, Inc., had won the contract for James Bay under mysterious circumstances, despite the fact that Bourassa's handpicked administrator, Pierre Nadeau, had already awarded the job to a consortium of three Quebec firms. At the time of the hearings, the company was facing charges of bribing New Jersey officials to snag an oil pipeline contract — charges on which Bechtel would soon be found guilty and fined — and the Cliche commission posed another public relations nightmare.

According to Nadeau's testimony, he and Paul Desrochers, the man known as Bourassa's fixer, had flown to New York for a meeting with Bechtel's top brass on what he later discovered was its corporate jet. To Nadeau's astonishment, the trip was not to explore reopening the bidding process, but to toast a contract already wrapped up by the premier's office in what journalist Matthew Fraser termed "a tacit deal at the highest political level." Having been duped, Nadeau also found himself excluded from the celebratory dinner with Stephen Bechtel. "They knew I wouldn't get my hands dirty," he testified.

For Bechtel, such revelations threatened more than the corporate image. The company had negotiated a percentage contract tied to costs, which had already ballooned from $4 billion to $12 billion, and in 1974 alone had earned $100 million — the first instalment of an ongoing windfall that the Cliche hearings put at risk.

It hardly seems surprising then that Chase, Bechtel, and the other major U.S. stakeholders in Hydro-Québec kept a close watch on the Cliche hearings. Nor was it unusual that yet another boardroom south of the border was also eyeing the commission's leading media star who, like Mackenzie King before him, had established a reputation for settling irksome strikes to his employers' satisfaction. For James Bay had not been the only provincial construction site to feel the muscle of the powerful Fédération des Travailleurs du Québec led by Louis Laberge.

During the previous year, the Iron Ore Company of Canada — owned by a consortium of six U.S. steel mills — had been battling the unions in the mining port of Sept-Iles on the St. Lawrence's north shore. The work stoppages had been wreaking havoc with the startup schedule and costs of a new Iron Ore smelter, not to mention with local bonhomie. "They were carrying guns on the streets of Seven Islands," Mulroney later told his friend and biographer

L. Ian MacDonald. "The Iron Ore Company was trying to put up new plants and they couldn't because of the violence in the construction industry."

Midway through the Cliche commission, Mulroney got a call from Iron Ore's longtime president, Bill Bennett, inviting him to dinner at Montreal's Chinese restaurant Ruby Foo's. Bennett was no stranger. Six years earlier, he had hired Mulroney to settle a strike at the company's Quebec North Shore and Labrador Railway. During those tense talks, they had spent nearly two weeks huddled in the Château Frontenac in Quebec City, and, later, Bennett had rewarded Mulroney with a television set and more legal work. For the American owners of Canada's largest ore producer, the high-priced young labour lawyer had already proved himself an effective hired gun. Now Bennett was summoning Mulroney to meet his bosses, the big boys from Cleveland who ran the company's chief shareholder and managing partner, the M. A. Hanna Company.

Founded by Hanna in 1949, Iron Ore existed for one purpose: to blast the ferrous deposits from its two open-pit mines in northern Quebec and Labrador, then load them aboard the company's rail lines and Great Lakes fleet for transport to the steel ovens of its Ohio Valley owners. Led by Bethlehem Steel, the second-largest U.S. steelmaker, and Hanna's own spinoff, National Steel, which ranked not far behind, the consortium represented the kind of U.S. industrial clout that for decades had made Washington policymakers tremble. But since the 1973 Arab oil embargo had devastated its chief market, the auto assembly lines in Detroit, Big Steel was feeling the squeeze. By the time the Cliche commission began its hearings, the labour strife at Sept-Iles loomed as yet another threat to the consortium's balance sheets.

With Bennett due to retire in two years, Robert F. Anderson, an irascible former mining engineer slated for Hanna's presidency, was searching for a new face to front the Canadian operations — a northern branch-plant manager for Big Steel. Anderson needed someone with enough political clout to curry continued favour with the Quebec and Newfoundland governments, which controlled the company's crucial mining concessions, but his chief priority was to find a gloved fist to tame the unions.

His first meeting with Mulroney was late on a summer afternoon in Ruby Foo's deserted dining room and, despite Anderson's urgency to get back to Cleveland that night, he liked what he saw. "Brian and I, we clicked right off," he recalled, barking into the speaker phone at his retirement office in Fort Myers, Florida, his conversation regularly erupting in expletives and diatribes against the incorrigible meddling of governments.

A onetime U.S. Air Force engineer, Anderson had been sent as a young Hanna mining technician to evaluate the ore deposits in the Quebec bush long before the ground had been broken for the first mine. He had lived for months in a tent amid the stunted spruce and relentless flies, and, of all Hanna's global properties, he still had the softest spot for the Iron Ore Company. Known as Rapid Robert by his underlings, he talked as fast as he made multimillion-dollar decisions, and he expected the same brisk fealty from his troops. Anderson was the antithesis of the telegenic smooth-talker sitting across the table from him at Ruby Foo's. But beneath Mulroney's manicured charm he recognized another rough diamond from hard-scrabble roots. "We talked the same language," he said.

Within days of the Cliche commission's final report in May 1975, Anderson made a formal job offer, but Mulroney demurred. His Conservative friends were stepping up their pressure on him to run for the Tory leadership, which was to be decided at a convention early in the new year. Instead of being miffed, Anderson proved remarkably understanding of Mulroney's political dreams; in fact, over the next seven years, he and the Hanna brass appear to have gone to extraordinary lengths to help foster them.

But then, few corporations better understood that shadowy terrain where business and politics meet than the men who ran the consortium founded by Ohio senator Marcus Alonzo Hanna, one of America's most flamboyant nineteenth-century industrial buccaneers — and the man considered the father of the modern Republican Party.

A boyhood friend of John D. Rockefeller Sr. from their days at Cleveland's Central High, Mark Hanna was a legend himself — one whose name still winks from the theatre marquees and highrises on the city's skyline. He had masterminded the 1896 presidential campaign of another old friend, Ohio governor William B. McKinley, who promptly engineered a seat for Hanna in the Senate. McKinley would later accuse him of trying to commandeer the White House, but if Hanna failed in that takeover attempt, he was more success-ful in bending lesser political institutions to his will. In the course of stumping the country fundraising for McKinley, he had set up the structures that won him acclaim as the Republicans' first national political boss. In his speeches, Hanna seldom failed to note both the right and the obligation of entrepreneurs to have their say in the nation's affairs. And historians have credited him with transforming the party of Abraham Lincoln into an ideological haven for Big Business.

For the next century, his firm's political affections would never stray from the Republican fold. By the Second World War, when Howard Hanna, the senator's nephew, chaired the company, its pres-ident was George Humphrey, a Michigan lawyer whom Dwight Eisenhower later summoned to Washington as his secretary of the Treasury.

On the eve of Washington's entry into the war, as the Pentagon worried about the longevity of the nation's chief iron ore reserves in Minnesota, which were crucial to the massive American arms build-up, Humphrey looked north and gambled on developing a Canadian mine to ensure U.S. long-term strategic interests. He negotiated Hanna's backing to explore a desolate tract of Quebec and Labrador which had been staked by Jules Timmins, the Ontario gold king, and a band of New York mining promoters. But it was not until 1949 that the deal finally went through.

During those protracted negotiations, Humphrey had learned the value of having an ally within the Canadian government. Whenever he needed friendly counsel or a favour, he had turned to C. D. Howe, Mackenzie King's American-born minister of munitions and supply, who took more than passing interest in the grandiose mining scheme. Not only did Howe share a first-hand understanding of the importance of ore reserves to any future allied war effort, but he had also worked closely with the U.S. Defense Department to build a military airfield at Goose Bay, Labrador, a pivotal link in the defence of the North Atlantic.

Dubbed Mackenzie King's "minister of everything," Howe had personally intervened to allow Hanna's private railway incorpora-tion within Canadian law; and, when tax breaks were being weighed, it was he who gave his blessing to the consortium's deci-sion to incorporate the Iron Ore Company of Canada in the United States. To some Canadians who already feared Washington's long reach, it seemed not without irony that the first board meeting of the firm that would control the country's largest ore reserves was held in Delaware, the state with the most secretive corporate filing regulations and the least onerous corporate tax provisions.

In promoting the project to his Cleveland partners, Humphrey had trumpeted the value of ore reserves in a friendly neighbouring country with a stable government — a government in whose continuing stability America's major steelmakers now held a stake: the consortium's mills had signed contracts to purchase close to 10-million tonnes of ore a year for the next twenty-five years.

Orchestrating the complex financing, Humphrey had launched an initial offering of $265 million in stocks, bonds, and debentures underwritten by two of Wall Street's most respected investment bankers, Harriman-Ripley and Kuhn Loeb. Three other blue-chip houses, Morgan Stanley, Lehman Brothers, and Goldman, Sachs, took a minority share of the action. To quiet Canadian critics railing against the colonization of the country's natural resources, Humphrey had also been obliged to bring in two Toronto brokers, Wood Gundy and Dominion Securities. But most of the initial $100 million bond issue — which did not mature until 1977 — had been underwritten by Wall Street and snapped up by a syndicate of fifteen American life insurance companies. More than two decades before many of the same investment houses put together the mammoth James Bay and Churchill Falls financings, that group of U.S. powerbrokers already had acquired a long-term interest in events north of the 49th parallel.

Once Humphrey's vision was financially afloat, he had invited an array of firms, from Montreal's C. D. Howe Company to Morrison-Knudsen Corporation of Idaho, to claw two mining towns, a 575-kilometre railway line, a massive loading dock, and a deepwater port out of the wilderness. For the early U.S. investors in the Iron Ore Company, carving a mining complex out of the uncharted Quebec bush was the stuff of romance — a heady fling at America's last frontier. Nor, for some, was the geography unfamiliar. Since the turn of the century, generations of Rockefellers and other American bluebloods had been jetting into the exclusive Adams Club on Quebec's Moisie River to fly-fish for wild Atlantic salmon. So sacred was that pastime that, when the planned route for Iron Ore's railway line threatened the Moisie's spawning grounds, Humphrey had quelled the outrage rippling through Eastern seaboard boardrooms by agreeing to build an alternative fishway; in the interim, he arranged to have the prized salmon transported upriver in bags slung from the company helicopters.

In July 1954, when Iron Ore's first shipment was loaded aboard the SS *Hawaiian* at a gala ceremony in Sept-Iles, *Time* magazine hailed it as "one of the great hands-across-the-border industrial ventures of modern times." By then Humphrey was secretary of the Treasury, but among the blue-chip crowd of 6,000 flown in for the occasion, nobody had deemed it odd that one of the most powerful members of Eisenhower's cabinet should preside over the launch of an iron ore plant in the obscure Canadian wilds.

At the height of the Korean and Cold wars, there was little doubt about the Iron Ore Company's importance to U.S. national security. When the construction was in jeopardy because the enormous tonnage of the earth-moving equipment confounded its hired DC–3s, a U.S. Air Force flying boxcar and crew had suddenly materialized to take over the job, complete with eight senior U.S. military officers to supervise what they dubbed Operation Ungava. Later, Schefferville, the mining town that Iron Ore had built, was chosen as the site for a radar base on the Mid-Canada line, part of the grid operated in conjunction with the Distant Early Warning (DEW) line by the joint North American Air Defense command out of Colorado.

For Hanna, such government collaboration was routine. When the Korean War threatened American nickel supplies, the U.S. government contracted to buy the entire output from the company's Oregon mines for a strategic stockpile — an arrangement that would later become the subject of a Senate investigation.

In return, Hanna had learned to make its needs heard in the corridors of power. Ever since Iron Ore's founding, the board in Cleveland had been pressing both the Canadian and the U.S. governments for what would become the St. Lawrence Seaway; from its opening in 1957, M. A. Hanna's fleet of Great Lakes freighters was the seaway's largest customer.

In 1958, in order to construct a massive concentrator complex, Hanna had called on Mr. Stephen Bechtel's master builders. By then, the San Francisco firm had become the company's primary contractor, but the Iron Ore project would pay off many times over for Bechtel, which had already made its mark building the Hoover Dam and stringing the Transarabian pipeline across the deserts of Saudi Arabia. Its success at subduing the subarctic terrain would bring the company a succession of multimillion-dollar Canadian mega-projects — among them, Hydro-Québec's grandiose scheme for rearranging the rivers flowing into James Bay. In recognition of its key role, Stephen Bechtel had been given a seat on Hanna's board, which he still held when Anderson recruited Mulroney.

When Humphrey left cabinet to return to the company, he had again prevailed on his old friend C. D. Howe, this time to find a well-connected Canadian to run Iron Ore. As it turned out, Howe had the perfect man for the job: his former executive assistant, Bill Bennett, whom he had put in charge of the government's top security uranium mining corporation, Eldorado Nuclear, one of the main sources for the U.S. military. From there, Bennett had moved on to head Atomic Energy of Canada and the Canadian British Aluminum Company, one of whose shareholders happened to be the Quebec North Shore Paper Company, owned by Colonel Robert McCormick. In 1960 Bennett signed on with Iron Ore in Montreal, where he stayed for the next seventeen years.

During those years, it had become increasingly obvious how dependent the company was on its friends in high places. In 1969, when Pierre Trudeau's government brought down a White Paper on taxation that would have wiped out the mining industry's traditional writeoffs, Iron Ore threatened to cancel a planned $290 million expansion unless the proposals were dropped. The cabinet had attempted to calm the furore by calling a task force, one of whose members would shortly be elected the youngest premier in Quebec's history: Robert Bourassa. Only after Bourassa's intervention on the company's behalf, in fact, did Trudeau's then finance minister, John Turner, introduce a bill to compensate Iron Ore for its losses due to the changes in the law. Later, Turner would join Bechtel's board.

That $10 million settlement had contained all the makings of a major controversy, but, curiously, the Iron Ore bill slipped through Parliament unnoticed — in part, thanks to the adroit manoeuvrings of one of Turner's top aides. Nearly two decades later, Mulroney would appoint that former finance department official, Simon Reisman, as his chief free trade negotiator with the United States.

By the summer of 1975, Bennett was touting Mulroney as his heir — a canny political operator who understood Cleveland's corporate agenda and whose contacts crossed Canadian party lines. Even when Mulroney shelved Anderson's first offer in favour of a run at the Tory leadership, Hanna seemed in no hurry to find another candidate. Days after his loss to Joe Clark, Anderson called from Cleveland to commiserate. Then he flew up to Montreal for another meeting to reiterate his previous offer.

As Anderson is now careful to point out, the job description was not quite the same as the one since incorporated into the Mulroney legend. "Let me correct you," he growls into the phone from Fort Myers. "Brian was never the head of Iron Ore. I was chairman and I was the CEO. He reported to me. He couldn't go ahead and do anything basic without checking it out with me and my board."

D URING a leadership bid so lavish that he had been dubbed the "Cadillac candidate," there had been endless media speculation about Mulroney's campaign finances. Only his longtime client, Paul Desmarais of Power Corporation, had owned up to donating $10,000 — an admission widely regarded as an understatement. Despite Mulroney's repeated promises of full disclosure, he was the only Conservative candidate who did not keep that vow. The *Montreal Gazette* had reported that he spent $345,000 — twice Clark's total — and he would later claim that he incurred such heavy campaign debts that it took his former law partner, Arthur Campeau, three months to negotiate his plum five-year contract with Hanna. According to biographer MacDonald, that initial $180,000-a-year deal was "back-loaded," meaning it swelled the longer he stayed with Iron Ore, and included share and pension benefits that would assure him "lifetime financial security."

In retrospect, there seems no doubt that his seven years in the employ of Big Steel gave him the economic freedom, not to mention the credibility with the U.S. and Canadian business elite, to pursue the prime ministership. As modest as Iron Ore's three-room office space was on Sherbrooke Street, its presidency came with convenient perks: four tickets to the Montreal Forum in a high-profile box behind the Canadiens' bench and membership in the Mount Royal Club, the bastion of Anglo power in Quebec, whose rolls included Stephen Bechtel and Robert Anderson. Schmoozing over three-hour lunches at the Ritz-Carlton Hotel with his press pals and partying hard with the likes of Ross Johnson, the head of Standard Brands, another U.S. branch plant, Mulroney cut a dashing figure on Montreal's *nouveau riche* scene, moving easily from the longshoremen's halls on the port to the salons of Westmount, where he lived with his bride, Mila.

Although Iron Ore owned a lumbering propeller fleet, he convinced the Hanna board of directors he needed something speedier to cut down the flight time to Cleveland. The second-hand de Havilland executive jet he acquired from Nelson Skalbania also came in handy for political missions — transporting his backroom operative, Montreal lawyer Michel Cogger, from Ottawa or flying influential friends like Desmarais to the Iron Ore fishing lodge on Quebec's Lac Koberdoc. There, where the speckled trout were both fat and compliant, he often entertained the cronies who would craft his next leadership bid.

Iron Ore also brought the Mulroneys one of the most coveted addresses in Montreal. Not quite a year after he joined the company, Mila Mulroney, using her Serbian maiden name, Pivnicki, bought an elegant three-storey stone house at 68 Belvedere Road, on the summit of Westmount's most coveted slope, for $1, "plus good and valuable consideration" — the usual legalese for concealing the terms of a transaction. Even those around Mulroney concede he scored a deal: a reported 4 percent mortgage — never officially registered — from Iron Ore. In 1981, the year he began secretly planning his next leadership campaign, the company bought the house back from him for $500,000, and for the next two years the Mulroneys rented it for only $1,100 a month. In June 1983, just weeks after he won the Conservative leadership, which obliged him to move to Stornoway, the official opposition residence, Iron Ore put 68 Belvedere Road up for sale for $750,000; the big house on the hill had apparently outlived its usefulness.

Within a year of joining Iron Ore, Mulroney ascended from the executive vice presidency, as promised, to take over the presidential suite. By then Bennett had become disenchanted with his onetime protégé and actively opposed his promotion. His backing had been contingent upon Mulroney giving up politics, but it swiftly became clear he had no intention of doing that, despite his convention defeat. "There was always a very noticeable friction between Bennett and Mulroney," recalls Richard Geren, who ran Iron Ore's mining operation. "Bennett told me, 'You know, I recommended Brian originally, but I don't know I'd do it now.' But Mr. Anderson overruled him."

On the day of his appointment, Mulroney unabashedly announced to Geren, "I don't know a damn thing about mining and I'm not inclined to want to know; I'm going to leave it to you." He might not have been much of a hands-on manager, nor was he well acquainted with the finer points of a balance sheet, but those were not the qualities that Hanna had sought. Every day for seven years he reported by phone to Anderson, who sums up Mulroney's responsibilities succinctly: "Primarily, labour relations."

By the dog days of the 1970s, with the humiliating end of the Vietnam War and the energy crisis wreaking havoc on the U.S. economy, the industrial heartland of America had been rechristened the Rust Belt. Across the Midwest, steel plants were shuttering and facing bankruptcy. The uneven ore grades being dynamited out of Schefferville could not be turned into the pellets that modernized mills were demanding. What the company needed was not a financial wizard, but a gladhander who could finesse layoffs with Canadian unions, politicians, and the press. By 1981, the year Ronald Reagan swept to power in Washington, Mulroney was performing that task so well that his contract was renewed with even more lavish inducements and an invitation to sit on Hanna's board.

Already, the company had dispatched him abroad, ostensibly in search of new foreign markets. But those trips also gave Mulroney an opportunity to hobnob with world leaders and hone his international diplomatic skills. Anderson took him to China for a week, and, after a particularly profitable year at Iron Ore, he rewarded the Mulroneys and Gerens with a tour of Hanna's ore properties in Brazil, where the company had also taken an active interest in maintaining stability. In 1964 Hanna had helped the CIA engineer a military coup against the government of President João Goulart, which had threatened to expropriate its holdings. The corporation had even put its trucks at the service of the generals. Later, Mulroney would claim the South American trip had convinced him of the wisdom of a hemispheric trade agreement, despite the ominous implications: it was precisely the competition from those Brazilian mines that would force Iron Ore to close part of its Quebec operations.

Another jaunt to Romania, arranged by his Conservative ally Robert Coates, a Nova Scotia MP, was billed as a marketing mission, but it proved more valuable to Mulroney's political aspirations. Carting along Coates and his former university pal, Patrick MacAdam, the company's part-time lobbyist in Ottawa, Mulroney won an effusive audience with dictator Nicolae Ceausescu, then Washington's favourite intermediary to the communist bloc. "I have never seen Ceausescu in such good form," marvelled Canadian ambassador Peter Roberts in his cable back to External Affairs. "Full hour longer than he usually gives to such calls. And I think it was unusual that at the end of the meeting he accompanied us out the door and down the corridor to the head of the stairs, where he stood and chatted just like anyone else."

If Mulroney dazzled the despot of Bucharest, the deal he was negotiating quickly became a company joke: Ceausescu was offering to pay for shipments of iron ore with Romanian-made tennis shoes. But the trip did boost Mulroney's confidence in his future. As Roberts noted, he and his party had been billeted at a hotel normally reserved for high-ranking communist officials. And Ceausescu not only made it clear that he knew of Mulroney's 1976 leadership bid, but encouraged him to try again. Pointing out that he had once hosted another defeated candidate in the very salon where they were meeting, Ceausescu offered Mulroney that comeback as an inspiration: the presidency of Richard Nixon. According to Mulroney's travelling companions, his vote of confidence had a wondrous effect: no sooner did Mulroney land back in Montreal than he announced he was going to stop drinking and get back in political fighting shape.

Like Mackenzie King's toils at the Rockefeller Foundation, the Iron Ore presidency provided a convenient apprenticeship for 24 Sussex Drive. "Paul Desmarais told me once that Mulroney's growth at Iron Ore was an essential stage to his becoming prime minister," L. Ian MacDonald recalls. Presiding over a company whose entire output was shipped to U.S. industry, then returned to Quebec in the form of American-made cars, Desmarais believed that his protégé had come to understand a vital truth: according to MacDonald, "He learned about the interdependence of the two economies."

Anderson concurs. "I think Brian learned a lot from us," he says. "He learned how to operate — and when I use the word operate, I mean a lot of things. Nobody in government knows how to operate — I mean . . . make money!"

By 1981 the company's coffers were helping fund Mulroney's political dreams. In Ottawa, Patrick MacAdam was on an Iron Ore retainer, keeping an eye on Joe Clark's declining fortunes at Tory headquarters. And in Montreal, Mulroney arranged a consulting fee for Frank Moores, who had resigned from two controversial terms as premier of Newfoundland. Both charismatic charmers who shared a taste for booze and backstage political machinations, he and Moores had traded so many favours they had lost count.

When Mulroney wanted to impress his client Paul Desmarais, Moores appointed the Power Corporation chairman chancellor of Memorial University. And the premier had placed Mulroney's name in nomination at the 1976 party leadership convention with a spell-binding speech. After Mulroney lost, Moores liked to claim that he had helped him win his job at Iron Ore, which was Newfoundland's largest employer. Later, when the contract for aerial inspections of the company's rail lines came up for renewal, one former employee received a phone call from Iron Ore's president announcing that it would have to go to Moores, whose friend Craig Dobbin owned a St. John's helicopter firm; informed that the contract had already been awarded to a lower bidder, Mulroney unleashed a volley of expletives.

In 1979, after leaving office, Moores had moved to Montreal and set up his consulting firm a block from Iron Ore's headquarters on Sherbrooke Street. There, with help from MacAdam, he orchestrated the four-year campaign to dump Joe Clark — the essential stepping stone to another leadership convention.

Meanwhile at Iron Ore, Mulroney doled out campaign contributions to friends of differing political stripes, accumulating his own IOUs. Those donations were one sign that the company made budgetary provisions for greasing the political wheels — a standard practice in the United States, where Hanna was a generous contributor to both the Ohio and the national Republican Parties.

During Mulroney's 1983 leadership bid, Anderson acknowledges that Hanna "must have" provided substantial financial help; in the election a year later, Iron Ore appears to have done its part to bring him to power. In 1984 one of the largest contributions to the PC Canada Fund was a $50,000 donation from the Labrador Railways Association Ltd, a group that exists on no provincial or federal registry but could only be tied to the region's single train line: Iron Ore's wholly owned Quebec North Shore and Labrador Railway.

Certainly, Hanna's top brass was not disinterested in the Conservatives' fundraising campaign. Both Anderson and longtime board member R. L. "Tim" Ireland III, who was related to the Humphrey family interests, kicked in $1,310.80 each. Four years later, when Mulroney's re-election prospects looked dim, Iron Ore threw $100,000 into the PC Canada pot to become the Tories' second-highest contributor.

Nor was there any reason for the boys from Big Steel not to support him; for seven years, Mulroney had performed admirably for them. In 1978, after a four-and-a-half-month strike, he clamped down on the steelworkers' union and the brotherhood of railway workers, complete with a press campaign charging they had been infiltrated by Marxist-Leninists. Then, gradually, the layoffs began — 500 here, 700 there. During the next three years, the company's payroll shrank and its profits soared. In 1980 shareholders collected a dividend for the first time in nearly a decade, and a year later, Iron Ore reported record profits of $92 million. But, as *Le Devoir* revealed, instead of reinvesting that windfall in Canada, the company began transferring them back to head office in Cleveland.

A year later, it became apparent why. On November 3, 1982, Mulroney went on the radio in Schefferville to announce that Iron Ore was closing its vast open-pit mine, the town's sole reason for existence. According to Richard Geren, the writing had been on the wall for at least three years as the company squeezed the last earnings out of the mine. But Alfred Rouleau, the dean of Quebec's Caisse populaire movement, raged against the company's "immoral behaviour." When Mulroney showed up with a conciliatory two-hour speech announcing $10 million in severance pay — while conceding that the company railway would charge for transporting workers and their worldly belongings to Sept-Iles — the townsfolk glared at him in appalled silence.

By then, Mulroney had already drafted his own relocation plans. Three months later, after one of the most intricate covert campaigns in Canadian political history, his forces manoeuvred Joe Clark into calling for a review of his own Conservative leadership. Having pulled off that coup, Mulroney retreated to a luxury Florida compound to polish his last assignment for the Hanna board: an appearance in Schefferville before an all-party committee of the Quebec National Assembly that was investigating Iron Ore's abrupt mine closure.

It was, from all accounts, a masterful performance. Armed with a glossy brochure, Mulroney paid tribute to Hanna's corporate citizenship and termed the crisis that would leave Schefferville a ghost town "a new beginning." The region's iron ore could no longer compete in shrinking global markets with Brazil's, he said, as miners sporting "Save the North" buttons sat in the back row muttering "Brian Baloney." He offered dazzling scenarios for the town's "serious and solid future": as the site for a prison or a NATO training school — perhaps even a national park featuring a native handicrafts industry.

He never once mentioned "globalization," the corporate buzz-word that would be used nearly a decade later to explain away the collapse of Canadian manufacturing under the free trade agreement. But to many, Mulroney's role in sacrificing Schefferville to Hanna's larger corporate agenda foreshadowed his choices as prime minister.

Indeed, once in office, he would not forget his former mentors in Cleveland, where upheavals had shaken the board. In 1981, as he plotted his leadership bid, his ally Conrad Black — who had named Mulroney a director of two of his companies — launched a bitter $210 million takeover battle for a dominant stake in M. A. Hanna. During the hostilities, Mulroney had claimed neutrality as "the jam in the sandwich." But in his memoirs, Black later slammed him for "his propensity to truckle to the *desiderata* of those whose goodwill was most important to him." Still, the buy-out, through Norcen Energy, had injected millions into the steel consortium at a time it was mired in debt. Four years later, Black sold that 20 percent inter-est to his partners in Norcen: Trevor Eyton and the Brascan/Noranda team who would lead the Bay Street forces promoting free trade.

But in the spring of 1986, three years after Mulroney had left Hanna, the guest list for his first gala state dinner at the White House included neither Black nor Eyton but his old boss and bene-factor, Bob Anderson, and Hanna director Tim Ireland III.

In Ronald Reagan's Washington, after all, the M. A. Hanna Company had a special cachet. One of Mulroney's fellow directors, Stephen Bechtel, had contributed two of his top executives, George Shultz and Caspar Weinberger, to the cabinet, and in 1989 Shultz would return to Bechtel's board. Peter Grace, another key Republican fundraiser whom Reagan named to head a commission on government waste, also had ties to the Cleveland consortium. His W. R. Grace & Co. had forged a partnership with Hanna to acquire a minority interest in a half-dozen coal mines from West Virginia to Colorado. Although coal was under attack as a cause of acid rain, many of their joint ventures mined the more environ-mentally acceptable low-sulphur variety. And Hanna's 1983 annual report even detected a bright side to the increasingly militant green movement: the company's coal investments, it noted, "could stand to benefit from growing environmental and safety concerns."

Still, some environmentalists might have bridled at the paradox in Mulroney's first declaration when he arrived in Washington in September 1984: the prime minister who announced that his chief priority was to tackle the scourge of acid rain had just spent the previous seven years on the payroll of a U.S. corporate colossus that drew its profits from the Midwest's most polluting factories, oil wells, and coal mines. In fact, only five months before his election, the American Iron and Steel Institute — whose membership included Hanna and its shareholder mills — had petitioned Washington's Court of Appeals to force the rollback of even the most rudimentary smokestack emission regulations designed to combat acid rain.

4 Ties That Bind

NORTH OF THE PENTAGON, Virginia's Highway
123 veers by a forbidding office complex set back among the trees,
its identity signalled only by serious security and a discreet roadside
sign: the Central Intelligence Agency. Five minutes farther down
the highway, in an unassuming row of suburban townhouses, an
equally discreet notice marks the headquarters of Richard Wirthlin,
the pollster whose strategic wizardry brought Ronald Reagan to
power and would help install right-wing regimes around the globe,
from Edward Seaga in Jamaica and Yitzhak Shamir in Israel to
Margaret Thatcher and John Major in Britain.

If the United States has always seen itself as a light unto the
world, perhaps no president felt that sense of mission as keenly as
Reagan. For him, America was the mythic utopia, the shining City
on the Hill, a land designated for an extraordinary destiny by a
divine covenant. If the nation occasionally got off track, it was
nothing a little free market economics and military build-up could
not set right.

Not surprisingly, the unassuming Mormon who helped carry the
Reagan revolution abroad shared those convictions. Like other
members of the church Brigham Young had planted in the basin of
Utah's Great Salt Lake, Wirthlin believed in minimum government

interference and maximum free enterprise that would reward righteousness with prosperity. In his own multimillion-dollar business,
he had one rule: "I only work for conservatives," he said.

In 1979 Wirthlin exported his distinctive psychographic software
to a former Toronto ballet studio and set up a computerized data-
analysis system that would revolutionize polling in Canada. Within
six years, that system would play a pivotal role in Brian Mulroney's
1984 election victory, helping to craft his platform and daily
campaign message just as it had done for Reagan before him.

Later, with its ability to track shifting public attitudes and
values, Wirthlin's Political Information System (PINS) — run by his
flamboyant Canadian protégé Allan Gregg — would tell Mulroney
on a day-by-day and region-to-region basis which political hot
buttons to push as he gradually imposed a continentalist economic
agenda that had the support of scarcely half the country. Although
the Conservatives would borrow a host of other White House
backstage techniques to help reshape the nature of the Canadian
political debate, only Wirthlin's public opinion snapshots provided
a measure of their success — charting the exhaustion of public
outrage as Ottawa's policies relentlessly meshed with those of
Washington.

Given that influence, it seems remarkable how much Canadians
knew about Gregg, who inspired media awe for striding through
Conservative backrooms in his ponytail and earring, and how little
they heard about the quiet American in grey flannel who had taught
him the secrets of his trade and set him up in business. But then,
Wirthlin liked it that way. Ever since the fall of 1968 when a
chauffeur-driven limousine delivered him to a clandestine Pacific
Palisades address high in the hills above Santa Monica, where the
host turned out to be Reagan, he had toiled first in secret, then in
the shadows, for the American conservative movement.

The son of a small-time rancher in Utah, Wirthlin had first
glimpsed Canada as a boy when he and his father hauled horses to
livestock shows in Alberta. But he had forsaken the range for
academia, where he shone, acquiring a PhD in economics from the
University of California at Berkeley. Among his fellow Mormons,
whose patriotism has made them unusually numerous recruits to
both the FBI and the CIA, his choice of Berkeley would later
provoke suspicions of liberalism. But his doctorate was not something he took lightly. Even those in the shadows occasionally

demand their due, and to this day visitors to his office who refer to him as "Mr." are sharply corrected by the receptionist: "It's *Doctor* Wirthlin."

In 1968, when Reagan's backers first approached him, Wirthlin was chairing the economics department at Utah's Brigham Young University, where his pioneering survey research had won him modest fame among West Coast marketers and defence contractors. But in those days, political polling was still a work in progress. What intrigued Wirthlin were the possibilities of statistical projection which computer programmers had initially explored for ends that had nothing to do with democracy: their simulation techniques had been developed by the U.S. military for its war games. But where once the Pentagon's mainframes had been used to predict battle scenarios and even survival rates after a nuclear holocaust, Wirthlin and others were adapting that technology for peacetime conflict zones: retailing and politics.

Subcontracted for Richard Nixon's 1968 presidential race, he found his strategic counsel spurned by campaign organizers. But later that year, the party grapevine carried news of his simulations to the California money men who had handpicked Reagan for governor when he was still a roving ambassador for General Electric. Having footed the bill for Reagan's 1964 televised barn-burner on behalf of Barry Goldwater, summoning Republicans to a "rendezvous with destiny," they were ultimately grooming Reagan for the presidency; but first they were determined to return him to the statehouse for a second term. For them, the enormous cost of Wirthlin's system was no obstacle. From drugstore king Justin Dart to Holmes Tuttle, the largest car dealer in California, the archconservatives who would become known as Reagan's Kitchen Cabinet were self-made billionaires who controlled some of the state's largest fortunes.

For the 1970 governor's race, Wirthlin set up his Univac computer in an unmarked office, dubbed the Bomb Shelter, on Los Angeles' Olympic Boulevard, where he ran simulations of the vote. Even programming the best possible odds for Reagan's opponent, his projections showed the governor coming out ahead. For his upbeat candidate who hated bad news, that forecast alone worked wonders: buoyed by Wirthlin's assurances, Reagan was transformed on the hustings. Four years earlier, a team of behavioural scientists had rehearsed him in a crash course on current events crammed into eight black binders, leaving him floundering whenever the campaign strayed from his tightly controlled script. But this time Wirthlin's high-tech plumbing of the public subconscious had reduced the issues to a few memorable concepts, and Reagan sailed onstage armed with the breezy one-liners he loved.

Wirthlin's massive phone banks, run out of Provo, Utah, where the accents were deemed regionally neutral, tabulated what issues provoked public emotions and why. Instead of measuring the reaction to a candidate's pronouncements, his PINS techniques helped craft that message from the start, then finetuned it by tracking its echoes through narrow demographic and regional slices of the population. One result was a platform that featured Reagan's first attacks on the welfare system. Years later, writer Roland Perry would paint Wirthlin as a puppetmaster pulling the candidate's strings in a book entitled *Hidden Power: The Programming of the President.*

With Reagan's re-election, Wirthlin set up his Decision Making Information (DMI) in Santa Ana, the capital of Orange County in the suburban sprawl south of Los Angeles. There, in the heart of right-wing Republican country, he began positioning his client for the next stop on the Kitchen Cabinet's political itinerary — a 1976 bid for the White House — when a Toronto Tory approached him about bringing his techniques to Canada.

Nearly two decades later, Wirthlin would recall that overture for a Canadian reporter. By then, he had moved to Virginia and rechristened his company the Wirthlin Group, a name scrawled across his letterhead and out front on the glass doors of his townhouse office. But he would pointedly note that the official legal designation of the firm was not the Wirthlin Group or even Decision Making Information; it was Decima.

Wirthlin would offer that fact unasked, but with a knowing smile. And from a man who had spent his career taking the emotional pulse of the populace, calculating the impact of a single word on a specific neighbourhood or class, it would appear to be no idle observation. In Canada, as he well knew, Decima was a name synonymous with Allan Gregg. But with a simple, seemingly offhand remark, Wirthlin was making one thing perfectly clear: despite all the adulatory column inches devoted to Gregg, *he* had started Decima, the firm that had helped bring Mulroney to power and kept him there for nine years. Richard Wirthlin was claiming parentage of the Conservative revolution in Canada.

RICH Willis was flipping through the American newsmagazines that had piled up in his office when he came across a story on the man *Time* dubbed "the guru of the modern political campaign." From his desk at Sherwood Communications, the holding company for Foster Advertising, a pivotal cog in Ontario's Big Blue Machine, Willis put in a call to Santa Ana. Wirthlin agreed to hear him out on an upcoming trip to New York.

When they met in the pollster's corner suite at the Plaza Hotel, there was an instant rapport. Not only were both hard-core conservatives, but Wirthlin's manner and Mormon background assured discretion, which was what Willis required. He was shopping for a secret assessment of how one well-known but wary Conservative might fare in the party's upcoming 1976 federal leadership contest: Ontario premier William Davis.

Working out of DMI's offices in California, Wirthlin confirmed Davis's fears: his federal ambitions were likely to be foiled by his Alberta rival, Peter Lougheed, who would soon throw his support behind Joe Clark. But that exercise convinced the Ontario team to hire him as the party's new pollster. Already Wirthlin's novel tracking techniques could offer a moving picture of a campaign in progress.

For the Tories, it was not unusual to turn south of the border for political wisdom. Their affable Maritime Machiavelli, Dalton Camp, and his American-born brother-in-law, Norman Atkins — who would serve as Mulroney's 1984 campaign chairman — had long enjoyed ties to the Nixon administration. In 1971 they hired Nixon's pollster, Robert Teeter, who ran Market Opinion Research out of Detroit. A year after Teeter helped engineer Bill Davis's election in Ontario, the federal Conservatives had hired him to poll for Robert Stanfield in the 1972 election.

For a party so long out of power, the Republicans offered both hope and sophisticated campaign techniques. After Stanfield's loss, national director Malcolm Wickson had taken his deputy, John Laschinger, on a field trip to the Ohio Republican Party headquarters to study the new U.S. direct mail methods that the Reagan campaign later perfected. Back in Ottawa, Laschinger had meticulously followed the counsel of a crusty Ohio party boss for choosing a mailing list on which to build his computerized fundraising base — prompting the Tories' first appeals to those Canadians on the subscription rolls of *Playboy* magazine.

But other links were also being forged with the Republican high command in Washington. Wickson brought in fundraising expert Robert Odell, who would return to work every Conservative campaign over the next decade and a half, including Kim Campbell's. And in 1979 Teeter introduced Paul Curley, the Tories' new campaign chairman, to Bill Brock, a former Tennessee senator who had become the head of the Republican National Committee. Invited by Brock to Washington, Curley was stunned by his red-carpet welcome and the bloodlust of a new generation of conservative true believers who were happy to share the latest voter-targeting tips and take-no-prisoner commercials.

"It was so negative, it was outrageous," Curley recalls. "What they did on TV — calling people liars, thieves — I came back and said, 'Geez, that stuff won't work here.' First of all the Canadian public wouldn't put up with it and second you'd never get it on the CBC." Ironically, more than a decade later during Kim Campbell's disastrous 1993 race, which Curley helped orchestrate with Allan Gregg, he would be proved partially right: public outrage would force the Conservatives to pull a televised spot focusing on Jean Chrétien's half-paralysed face and questioning his capacity to appear prime ministerial.

Throughout the 1970s, cross-border party ties would continue to grow. But in 1975 when Willis called Wirthlin, he was reaching outside them — making an alliance with Reagan's California machine, which was still considered too outrageously right wing for the tastes of the East Coast Republican establishment. At the time, his move was based less on ideology than on pragmatics: by then, the Conservatives were disenchanted with their high-priced Detroit pollster. Although Teeter had set up a satellite operation across the river in Windsor, some Tories had taken to griping that the only time he turned his thoughts to Canada was on the flight to Ottawa. Later, when Wirthlin inquired why the party had sought out his services, one official cracked that it was because they figured the plane ride from Los Angeles took longer than the one from Detroit. "We were having trouble getting information out of Teeter," Willis confirms. "He just wasn't paying attention."

Wirthlin not only paid attention, but he took Willis under his wing, hosting him at the 1976 Republican convention in Kansas City where Reagan's presidential hopes were narrowly dashed by

Gerald Ford. There, Willis met the key players who would orchestrate Reagan's next White House bid: Lyn Nofziger, his rumpled press secretary; Roger Ailes, his rambunctious adman; and Michael Deaver, his former right-hand-man in the statehouse, who had built a public relations firm around booking Reagan's speeches and syndicated weekly radio commentaries.

Two years later, Willis convinced Wirthlin to set up a polling branch plant in Toronto. He turned the negotiations over to Tom Scott, the chairman of Sherwood Communications, who established a 50–50 partnership with Wirthlin's Decision Making Information. Sherwood was to provide the Conservative and corporate connections, DMI the analytical know-how and top-secret software.

To run it, Wirthlin agreed to send Ron Hinckley, his executive vice president of operations, to Toronto from Santa Ana. But Scott insisted on including another employee in the arrangement, complete with an initial 10 percent share of the stock: Allan Gregg, the shaggy whizkid who had arrived at Conservative headquarters to do research as a Carleton graduate student and had stayed, dazzling Joe Clark's aides with his statistical prowess, his shared Alberta roots, and his sideline as a rock band manager.

Gregg had so impressed Tory strategist Bill Neville that Neville nominated him for a 1978 State Department grant to study American polling techniques. During that U.S.–funded swing through California, he met Wirthlin, whose tracking apparatus he realized was light years ahead of his competitors' methodology. As Gregg tells it, it was he who returned home and persuaded the Tories to import Wirthlin's expertise. But neither Wirthlin nor Hinckley have any memory of meeting Gregg on the tour. What they do recall is the stumbling block of Trudeau's Foreign Investment Review Agency, which required a Canadian to head the new firm. As Willis puts it, "We needed a Canadian front man."

Gregg proved the perfect choice. Not only did he translate Wirthlin's program for the Tories, but he added his own innovations. In fact, so expert did he become that after their 1981 campaign for Davis — targeting select households with personal letters from the premier addressing specific concerns — Wirthlin invited Gregg to a New York media seminar to showcase their handiwork.

But in Canada, where the Conservatives had no desire to draw attention to their new U.S. pollster, a crisis erupted over what to call the partnership. Wirthlin offered the solution: Decima — a name that already had a history of dissimulation. After the 1976 elections that brought Jimmy Carter to power, he had worried he would be shut out of federal contracts; in a sly semantic move, his accountant had come up with a contraction of Decision Making Information — Decima — which Wirthlin incorporated as the firm's holding company. He printed up a Decima logo and letterhead, used only when Wirthlin was bidding on work from the Democrats.

In Canada, once again, Decima was adopted as a convenient cover — apparently free of American associations that might offend nationalists. But true to his profession, Wirthlin tested the red, white, and blue logo on a Toronto focus group, whose reactions his team studied through a one-way mirror. One participant observed it looked like the American flag. Behind the mirror, one of Wirthlin's pollsters snickered, "If only you knew: an American accountant thought it up!"

After Gregg's work for Joe Clark's election in 1979, Decima was poised for a bonanza of federal contracts. But before they materialized, the government fell. Ironically, one of the items on the agenda of Clark's final cabinet meeting was the approval of a FIRA exemption that allowed Wirthlin to become Decima's half-owner.

With another election looming, Hinckley spent his Christmas holidays scrambling to install the firm's new Toronto phone banks; no matter how neutral the Utah accent, the Tories could not be caught conducting voter surveys out of Provo. But by the time the balloting rolled around, he was braced for disaster. He booked off for a Florida vacation, forewarned by Clark's shrinking numbers.

Suddenly Decima's prospects looked bleak. Its quarterly survey report aimed at corporate and government clients had signed up only two subscribers. Nor had Sherwood and DMI solved a contractual wrangle, which was piling up lawyers' fees and saddling the fledgling company with debt. In the summer of 1981, when Gregg came up with a new group of investors to buy out DMI's share, Wirthlin leaped for the exit.

By then, he had bigger fish to fry. A year earlier, he had provided Gregg and Hinckley ringside seats in Detroit's Joe Louis Arena where the Republican national convention annointed Reagan as its presidential standard-bearer. As chief campaign strategist, he went on to target the disaffected blue-collar Democrats who assured Reagan's landslide, orchestrating the muscular, tall-in-the-saddle message that spoke directly to their economic and patriotic angst.

After the election, Wirthlin had the opportunity to write himself a pivotal role in the White House. But he preferred to stay in the private sector, where DMI could profit from a $1-million-a-year contract with the Republican Party, not to mention foreign government work. Meanwhile, he remained on virtual full-time call to Reagan. From his headquarters across the Potomac, he set forth a governing strategy based on what he termed a "perennial campaign" — an approach that Gregg would later bring to Mulroney's government. For the next eight years, Wirthlin monitored each fluctuation in the public pulse and helped calibrate Reagan's responses, from the chest-thumping highs of the Grenada invasion to the lows of the Iran-Contra scandal, shoring up the myth of the Teflon president.

During that time, Wirthlin stayed in touch with his former Canadian partners. "There wasn't anything I couldn't get access to," Willis says. "Anything we asked for, they delivered. I remember going to Republican conventions and being treated like a cock of the walk."

Later, with Mulroney's election, Gregg's virtuosity with Wirthlin's PINS software would turn Decima into the most celebrated public opinion house in the country — a profit mill whose status was assured by its contract with the ruling party. But unlike his mentor, he would seize the public spotlight, becoming a blunt apologist for the government's policies while professing a neutral scientific allegiance to the numbers he ran. His enemies would gloat that his worst mistakes were not his strategy calls, but taking to the microphones to spell them out afterward. Where once pollsters had been invisible, Gregg would become a media star whose image was as familiar as that of his most important client — and increasingly more favourable. "By giving Allan a machine behind him, we gave the Tories their own indigenous polling capability," Hinckley says. "But Allan spearheaded the popularity of the pollster; he was the first to give it the pizazz."

The pollster's job, Gregg once said, was to offer advice "totally unfettered by any moral notion of what is good, bad, right, or wrong." But at a private banquet for Ottawa insiders in 1991, he would stun his audience with a scathing lampoon of his profession, arguing that even the most unlikely dolt could get elected with the right polling and packaging.

By that time, Gregg and Wirthlin would come to a parting of the ways that was more than philosophical. When they worked for rival camps in the Israeli election, Wirthlin would take satisfaction when his Likkud candidate whipped Gregg's client in the Labour party. But curiously, their business links would come virtually full circle. In 1989 Gregg sold Decima to international public relations giant Hill & Knowlton, whose exclusive pollster at the time was his old boss, Richard Wirthlin.

After Wirthlin's departure from Decima, Hinckley too packed up for Washington, where his career underlined just how closely public opinion was tied to U.S. national security interests. After a stint as Wirthlin's point man within the presidential bureaucracy, he moved on to the National Security Council, where he set up a crisis management centre to instantaneously process information pouring into the White House situation room during strategic alerts such as the Soviets' downing of Korean Airlines flight 007 or the suicide bombing of U.S. Marine barracks in Beirut.

Later, after advising George Bush on foreign policy during the 1988 elections, Hinckley was rewarded with a patronage plum. As director of audience research for the United States Information Agency, the government's foreign propaganda arm, he measured the effects of the Voice of America's broadcasts in the years leading to the collapse of the Soviet empire. And helping to orchestrate the campaign to vilify Saddam Hussein before the Persian Gulf War, he was instrumental in marshalling international support for the U.N. vote that legitimized the U.S. bombing of Iraq.

But no matter how compelling Washington's farflung public opinion interests, Hinckley kept an eye on the polling apparatus he had erected in Canada. In 1983, when the Conservatives ousted Joe Clark in favour of Mulroney, he was not surprised. In fact, whenever visiting Tories recounted how Mulroney had to be persuaded to trust Allan Gregg in the 1984 campaign — still wary of his loyalties to Clark — Hinckley could scarcely conceal his amusement. "Allan got going with Mulroney behind closed doors a lot earlier than he said he did," he insists. "He was doing some confidential polling for Mulroney and meeting with his henchmen when I was still there, and I was there until 1981." In 1981, as president of Iron Ore, Mulroney was denying any interest in a return to the leadership fray — a posture he would maintain publicly for the next two years. "All I know," Hinckley says, "is Allan didn't want me to breathe a word of this."

IN the cramped White House press room that Richard Nixon had erected over the former presidential swimming pool, Bill Fox wedged his fullback's bulk into the standing-room-only space in the rear. In the centre, rows of upholstered theatre seats, some with tiny brass plaques on their arms, were reserved for the U.S. media elite: network news stars like Sam Donaldson and Lesley Stahl in the front, the lesser lights fanning out towards the back in descending rank.

At the daily noonhour briefing by deputy press secretary Larry Speakes, a reporter from a regional Nebraska paper boasted more status than Fox, newly posted to Washington in December 1981 as the correspondent for the *Toronto Star*, Canada's largest newspaper. After all, what counted in the U.S. capital was not circulation but congressional votes, and, as a Canadian, Fox was incapable of delivering those.

Still, consigned to the equivalent of media Siberia, he gloried in his assignment — one that would provide unwitting tutelage for his job as Mulroney's communications czar two years later. Even on the fringes of the White House press corps, he had a front-row seat on the extraordinary media management operation created by Michael Deaver, the caretaker of Reagan's image, whose techniques Fox would import to Ottawa.

From Richard Wirthlin's running measure of the public mood — which helped draft the official White House line-of-the-day — to Deaver's tight rein over Reagan's every appearance, no administration had ever elevated the manipulation of the news to such a central role in its philosophy of governance. So crucial had controlling the media become that, in 1983, deputy White House press secretary Leslie Janka quit, charging, "The whole thing was PR. This was a PR outfit that became president and took over the country."

But as Deaver saw it, the press was the filter through which most Americans received their information, and no effort was spared to make sure the right story — the White House story — got out. How else to win public support for Reagan's economic policies, which were actually at odds with what the majority of Americans were telling pollsters they favoured?

Every morning Deaver's team met with one question: What do we want the press to cover today? Cutting back Reagan's press conferences, he staged events to feed the yawning media maw its daily sound bite, complete with compelling visuals. Playing the press like a three-ring circus master, he threw so many briefings and photo opportunities at journalists that no time was left for unpredictable enterprise reporting. "Manipulation by inundation," Deaver called it, and, as a reporter, Fox might have been appalled at the scorn White House operatives showed for his profession. But no sooner did he join Mulroney's team than he began working with Allan Gregg to duplicate the Deaver-Wirthlin partnership on Parliament Hill. Nor could they have served a more enthusiastic employer: an incurable newshound, Mulroney blamed every drop in the polls on poor media coverage.

Fox insists that his Washington apprenticeship was accidental. When he arrived in the U.S. capital, he had no thought of crossing over to the other side of the media barricades — "the equivalent," he says, "of crossing the River Styx." A feisty fireplug from Timmins, he was not unaware of his bar-room Irish charm and, in Ottawa, he was a popular, aggressive reporter with friends on both sides of the aisle — indeed, even in the wings, where he regularly covered the breakfasts held by dissident Tories plotting Joe Clark's overthrow.

Among his Liberal chums was Ed Lumley, Trudeau's minister of international trade, on whose government jet he hitched a ride to Washington. Eddie, as Fox called him, was making one of his first pilgrimages to talk up a free trade agreement with his counterpart Bill Brock — by then Reagan's U.S. trade representative. The subject was anathema to Fox's bosses at the *Star*, but he had no trouble making page one as he chronicled the Reagan administration's increasingly unvarnished hostility to Trudeau. Still, in the city that Reaganauts loved to refer to as the capital of the Western world, Fox found scant interest in what was happening north of the border.

But when Mulroney snatched the Conservative leadership from Clark, American colleagues started to call him, inquiring about Trudeau's new challenger. As it happened, Fox was in a privileged position to fill them in. More than a decade earlier as the Montreal correspondent for Southam News Service, he had struck up a friendship with the well-connected labour lawyer whose name he had spotted at the top of his predecessor's contact list.

Both Irishmen from gritty resource towns, they had grown up far from the intellectual smugness of Toronto or Montreal. Over regular three-hour lunches, they discovered a shared taste for booze and political gossip. Mulroney had cultivated a half-dozen close friends in the media, but covering his abortive 1976 Conservative leadership bid, Fox often found himself the only reporter on the campaign plane, hopping between obscure whistlestops. Soon it was "Foxie" and "Bri," their raunchy jock talk drifting into an affection that he admits overstepped journalistic bounds. Not long afterward, they had traded invitations to the christenings of each other's children.

During his Washington days, as Mulroney was positioning himself for his coup against Clark, Fox swears that they did not keep in touch. But in 1983, when the *Star* flew him back to Ottawa to cover the Tory leadership vote in Ottawa, he allowed himself one indiscretion: from his post on the convention floor, milling with other reporters in front of Mulroney's box before the final ballot, he flashed a thumbs-up sign at his old drinking buddy, who would promptly be declared the victor.

Back in Washington months later, Fox received an urgent summons from a mutual friend for a confidential meeting with the Conservatives' new national director, Janis Johnson, who also happened to be Frank Moores's estranged second wife and one of Mila Mulroney's close friends. In Ottawa, Johnson confided what had already become clear to the party's worried brass: their new leader was floundering on the campaign trail. When Mila or one of Mulroney's cronies was not along to swap stories on the interminable flights through smalltown Canada, Mulroney was lonely and increasingly glum, a dud on the hustings. Finally, he himself put in a call to Fox: "Look," he said, "I need some help."

Astoundingly for a politician so enamoured of the press, Mulroney's media operation was in a shambles. He had apparently failed to hire a press secretary. As it turned out, he had been holding the job open for Fox all along. Within a day their deal was done. But when he accepted, Fox made it clear he was not interested in serving as the traditional hired gun, firing press releases at his former colleagues; he wanted a say in crafting strategy and his accustomed place in the inner circle. "I was only going to do it," he says, "if I was part of senior management."

In an era when television had replaced the smoke-filled backroom as political kingmaker, Fox immersed himself in books about communications and campaign tactics. But it soon became clear that his most influential education came from his two-year exposure to

Deaver's meticulously orchestrated White House productions. In Ottawa, Fox's reporter friends were stunned when, in response to a media question, he himself answered it on the record and on camera — just as he had watched Larry Speakes do for Reagan. Not that Fox went as far as Speakes, who would later admit that he had twice manufactured quotes from the president — a confession that would cost him his job as head of communications for Merrill Lynch.

Rumpled and hot-tempered, seldom afraid to speak his mind, Fox presented a stark contrast to the slick, Southern unflappability of Speakes. But he had grasped the basic rules of the media manipulation game: control the message, keep it simple, and repeat it incessantly. Following Speakes's example, he took to cutting off unwelcome questions and tightly limiting exposure to his gregarious boss, who was used to palling around with the boys on the bus. The photo opportunity became a fixture on Parliament Hill, and every trip, no matter how mundane, was carefully pre-scripted to provide the daily visuals for television.

But for all Fox's efforts, Mulroney was still not making headlines. With the Liberal race to succeed Trudeau monopolizing media attention, his strategists had decided to concentrate on campaigning in the boondocks. But as his popularity plummeted by 30 percent, even that boony strategy seemed to be backfiring. By the late spring of 1984, when Fox flew to Washington to set up Mulroney's first official visit as opposition leader, there was an urgency to his mission. "We'd disappeared from the media radar screens for three months," he says. "We needed something to happen quick."

The White House seemed happy to oblige. Not only were Reagan and his officials delighted at the prospect of a Conservative coming to power in Ottawa, but they found themselves with what the French call an embarrassment of choices: John Turner, the man most likely to succeed Trudeau, already had the trust of the two most powerful members of the U.S. cabinet, George Shultz and Caspar Weinberger, from his days on the Bechtel board and his frequent visits to the capital as finance minister. For Mulroney, Turner represented a rival for Washington's affections — another reason to solidify his ties to the White House. "By then, the Americans were very interested," Fox says. "They wanted to get a look at him."

Playing Mulroney's one-man advance team, Fox worked with a half-dozen State Department and National Security Council officials, but Deaver was the key — keeper of the president's schedule and arbiter of his public gestures. The man whom *Time* magazine had dubbed the Vicar of Visuals agreed to give Mulroney a forty-minute get-acquainted chat with Reagan and Vice President George Bush in the Oval Office — and a photo opportunity in the Rose Garden. The only White House photo op of the day, it won Mulroney coveted space in the *Washington Post*, his profile silhouetted beside Reagan's in symbolic solidarity — precisely the signal Fox wanted transmitted to front pages back home. The *Post* story barely mentioned the Conservative leader in its text, but no matter: as Fox had come to understand, pictures were the medium that carried the message.

On the Washington beat, he had learned that the U.S. press pack only took notice of a foreign leader who fit into the capital's lead story. When Mulroney emerged from the White House, Canadian reporters pummelled him with questions about steel quotas and acid rain. But he rated mention in the U.S. press because Fox had drafted a declaration that meshed with Deaver's line-of-the-day on reviving stalemated arms control talks: Mulroney assured American reporters that he had come away convinced of the president's sincerity in wanting to get the negotiations back on track.

At a time when the White House was determined to disown Reagan's hawkish past, that kind of communications *quid pro quo* quickly cemented relations between Fox and Deaver. Never before in the memory of Patrick Gossage, the Canadian Embassy's press counsellor, had the administration made such a fuss over an opposition leader. For Gossage, the camaraderie was a bitter reminder of the countless brushoffs he had endured on behalf of his former boss, Trudeau. In a town where the smallest symbols are barometers of status, he observed that Speakes presented Fox not with the traditional paperweight as a gift but a prestigious White House medallion in a velvet-lined box.

Later, Fox confided to Gossage his thrill at riding up the driveway of 1600 Pennsylvania Avenue as part of the official party, a Washington insider at last. "These people were really blown away with being at the White House," Gossage recalls, "in a way that Trudeau's people never were."

Still, Fox was amused as Speakes greeted him like a long-lost friend, struggling to recall some encounter during his former incarnation in the White House press corps. "Obviously we hadn't met before," he chuckles. "I mean, I was one of the *scribinis* — and as a

Canadian, the lowest of the low. I loved to rub it in: I'd say, 'Larry, even your deputies didn't return my calls.'"

Mulroney's international debut proved a singular success — even snatching ink from Turner, who had just won the Liberal leadership the previous weekend. Making his rounds with Conservative foreign affairs critic Sinclair Stevens, he won audiences with Shultz, Commerce Secretary Malcolm Baldrige, and Treasury Secretary Donald Regan, as well as key congressional Democrats.

But one of his most prized stops was a breakfast with the editorial board of the *Washington Post*. Mulroney emerged from publisher Katharine Graham's private dining room to declare that he had given the Americans a scolding for ignoring Canada: "You know, unless you're Wayne Gretzky or a good snowstorm, you never get mentioned down here." Throughout his nine years in office, he would energetically court the U.S. press, singling out network correspondents by their first names and plunging into despondency whenever an American trip failed to rate coverage.

Later, U.S. correspondents in Ottawa would joke about being able to breeze into his prime ministerial office uninvited, while their Canadian counterparts were often treated like pariahs. On assignment in Haiti, a former *Los Angeles Times* bureau chief mocked that access to *Toronto Star* reporter Linda Diebel, as if Ottawa, too, were some over-eager Third World outpost. But Mulroney's esteem for the American media was not always returned. According to a participant at his *Washington Post* breakfast, he had barely walked out the door when Ben Bradlee, the paper's legendary executive editor, turned to his colleagues and pronounced his verdict. "Lightweight," Bradlee cracked.

On his advance trip, Fox had leaned on the embassy to host one of the glittering soirées that had turned Ambassador Allan Gotlieb and his wife, Sondra, into the toast of Embassy Row. As he made clear in no uncertain terms, it had to feature their A-list of invitees from the Reagan administration. "We were anxious to show we were well received," he says.

Gotlieb had demurred, noting that it might be difficult to lure cabinet luminaries out for an opposition leader. Fox suspected the ambassador was hedging his bets. "My job was to fix him with my beady eye and say, 'We want the A-list,'" he recalls, "'and I'll leave it to you to think about it overnight.'"

As Fox tells it, his veiled threat left the embassy staff reeling.

Gotlieb took to the phones, calling in his markers. The next morning at 5 A.M. when Fox crawled back to his hotel from a night on the
town, he found his message light flashing: the stipulated guest list
was indeed taking shape. "Had I not been satisfied we were going to
get the A-list, I would have cancelled the dinner," he says, "because
I know what wall-poster journalism is. The stories would have read:
only the bums showed up. I knew what the consequences would be
to Brian."

Fox had every reason to be acutely aware of the power of media
ridicule. During Joe Clark's round-the-world tour, a report on the
prime minister's lost luggage had turned him into the laughing-
stock of the Ottawa press corps — the butt of pundits such as
Mulroney's pal Allan Fotheringham. Any image-maker knows a
politician can recover from many a slur, but rarely from having
become a national joke. As Fox admits, "We didn't want any
'luggage tour.'"

For Mulroney, Gotlieb's dinner at the ambassadorial mansion on
Rock Creek Drive was the crowning glory of his trip, proof of his
embrace by Reagan's White House. Gathered in his honour were
seventy-two of Washington's most esteemed powerbrokers, including Deaver, Weinberger, and Attorney General William French
Smith, once the president's personal lawyer in California. Most surprising of all was the presence of CIA director William Casey, who,
unlike the rest, had never been known as one of the capital's social
butterflies.

A mumbler who was celebrated for leaving fellow diners splat-
tered in food, Casey was a zealous Cold Warrior who saw the world
in terms of black and white — communists or free enterprise
tycoons like himself. The CIA's analysts had been keeping a close
watch on Mulroney, who was already a favourite of Wall Street,
where Casey had plied his trade as a shrewd tax lawyer. But
distrusting his bureaucracy almost as much as he did Congress, he
had more than a passing interest in taking a personal measure of the
candidate most likely to replace Trudeau. That dinner, according to
Charley McMillan, "gave Mulroney an incredible inner confidence.
And it anchored a sense in the Americans that Canada–U.S.
relations could be better."

But for the press, the evening also provided a glimpse of Fox's
news-management style to come. Most of the twenty-six Canadian
journalists covering Mulroney's visit found themselves reporting on

the event from the pavement outside, where they were obliged to forage for scraps from exiting U.S. media superstars such as Ben Bradlee. Like the Reagan White House, Mulroney's government would focus its affections on the owners and the top editors of the Canadian media, flattering them with dinner invitations and off-the-record phone calls that disguised spin control with intimations of insider lowdown. Meanwhile, their less malleable employees on the beat were often treated with contempt. Information and access became a commodity judiciously doled out by the prime minister's press office, which rewarded the most favourable coverage with weekends at Harrington Lake or tête-à-têtes at 24 Sussex Drive.

On the embassy guest list, Fox had included two senior TV correspondents, the CBC's Joe Schlesinger and CTV's Craig Oliver — and only then on an off-the-record basis — but no print or French-Canadian journalists. When Canadian Press reporter Carl Mollins filed a story on that oversight, Fox was irate: not only had it tarnished Mulroney's shining moment but it had upstaged any other coverage in the Quebec press. The next morning, Mollins was still in the shower when Fox pounded on his door in Georgetown, thundering at the reporter's wife: "Tell Carl I'm looking for him."

Neither Deaver nor Speakes would ever have made such a move. At the White House, muscle-flexing was more subtle. When Dan Rather attacked Reaganomics, Deaver dined with CBS chairman William Paley, noting that he was thinking of persuading the Federal Communications Commission to stop rating newscasts — a prospect that would have devastated the network's ad revenues. But Fox preferred a pit-bull style. He threatened to tear the lungs out of his former *Toronto Star* colleague Joe O'Donnell, then claimed it was a joke.

After Mulroney's election, Fox made a handful of solo trips back to the White House for further tips on honing the prime ministerial media operation. On one visit, he conferred with right-wing zealot Pat Buchanan, who would pen a column for the *Washington Times* entitled "Annex Canada One Day?" Buchanan railed against Mulroney's wishy-washy conservativism, urging Fox to define the government's ideology. "I remember him telling me Mulroney was a communist because of Medicare," Fox chuckles. "I was conscious in a dozen different ways every day there that I wasn't an American."

But, increasingly, his press office aped U.S. presidential pageantry. For Mulroney's first meeting with provincial premiers in early 1985,

Fox arranged his press conference appearance not seated at the usual table, but behind a White House–inspired podium studded with the Canadian coat of arms. When Fox announced Mulroney's arrival with "Ladies and gentlemen, the prime minister," the hoots of derision from the assembled scribes, who began humming "Hail to the Chief," put an end to that flourish.

But those missteps failed to dim his enthusiasm for the gospel according to Deaver. Beneath the image-maker's casual, even off-hand veneer, Fox saw a canny understanding of television's power to convey more than one message at once. Deaver had posed Reagan at a B–1 bomber factory announcing yet another whopping defence contract — in front of a gigantic sign reading "Prepared for Peace." "He had a real genius to understand TV's ability to communicate complex issues," Fox says. "Everybody says television can only convey simple messages, but it's not true. He also understood how you communicate at a multiplicity of levels."

Control was Deaver's byword, and it would soon become Fox's as well. But he could never make his American counterparts understand that the difference in political systems prevented him from keeping Mulroney in quite the same magnificent isolation as Deaver kept Reagan. "They'd pound the table and talk about controlling the agenda," he recalls. "And I'd say, 'Well, that's okay when you've got the Rose Garden and a White House spokesman, but Question Period is another matter.'"

Still, he restricted press access to scrums in the corridors outside the House of Commons, where the media was left scrambling after the prime minister like a yapping mob. And when Reagan arrived in Ottawa in the spring of 1987, Fox showed his mastery of dissent. Protestors were issued permits and herded onto a site far from Parliament Hill or the presidential motorcade, allowed to demonstrate before Air Force One landed. Public fury was channelled into a quaint side show, complete with papier-mâché floats — all orchestrated by the press secretary's brother, Robert Fox.

But nothing illustrated his obsession with control more clearly than the gag order issued to the entire civil service within weeks of the election. During Mulroney's Washington blitz as opposition leader three months earlier, Fox concedes that they had "kind of hatched" plans with the White House for a swift follow-up trip as prime minister. But Mulroney was furious when news leaked out of his first official pilgrimage to Washington. Three top bureaucrats were summoned to the Prime Minister's Office, where an accusatory chill hung in the air.

Pointing out that the leak had sprung from Washington, not Ottawa, they shifted uneasily from foot to foot, assuring him they were already preparing a briefing book for his American visit. Fox stared down the seasoned trio. "What makes you think you can give us advice?" he demanded icily.

As one participant later recalled, "They didn't trust the bureaucracy. They thought we were all Liberals and were going to be resisting all the changes they wanted to make with the United States." Fox admits those suspicions. "Once you're elected," he snorts, "they come thundering over the horizon like the Mongol hordes: 'We'll take over everything.'" But in fact, his show of force was a message specifically targeted at Marcel Massé, undersecretary of state for external affairs, the most certain Liberal — and the suspected source of the leak. "I was instructed to deliver a commentary that the prime minister didn't want to deliver," Fox explains.

That intimidation would soon be expanded into official policy with an order to the federal bureaucracy in general, and all 4,000 employees of External Affairs in particular, forbidding them to talk to the press, even socially, without express permission. Ironically, at External Affairs the order was issued over Massé's signature. For months afterward, diplomats avoided reporters, terrified of reprisals. Although the order was later disregarded, it was never legally rescinded throughout Mulroney's mandate. The threat of firing hung over any External mandarin tempted to question the government's foreign policy, above all its continental drift.

Paradoxically, secrecy held sway in Ottawa to an extent that would never have been tolerated in Washington. To sell the free trade talks — which had the support of less than 50 percent of the populace — Fox drafted a sophisticated strategy that treated them not as a commodity to be hyped, but as a potential disaster to be downplayed. Like Deaver pitching Reaganomics, the government was faced with manufacturing consent for a policy at odds with popular sentiment. The solution was to treat it as some toxic waste spill — an exercise in damage control.

In September 1985, less than a week before Mulroney officially announced his launch of negotiations, a leaked memo from Fox's office showed that — just as Deaver drew on Richard Wirthlin's polling — he relied on Allan Gregg's reading of the public psyche.

"The majority of Canadians do not understand fully what is meant by the terms free trade, freer trade or enhanced trade," the memo reported. "The popular interpretation of free trade appears to be keyed to the word 'free.' It is something for nothing — a short cut — to economic prosperity . . . But are respondents really thinking when they express their opinions on free trade? Gregg suggests not, calling the free trade issue a 'non-brainer.'"

Instead of correcting that ignorance, Fox's tactics called for capitalizing on it: "Benign neglect from a majority of Canadians may be the realistic outcome of a well-executed communications program," he argued. "It is likely that the higher the profile the issue attains, the lower the degree of public approval will be."

In fact, thanks to a massive campaign by opponents, the free trade debate so transfixed the nation that it almost cost Mulroney the 1988 election. Four years later, as the government faced a similar uphill fight with the North American Free Trade Agreement, the transcript of a taped August 1992 conference call among top government fig-ures plotting PR strategy was leaked to *Maclean's*. The tapes revealed that the government's own polls showed only 45 percent support for NAFTA. But again those officials betrayed a steely determination to push ahead with the pact at all costs. Dismissing opponents as "that old left-wing, crypto-communist, anti-free trade, NDP–Liberal con group," Jim Ramsay, a longtime Tory operative who was then chief of staff to Trade Minister Michael Wilson, called for a counterattack. "As you can see we're moving the numbers," Ramsay reassured his fellow bureaucrats. "I guess the opposition have left us these empty heads to fill and we've been getting in there."

But if there was one issue on which Gregg and Fox seemed inca-pable of moving the numbers, it was Mulroney himself. Despite the most sophisticated media machine in prime ministerial history, his polls plummeted as consistently as his credibility. By 1991, Gregg's public soundings showed that a majority of Canadians harboured a visceral dislike of the man whose public appearances were haunted by placards reading "Lyin' Brian"; they also registered a pervasive sense of national disempowerment and despair. "In the seven years we have been doing this research," Gregg worried, presenting Decima's annual poll to *Maclean's*, "we have never identified a blacker mood."

Still, steadily, relentlessly, undeterred by those declining num-bers, Mulroney continued to impose Reagan's neoconservative economic agenda on the nation. Contrary to the popular conception of a government crafting policies in slavish response to the polls, he and his spin control operatives used the polls to measure the limits of their flexibility in pushing unpopular economic policies on Canadians.

But as he wound up his Washington debut in June 1984, Mulroney delivered his own line-of-the-day, which ought to have provided a glimpse of whose approval he would be currying. On the tarmac at Andrews Air Force Base, he recounted his conversation with Reagan in the Oval Office to a gathering of reporters: "I said, 'Look, if I were the president of the United States and I got up in the morning, my first thought would be, Thank God I've got Canada as a neighbour. Now, what can I do for Canada today?'"

5 Clearing the Air

THE CIVIL WAR was Russ Wunker's passion — an exercise in betrayal and tactical miscalculation that had nearly rent asunder the tentative American union. For the son of a U.S.–born resort owner from Haliburton, it was not an unusual hobby: Wunker had spent his undergraduate years at New York state's Nyack College, where he organized the campus for Richard Nixon and Spiro Agnew, then earned an M.A. from the University of South Florida in Canadian-American relations. But back home, charged with coordinating the Tories' annual general meeting in February 1981 — the first since Joe Clark had so ignominiously fumbled his grip on power — Wunker sensed that a civil war was threatening to tear apart the Conservative Party. Treachery was in the air, and across the country knives were being quietly sharpened for Clark — some less quietly than others.

The most obstreperous rebels were clustered around maverick York North MP John Gamble, a loquacious, bantam-weight tax lawyer from the northern Toronto suburb of Markham and the party's extreme right wing. In 1979 Gamble had snatched his riding from under the astonished nose of Trudeau's defence minister, Barney Danson, with dogged grassroots organizing and relentless coffee parties. Nine months later when Clark's government toppled in a disastrously misjudged nonconfidence vote, he was apoplectic. Soon afterward, in his recreation room on a subdivision cul-de-sac, a tiny band of fellow malcontents gathered to begin fomenting demands for a review of Clark's leadership.

Setting up the PC Review Committee, the first public sign of dissent within party ranks, their movement quickly spawned a catchier tag: ABC — Anybody But Clark. As Gamble saw it, "Clark had blown his chance. But the issue for a lot of us was that he was not a conservative, in any case."

For the next three years, Gamble became the standard-bearer for revolt, the lightning rod for sporadic media attention to the growing dump-Clark movement. Others, too, were working towards the same ends: MPs such as Nova Scotia's Elmer McKay and Ontario's Paul Dick, who would later become associate minister of defence, were tracking discontent in the caucus. And in Montreal, Frank Moores, a former party president who loved to regale drinking companions with his uncanny Clark imitations, had begun wielding his charm and cross-country contacts to organize for Mulroney. Like Gamble, many of the key players in that plot would turn out to have curious ties to the Reagan administration — above all, to its extreme right wing, which was then aggressively fostering its own covert national security agenda around the globe.

But as they discreetly built support for a leadership review, paving the way for Mulroney's takeover of the party's top post, they were content to let Gamble seize the spotlight and take the heat. "It didn't take courage," he says. "It took complete absolute reckless abandon to speak out. And people were absolutely delighted I was doing it and not they."

Not that Gamble had ever shrunk from airing his sentiments. He had risen in the House to denounce sending condolences to Yoko Ono after John Lennon's assassination, branding the dead Beatle a "leader of the drug culture." And in his regular peppery parliamentary interventions, he routinely railed against the evils of bilingualism, immigration, homosexuality, the metric system, and the CBC. But his favourite target was foreign aid, which he accused the government of using to molly-coddle communism around the globe. That charge was hardly surprising considering that one of his longtime associates was Paul Fromm, a former member of the neo-Nazi Western Guard and founder of Canadians for Foreign Aid Reform (C-FAR), a controversial group with xenophobic overtones.

In Clark's caucus, Gamble's views left him an isolated figure, not infrequently the butt of jokes. But in some American circles that had just swept Reagan to power, his tirades might have passed as humdrum fare. In 1980, as his fury at Clark was beginning to fester, he was invited to Taiwan for the thirteenth annual convention of the World Anti-Communist League (WACL), a secretive coalition of ultra-right-wing organizations from around the world, including the newly resuscitated American conservative movement.

Co-founded in 1966 by the governments of South Korea and Taiwan's General Chiang Kai-shek, the organization had begun as a militant front against encroaching communism in Asia, complete with its own CIA–backed Political Warfare Cadres Academy on the outskirts of Taipei. But as other chapters signed on representing far-right parties in Europe and military dictatorships in Latin America — even the virulently anti-communist royal family in Saudi Arabia — the league became a crucial instrument of international outreach for two regimes that increasingly found themselves international pariahs. With a growing number of nations recognizing mainland China, WACL evolved into a surrogate foreign service for Taiwan, courting politicians and parliamentarians abroad. On lavish all-expense-paid junkets to Taipei or Seoul, VIP guests were fêted at parades and stadiums full of flag-waving schoolchildren, which tended to leave a lasting glow of goodwill.

In Canada, which had no diplomatic relations with Taiwan, WACL had found fertile recruiting ground on Parliament Hill through one of its international subsidiaries, the Anti-Bolshevik Bloc of Nations (ABN). An alliance of hardline anti-communists, ranging from nationalist Croats and Ukrainians to Baltic immigrants who were fighting Soviet occupation of their homelands, ABN's Canadian chapter was headquartered in Toronto under a Ukrainian-born engineer named Orest Steciw. With regular seminars in ethnic communities and its annual Captive Nations Day gala, the group had won a sympathetic ear from a handful of Conservatives in the House: Edmonton's David Kilgour, and Donald Blenkarn and Otto Jelinek in Ontario. Even Michael Wilson, who had a large immigrant population in his riding, was often a patron of official functions.

Still, when Steciw met John Gamble, a longtime activist in the far right, he rejoiced at his luck. Other MPs preferred to downplay their support, but Gamble, who regularly denounced Trudeau as a communist, had no such reticence. "Here was an MP who said what he meant," Steciw explains. "We were like a voice in the wilderness then, and he was a bright light. We were desperate."

Through Jelinek, Gamble soon received an invitation to the annual shindig of ABN's parent, the World Anti-Communist League. His visa was arranged by Patrick Chang, then Taiwan's trade commissioner in Toronto, whom the government would later deport for engaging in banned diplomatic activities — including orchestrating trips for scores of MPs.

In Taipei, Gamble found himself accorded the usual red-carpet treatment. Booked into a luxury hotel, he was promptly whisked off to meet Dr. Ku Cheng-kang, WACL's octogenarian honorary chairman-for-life, who had been a member of Chiang Kai-shek's Supreme National Defence Council and who still ranked as one of the top members of the island's ruling Kuomintang. "Dr. Ku had no interest in anything but communism," Gamble recalls. "He had a one-track, one-dimensional mind, and no attention was ever given to anything else."

With Ku, Gamble joined other foreign guests pegged to address a raucously enthusiastic crowd of 4,000 Taiwanese who applauded his every line, despite the fact that most spoke not a word of English. For an opposition backbencher, it was a heady experience. Gamble's subject was Trudeau's collusion with communist regimes around the world through foreign aid — a guaranteed crowd-pleaser. The Taiwanese were not the only ones impressed by the force of his convictions. At that meeting, Gamble met dozens of American ultra-conservatives, among them Edwin Derwinsky, who would soon become secretary for veterans affairs in Reagan's cabinet.

But it was not until the next WACL conference a year later that he made the acquaintance of a gentleman who was far more instrumental in White House foreign policy, serving the president in tasks requiring infinitely greater discretion than politics allowed: retired Major General John Singlaub, a former CIA deputy station chief in Korea who had trained U.S. Ranger troops in Vietnam. A brisk, highly decorated patriot who had held on to both his hardline beliefs and his brushcut, Singlaub had come to the 1981 conference in Taiwan to take the measure of his new assignment — harnessing WACL as an activist web to support Reagan's covert anti-communist crusade around the globe.

From the moment he took office in January 1981, Reagan had charged his friend and CIA chief William Casey with launching a series of clandestine military insurgency movements in eight countries, from Afghanistan to Angola and Cambodia. Having already run afoul of Washington's regulators in previous government service, Casey had devised a master plan to shield those so-called black ops from the whims of congressional funding and oversight: he privatized the administration's covert foreign policy, setting up a complex, corporate-style, off-the-books network that spanned the globe and was initially called Project Democracy. Later, as the administration began soliciting donations from wealthy conservatives and foreign governments, juggling offshore companies and Swiss bank accounts, it would become known simply as The Enterprise.

To finance a massive airlift of arms to the mujahadin forces in Afghanistan, Reagan had turned to the royal House of Saud: in return for Riyadh's bankrolling of the Afghan resistance, the White House agreed to lobby for the export of AWACS radar surveillance planes to the Saudis. But elsewhere, including Nicaragua, where the Sandinistas had overthrown Washington's pet dictator, Anastasio Somoza, guerrilla forces had to be recruited and trained. Casey called on Singlaub, a member of his Office of Strategic Services (OSS) team who had parachuted into Nazi-occupied France and gone on to become an expert at building jungle insurgencies. Coordinating logistics, weapons shipments, and fundraising from his home base in Phoenix, the general reported indirectly to the White House through a young Marine liaison officer at the National Security Council, Lieutenant-Colonel Oliver North.

For Singlaub, WACL offered a worldwide support and funding infrastructure run by zealots who shared Reagan's obsessions, as well as a penchant for secrecy. But the league also presented a public relations problem. Over the previous decade, a handful of horrified conservatives had gone public with their discovery that WACL's rolls included former Nazi collaborators, documented war criminals, and leaders of paramilitary death squads in Argentina, Honduras, Guatemala, and El Salvador. The Anti-Defamation League of B'nai Brith had denounced it as a "gathering place for extremists, racists, and anti-Semites," and former British MP Geoffrey Stewart-Smith had quit, blasting it as "an anti-Semitic international."

In making their case, Jewish critics had frequently pointed to Patrick Walsh, the founder of WACL's Canadian chapter, then called the Freedom Council of Canada. By the 1970s, Walsh had achieved notoriety for running a thriving right-wing press out of tiny Flesherton, Ontario, where he and his partner Ron Gostick churned out titles such as *Anne Frank's Diary: A Hoax*, which dismissed the holocaust as so much fictional nonsense.

In 1981, when Singlaub arrived in Taipei, he was already worried about putting a new face on WACL's Canadian subsidiary, and the loquacious Markham MP had convinced him he was just the man for the job. Gamble had delivered another of his anti-Soviet stemwinders. "What is our purpose?" he thundered to the crowd. "To destroy communism! To eradicate this blight on mankind, this scourge, this pestilence!" Gamble found Singlaub "a fine man — very self-sacrificing, hard-working, honest," and, within months, he formally joined up. Gamble would later arrange similar Taiwan junkets for other like-minded MPs: his parliamentary pal Donald Blenkarn, by then the influential chairman of the Tories' finance committee; Felix Holtmann, the Manitoba pig farmer whom Mulroney named to head the House committee on culture and communications; and Ontario member Murray Cardiff. When the Iran-Contra scandal broke, they and their colleagues in ABN would close ranks, spurning questions about the meetings they had attended where support for Reagan's freedom fighters around the world had become Topic A. Asked about his trip and his own meeting with Singlaub, Blenkarn would shrug: "You want to pay my way to Taiwan? Sure. Why wouldn't I go?"

But it was Gamble with whom Singlaub established the closest ties — and whom he would later tap to co-chair WACL's North American chapter as he threw himself into organizing arms and financing for the Contras. In fact, over the next two years, at the very moment Gamble was noisily fronting the dump-Clark movement, he and his ABN friends were quietly forging links with WACL and that dark underbelly of the Reagan administration which had the blessing of the occupant of the Oval Office himself. During those years, Singlaub became a frequent visitor to Canada, drumming up support for Reagan's rollback of communism around the globe, but especially in Nicaragua. "That was his pet peeve," Steciw recalls. At a time when the excitement of the Reagan revolution was still fresh in the air, a tiny band of Canadian right-wingers had hooked into its zeitgeist — none more zealously than John Gamble, who was caught up in a rollback operation of his own.

At the party's 1981 annual general meeting in Ottawa, Gamble and his fellow rebels had succeeded in engineering a vote on Joe Clark's leadership. Clark had won by a healthy 66.4 percent, and party organizers like Russ Wunker breathed a sigh of relief. But contrary to their expectations, the anti-Clark movement did not wither away. "Gamble was just this ongoing thorn," Wunker concedes. "He was shaking up the party."

In fact, while Wunker regarded the rebels' 33 percent support as a defeat, John Morrison, the chief organizer of Gamble's dump-Clark operation, saw it as a promising sign of victory to come. "It was," Morrison says, "far beyond our expectations."

IN the spring of 1981, shortly after the Conservatives' annual meeting, John Morrison set up the Committee for a PC Leadership Convention in his suburban Toronto home. There, he stepped up his anti-Clark campaign, working to take over a moribund political vehicle called PC Metro, then staging a well-publicized vote on Clark's leadership.

Meanwhile, Morrison dispatched his friend Gordon Jackson, another veteran of Gamble's election campaigns, to Washington to plug into the American New Right, a coalition that had once been dismissed as the radical fringe. For Reagan's 1980 campaign, those groups, which ranged from Jerry Falwell's religious right to the followers of the Reverend Sun Myung Moon, had come together under the umbrella of the National Conservative Political Action Committee, known as NCPAC, whose specialty was targeting liberal Democrats with vicious attacks.

Founded by a young Connecticut right-winger named Terry Dolan — whose brother Anthony, a White House speechwriter, had penned Reagan's evil-empire address — NCPAC had spent more than $1.2 million in the 1980 elections to run negative, even shocking, campaign commercials; in the process, it had defeated Democratic senators Birch Bayh, Frank Church, and George McGovern. With millions to spend, thanks to NCPAC's fundraiser Carl "Spitz" Channell — who would later be indicted for illegally raising $10 million for the Contras — the group had honed the low blow and the campaign dirty trick to slick precision.

In September 1981 Jackson and Morrison brought Dolan to

Toronto's Harbour Castle Hotel, where he shared his secrets with an audience of some of the country's wealthiest ultra-conservatives. Among them were insurance magnate Colin Brown, founder of the National Citizens' Coalition, and Harold Siebens, a Calgary oil millionaire who was footing the bill for Dolan's visit. An American who had made his first fortune in St. Louis selling sporting goods to the U.S. military, Siebens had retired and driven north to Alberta, where he promptly made a second killing on the oil boom. A fervent libertarian, he had become one of the chief financiers behind Vancouver's ultra-conservative Fraser Institute. And during Mulroney's 1984 election campaign, his family's Candor Investments Ltd. would contribute $150,000 to become the largest single donor to the PC Canada Fund.

Even addressing that like-minded audience, Dolan plied his trademark shock tactics. A conservative revolution would never happen in Canada, he taunted his listeners, because none of them had the courage to stand up for their beliefs. Siebens promptly coughed up for a poll on the prospects for a leadership convention, and Morrison stepped up his own brand of negative campaigning. Speaking to Tory groups across the country, he fanned controversy over Clark in the media and through party mailings. By late 1982, another annual general meeting had been scheduled for the new year in Winnipeg, complete with a vote on Clark's stewardship. "We'd forced the issue," Morrison says.

Instead of an attack on the party leader, his strategy was centred on a sly, apparently benign catch-phrase: in order for the party to go forward, it had to clear the air. "Clear the Air" became the righteous exhortation on lapel buttons and delegates' lips — one even the hapless Joe Clark himself adopted in a speech. Then it was only a matter of raising the stakes — defining what would constitute a win for the party leader this time around. When Otto Jelinek suggested the caucus would revolt if Clark did not better his last showing and call a leadership convention, Morrison and company let out a cheer.

Under any other terms, Clark's 61 percent support at Winnipeg would have constituted a win. But as news of the vote — and his decision to submit to the will of a leadership convention — swept the hall, pandemonium broke out. TV cameras zeroed in on the pint-sized mustachioed MP who had just delivered a harangue in a hotel room across the street. John Gamble could see fists raised in his direction and hear angry, tearful shouts of "See what you've done." A prominent Tory even slapped one of his aides. "There were a lot of people in the background working feverishly for the same thing," he snorts. "But they all stayed in their rooms."

Gamble promptly found himself shunned — a condition that persisted throughout the leadership campaign to come. He knew he didn't stand a chance of winning, but he threw his hat in the ring anyway, expecting seventy or eighty votes. Instead, he got a humiliating seventeen. "A massacre is difficult to swallow," he concedes. Gamble had, by then, served his purpose. "His chief claim to fame was taking out Joe Clark," says Peter Regenstreif, the strategist for rival Peter Pocklington. "And he did, beautifully."

Surprisingly, one person who had tried to talk Gamble out of running was John Morrison. By then, Morrison had gone to work for the candidate who would most clearly benefit from his efforts to reopen the party's top post: Brian Mulroney.

But when he showed up for his first meeting with Mulroney's closest collaborators, Frank Moores and Fred Doucet, someone pointed out that his presence could raise awkward questions about whose interests he had been serving during the dump-Clark campaign. On the advice of another of Mulroney's longtime friends, Morrison spent the rest of the leadership race toiling under an assumed name, Morris Johnson.

IN January 1981, on the day after Reagan's Inauguration, Russ Wunker had placed a call to the Republican National Committee in Washington, where most of the party's top brass had just left for jobs in the new administration. He had literally caught the party in the middle of changing the guard. Dave Turner, the new second-in-command, was testy when he picked up the phone. What could the Republicans possibly want from a bunch of defeated Canadian Conservatives? "I said, 'We're your type of people,'" Wunker argued. "We're soul-mates and we've just come through a miserable defeat like you guys did after Watergate. How did you turn yourselves around?"

Armed with a letter from Joe Clark designating him the Tories' official liaison with the Republicans, Wunker made a trip to Washington, where Turner not only became a friend but one of the party's increasingly numerous links with U.S. Conservatives over the next

two years. Turner arranged appointments on Capitol Hill for visiting MPs and found slots for a handful of Tory riding officials in the
Republicans' training courses for campaign managers. "He opened
doors for us, set up meetings for us," Wunker says, "even meetings
the embassy told us they couldn't get."

But in 1982 Turner also called to send up an alert. "Who are these
guys sniffing around down here?" he asked. The guys turned out to
be Toronto pollster Michael Adams, who had been sent to
Republican headquarters for campaign hints by his new client: the
Edmonton Oilers' colourful millionaire owner Peter Pocklington,
better known as Peter Puck, who was also waging his own war
against Clark — with his own ties to the American conservative
movement.

A regular in Palm Springs, where his frequent golfing partner was
Gerald Ford, Pocklington's own politics lay far to the right of the
former president. As a disciple of Ayn Rand, he was a fervent libertarian who believed governments should get out of business's way;
he had celebrated his faith in an unfettered marketplace on the hull
of his speedboat, the *Free Enterprise*. Many of his enthusiasms,
including his call for a flat tax, owed their origin to the two ultra-
conservative think tanks whose alumni had most influenced the
Reagan administration: California's Hoover Institute and the
Heritage Foundation in Washington. But then Pocklington had
always looked southward for his inspiration. "Without Americans,
the world would probably be back in the caves," he says. "They're
the only people with the patriotism and the courage to stand up for
what they believe in. The United Empire Loyalists on this side of the
border — they're more into: 'What can we get from government?'"

Like most of his fellow Albertans, Pocklington loathed Trudeau,
whom he still terms a Maoist. But he had only slightly less antipa-
thy towards Joe Clark, whom he deemed not a conservative at all. In
1981 the man who owned Wayne Gretzky began importing other
stars to Edmonton as guest speakers at a series of political lun-
cheons he sponsored: from Moral Majority leader Jerry Falwell to
Henry Kissinger and his golfing partner Gerald Ford, all were prominent U.S. Republicans who championed an idea still rarely aired
north of the border — continental free trade. "Even then, my
American friends all believed in it," Pocklington says. His luncheon
series was "to educate the people of Edmonton that there was
another way of doing things."

One of Pocklington's biggest draws was Kissinger's former deputy Alexander Haig, the blustering four-star general who had just been forced out as Reagan's first secretary of state. Setting up his own consulting firm, Worldwide Associates Inc., Haig had signed up a handful of defence contractors such as United Technologies Corp., on whose board he sat. He regularly dropped by its Montreal subsidiary, Pratt and Whitney Canada, which a parliamentary committee would later investigate for selling helicopter spare parts to Iran. And in the years leading up to Mulroney's election, the general was a frequent visitor to Canada, where he counted Ontario premier William Davis among his friends; in 1983 Haig had been the star attraction at a Toronto fundraiser for one of Davis's cabinet ministers, Nick Leluk, a strong supporter of the Anti-Bolshevic Bloc of Nations.

But Haig had other interests in the country than its defence industry. Among his clients was Amway Corp., the U.S. direct sales giant based in Ada, Michigan, on the outskirts of Grand Rapids — Gerald Ford's hometown. At the time, Amway was engaged in a multimillion-dollar tax battle with the Trudeau government which Haig would later claim he had helped resolve. In 1982, after a protracted fight, Amway pleaded guilty to four criminal charges of evading $148 million in back taxes and customs duties over fifteen years, and paid a $23 million fine.

But the corporation was appealing that judgment. The case had outraged its elderly founders, Jay Van Andel and Richard De Vos, both ardent free-marketeers with more than the usual corporate connections to the White House. A close friend of Reagan's, De Vos had served as finance chairman of the Republican National Committee.

Throughout the Conservative leadership campaign, Amway's name would repeatedly resurface as the suspected financier behind those candidates who had done the most to agitate against Clark and to open up the race: Gamble and Pocklington. In 1982, at the height of his militancy, Gamble had been invited to address one of the corporation's regular pep rallies in Columbus, Ohio. There, on the occasion of American Heritage Day, 9,000 of its Canadian distributors were being whipped into the usual frenzy of U.S. patriotic zeal and zest for free enterprise, and Gamble's attack on the taxation system further enraptured them. "For a politician, it's an absolute miracle," he says. "Before I could finish a sentence they were screaming."

Gamble denied that his funding came from the cosmetics and cleaning empire. Not that he would have objected if it had. But in spite of his efforts, he claims most of Amway's support went to Pocklington, who, after a $50,000 speaking tour in twenty cities, threw his own hat into the Tory leadership ring on the day after Gamble's announcement.

Pocklington had been introduced to both Van Andel and De Vos by his friend Jerry Ford. Not only did he share their fervour on the subject of minimalist government, but he had made three of his speeches to Amway conventions, spouting quotes from Benjamin Franklin and Abraham Lincoln. One of Pocklington's chief organizers, Bill Campbell, who had run Republican campaigns in the United States, had hooked into the company's networks, packing riding association meetings in British Columbia and Alberta — almost taking over Clark's own constituency. Distributors who had just been recruited as new party members littered the hockey mogul's rallies across the West, some gleefully sporting buttons with Peter Puck's picture above the boast, "I did it Amway." But Pocklington waves off the reports of support as "a lot of rot." "Maybe 5 percent of the crowds were Amway distributors," he says.

In the end, at the party's leadership convention in Ottawa, he fared only slightly better than Gamble: Pocklington garnered a mere 102 votes — twenty-five of which his strategist Peter Regenstreif, had borrowed from Mulroney supporters in the Alberta caucus to help him avoid first-ballot humiliation. Pocklington promptly marched over to Mulroney's box with another defeated contender, Michael Wilson, in a move that had been prearranged earlier.

After the tumult and the shouting of the convention had died, party reconciliation was the order of the day. But it did not pass unnoticed that, of all Mulroney's leadership rivals, only his old pal, Peter Pocklington, was included in the celebrations for his inner circle on the night of his victory. Indeed, his presence provoked questions: Had he been a genuine rival or merely a decoy for Mulroney all the time?

As the new Tory leader's biographer, L. Ian MacDonald, would point out, Pocklington's campaign had proved exceedingly helpful: not only had his lack of parliamentary experience diluted those same accusations against Mulroney, but as an Albertan he had siphoned off support from Clark. Pocklington had also provided another service: he had staked out the ideological ground that Mulroney would later claim in an apparently stunning about-face. Like the most serious challenger, John Crosbie, he pumped for free trade with the United States in every debate, allowing Mulroney to oppose it — a far more popular line, according to the polls of the time.

"He was against it," Pocklington says, then makes a wry concession. "Well, I guess he was not all that much against it. Brian was a very political person; he knew you didn't win elections like that, whereas I just came out with it." It is Pocklington, in fact, who best sums up their respective roles in the leadership race: "He was there to win," he says. "I was there more to talk about ideas."

In fact, many of those ideas were shared by Mulroney's chief aides. When Pocklington sent Michael Adams to the Republican National Committee in Washington, the pollster was dazzled by the entrée that his client's name won him. Among those he met was the party's senior adviser on foreign affairs, Richard Allen, Reagan's former national security adviser.

A longtime activist in the Republican right wing and a former official in the Nixon administration, Allen had been forced out of the White House after a minor scandal: he had accepted $1,000 from a Japanese publisher for setting up an interview with Nancy Reagan. Allen had never personally profited, but when the cash was found in his White House safe along with other Japanese gifts, his enemies pounced on that excuse to demand his resignation.

Still, he retained strong ties to Reagan's inner circle, as well as a prestigious perch at the Heritage Foundation. Allen's loyalty was considered beyond question: during the 1980 election he was one of the key Republicans who met with Iranian emissaries offering purported deals on the American hostages in Teheran — and the threat of a so-called October Surprise that the party feared would derail Reagan's hopes at the ballot box in November. By the time Adams met Allen, he was in charge of the Republicans' international outreach, linking the party with other right-of-centre groups around the world.

For years, Allen had pitched the notion of a North American economic union, and, as a result, he harboured more than a passing interest in Canada, where the mere mention of Trudeau's outings to Cuba could detonate a tirade of outrage. Meeting a Canadian, he still inquires: "Are you a left-winger tree-hugger or a Comm-symp type? I'm a Reform Party guy myself."

In Adams, Allen sensed a kindred conservative spirit — and an opening to the Tories north of the border. Adams drafted him for the advisory board of a polling newsletter for U.S. corporations he was then trying to launch, and for the next two years Richard Allen appeared on Adams's *Focus Canada* letterhead.

During that time, the Republicans' national security chief networked energetically among the Conservatives. He and the chairman of the Republican National Committee, Frank Fahrenkopf, came to Ottawa for a Senate reception. And as a leading member of the International Democratic Union — a global conservative alliance — Allen spent the months after Mulroney won the Tory leadership helping Russ Wunker organize the union's 1984 annual conference in Vancouver; he had invited a group of Tories to fly to Dallas afterward as his guests at the Republican convention. When the Liberals' September 1984 election call undid those plans, Allen bailed out Wunker by arranging to transfer the union's festivities to Australia.

But in May 1984 Allen was in Toronto on another mission. Invited as the keynote luncheon speaker at a private business seminar thrown by Michael Adams, Allen seized the occasion to plug his pet scheme for a continental union. Raising the spectre of mounting protectionist pressures in Congress, he warned that Canada ought to start lobbying in Washington to raise its profile, or Americans would take it for granted.

Not that Allen himself could have been accused of any such lapse. After an interview for CBC's *Morningside*, the show's guest host Patrick Martin and his producer were leaving Allen's room at the Inn on the Park when they had what seemed a curious encounter. In the hallway, on his way in to see the former U.S. national security adviser, was Charley McMillan, the York University business professor serving as chief foreign policy adviser to Brian Mulroney, who was by then leader of her majesty's loyal opposition.

As a fellow free-trade enthusiast and expert on Japan, McMillan was, in fact, one of Allen's old friends, and during those years they regularly consulted by phone. But when Martin and his producer asked why they were meeting, McMillan squirmed: he was at the hotel with Mulroney, he said, on an "unpublicized" visit. At the time, the *Morningside* team wondered if they had stumbled on a story, then decided against pursuing it. But years later, after nearly a decade of Mulroney's continental enthusiasm, the question still haunted one of the journalists: Why — four months before the federal vote — was the opposition leader meeting so clandestinely with one of Ronald Reagan's veteran foreign policy fixers?

McMillan says it was Allen's first introduction to Mulroney — "purely social." With his campaign eclipsed by the Liberal leadership race, "Mulroney probably gave him a rundown on how he thought things would go." But within a month, the opposition leader was also due for his first visit to the White House, and he had a great deal riding on the trip's success. As McMillan acknowledges, "Allen still had clout with the Reagan administration — no question about it."

By the time the trio met at the Inn on the Park, Russ Wunker had found himself displaced as the Conservatives' liaison with the Republican machine. His Washington contact, Dave Turner, had come up to Ottawa for the 1983 Tory leadership convention, and later would sit with Wunker in campaign chairman Norman Atkins's hotel suite on election night as news of the Conservative rout poured in. But afterward, both suddenly found themselves ignored by the Mulroney camp.

"I could never get Mulroney to reappoint me in any relations with the Republican National Committee and Washington," Wunker says. Indeed, the U.S. dossier became the personal beat of Mulroney's closest aide, Fred Doucet. As Wunker concluded, "They seemed to want to do their own thing."

OUTSIDE the Waldorf Astoria, limousine gridlock was playing havoc with Manhattan rush-hour tempers. But inside the grand ballroom, where 1,400 of the continent's corporate movers and shakers had gathered in black tie and anticipation on a chill Monday night in December 1984, mellowness was being served up with the champagne and canapés.

Mellowness was, after all, Ross Johnson's stock-in-trade. With his breezy country-club banter and his raucous, expletive-riddled anecdotes, the vice-chairman of Nabisco Brands had a way of forging instant intimacy, especially with powerful men. And seldom had so many powerful men come together than the crowd Johnson had helped assemble for the 306th dinner of the venerable Economic

Club of New York, to hear his old friend Brian Mulroney announce that Canada was "open for business again."

The pair had struck up a fast friendship more than a decade earlier in Montreal, when Mulroney was still a lawyer-about-town and Johnson the president of Standard Brands Canada, the subsidiary of a stodgy U.S.–based grocery giant. But they had immediately recognized in each other a shared taste for power and life in the fast lane. With his band of Standard Brands executives whom he had dubbed the Merry Men, Johnson never let nine-to-five life interfere with his revelries, haunting the city's best watering holes with Mulroney and dispensing nicknames to all he met. His own summed up his position in the social pecking order: the Pope.

Like Mulroney, Johnson had been taken under the wing of one of the city's corporate titans, Paul Desmarais, who had sponsored him for membership in the Mount Royal Club. But he, too, had come from humble roots, the son of a Winnipeg hardware salesman. At the University of Manitoba, where he presided over his fraternity's pranks, he had already established his reputation as a master of schmooze, but behind his deceptively casual mien lay a tactician's mind and a restless ambition. And like Mulroney as well, he had no trouble in pinpointing the exact location of the brass ring: the other side of the border.

Ever since his early days as an accountant at Canadian General Electric in Montreal, Johnson had chafed for a promotion to the American head office, and at Standard Brands finally his chance had come. Named to head the country's international division in New York, he began his climb towards the presidential suite. Hanging out with sports stars like Frank Gifford and Bobby Orr, he was careful to cultivate his own board, one of whose most powerful members was a fellow Canadian who took a shine to him: Earle McLaughlin, then chairman of the Royal Bank, who would later begin the push for free trade talks.

Johnson vaulted into the CEO's post at Standard Brands in 1976, the same year Mulroney made his first abortive leadership bid. And the two had stayed in close touch as Mulroney plotted his political revenge at Iron Ore and enjoyed a visitor's perks in New York, where Johnson was soaring in corporate America's loftiest circles. Within a year, he had merged his company with Nabisco, to become head of America's nineteenth largest industrial corporation.

He counted among his pals Jim Robinson, the young Georgia

dynamo who had just taken over American Express, and Rawleigh Warner, the chairman of Mobil Oil, who sat on the American Express board, where Johnson himself would soon be offered a seat. Another corporate titan whose favour he curried was Dwayne Andreas, the chairman of the world's largest agribusiness, Archer Daniels Midland. The man known as the "king of corn and clout" would also invite Johnson onto his board, and in 1988, as chairman of the presidential commission to celebrate the bicentennial of the U.S. Constitution, Andreas would hand him the prestigious job as his vice-chair. A veteran cultivator of politicians both at home and abroad, Andreas understood well that his corporate fortunes rested on agricultural subsidies and other goodwill from governments around the world.

Many of those with whom Johnson forged friendships during his early charm offensive in New York would come to play pivotal roles in Canada during Mulroney's nine years in power. But few would become more controversial than Martin Davis, the CEO of Gulf + Western, the owner of Paramount Pictures. A legend even among fellow self-made men, Davis had begun his business career at fourteen as a runaway, peddling newspapers at Grand Central Station and, after a stint in the army, had wangled a job as an office boy at Samuel Goldwyn studios. In 1987 Johnson would cap their decade-long friendship by inviting Davis onto the board of his expanded grocery and tobacco conglomerate, RJR Nabisco, only to have that generosity rebound: during his disastrous attempted takeover of the company, Davis would help vote him out.

But in 1984, as Mulroney swooped into New York to address the Economic Club, Davis was still one of Johnson's key cronies — and a man with more than the usual corporate interest in what the new Canadian prime minister had to say. Only days earlier, Gulf + Western's publishing division had snapped up Prentice Hall, including its Canadian subsidiary, which was now subject to a ruling by the country's revamped investment review agency .

Nor was Davis alone in wanting to eyeball Mulroney. Many — prodded by Johnson — had contributed to his campaign, often through their Canadian branch plants. Through his own subsidiaries, Nabisco Brands Ltd., and Nabisco Brands Investments Ltd., both in Toronto, Johnson's firm had anted up at least $80,500 for the Conservatives' 1984 election effort — only the first of its many generosities to the government.

In the three months since Mulroney's win, Johnson had become his unofficial Pied Piper in New York. Nabisco had taken the lead in financing an eight-page advertising section in the *New York Times*, scheduled to appear the day after the prime minister's Economic Club speech, heralding his new regime's virtues: Nabisco's own full-page ad saluted Mulroney as "the right man in the right place at the right time."

Working with former New York consul general Ken Taylor, who was still the toast of the city for smuggling U.S. diplomats out of Teheran — and whom Nabisco had just hired for intergovernmental duties — Johnson had hustled a stellar guest list for Mulroney's Manhattan debut. Sprinkled among the corporate elite were David Rockefeller, General Electric chairman John Welch, and Johnson's friend, *Time* publisher John Meyers, whose magazine had just featured the prime minister on its cover.

At a dais flanked by red-coated Mounties, Johnson had introduced Mulroney to the first of eleven ovations. It was, as *Maclean's* columnist Peter Newman saw it, a love-in. "Most Canadians don't realize that Mulroney is genuinely at home with the Wall Street barons who turned out for him," Newman raved. "He played them as masterfully as Johnny Carson."

In fact, Mulroney was a hit without a single one-liner — without, in fact, saying a word. Already, three days earlier, he had tabled legislation to take the last teeth out of FIRA, rechristening it Investment Canada and charging it with a responsibility to foster, not scrutinize, foreign takeovers. "The government of Canada is there to assist — and not harass — the private sector in creating the new wealth and new jobs that Canada needs," he declared to yet another round of applause.

But the biggest cheers greeted his vow to scrap the National Energy Program and its "odious" back-in provision, which had demanded a 25 percent share of all oil found on federal land, even on discoveries that pre-dated the policy. What U.S. oilmen most hated was that retroactive clause that had changed the rules in mid-play. "There shall be one game — building Canada — and one set of rules," Mulroney announced as the room went wild.

Some of his advisers might have been pushing those moves out of ideology, but as Charley McMillan once noted, "Mulroney is about as ideological as a coffee pot." It was his apprenticeship in a U.S. boardroom that had given him what McMillan called "an MBA in corporate networks and decision-making." And at last in the Waldorf Astoria, he was speaking to the constituency he knew best.

Already, barely two months into office, Mulroney was delivering the key provisions corporate America had demanded. All that remained was to open up Canadian markets through a free trade pact that would have historic ramifications in creating what the Waldorf crowd liked to call a level continental playing field. And in that stormy debate to come, Ross Johnson would again have a role to play.

6

Godfathers

IN THE ELEGANT WHITE HOUSE SALON folksily known as the Family Dining Room, Paul Robinson beamed over the pheasant consommé and sea bass like some proud godfather at a christening. And, in a way, he was. Four years after he had helped sweep Ronald Reagan to the place of honour down the table, here he sat in September 1984 officiating at the first White House luncheon for Brian Mulroney, another old friend he had shepherded towards power — discreetly, of course. But as it turned out, not quite discreetly enough for the liking of some of Reagan's handlers.

Months earlier, the State Department had finally succeeded in putting a muzzle on Reagan's ebullient ambassador to Ottawa, whom *Maclean's* columnist Allan Fotheringham once characterized as "the only bull who carries his own china shop around with him." Ever since his 1981 political appointment, Robinson had distinguished himself by telling Canadians exactly what he and his boss thought of Trudeau's policies. Big, burly, a former high school defensive end who had been dubbed "John Wayne in pinstripes," he was far more verbose than the Duke had ever been, but he shot straight from the mouth.

Never sullying his discourses with diplomatic niceties, Robinson made headlines virtually every time he spoke. As he swept across the country, a blustering proconsul for Reagan's imperial presidency, he had scorned the metric system as "rubbish," lambasted Trudeau's FIRA for its "nitpickers," and dismissed a protest against U.S. cruise missile tests as nothing for Washington to worry about — "no bigger a crowd than you get at a ballgame." After one of his regular attacks on the country's lacklustre defence spending — he once made three such speeches in a single week — he told a dissenting audience member who approached him later to "Shove off!" The gentleman in question turned out to be John Miller, deputy managing editor of the *Toronto Star*, who proceeded to record the encounter on the paper's front page.

Robinson prided himself on his forthrightness: "I have done this intentionally," he bristled to the *New York Times*, which had been alerted to his antics. But even when his intention was to reassure, he managed to offend, blithely declaring that he saw no reason for Canadians and Americans not to get along since they were, after all, "two peoples with interchangeable parts."

Back in Washington, the professionals at the State Department might cringe, but they knew that, as one of Reagan's earliest supporters, Robinson was untouchable. Soon after he arrived in Ottawa, one of his embassy staffers had responded to his instructions by noting, "We'll check that with State." The ambassador had seized the occasion to make one thing perfectly clear. "I said, 'You check it with State,'" he recalls, "'and it's the last thing you'll be doing here.'"

Still, even he had finally been chastened in May 1984 — four months before Mulroney came to power and a month before the Liberal leadership convention — after lumbering into the Canadian electoral waters. Responding to a reporter's query, Robinson had observed that, whether the new prime minister turned out to be Brian Mulroney or John Turner, both of whom had "an honest understanding of business and the realities of this world . . . the future of our relationship cannot help but improve."

State had gone ballistic about a comment that could be construed as meddling in another country's internal politics — a pastime for which Washington was not exactly unknown. In fact, Robinson had been cultivating Mulroney as a prime ministerial prospect since the earliest days of the Reagan regime while a handful of other U.S. officials were quietly nurturing a Canadian constituency for the centrepiece of Reaganomics, free trade. But he had agreed to put a lid on it until the Canadian elections were over and Reagan had secured his own bid for a second term in November.

When Mulroney arrived in Washington late on the evening of September 24, 1984, Robinson had been standing in the dark at Andrews Air Force Base to greet him. But for the rest of the visit he kept an uncharacteristically low profile for a man who, at six-foot-four, loomed over any room. Still, with his silver sideburns curling above pink jowls and prosperous tailoring, he could scarcely be missed, grinning like some oversized cat who had swallowed the canary. For with Mulroney's ascension to power, Robinson felt that at least part of his mission in Ottawa was on track — a mission which had begun in late 1979 in the Grand Ballroom of the New York Hilton when Reagan announced he was making one more try for the White House.

As the finance chairman for the Illinois Republican Party, Robinson had been the first state chair to throw his weight behind a candidate then regarded as a longshot. Ideologically, it was a match made in heaven. A former U.S. Navy officer during the Korean War, Robinson was a stalwart of the Republican Party's far-right wing, a champion of North Carolina senator Jesse Helms, and a fervent anti-communist who, during his Canadian posting, would refuse to meet with leaders of the New Democratic Party. "I just thought socialism had no spot on the continent," he growls still.

As a zealous free-marketeer, it seemed no accident that Robinson hailed from the city regarded as one of the cradles of Reaganomics, where an owlish University of Chicago economist named Milton Friedman had published a 1956 manifesto, *Capitalism and Freedom*, whose title embraced Reagan's twin obsessions. Like the flinty self-made millionaires in the California Kitchen Cabinet, Robinson embraced Friedman's monetarist theories with evangelical zeal.

Although the Canadian press routinely referred to him as a Chicago insurance broker, that quick sketch sorely understated his financial heft: he had built his Robinson Incorporated into one of the largest mass-marketers of group insurance in the world. Pioneering policies for bank credit card holders and some of the largest American and British professional associations, he would later become the exclusive broker for Visa USA Inc. For years, he had been making business trips to Canada, where he had an affiliate and felt a special kinship for the country: his great-grandparents had immigrated to Illinois from Elgin, Ontario — a story he loved to tell — and he had unearthed photos and the deed to their ancient stone farmhouse, although he never did manage to visit it during his four-year posting.

Robinson had offices around the world — Britain, Australia, and New Zealand as well — but only in the English-speaking world. He never trifled with more exotic locations. "If they don't speak the language, well, forget them," he says. Given that predilection for things Anglo-Saxon, he had been astounded to sit in the New York Hilton ballroom five years earlier at Reagan's $500-a-plate presidential kickoff and hear his candidate call for a vaguely defined continental trading zone, dubbed a North American Accord, which would include both Canada and Mexico.

As Reagan waxed rhapsodic over the prospects for "a continent whose three countries possess the assets to make it the strongest, most prosperous and self-sufficient area on Earth," Robinson had recoiled in horror. "I was in favour of U.S.–Canada," he says. "But Mexico! Even the language is different, the mores are different. It surprised me to include Mexico."

His astonishment was shared by many both north and south of the U.S. border, where the leitmotif of the last century had been a wariness of anything that smacked of American hegemony. But Reagan's press secretary Lyn Nofziger had assured the quizzical American media that his boss had consulted the governments of both Mexican president José Lopez Portillo and Joe Clark before unveiling the proposal.

Beneath Reagan's utopian rhetoric, in fact, most political analysts got his subtext. At a time when the United States was convulsed with its second energy crisis in five years — when outraged motorists were lining up at the gas pumps as Iran's new ayatollah wreaked his revenge on the Great Satan — Reagan was signalling his commitment to a concept long pondered in national security circles: making America less dependent on the vagaries of Middle Eastern oil imports by tapping into the vast energy wealth of its continental neighbours. There were only two stumbling blocks to securing such access in an oil crunch: Mexico's stringent government monopoly of its petroleum reserves, enshrined in Article 27 of the country's constitution, and Canadian energy policy, which gave the country first call on its own oil. According to Richard Allen, who was then Reagan's foreign affairs adviser, the North American Accord — the rough draft for NAFTA — was an attempt to make an end-run around those barriers to continental energy reserves.

Allen takes credit for coming up with the concept shortly after the Iranian revolution. He and California public relations whiz Peter Hannaford had pitched the idea to Reagan as a way of pre-empting one of his strongest rivals for the Republican nomination, Texan John Connally. "Connally had come out for a North American energy alliance," Allen recalls. "But whenever you said energy, the Mexicans and Canadians thought it was an energy grab, so we just called it a North American Accord. The idea was not to define it, because that's where you got into trouble."

Another backroom player in the campaign had already been working with Mexico on trade talks. In the mid-1970s Myer Rashish, a neoconservative economist who had set up the first U.S. Trade Representative's Office, had been hired by former Secretary of State Henry Kissinger and his mentor David Rockefeller to come up with a policy that would access the vast cash reserves that Mexico was harbouring from its oil bonanza. Organizing a dozen corporate heavyweights, including George Shultz, then still at Bechtel, and oil tycoon Robert Anderson of Atlantic Richfield Corp., Rashish had dubbed them the Mexico Study Group and had flown them all to Mexico City on Rockefeller's private jet. At the presidential palace, Los Pinos, they had been enthusiastically received by Lopez Portillo, but, in the dying days of the Carter regime, nothing came of their report, which saw the solution to U.S.–Mexican tensions as free trade. "Of course, we weren't talking of complete free trade," Rashish admits. "That would have been much too bold for the Mexicans — another design of American imperialism."

After Reagan's landslide victory, Allen conscripted Rashish for the transition team and dusted off the North American Accord, which had been waylaid during the domestic campaign. Attempting to drum up trips for the president-elect to both Ottawa and Mexico City, they found Trudeau otherwise engaged. But Lopez Portillo had once again been keen — so keen that he had even showily defied Mexico's constitution, which forbade his leaving the country without congressional permission. To greet Reagan, he strode across the border bridge at El Paso, presenting him with a stunning Palomino. In return, Reagan had given him a rifle.

As Reagan's first undersecretary of state for economic affairs, Rashish had the globe as his beat, but he admits he "kept Mexico and Canada as special clients." Finally nailing down a trip to Ottawa as Reagan's first foreign visit after taking office, he watched as the two leaders talked past each other — Reagan recounting Israeli jokes in response to Trudeau's worries over the Middle East, the prime minister barely masking his scorn — and swiftly realized it was not the most opportune moment to broach a continental common market.

The concept soon vanished from public consciousness, dismissed by pundits as another loopy notion from the president's rumoured shoebox of yellowed press clippings. But quietly, in boardrooms and bureaucrats' cubbyholes, a small band of men on both sides of each border were still talking it up. One was John Gavin, who had succeeded Reagan as head of Hollywood's Screen Actors Guild and been rewarded as his ambassador to Mexico City. Another was Paul Heron Robinson Jr.

The accord was on Robinson's mind when he landed in Ottawa in July 1981 to take up his post. Within months, he had sought out Brian Mulroney. The U.S. consul general in Montreal had touted the young president of Iron Ore as a comer and, that fall, he had arranged a small private dinner for Robinson to meet him. During that get-acquainted session, Mulroney had displayed the same brash charm and wit that had captivated other older, influential Americans who had become his mentors. "He was a straight shooter," Robinson recalls, "and we just got on famously."

The ambassador was convinced he had found a kindred political spirit. Mulroney vented his horror at Trudeau's new National Energy Policy, which had put a brake on oil drilling with its contentious retroactive claims, and echoed the administration's outrage at FIRA. Nor was Robinson left with any doubts that the Iron Ore president, who had just been elevated to Hanna's board in Cleveland, shared his passions when talk turned to the delicate subject of free trade. In fact, Mulroney had been mulling over the notion for three years with Duncan Edmonds, a former Clark adviser who was a close friend of Richard Allen's and had become one of the cheerleaders for continentalism in Ottawa; at Iron Ore, Mulroney had even taken to pressing copies of Edmonds's draft Treaty of North America upon acquaintances. But as he reminded Robinson, having brought down Wilfrid Laurier's government in 1911, the subject would require deft positioning on the Canadian public agenda. Still, for Robinson, Mulroney represented a hot Conservative prospect with exactly the credentials that appealed to the Reagan faithful: "I felt as a businessman," he says, "we'd be able to do business with him."

The thought was bracing as he kicked off his four-year diplomatic stint: no more of Trudeau's arrogant intellectualism, no more snipes at superpower imperialism or anti-American posturing. In Mulroney, he had found a savvy political operator with "a sense of mission and a confidence — and he understood us." As Robinson later told his hometown paper, the *Chicago Tribune*, "I saw him then as a man on the rise — a friend of America."

NEITHER can agree who called the other first. But shortly after he landed in Ottawa in the summer of 1981, Paul Robinson had a visitor in his huge panelled ambassadorial lair directly across the street from the Parliament Buildings. His caller was already a familiar presence around the American Embassy: a balding, implacably upbeat international trade lawyer named Tom d'Aquino, president of the Business Council on National Issues. In fact, d'Aquino would broker the council's corporate interests with such success during the Mulroney years that *Canadian Forum* termed him the "de facto prime minister."

As head of BCNI, d'Aquino was the front man for 150 CEOs from the country's largest corporations, at least one-third of them subsidiaries of American-based multinationals. The council had been founded five years earlier as an organizational riposte to a crack by former NDP leader David Lewis about "corporate welfare bums." In the aftershocks of the energy crisis, when business had begun mobilizing around the world to protect its faltering interests, a tiny band of Toronto executives had realized that corporate Canada too lacked any voice in the volatile public debate. Or, as Tom d'Aquino later put it, that voice had degenerated to "little more than a squawk."

The council had been set up in 1976 with only a dozen original members led by Noranda's Alfred Powis, Canadian Pacific's Ian Sinclair, Power Corporation's Paul Desmarais, and the Royal Bank's Earle McLaughlin, chairman of the biggest of the country's chartered banks. But its driving force had been Bill Twaits, then retiring as chairman of Imperial Oil, the Canadian subsidiary of Exxon, which had begun its life as John D. Rockefeller's Standard Oil of New Jersey. In fact, Twaits had even tapped one of his executives, Bill Archbold, as the council's first executive director, and given it space in his office in Toronto.

But for the next four years, BCNI had been a random and muted presence on the Canadian political scene. To correct that, the council had hired d'Aquino as its Ottawa lobbyist. Although once a Trudeau speechwriter, who claims credit for coining the phrase "the just society," he had left government in 1972 for London and a job with an international consulting firm. There, where the European Common Market was struggling to be born, d'Aquino says that the notion of a continental economic union had "captured" him. Certainly, it had transformed him into what he now calls an internationalist — which turns out to have nothing to do with the United Nations and everything to do with corporate globalization.

Tom d'Aquino's newfound enthusiasm had meshed perfectly with the philosophical drift of his clients, mainly U.S. multinationals such as Ford. With operations scattered across Europe, they chafed at the differing requirements for doing business in each country — requirements that could dictate costly adjustments in everything from assembly line procedure to customs duties and repatriation of their profits back to head office. After all, if those differences could be wiped out in Europe through a common market, why not around the world?

"I got very caught up in the problems of the multinationals," d'Aquino says with his characteristic relentless pep. "I was fascinated how the transnational corporation was the train that was leading the world economy — really pushing the frontiers." Some of those frontiers, as it happened, were national identity and sovereignty. "We were watching an entirely new concept of economic globalization," he says, "and I brought all that back to Canada with me."

Setting up his own firm, Intercounsel, on the eighth floor of Ottawa's Royal Bank tower in 1975, d'Aquino also brought back some of his multinational accounts: among them was Gulf Canada, a subsidiary of the Pittsburg-based giant founded by the Mellon family — whose interests were also represented on the board of M.A. Hanna.

In the late fall of 1980, weeks after Reagan's election, d'Aquino had received a summons to lunch from Alf Powis and Bill Twaits. Over the genteel white linen of the Toronto Club, they had reissued a year-old invitation, asking him to run BCNI full time and, not incidentally, to revamp its image. Three months later, the sign on Intercounsel's door came down, replaced by gold lettering announcing the Business Council on National Issues. Inside, d'Aquino's staff of seven had stayed on, eventually ballooning to twelve. With an annual budget of $1 million, they churned out the thick gilt-covered reports that became BCNI's trademark and, during the Mulroney years, often government policy — occasionally transformed word for word into legislation.

In the beginning, BCNI had blatantly patterned itself on the U.S. Business Roundtable, the lobby of 196 top Fortune 500 corporations whose enormous influence with congressmen and the Reagan White House was uncontested: only CEOs could be members; no underlings allowed. As CEO of the CEOs, d'Aquino bridles at the suggestion of an American model. Unlike the roundtable, he argues, BCNI has not confined itself to economic issues. He points to one of the council's first blue-ribbon task forces — designed to mirror royal commissions and, under Mulroney, taken even more seriously — which focused on Canadian social policies. But like BCNI's other preoccupations, those policies were a key to the continentalist economic agenda: national health insurance and other skeins of the social safety net were the chief distinctions that set the country apart from the United States — and one of the chief obstacles in creating a level economic playing field for a North American trading zone.

In fact, one of BCNI's first crusades seized on a cause that would dispense with many of those gripes that multinationals had with Ottawa: free trade with the United States. In many ways a misnomer, it had less to do with trade — more than 80 percent of which was already duty free — than with harmonizing the laws and policies in both countries, the better to do global business. Raising the spectre of U.S. protectionism — the notion of a Fortress America that would block Canadian imports — its apologists at BCNI and elsewhere provided a compelling rationale for dismantling the regional incentives and social programs that U.S. industrialists liked to brand subsidies.

As soon as they met, Tom d'Aquino and Paul Robinson recognized in each other a shared vision. At BCNI's offices and its regular lavish dinners for its blue-chip members, Robinson became a frequent speaker who found a receptive audience for his rambunctious patriotism. But he quickly realized that neither he nor the Reagan administration could be seen as the instigators of any continental trade initiative. "I knew it had to come from the Canadians," he explains. "For one thing, Canadians always told me that. If it got out that it was an American idea, I knew it would be dead."

In the fall of 1981, d'Aquino and a handful of top BCNI officials had huddled in Toronto to chew over shaping that issue, which had confounded Canadian governments over the previous century. At the time, as d'Aquino admits, "if we'd polled all our members, you would have found an overwhelming majority against free trade." It was just one example of how BCNI more often pursued the transnationals' agenda than the dictates of its own Canadian membership, but that reluctance did not deter the group. They commissioned one of BCNI's task forces under Alf Powis to make the free trade case — or, as d'Aquino would later boast, to sell it "quietly." Discretion, they knew, was all. The problem was what to call their inquiry without giving the game away. As d'Aquino points out, "You couldn't say 'free trade.'"

It was a semantic problem that he and Robinson had wrestled with ever since their first meeting at the U.S. Embassy months earlier. The ambassador, who had never shrunk from calling a spade a spade, would shake his head at d'Aquino's list of flannel-mouthed phrases to veil their grand continental design. "Tom had eight other things to call it," he chortles. "He said, 'Why don't we call it Freer Trade?' I said, 'Tom, that's so transparent, they'll see through it!'"

Other labels they pondered were Liberal or Liberalized Trade — but both had partisan echoes. Then d'Aquino came up with what Robinson dubbed "a real mouthful": a Trade Enhancement Agreement — or, as they joked, "TEA for two." When d'Aquino tried it out on Robinson, the ambassador grimaced. "Tom, that ain't a winner," he said.

But three years later, when Mulroney came to power in September 1984, BCNI — which had just taken its first major role in a federal election — had a report waiting to provide him with the policy ammunition to peddle free trade. Its title: "The Canada–United States Trading Relationship and the Idea of a Trade Enhancement Agreement." Overnight, after a campaign in which Brian Mulroney had given voters the distinct impression that he did not even want to consider the subject, TEA for two was already being served at 24 Sussex Drive.

SNOWDRIFTS had slowed Toronto traffic to a claustrophobic crawl and an icy wind howled through the skyscraper canyons. Climbing out of his limousine at 7:30 on a frigid January morning in 1983, Bill Brock shuddered at the climate in which he had been obliged to carry out his secret mission. With a discretion usually reserved for covert intelligence operations, he was breakfasting with the top trio of BCNI: Tom d'Aquino, Alf Powis, and Rowland Frazee, who had succeeded Earle McLaughlin as chairman of the Royal Bank. In the bank's splendid presidential dining room, Brock warmed at the sight of a 3-metre lemon tree sprouting real lemons, not to mention the delicate subject under discussion: how to sell the idea of a comprehensive trade agreement on this inclement side of the border.

The millionaire heir to a Tennessee candy fortune, Brock was a dedicated free trader whom Reagan had rewarded for chairing the Republican National Committee during his election campaign by naming him the U.S. trade representative, or, as he was known in Washington parlance, the USTR. His goal had been to carve out a new round of multilateral trade talks, but a quick trip around the world had dashed his hopes; the leaders in both developing countries and the economic powerhouses of Europe and Asia had made clear their distrust of any such initiative that the Reagan administration might use to retailor the world trading system to its liking.

But beneath his courtly Southern manners, Brock had never hesitated from tactical hardball. If the world would not come to the negotiating table with a carrot, he offered a stick: the threat of a series of bilateral treaties that would eventually leave Washington at the hub of any new global round. Brock's first pact with Israel had been greeted as a yawn. The country was seen as a U.S. pawn — dependent on its annual congressional foreign aid allotment for its very survival — and not a very powerful one at that: the entire trade between the two nations was negligible.

Canada offered more propitious prospects. America's largest trading partner, Ottawa also prided itself as an honest broker for other nations in Washington's court. A Canadian agreement would have a reassuring resonance in distant capitals, providing the pattern on which deals with the rest of the world could be cut.

But Brock had another reason for meeting Frazee, Powis, and d'Aquino that chill January dawn: even more than others in Reagan's cabinet, he had been infuriated by Trudeau's nationalistic measures — what Paul Robinson derided as the "Canadianization" of Canada. In 1981, rumours that the Liberals were considering drafting a new national industrial strategy and putting more teeth in FIRA had so enraged him that he had sent off a blistering nondiplomatic note threatening retaliation. Unbeknownst to Canadian officials, Brock had even convened a committee of his most combative young lieutenants to come up with punitive measures. "We were discussing options to teach Canada a lesson," admits Bill Merkin, who would later become the deputy U.S. free trade negotiator. "The most draconian was to cut off the capital markets, or just have an official U.S. government statement saying not to invest in Canada."

Ironically, it was Paul Robinson who had stepped into the breach to stave off those threats. Flying to Washington, he had stormed into the next cabinet meeting and enlisted Al Haig and Treasury Secretary Donald Regan against Brock. "My argument was: Canada is not Bulgaria," he says. "In fact, we may have better relations with Bulgaria. We can't treat Canada like it's just another country." Then, his protective instincts stirred, Robinson had roared back to Ottawa to orchestrate a hush-hush meeting at his residence over Thanksgiving weekend between Regan and Finance Minister Allan MacEachen, who agreed to publicly disavow the rumoured plans in his next budget.

Later that year, Brock had tried to exclude Canada from a regular quadripartite meeting with Europe and Japan, and again Robinson had intervened, going over the USTR's head and trading on his friendship with Reagan, to get the event cancelled instead. But those territorial tussles had made bitter enemies of the two key players from Reagan's administration who would work behind the scenes to pave the way for free trade talks. Whenever Robinson heard politicians or reporters rhapsodize over Brock's Southern charm, he could barely contain his bile. "The Canadian press was trying to make me look like an ogre," he says, "when what was really happening was I was saving the relationship."

Later, when Brock came to Ottawa to meet with d'Aquino and Canadian officials trying to nudge the free trade initiative forward, he assigned Merkin to keep Robinson out of his hair. On one trip, the quiet bureaucrat had found himself with a baseball bat in his hand in the backyard of the ambassador's elegant residence, where Robinson, a diehard Chicago Cubs fan, had set up a pitching machine.

But Brock had agreed with Robinson on one thing: as he told Frazee, Powis, and d'Aquino, if ever there was to be a free trade agreement, the demand would have to come from the Canadian side.

ED Lumley had no patience with his nationalist confrères in Trudeau's cabinet, which was already splitting over the issue of free trade. The gregarious former Coca Cola bottler from Cornwall had scarcely been named the Liberals' minister of international commerce when he showed up on Bill Brock's doorstep in Washington. Officially, he was there to explore trade talks that would cover only a few sectors, such as steel. But unofficially, he wanted the whole kit and caboodle on the table — a wide-open comprehensive free trade deal.

A week after they met, the minister called again from South America, where he was hosting a Canadian export show. He would pick Brock up for their next meeting in Ottawa in his government jet, he said, if they could make a tradeoff: a little weekend detour to the Superbowl in Detroit, where surely the U.S. trade representative could wangle tickets. Brock snared four seats on the 50-yard line, just behind Vice President George Bush, and invited Merkin along. "They got on like a house on fire," Merkin recalls.

Back in Ottawa, Lumley conferred regularly with Paul Robinson, plotting their continental battle plan. They too spoke the same language — the brisk, unsentimental vocabulary of business which had no patience with borders. More than a decade later, Robinson still counts Lumley a friend, underlining his singular achievement: "He shackled FIRA." By 1983, thanks to Lumley's accommodations, 93 percent of FIRA applications were being okayed, and the ambassador was trumpeting to the Chicago Board of Trade that the agency had been reduced to "a lapdog."

With Mulroney poised to take over the Conservative Party and Turner positioning himself in the Liberal camp, Robinson had kicked off the year by striding into the U.S. Embassy on the first day of January 1983 and announcing to his troops that it was time to unleash a free trade blitz — full throttle ahead and damn the torpedoes.

Two months later, Bush landed in Ottawa on an official visit, beginning his role as the administration's point man with Canada — a brief he would personally oversee even during his own presidency. Perusing the vice president's itinerary, External Affairs officials were stunned to note that he was scheduled to spend an hour at the Château Laurier with Tom d'Aquino and a handful of top Canadian

CEOs. Proposed by Paul Robinson, who let External know it was none of the department's business, the gathering was the group's first follow-up with the White House since its secret session with Brock.

In Bush, whose Texas oil friends had long been irate over FIRA, d'Aquino and the BCNI found an enthusiastic booster for the notion of a continental trade and energy pact. Nor were they unaware of the import of their meeting: later they lined up around the vice president to immortalize the moment in a snapshot that would enjoy pride of place in a silver frame on d'Aquino's pine bookshelves.

By then, Brock's USTR commandos had also teamed up with their counterparts in the bowels of the Ottawa bureaucracy, where another band of true believers was toiling to advance the continental cause. Their leader was Derek Burney, a trade veteran who had been promoted to head the U.S. desk at External and who would later personally oversee the negotiations from Mulroney's office. As one of the chief organizers for the 1981 economic summit in Montebello, Burney had forged early links with Michael Deaver and the Reagan administration, and he was more than receptive to their celebration of the corporate imperative. As a brusque, no-nonsense foot-soldier on the trade side of the diplomatic corps, he had been dispatched to Germany during Trudeau's fling with the Third Option — trying to wean the country from its U.S. dependence by seeking new foreign markets. There he found executives appalled by Canadian investment restrictions. He soon concluded that the Third Option was a dud: Europe, then plunging into its own recession, could never replace America as an export market.

In 1981, shortly after the Montebello summit, he had begun a review of Canadian trade policy with deputy trade minister Robert Johnstone, whom Mulroney would later post as consul general to New York. During the next two years, Burney and his trusty sidekick Michael Hart met repeatedly with BCNI and other business groups, giving corporate Canada unaccustomed input into a policy process that traditionally had been guarded jealously by External's mandarins. In August 1983 they presented their report to Gerry Regan, a former Nova Scotia premier who had succeeded Lumley in the trade portfolio and who shared his continental enthusiasms.

Blandly entitled *Canadian Trade Policy for the 1980s: A Discussion Paper* and crammed with tedious bureaucratic jargon, that review would later be pegged by Burney as one of the key philosophical stepping stones in building an argument for free trade talks within the Ottawa establishment. Despite its inordinately cautious language, Regan too had treated it as a milestone. Highlighting its plug for sectoral free trade negotiations with the United States, the minister made headlines — and in the process opened the charged debate in the press.

In Washington Bill Brock promptly endorsed the report — not that it surprised him. Weeks earlier, long before most members of Trudeau's cabinet had seen it, Burney had provided Brock with a draft copy through his friend, deputy USTR Mike Smith. Indeed, as officials relate the backstage story of the prelude to free trade talks, one aspect stands out: the conspiratorial glee with which a tiny band of officials joined efforts to put the issue on the Canadian agenda through a mixture of guile and outright deception.

Even the review's conclusions were a charade of sorts. Those few analysts who bothered to plough through Hart's leaden, carefully qualified prose would have discovered that the report actually recommended not the sectoral talks Regan underlined, but an across-the-board trade deal. While pointing out that, for the moment, such a step remained too politically contentious to dare, it noted that "at some point in the future" with more public support, such a comprehensive negotiation might fly.

In fact, Burney admits he always knew the sectoral approach was doomed; his American counterparts had already assured him of that. Not only were there not enough sectors where equal tradeoffs were possible between the two countries, but the concept simply held no interest for the free market purists in Washington. "I had no doubt the sectoral talks would go nowhere," Merkin agrees.

True to that prediction, the negotiations bogged down. Then, to the Liberals' surprise, Brock and his team backed off. They had already read the political winds from the north — correctly as it turned out. "In Washington, there was a feeling that with a change of government it would work," Merkin says. "Despite Lumley and others, there was an assumption that, if another party came in, especially one reported to be closer to the business community, we could probably get a deal."

CRISS-CROSSING the country, ever vigilant for Washington's interests, Paul Robinson had followed the gathering revolt against Joe Clark within Conservative ranks with as much objectivity as he could muster. In a cable to George Shultz, the U.S. Embassy would later characterize Clark as a "plodding and uncharismatic figure whose quirky physical mannerisms are the butt of numerous jokes" and who had "disasterously [sic] bumbled away power." Robinson had nothing against him personally. "He was a good man," he says pointedly, "as a foreign minister."

But like a Chicago Cubs' scout who had picked out a star prospect on an obscure farm team, Robinson was convinced that in any leadership contest Brian Mulroney would carry the day. In the spring of 1983, when he heard of the suicidal conditions Clark had set for retaining his post, he shook his head in disbelief. "I thought," Robinson chuckles, "now it's open!"

During that year's leadership convention, Mulroney had nothing good to say on one subject: "Don't talk to me about free trade," he thundered to a questioner. "All that would happen with that kind of concept would be the boys cranking up their plants in the United States in the bad times and shutting their entire branch plants in Canada. It's bad enough as it is."

If those comments would turn out to be prophetic, they also failed to reflect the history of his thoughts on the matter. Duncan Edmonds had a clear recollection of Mulroney sitting in the panelled hush of the Mount Royal Club five years earlier enthusiastically expounding on the subject. And within days of his election, it had suddenly found a place in his affections — and on his agenda — again. As for his apparent about-face, Bill Fox, who still serves as a freelance spin doctor for his old boss, reports that Mulroney now claims he was misquoted. "On the campaign, he said, 'I don't believe in *unfettered* free trade,'" Fox dutifully points out. "He says the adjective got lost."

Whatever got lost, or even temporarily disowned, it did not bother Robinson: politics, after all, was politics and nothing mattered if you failed to win. Throughout the Tory leadership campaign and the election a year later, he watched indulgently from the sidelines as his young friend swept to successive victories. With Mulroney finally in power, the ambassador never doubted his commitment to a continental free market. "We were both for it," Robinson confirms. "But he didn't really go fast-forward until he was elected."

The speed of that switch was nothing short of dizzying. Within weeks of his election, armed with BCNI's recommendations and Burney's policy review, Mulroney had instructed Trade Minister James Kelleher to inform Brock that Ottawa was ready to start exploring the road to negotiations. Two months later, Finance Minister Michael Wilson's first budget statement, *A New Direction for Canada: An Agenda for Economic Renewal*, had carried a little-noticed section — again worded in dry euphemisms — committing the government to "a careful analysis of options for bilateral trade liberalization with the United States."

Later that November, former Liberal cabinet minister Donald Macdonald, a corporate lawyer who had garnered the nickname "Thumper," had added his own partisan imprimatur to the free trade juggernaut. In upstate New York, at a gathering of the Council on Foreign Relations, one of the Rockefellers' favourite philanthropies, Macdonald suddenly pre-empted his own royal commission report on the Canadian economy by nearly a year to declare that free trade was a "leap of faith" which the country had no choice but to make. So necessary was the move to the health of the nation, Macdonald ventured, flexing a metaphor, that it was worth even "risking a coronary."

Listening to his testimonial, some fellow delegates feared succumbing to precisely such an attack. "One man's leap of faith is another's Russian Roulette," protested nationalist economist Abraham Rotstein. York University historian Jack Granatstein dubbed it "more like a leap into the dark. No one knows the economic consequences of free trade with the Americans." But even those critics agreed that Macdonald's vote of confidence served as one of the key milestones on Mulroney's road to free trade, giving it the gloss of approval from a Liberal pillar of Bay Street. Nor were they surprised later when Mulroney rewarded him with a posting as high commissioner to London.

Gradually, the intricate pieces of the continental puzzle were falling into place. Mulroney appointed Burney, who had already accompanied him on both his trips to the White House, as maestro of the production that would set his stamp on the coming decade of Canadian-American follies — the Shamrock Summit extravaganza to be held in Quebec City. There, his televised duet with Reagan inspired Liberal commentator Eric Kierans to sum up many Canadians' sentiments on CBC's *Morningside*: "The general impression you get," Kierans cracked, "is that our prime minister invited his boss home to dinner."

But if the hype and musical hoopla of the summit had riveted, and appalled, the nation, it also evoked some shimmering Hollywood set — a false front. Backstage, behind the glitz and sequins, another story was unfolding — one that would irrevocably change the country's fate. Behind the closed doors of a Château Frontenac salon, Mulroney and Reagan signed off on an obscurely worded statement, agreeing to start preliminary trade talks.

If most journalists covering the twenty-four-hour Quebec City spectacular failed to catch on to that formalized leap of faith, they could hardly be blamed. After years of nudging Bill Brock towards an understanding of just how explosive the term "free trade" was in Canada, Burney had made sure that the dread phrase was nowhere in sight. Instead, the final communiqué called for "measures to enhance access to each other's markets" and "a program to explore further means to facilitate and increase trade and investment" — eye-glazing bureaucratese meant to obscure the undertaking. "It was," Burney concedes, "as vague as we could make it."

Despite that tactical victory, within days Burney was in despair. In a cabinet shuffle, Reagan shifted Brock to the labour portfolio. "The guy we'd been nursing along through all the taboos — don't mention free trade, all of that — the godfather on the American side," he lamented, "all of a sudden he was gone."

Four months later, Brock's rival for that title was gone as well. In July 1985 Paul Robinson submitted his resignation as ambassador. He had staked out the first territorial imperative for Reagan's North American Accord: a trade pact was already taking shape on the horizon. "The Shamrock Summit legalized it," he says, "made it a formal issue." It was up to both countries' bureaucrats to carry the ball forward. As Tom d'Aquino pointed out, the gameplan had already been laid out in Quebec City: "It was very important symbolically in terms of sending a signal to recalcitrant officials on both sides to really get aboard and serve their masters."

At the signing session in the Château Frontenac, Robinson had sat on Reagan's left, basking in what he knew to be a historic moment and savouring the president's own pleasure in the first step towards exporting his free market faith. "Reagan opened up,"

Robinson recalls. "He said the origin of all this was the repeal of the Corn Laws in England in the 1870s, which led to the biggest commercial empire in history. He went on for quite a long time about it — and all with no notes." (In fact, the Corn Laws were repealed in 1846.)

Since Mulroney's election, Robinson had kept in constant touch with him, never failing to point out to visitors how, from his own baronial digs, he could stare out across Wellington Street and straight into the Prime Minister's Office. When they weren't talking on the phone directly, Robinson was on the line to Mulroney's chief aide, Fred Doucet. "There were a lot of things I could dump on Fred," Robinson says, "and he on me."

Certainly, he never found a problem winning an audience with the prime minister for visiting U.S. politicians and corporate poobahs. "Mulroney loved Americans," recalls Lucien Bouchard, his former friend and cabinet minister. "No matter how lowly a congressman was in town, he'd make time to see him."

But just how close Robinson was to Mulroney and his longtime cronies would not become clear until after his retirement. In early 1986, less than a year after he stepped down as ambassador, Robinson would become a director of Government Consultants International, the controversial lobbying firm founded by Frank Moores, master strategist of the dump-Clark movement.

GCI, which included Patrick MacAdam and Fred Doucet's brother Gerry, had already earned notoriety for raking in more than $28 million in billings during Mulroney's first two years in power. But notoriety did not discourage Paul Robinson. When asked why he had been named to Moores's board, he blithely replied that it was to drum up U.S. business.

In the years to come, Robinson would remain a recurrent presence on the continental landscape he had done so much to alter — surfacing regularly in Ottawa, where he and his wife kept an apartment. Later, serving on the board of the Canada–U.S. Fulbright Fellowship foundation, he demonstrated that, although the Evil Empire had by then imploded, he himself had remained constant: at a November 1992 board meeting in Chicago, he left the foundation's Canadian directors speechless with a rousing tirade against the short-sightedness of the citizenry north of the border which failed to understand how much Canada still needed Washington's military muscle.

Before Robinson resigned, he had given Mulroney advance warning, and Doucet had called back with a question: "He said, 'What
kind of a letter do you want?'" Robinson recounts. "'One that tells
the truth or do you want one you can give to the press?'"

Robinson opted for a farewell missive that he promised not to
show the media until after the prime minister left office. On the
morning of June 1993 when Mulroney relinquished the party reins
to Kim Campbell, Robinson finally read it aloud to a reporter over
the phone. As it turned out, the letter was merely florid praise for
the ambassador's fostering of Canadian-American relations. The
only passage that might have raised eyebrows was startling chiefly
because of its timing. Written in the summer of 1985, weeks before
the official launch of free trade talks, it already invoked a continental
vision: in it, Mulroney credited Robinson with helping "to cement
the bonds that make Americans and Canadians . . . common heirs
to a continent."

By then those sentiments hardly seemed the stuff of potential
scandal, but Robinson remained acutely protective of the leader in
whom he felt such an avuncular pride. He would hang Mulroney's
letter over his desk at Robinson Incorporated, on Chicago's LaSalle
Street, but for years, whenever Canadian journalists dropped by, he
would take it down. He worried that it might hurt the man who had
proved such a friend to Washington if the press — or worse, the
socialists — ever got hold of it: "They'd say, 'See, here's this Prime
Minister playing up to the Americans again.'"

7

Singing in the Acid Rain

AIR FORCE ONE nosed towards the gigantic flood-lit hangar at Quebec City's Ancienne Lorette airport like some over-sized Hollywood prop. Its cabin door swung open to disgorge half the U.S. cabinet, most attempting some dutiful nod to the White House theme-of-the-day, which called for the wearing of the green. Even the sombre George Shultz, whose aides referred to him as The Buddha, sported a lime pocket handkerchief, albeit sheepishly, like some teenager caught in an uncool school play. But to Michael Deaver, the producer of the March 1985 Shamrock Summit extravaganza, all that mattered was that the assembled U.S. network cameras caught the star of the show, Ronald Reagan, stepping out in a telegenic emerald tie.

At the sight of him, gasps rippled through the White House press corps lined up at the end of the red carpet, where Brian Mulroney waited to greet him. But the astonishment was not, alas, because of the president's Irish sartorial flair. "The hair!" a *Washington Post* correspondent whispered, as the TV lights caught the presidential pompadour gleaming an unusually harsh shade of chestnut. The twitter among the media almost drowned out Reagan's assertion that, for Washington, there was "no more important relation-ship today" than the one with Canada. "Except," cracked a scribe, "the one with Grecian Formula #10."

But that disconcerting visual was the only lapse in this, Michael Deaver's penultimate outing as the president's master political impresario. Four months earlier, he had flown into Quebec City like a conquering general with a thirty-man "pre-advance" team — the first of four planning waves that left Bill Fox and Mulroney's half-dozen aides spectators at their own party. As steadily expanding U.S. crews took over the Château Frontenac, setting up what they termed the Quebec City White House, Deaver had scouted each historic nook and cranny for prospective visuals. Driving the motorcade route and pacing the meeting sites, he had meticulously plotted each camera angle in what would become a giant $2.6 million photo opportunity.

For most Canadians, the summit was the first glimpse of Reagan's politics of illusion at its most dazzling and disturbing. Outside, temperatures were glacial and an overnight blizzard had necessitated a frenzy of snowploughing, but inside the hangar, huge heating fans held nature in abeyance for the cameras. Still, the media lights gave the scene a surreal brightness, as if the hokey St. Patrick's Day welcome was indeed unrolling on a sound stage, far from reality.

With more scarlet-coated Mounties littering the hangar than the chorus of *Rosemarie*, no visual symbolism had been left unexploited, even if it did not always produce the desired effect. Behind the podium, billboard-sized flags of the two countries melted into each other in an ominously seamless union. And amid a handpicked crowd of Quebec Conservatives, one held up a puzzling sign: "Welcome home Brian and the Gipper."

Other, less polite placards reading "Yankee Go Home" and "Keep Your Chin Up, Brian, Big Brother is Here" had been banished downtown to the Place d'Armes, out of the Americans' sight. Only one bilingual billboard protest had been permitted in Lower Town, where network cameras were alerted to its presence: "Stop Acid Rain," it read, above a cheery green shamrock. Outside the Château Frontenac, as soon as the U.S. cameras hove into view, two hundred apparently random citizens hoisted red-and-white anti-acid-rain umbrellas studded with discreet maple-leaf logos.

The acid rain issue had, in fact, thrown an anxious pall over the summit preparations for months — a stumbling block that had more to do with style than substance. As a prescient State Department briefing memo had noted, although it was the most visible topic on the environmental agenda — and the one where the countries' differences were most pronounced — Mulroney was "unlikely to make substantive changes in the acid rain positions inherited from the Liberals." The memo went on to warn that, "after a 'honeymoon' period with the US, the new government may well pick this topic as suitable to demonstrate [its] independence of Washington. Mulroney, however, does not appear to take [an] intense personal interest."

The problem was, as another State analysis put it, the new prime minister needed "to show his pro–U.S. tilt is paying off." And for Mulroney's next eight years in office, acid rain would become the barometer to measure the highs and lows of bilateral relations. Any attempt to ignore the problem during the summit could undercut the far more crucial issue at stake for Washington: the delicate pre-negotiations for a free trade pact.

Already, Larry Speakes had almost blown that exercise by burbling to Washington reporters that "We are literally on the verge of something truly big in the trade area. We believe a new trade relationship could be a blockbuster of North American economic news." Panicked Canadian officials had stepped in to warn him about the sensitivity of the subject back home, where the PR ground had not yet been tilled. Thus, while the agreement to begin exploring free trade talks came to be couched in increasingly obscure verbiage — veiled from all but the corporate and bureaucratic cognoscenti — the acid rain issue acquired even higher-profile urgency as a smokescreen. "It was," as summit organizer Derek Burney termed it, "a diversion."

But what form that diversion would take was another matter. Reagan was hostile to any measure that meant the regulation of business — a neoconservative heresy. And two months earlier, a group of industrial state senators had extracted a promise from him that he would not foist costly new measures on them to reduce emissions. Their fears appeared groundless considering that the administration's environmental record had become an embarrassment even to many Republicans. Reagan's Environmental Protection Agency (EPA) was still struggling to recover from a payoff scandal, and his former interior secretary, James Watt, had outraged the green movement by trying to sell off public lands to mining companies and referring to the Audubon Society as a "chanting mob."

Anne Gorsuch Burford, his first EPA administrator, had refused even to use the phrase "acid rain," referring instead to "non-buffered precipitation." But after her forced departure in 1983, White House handlers had brought in William Ruckelshaus to put a more credible face on the agency. To defuse the public outcry, Ruckelshaus had urged a $1 million commitment to fight acid rain. But Reagan and his hardline budget director David Stockman had vetoed any such spending. The president had betrayed his disinterest in the portfolio by repeatedly failing to recognize Ruckelshaus at meetings, then addressing him as "Don."

As it happened, acid rain was one of those issues on which Ronald Reagan held strong opinions. During the 1980 election, he had stunned Deaver by ad-libbing to a steeltown crowd in Steubenville, Ohio — the state with the highest sulphur dioxide emissions — that acid rain came from trees. The remark haunted his campaign as environmentalists festooned roadside forests with placards taunting "Killer Trees!" and "Cut Me Down Before I Kill Again!"

Not that the ridicule had changed his mind. At least two cabinet planning meetings were held in the weeks before his departure to Quebec City and, during one, a former administration official recalls, the acid rain issue was still being pondered when "Reagan came out with, 'Trees pollute more than people.' I looked around to see if everybody had a straight face — and they did. I was nervous that I'd break out laughing." As he recalls, the preoccupation of those meetings "was how to give Mulroney something without giving him something — something face-saving that wouldn't mean anything. That's how the whole envoy thing came up."

The "whole envoy thing" — later the subject of congressional and FBI investigations and a criminal indictment against Michael Deaver — was a compromise whose authorship would remain in dispute for years: a proposal for each leader to appoint a personal high-profile acid rain emissary to further study the problem. In Quebec City at the time, Deaver was getting the credit for the idea — and dubious credit at that.

Emerging from the Château's Petit Frontenac salon after his first brief meeting with Reagan, even Mulroney seemed bent on shuffling the contentious announcement out of the way before it could mar his show. "We did not work a miracle," he intoned apologetically, "but we did take a significant step forward."

Among the howls of disagreement, Michael Perley, co-founder of the Canadian Coalition on Acid Rain, denounced the gesture as "a disaster" and the *Montreal Gazette* offered a damning assessment: "The choreographed cheer in Quebec City cannot disguise the fact that the Mulroney government suffered an abject defeat on acid rain," its editorial declared. "All the agreement means is that action on reducing acid rain of U.S. origin is at least a year further off. How many more lakes will be dead by then?"

For acid rain activists, the capitulation was the first indication that the new government's resolve was faltering when it came to pressing for a clean-up of those U.S. industries that produced most of the damaging sulphurous emissions wafting northward into Canada. "We were very concerned that Mulroney would have fallen for this," says Perley. "I wanted him to say: 'If this is the best you're offering, forget it,' and walk away."

But even more distressing to those in the clean-air crowd was the choice of the emissaries themselves: instead of distinguished scientists or environmentalists, both governments had appointed political loyalists with a reputation as backroom fixers. As Fred Doucet, who had taken over the U.S. dossier in the Prime Minister's Office, put it, the task required "artists in politics."

Filling that job description, Drew Lewis, Reagan's former secretary of transportation, had broken the U.S. air traffic controllers' unions during the 1981 strike that signalled the administration's assault on labour. Within the party, he had a reputation as an aggressive, take-charge administrator with well-honed political instincts: when Reagan's Kitchen Cabinet had worried that his presidency was foundering, they had tried to draft Lewis as his chief of staff. As a Pennsylvania Republican with impeccable connections to the coal and oil fortunes that had made the state the highest source of sulphurous emissions after Ohio, Lewis also had an acute appreciation of the exigencies of industrial America. In 1983 he had left government to return to business himself, becoming chairman of Warner-Amex Cable, which was then a division of American Express.

Not only was he a close friend of Amex chairman Jim Robinson, who would soon become the unofficial U.S. point man on the Canadian free trade pact, but Robinson's glamorous second wife, Linda, also worked as Lewis's public relations chief at the time. The daughter of radio star Freeman Gosden, who played Amos in the *Amos 'n' Andy* series, she grew up in Hollywood, where Ronald

Reagan was a frequent dinner guest, and later worked in his presidential campaign. In 1980 she had been press secretary to Bill Brock at the Republican National Committee, before becoming Lewis's chief spokesperson at the Transportation Department, then following him to Warner-Amex, where she met and married Robinson.

Given her corporate and political cachet, not to mention her nightly star turns on the New York social circuit, Linda Gosden Robinson was no ordinary staffer as she swooped into acid rain meetings with Drew Lewis in her Oscar de la Renta suits and serious diamonds. "We're doing this for you all," she would tell her Canadian counterparts, underlining Lewis's $1-a-year status. But as his assignment ended and Amex sold out its cable interests, they would note that Linda Robinson made $1 million from the deal — enough to start her own PR firm, where her clients would include another close friend, Mulroney's pal Ross Johnson.

As for the prime minister's envoy, who could argue that "Brampton Bill" Davis, the man who had ruled Ontario behind an inscrutable haze of pipe smoke for fourteen years, did not grasp the art of cosmetic politics? As he himself once acknowledged, "Bland works." A master of the middle-of-the-road who had cautioned his party not to follow the extreme prescriptions of Reagan or Margaret Thatcher, Davis was also someone to whom Mulroney owed a great deal. In May 1983, with uncharacteristic emotion, he had taken himself out of the Tory leadership race, putting his Big Blue Machine — including campaign strategist Norman Atkins — at Mulroney's disposal. The prime minister and his cronies were acutely conscious of that IOU, and two years later, when Davis stepped down as premier, a man disheartened, Mulroney flattered him with regular phone consultations.

But Davis also boasted his own ties to the Reagan administration which had a stake in the Shamrock Summit's success. For more than a decade, as Richard Wirthlin helped shape his victories, the premier and his aides had forged connections with the California Reaganauts. Unbeknownst to most Canadians, Davis also had another link to the Reagan camp: Ambassador Paul Robinson.

In 1981, when Robinson had first called on the premier at Queen's Park, he found a remarkable personal touch: Davis had pulled out the yearbook from Hinsdale High, the ambassador's alma mater in a western suburb of Chicago. Cracking it open, Davis had flipped to the senior class picture and Robinson's football exploits, then to the junior class that featured Robinson's wife-to-be, Martha. "He didn't know what I was up to," Davis recalls. Then the premier turned to the freshman class photo and pointed to a pretty blonde: his own wife, Kathleen Louise Mackay. With that, their friendship was sealed.

Davis takes credit for helping Robinson understand that Canadian acid rain activists were "not some sort of radical element." Robinson, in turn, claims that it was his idea to defuse the issue by naming what he calls a presidential commission — a boast he would later swear to under oath at Michael Deaver's trial. "I said I did it," Robinson declares, "and helped get him off the hook." The ambassador also insists he was behind Davis's assignment: "I remember telling Fred Doucet," he says, "'You've got to put Davis on that committee.'"

With the envoy's job, Mulroney was again prevailing on Davis for a favour. At the news of his appointment, Perley and the acid rain coalition were furious: as premier, he had personally blocked action against the province's two worst polluters, Inco's smokestacks in Sudbury and the government's own Ontario Hydro. Only two years earlier he had resisted federal pressure to set provincial sulphur dioxide abatement standards. "I am not prepared to have the government create an economic problem for Sudbury," he had declared, calling for a wait-and-see approach.

Davis's penchant for putting off tough decisions was so famous that, at a farewell roast, longtime assistant Clare Westcott saluted him for having "made procrastination a vital and important instrument in the running of government." Certainly, it was a gift tailor-made for his new post.

When Davis accepted the job, he waved off the first title offered — ambassador — as too grand for a politician who had cultivated a pipe-and-slippers image. Besides, it raised expectations, and, as he repeatedly reminded an aide later, you don't appoint a royal commission unless you already know what it's going to find. Davis understood perfectly the diplomatic subtleties of his task. "I knew this was an opportunity to ease the political pressures on the prime minister here," he says, "and have a report that was somewhat inconclusive for the White House."

IN the press room set up in the old Quebec Court House, Fred Doucet was trying to explain his boss's accommodations on acid rain to Shamrock Summit reporters. But as he wound up, a vivacious brunette in a purple coat was already moving among the media handing out buttons reading "No More Blarney." As co-founder with Michael Perley of the Canadian Coalition on Acid Rain, Adèle Hurley had made her way behind the summit's stringent security lines to perform a task at which she had become expert: dispensing quotable quotes.

Still, she did so in the politest possible terms. "The prime minister was trying to be a good host," her carefully worded press release stated, "but we're disappointed. The appointment of acid rain envoys is essentially a face-saving gesture for the President, who remains committed to the use of the North American environment as a garbage dump."

Hurley had her reasons for being so genteel. For if she and Perley were disappointed about Mulroney's appointments, they were not surprised: Doucet and other government advisers had consulted with them before the announcement. What virtually no one knew at the time was that the two-million-member Canadian Coalition on Acid Rain, one of the country's most vocal and effective environmental groups, was the brainchild of the Tory cabinet — specifically of Fisheries Minister John Fraser.

Indeed, that tie to the government, which had endured for more than five years through both Conservative and Liberal regimes, would become increasingly awkward as Mulroney took power and displayed a see-sawing ambivalence towards the coalition's chief *raison d'être*: lobbying Washington to clean up its act on acid rain.

A Vancouver lawyer who specialized in resource issues, and also a devoted salmon fisherman, Fraser had served as Joe Clark's environmental minister in 1979. In that portfolio, he had seized on acid rain as his *cause célèbre* and had pronounced the sulphurous belchings drifting north from the Ohio Valley's utilities and steel mills "an appalling situation." But he had optimistically predicted that a little diplomatic muscle-flexing would do the trick. "The United States cannot afford to have hostile Canadians for neighbours," he had argued.

But Fraser had landed his job just as the environmentally friendly administration of Jimmy Carter was forced into an about-face, courtesy of the decade's second energy crisis. Amid panic over cutting down on U.S. oil consumption, Carter had unveiled a conservation plan that called for burning even more high-sulphur, acid-rain-producing coal. With disgruntled friends in Carter's EPA, Fraser had begun to hatch a plan to turn acid rain into an American public issue — through Canadian pressure — which would force the White House to see the error of its ways.

But Clark's government had fallen and Ronald Reagan had swept into the White House, launching a frenzy of deregulation in Washington. For U.S. clean air advocates who suddenly found themselves out of fashion, Canadian activism became their last best hope. In March 1981, in a speech to environmental lawyers sponsored by the Canadian and American bar associations in Banff, Jim Moorman, a burly, bearded attorney from Carter's Justice Department, had spelled out a step-by-step strategy for Canada to lobby for acid rain legislation in Washington.

In his audience, Fraser, who had won an opposition seat on Parliament's new bipartisan acid rain committee, was intrigued by the precision of Moorman's ten-point plan. After the session, he grabbed a copy of the text, which he passed on to John Roberts, his Liberal successor in the environment portfolio, with whom he was working closely. At last, Fraser thought, here was a way to take the issue out of the hands of what he had come to scorn as "the striped pants set."

Within two months, Moorman's speech, entitled "The Role of Canadian Citizens in Dealing with the United States on the Acid Rain Question," had become the blueprint for Ottawa's strategy towards Washington on the issue — a strategy that would last for the next decade. Indeed, some analysts even credit Moorman's analysis as the inspiration for the overall foreign policy approach to the United States adopted later that year by the Department of External Affairs and its top mandarin, Allan Gotlieb.

As ambassador to Washington, Gotlieb would ply the thesis that Moorman laid out in his Banff speech: in the U.S. capital, the traditional role of the political parties had collapsed and had been taken over by lobbyists; if Canadians wanted to win attention for their case, they would have to join in what Moorman branded that "terribly high-powered floating crap game." In short, they would have to do just what the coal and steel industries were doing — lobby.

Not only congressmen and their staff would have to be cultivated, but also the media, obscure U.S. regulatory agencies, and American grassroots organizations whose interests meshed with Canada's. In the crunch, Canadians should even be prepared to take their case to the U.S. courts, Moorman said. But he cautioned against using the embassy or any other direct arm of the government, which would likely provoke cries of foul from U.S. industry — not to mention a backlash. Instead, he recommended hiring Washington professionals to do the job.

Fraser was mulling over that counsel when he was a guest speaker at an international acid rain conference in Toronto sponsored by the Ontario Federation of Naturalists. There, he was impressed by Hurley, who worked as an environmental researcher for Ontario Liberal leader Stewart Smith. Later, she found herself invited to a dinner with him at the city's Sutton Place Hotel, where he unveiled Moorman's game plan to a group that included Michael Perley and Monte Hummel, executive director of the World Wildlife Fund. By the time dessert and coffee arrived, the group had nominated Hurley for a trip to Washington to study how they would mount a lobbying operation in the U.S. capital.

At twenty-six, having never been out of the country, she was petrified. She called Moorman with trepidation. Ironically, Hurley's very lack of sophistication captivated him. "I thought she should be the lobbyist in Washington," he says. "She's a very attractive person in a wholesome way and she seems completely without any guile. She's someone you want to help."

Most importantly, Hurley fit one of Moorman's key instructions: if Canadians were going to take on Americans, they should do so "in good temper." He argued that "one thing Americans admire about Canadians is their politeness and civility. We're sort of tired of screamers. If Canadians flipped into one more scold, Americans would quickly tell you guys to buzz off and start pointing out what you were doing wrong."

By then, Hurley, Perley, and Fraser were beginning to agree. Interviewing prospective U.S. lobbyists, they found the résumé of one New York duo strewn with grammatical and typographical bloopers. "We knew we weren't exactly dealing with the top drawer," Hurley recalls. "They were very hired-gun-type guys. Michael said, 'These guys could be working for us on Monday and the coal industry on Tuesday.' Then we thought: we know more about this than they do."

Within a year, Hurley was on her way to Ronald Reagan's Washington with the blessings of Environment Minister John Roberts as the government's own acid rain agent abroad. In the U.S. capital, where the 1980s' romance with corporate might was still in its first flush, she had previously attended a coal industry convention, horrified at the self-congratulatory mood in the air. "They were celebrating: they were going to undo everything that Carter had done," she recalls. "I could see environmental groups were going to be on the outs, so I could not afford to hitch my wagon to them. I thought: Whose slip stream can I get into? Who has money and power and influence — and is not a creep?"

Hurley hooked up with a rumpled British public relations expert named John Adams, who represented the American Environmental Equipment Manufacturers, the makers of the smokestack scrubbers that any acid rain legislation would require. "I figured they were closer to business," she says, "so maybe they'd hang out with Republicans."

In fact, Adams provided more than bipartisan contacts. He rented her an office in his K Street suite, complete with its own brass plaque on the door, unlimited access to the latest in environmental literature, and space in his newsletter. Overnight, the Canadian Coalition on Acid Rain was in business in the heart of U.S. lobbyists' row.

A jungle of CBC cables and lighting tripods was rising above the broadloom in Hurley's new Washington offices. Adrienne Clarkson, the co-host of the network's *fifth estate* who had turned up to film a segment on Hurley entitled "Lobbyist," marvelled at the posh setup. "How do you do all this?" she inquired.

For Hurley and the acid rain coalition, that was, in fact, the rub. Moorman had warned that, unlike the Canadian coalition offices — which had received a $100,000 grant from Environment Canada — the U.S. acid rain lobby operation could not run on government grants. "You can't have the Canadian government financing American citizen groups," he said. "If that became well known, it would be viewed as phony — and improper."

Moorman and Hurley lived in terror of incurring the wrath of one of the most feared men in Washington — and the leading opponent of U.S. acid rain legislation: Michigan congressman John Dingell. As the immensely powerful chairman of the House energy and commerce committee, Dingell was so vigilant of the interests of his Dearborn constituency, home to the world headquarters of the Ford Motor Company, that he had won the monicker Tailpipe Johnny.

A bulldozer with hornrims and a steeltrap mind, he was noted for his 300-page Dingellgrams, harassing officials or fellow congressmen with questions that could tie them up for months. Dingell routinely rolled over anyone who stood in his or Detroit's way, and he had not taken kindly to Ottawa's push for legislation in Washington. After all, any measure against tall-stacks emissions could open the way to tailpipe controls on nitrous oxide, the secondary contributor to acid rain — a prospect that had mobilized the already beleaguered auto industry. Dingell was constantly on a collision course with the Canadian Embassy, and never bypassed an opportunity to point out that Canada was no innocent when it came to polluting: Inco, he repeatedly declared, belched more sulphur dioxide "than the Milky Way."

Moorman had warned that if Dingell got wind that the government was behind Hurley's lobbying, she could find herself hauled up before his subcommittee for a merciless — and damaging — grilling. She became obsessed with observing U.S. lobbying procedure to the letter, including signing in at the U.S. Justice Department's registry for foreign agents. But those forms also required Hurley to account for her funding.

Her initial stake had come from the Northern Ontario Tourist Outfitters, a group of resort owners in the acid rain coalition led by Dean Wenborne, the flinty American-born owner of a luxury fishing camp upwind of Sudbury on the French River. Like other lodge owners, Wenborne had seen the dying lakes and trout first hand. But the Outfitters' $17,500 stipend was running out. By the time Adrienne Clarkson showed up at the K Street office, Hurley was feeling the pinch. Then, primed by the *fifth estate* show, the coalition's direct-mail fundraising machine in Canada kicked in.

Still, the necessity of financing the Washington acid rain office — and keeping its accounts fastidiously separate from Michael Perley's government-funded operation in Toronto — would become a preoccupation for the next decade. In 1981 when the coalition mobilized the well-heeled cottage-owners of Muskoka, who also had a stake in the fight, fundraising took on a life of its own. Led by

Jeffrey Shearer, then the executive vice president of Comac Communications and the president of the Muskoka Lakes Association, the group hit upon a solution that had always worked for the wealthy stockbrokers and socialites among its membership: gala $100-a-plate dinners that attracted as many as 1,000 patrons to hear speakers like Allan Gotlieb and Massachusetts' senator Edward Kennedy.

One cottager donated the wine, artists ran off the posters and invitations free of charge, and Rosedale resident Joan Booth threw open her luxury home for the annual pre-dinner telephone blitz. The acid rain cause became so trendy that RBC Dominion Securities offered its phone banks to the volunteers drumming up contributions after hours. Pledges were flashed across the brokerage's electronic stock boards, and prizes were awarded for top sales — the coalition's discreet navy ties studded with golden acid rain droplets. "They were a very sophisticated design," Hurley explains, "because you had to be able to wear them into the Albany Club."

She speculates that the coalition owed its success to something visceral in the Canadian psyche: "For a lot of people, the movement was a way of keeping the cottage life alive all winter," she says. "The touchstone for all of them was the lake and the loons and gin and tonics on the dock."

Over a decade, the coalition raised an estimated $3 million and spawned a decidedly upwardly mobile environmental movement — many of whose members also figured on the rolls of the Conservative Party. "There came a time," Hurley says, "when it wasn't acceptable in polite society to dare to be against acid rain." Or at least in Canadian polite society. The coalition's Establishment credentials cut no mustard in Reagan's Washington, where the White House adamantly insisted on more research into acid rain.

Instead, Hurley focused her efforts on the U.S. media and Congress, where she forged an alliance with a group of New England senators — Vermont's Robert Stafford, a Republican, and Maine's George Mitchell, a Democrat; Mitchell lent her his help and occasionally even his office. But the coalition's key ally was California Congressman Henry Waxman, the chairman of one of Dingell's subcommittees and the leading voice against acid rain in the House. Hurley and Perley arranged acid rain tours to Canada for key congressional staffers and reporters from the *New York Times*, making sure to include a flight over Sudbury's stark sulphur-inspired moonscape and one swoop through Inco's bilious smoke-stack plume.

Gradually, as the press clips began mobilizing U.S. public opinion, Hurley also sought out alliances with American groups who had a stake in the issue, from foresters and anglers to New England canoeists. Then, in the midst of her consciousness-raising efforts, Hurley won help from an unexpected source: Reagan's Justice Department. Wielding an obscure 1938 law, it classified two National Film Board shorts — one entitled *Acid Rain: Requiem or Recovery* — as "government propaganda," a category previously reserved for wartime Nazi films. Having created an international incident, the administration ensured lineups around the block at Washington's Biograph Theatre for two documentaries that otherwise might have passed unnoticed.

By 1983 Hurley had other proof that her work was paying off: a poll by the U.S. National Wildlife Federation revealed that two-thirds of North Carolinians were now aware of the scourge of acid rain. "This is not a Canadian issue any more," she said.

Back home, too, things seemed to be looking up. As the 1984 election campaign got underway, the coalition prepared question-naires for the candidates, then released their evaluations in the form of acid rain report cards to the press. As Allan Gregg's polls made clear, the issue was an increasing worry among voters. Mulroney, at John Fraser's urging, had responded so convincingly with a promised plan of action that he won the coalition's top marks. Hurley and Perley were enthusiastic about his victory. "We had high hopes for him," Hurley acknowledges.

Those hopes still seemed well founded in the spring of 1985 as the Shamrock Summit approached. Two weeks beforehand, Environment Minister Suzanne Blais-Grenier had unveiled an acid rain package that allowed the government to come to the meeting with clean hands: a promise to cut Canadian sulphur dioxide emissions by 50 percent over nine years and to spend $150 million helping industries install scrubber technology. The coalition had been urging such a move on the previous government for years. Not only did it offer a riposte to Dingell, but it also called the White House's bluff.

Then suddenly, through Fraser, the coalition learned that instead of demanding genuine action on the issue from an administration with which he obviously had leverage, Mulroney had backed down. Hurley was shattered to learn he had agreed to the White House's envoy ploy — another U.S. stall. Even a former aide to one of the envoys admits that, while the prime minister argued it was a way to bring Reagan around on the issue, the dynamics of the situation were already clear: there was not going to be any significant follow-up. "I think Mulroney got suckered in bigtime. There was no intention really to do anything."

The coalition was all the more outraged at the choice of Davis. "We felt so stupid," Hurley says. "He'd been the premier when the smelters and Hydro got away with murder." She and Perley vented their sentiments in a letter to the *Globe and Mail*, decrying Davis's decade and a half of "studied indifference."

For any other environmental group, that might have been a natural, even timid, gesture. But Hurley and Perley promptly found themselves confronting the wrath of Doucet: he made it clear that the prime minister had not been expecting any flak from what he had perceived as the government's own tame green lobby. "Doucet was fawning over us in the early days because they really needed us," Hurley says. "But when we criticized the envoys, he went crazy."

Suddenly, the coalition felt a chill. During the following years, the message from the Prime Minister's Office became increasingly clear: stop making waves in Washington — and above all, stop criticizing Brian Mulroney. Finally, in 1988, Hurley and Perley found themselves summoned to the office of Environment Minister Tom McMillan, a P.E.I. party stalwart whose brother Charley had been the prime minister's senior adviser on relations with the United States. McMillan threw down a handful of press clippings on his desk: he accused them of sabotaging his efforts and knifing the government in the back. Then he let them know that the coalition's annual $100,000 grant from Environment Canada, which kept its Toronto office afloat, was in jeopardy — the first time any government had ever wielded such a threat. "It was really to put us on notice," Hurley says. "It was not very sophisticated bullying."

Through an appeal to Fraser, they staved off that financial weapon. But increasingly, the godfather of the acid rain coalition was helpless to protect his environmental protégés: in cabinet, his influence as a Clark Red Tory relegated him to the sidelines and, by late 1985, the Tunagate scandal had cost him his portfolio. Even when an emotional vote returned him as Speaker of the House, Fraser was largely powerless to intervene on the coalition's behalf with a prime minister capable of volcanic eruptions over critiques in the press. "John was just always there for us," Hurley says. "But gradually he was in no position to help."

With the Shamrock Summit, she realized, something had changed. Instead of remaining a bipartisan Canadian issue to wield against Washington, acid rain had become a pawn on the big board game of free trade. Over the next years, the more tense the negotiations became, the less noise Mulroney made on the issue — and the more the Canadian Embassy in Washington took its distance from Hurley's U.S. efforts. Rather than using the increasingly popular cause as leverage, the government treated it as a possible threat to congressional approval of the trade pact on which Mulroney had gambled his political fortunes.

Nor did it help that many of the corporations bankrolling the free trade campaign in Canada were the worst polluters: heading that list was Alf Powis's Noranda, a subsidiary of the Edper-Hees-Brascan group, whose smelter at Rouyn, in Quebec, had been rated the second highest source of sulphur dioxide emissions on the continent.

In retrospect, some in the coalition realized that they ought to have seen the Shamrock Summit extravaganza as an omen: only hours after announcing their acid rain envoys, Reagan and Mulroney had descended from their boxes in Quebec's Grand Theatre for a musical finale on stage. While Reagan and his wife, Nancy, barely mouthed the words to "When Irish Eyes Are Smiling," the onetime choirboy from Baie Comeau could not resist displaying his excellent tenor. With an exuberant flourish, Mulroney took the last cautionary line of their duet as his own solo: "Sure, they'll steal your heart away."

IN Jeffrey Shearer's publishing office at Telemedia in midtown Toronto, the most pressing environmental problem was not acid rain; it was the fumes from Bill Davis's pipe. "The room was choked with smoke," Adèle Hurley recalls — to say nothing of the acrid feelings in the air. In June 1985, three months after his appointment as an envoy, Davis had finally requested a meeting with the coalition's executive. But it became clear to Shearer, its president, and others that he still had no plan of action. When Michael Perley presented him with the activists' own wish list, including a request that Davis attend the annual meeting of Maritime premiers and New England governors later that month, the envoy remained non-committal. The exchange grew increasingly tense. When Davis fled an hour later, he found TV cameras waiting outside the door, which increased his fury. Steaming, he strode past the reporters, while Michael Perley informed the assembled microphones that the envoy did "not have his own agenda."

As a genius of backroom manipulation, the former premier did not take kindly to that media ambush. The next day, Shearer received a call from his boss, Philippe de Gaspé Beaubien, the chairman and owner of Telemedia, who also happened to be one of Mulroney's Montreal friends. "Now, Jeff," he said, "I just got a call from William Davis, who's one of the most influential politicians in this country, and he was wondering if you were doing this sort of thing as part of your job as president of Telemedia." Davis had put the acid rain coalition on notice not to mess with him.

Having despaired of winning action from the Canadian side, Hurley turned her attentions to Drew Lewis. Years earlier, in her grassroots organizing, she had worked with Pennsylvania anglers who had been galvanized by the fact that the Poconos' resort lakes were increasingly acidified. Through them, she met another group of the state's notables with a stake in the acid rain debate: dozens of wealthy Americans from Pittsburgh who owned palatial summer homes along the stretch of Muskoka shoreline at Beaumaris known as Millionaire's Row. Many were the descendants of Pennsylvania's coal barons, but they had been summering on Ontario's lakes for generations.

That August, at Hurley's urging, Joan Booth called on one of those Americans with a suggestion: through the social grapevine, she had heard that Drew Lewis was on a fishing trip a few miles north on Lake Ahmic. Why not ask him to drop by Muskoka for a casual chat about acid rain? As it turned out, Booth had chosen her intercessor well. Elsie Hilliard Hillman was one of the wealthiest women on the Eastern seaboard; she was also a former Pennsylvania delegate to the Republican National Committee and state co-chair of both Reagan-Bush presidential campaigns. Lewis might have passed up many invitations that cut short his fishing, but not one from Elsie Hillman.

During the following days, many who found Hillman's servants hand-delivering elegant caligraphy invitations to their docks along

Lakes Joseph and Rosseau felt exactly the same way. On a Sunday afternoon, Lewis arrived at the tony Beaumaris Yacht Club, which had once been Elsie Hillman's family home, where a crowd of moneyed Republicans had gathered — many pulling up aboard their antique mahogany launches.

Over Bloody Marys and cucumber sandwiches, the acid rain coalition signed up recruits for a new organization called American Friends of Muskoka, whose members soon received a tasteful personal note from Elsie Hillman soliciting donations to carry on Hurley's lobbying operation in Washington. Hillman also wrote a no-nonsense letter to Pennsylvania Senator John Heinz, the grocery heir whose first campaign she had co-chaired. As for their guest of honour, the afternoon clearly had an effect: within a month, Lewis was shaking up the White House.

In September, after another fishing trip to Muskoka with Davis, where a provincial environmental scientist took the envoys on a tour of the blight caused by years of sulphur-laced downpours, the pair had hopped a luxury-fitted federal government Challenger for a meeting with New England state governors in Springfield, Massachusetts. There, Lewis startled some of his own staffers by admitting what science had demonstrated all along but Reagan had refused to acknowledge: "It seems to me that saying sulfates do not cause acid rain," he announced, "is the same as saying that smoking does not cause lung cancer."

One former aide recalls the shock that registered on the face of Marty Smith, a deputy assistant secretary in the Interior Department who had been assigned to keep an eye on Lewis: "Marty went flying out of there so fast and called the White House. He knew they'd be apoplectic. The spin started almost immediately."

Although the White House media machine cranked up to counter the next day's glowing coverage of Lewis in the *New York Times*, it toiled in vain. Drew Lewis had PR whiz Linda Gosden Robinson in his employ for good reason. On the paper's editorial page, he emerged as the hero of the hour, while the White House was castigated for "squirming away from Mr. Lewis's candor; five years procrastination is enough."

The acid rain coalition saw Lewis's perceived rebellion as cause for hope. But it soon became clear that the U.S. acid rain envoy had gone as far as he was going to go. "I think Drew went out on a limb that one time," says a former official. "But I think he realized he was going to walk into a brick wall, so he was not going to push this thing because it was not ultimately in his best interests."

Suddenly Lewis let Davis know he was in a hurry to wrap up their mission. As one participant recalls, "Drew clearly wanted out. The object was to compress everything and get the report done." In fact, despite the elaborate efforts to show the envoys' commission as a joint bilateral project, the report ended up being written in Washington.

That fall of 1985, Michael Deaver, who by then had been hired as Ottawa's lobbyist, flew up to Toronto to confer with Davis over the wording. The Canadian envoy wanted some guarantee that the issue would not fall off U.S. radar screens. Deaver brushed him off with the assurance that the new EPA administrator, Lee Thomas, would see it received cabinet attention. He was miffed when one of Davis's aides, a former White House staffer, pointed out that the EPA chief was not, in fact, in Reagan's cabinet. "It became clear," says a former official, "that this was pretty meaningless. It was an exercise in damage control."

The group gathered again at New York's exclusive River Club for a final breakfast conference with Deaver, Drew Lewis, Linda Robinson, and Allan Gotlieb. Later, Mulroney's aide Fred Doucet worried that the report might raise hackles in Washington and hurt the trade talks; he intervened to water down even Lewis's covering letter to Reagan. Every effort was made not to offend the White House.

In their slim thirty-five-page report, Davis and Lewis acknowledged that acid rain was a "transboundary" problem — the first time a U.S. official had made that admission; indeed, nine months earlier, the White House had fought to keep that very word out of the Shamrock Summit's final communiqué. But the envoys' chief recommendation was a $5 billion joint venture with U.S. industry to develop and test new clean coal technology, with no hint of how that funding would be guaranteed.

For Lewis, once again, the report was a public relations triumph. Declaring to the assembled press in Washington, "We can't keep studying this thing to death," he was hailed as a man of immense acumen and political courage. But to acid rain activists, the report was a shallow semantic victory, which set back any meaningful clean-up program for years. Not only did the envoys reject clean coal technology that already existed in favour of further study, but they also ignored the smokestack scrubbers that had long been shown as the only effective means of cutting sulphur dioxide emissions. Their reason: "high socioeconomic costs" — in other words, Midwestern utilities, which had mounted a massive Washington lobby under the banner of the Edison Electric Institute, had balked at the expense, warning it would mean higher electricity rates.

But most deceptive of all was the fact that their recommendations were not new: part of the program they called for was already in place, complete with congressional funding that had even been supported by the coal industry's chief booster, West Virginia's fire-and-brimstone senator, Robert Byrd. For the coal states, the envoys' report was a boon, assuring five more years of stalling and a commitment to find ways to keep burning high-sulphur eastern coal, rather than alternative fuels. To environmentalists, the schizophrenic report was, like the Shamrock Summit that spawned it, a triumph of the politics of illusion. As an aide to one northeastern Republican senator quipped to Hurley after Lewis's press conference, "You guys got horn-swaggled."

But if the report at least registered official White House acknowledgment of the U.S. contribution to acid rain, Hurley and Perley handed that credit to Reagan's envoy, not to Mulroney's. Bill Davis likes to recount a meeting with Lewis at the White House immediately before releasing their recommendations, where a Reagan aide protested: "Hey, didn't you guys understand that you weren't supposed to accomplish anything?" But in Ottawa, when he presented his report to the media, he met a distinctly hostile reception. Under a barrage of questions, he was forced to admit that he had not pushed for any specific American commitments to lower sulphur dioxide emissions because Lewis had warned him they would be vetoed by the White House. Perley questioned whether the report was even worth Davis's $1-a-year salary.

In fact, as the *Globe and Mail*'s John Cruickshank discovered, Davis's acid rain mission had cost Canadian taxpayers much more than the single greenback that he had framed on his wall. The envoy's job eased the former premier's transition from public life with a prestigious berth that Cruickshank estimated had racked up $500,000 in expenses and perks. The post came complete with two offices, one in Ottawa and the other a three-room corner suite in a downtown Toronto tower, where Davis had transferred three members of his former Queen's Park staff: his secretary, his long-time executive assistant, and, on a part-time contract at the rate of $350-a-day, his former principal secretary, John Tory, the Ontario blueblood who would later become Mulroney's 1988 campaign chairman.

As his environmental adviser, Davis had chosen not one of the country's scientific or ecological experts, but Andrea Belanger, an American who had won high-profile political appointments in two Republican administrations before emigrating to Toronto to marry a Canadian film-maker. After working in the public relations office of Richard Nixon's first EPA director, William Ruckelshaus, Belanger had gone on to oversee the distribution of patronage plums in Gerald Ford's White House after the Watergate scandal — personally handing George Bush his papers as the new director of the CIA. In Toronto, she had worked for Davis's party liaison Pat Kinsella, and later for a Tory MPP. If anything underlined the fact that Davis considered his mission purely political, it was Belanger's appointment.

As the *Globe and Mail* reported, Davis's federally funded staff not only prepared his acid rain briefs; it also tended to his private business, which provided a handy supplement to his $50,000 provincial pension. During the course of his stint as an acid rain envoy — and before he joined the venerable Toronto law firm run by John Tory's uncle — the ex-premier had begun amassing a string of prestigious corporate directorships at the brisk rate of nearly one a month. Seagrams, Power Corporation, the Toronto auto-parts maker Magna International — everyone seemed to want his wisdom around the boardroom table. The most lucrative appointment was estimated to be to the board of First Boston Inc., the holding company for the New York investment bankers of the same name which were then leading the wave of mergers and acquisitions sweeping America.

But the appointment that gave acid rain activists most pause was one closer to home — and to nitrous oxide emissions from automobiles. Halfway through his envoy duties, Davis had assumed a seat on the board of the Ford Motor Company of Canada, which, along with its Dearborn parent, would lead the fight in both countries against any future tailpipe emission standards for the auto industry. As part of his director's fee, Ford had also provided him with a shiny new Lincoln.

Oddly, in Dearborn, John Dingell's hometown, Drew Lewis, too, would soon be asked to join the corporation's board. But if those directorships seemed an awkward fit for two men studying acid rain, so did Lewis's next career move. Five days after the release of the envoys' report, it became clear why he been in such a hurry to wrap up his assignment: he joined Union Pacific Corporation — a Pennsylvania conglomerate better known for its railways than for the fact that it holds substantial interests in trucking, oil, and coal mines.

IN late January 1986, two weeks after the envoys' report, Environment Minister Tom McMillan made a speech to the New York Board of Trade in which he called the Reagan administration's handling of the acid rain issue "a litmus test of whether Canadian–U.S. cooperation works both ways." It was a metaphor that his boss, Brian Mulroney, would live to regret. For the next four years, as the White House failed to budge on acid rain, it begged the question: given the litmus test his own government had set, was Mulroney making all the concessions?

The White House had greeted the report with the same level of enthusiasm it had reserved for the thinly novelized confessions of Reagan's daughter, Patti Davis, which had been published at the same time: Reagan ignored it. For three months, he avoided any comment on the subject, and even the normally chatty Larry Speakes confined himself to handing out a written response pronouncing the envoys' work an "earnest" effort. But that cryptic silence whipped up suspense, just as it was meant to.

In fact, U.S. environmentalists and acid rain champion Henry Waxman had pleaded with the Canadian Embassy not to press for endorsement of the report. They warned that it would lead to a five-year delay in real emission-control action. Later, Waxman would blame the Canadian government for "pulling the rug out from under us." The embassy dismissed him as just another congressman — infuriating its chief ally in Congress.

In Ottawa, where Mulroney was preparing for his March 1986 summit with Reagan in Washington, prime ministerial aides also shrugged off Waxman's unwelcome advice. Instead, the PMO continued to drum up an air of drama over any prospective presidential reaction to the report. Would Reagan endorse it? Wouldn't he? The press obligingly joined the buzz. To David Hawkins, a lawyer at Washington's Natural Resources Defense Council, Ottawa was merely falling for an old negotiating ploy — one that would later become a familiar pattern in Canadian-American relations. "It's almost as if the White House is running a prom and keeping the girls wanting invitations in the dark until the night before," he warned. "It will be such a relief when the phone finally rings, they will take anything."

When Mulroney showed up at the White House on March 18, 1986, he did indeed seem grateful for a gesture that might have been considered a minimum formality. He even thanked the president for his "sensitivity." In a ceremony in the Roosevelt Room, Reagan endorsed the recommendations of his own envoy which committed him to nothing more than requesting half the $5 million funding from an already budget-cutting Congress. The other $2.5 billion would have to come voluntarily from those very industries that had been battling acid rain bills for years. Later, Congress would fail to vote most of the appropriation, and the industry contribution would never materialize.

At his own press conference, Mulroney served up Reagan's crumb as a diplomatic triumph. "This is a front-burner issue," he crowed, waving off Hurley's scorn that it was "just an exercise in public relations." Such nay-saying, he proclaimed, was "silly."

Canadian officials boasted that Reagan had made the concession solely out of his enormous affection for Mulroney. But later the prime minister's aides would relate the wiles Mulroney used in order to provoke action, or even understanding of the problem. For weeks before his Washington visit, they had struggled to come up with examples to help the anecdote-prone president get the drift of acid rain damage: statistics on how it was eating away at the Washington Monument outside his window or even the facade of the White House. Finally they hit upon the perfect story. "You know that lake in the movie with Katharine Hepburn and Jane Fonda, *On Golden Pond*?" Mulroney asked Reagan. "Well, that's a real lake in New Hampshire, and, you know, it's been damaged by acid rain." Bingo! the prime minister had the president's attention.

But American officials offered another explanation for Reagan's reluctant capitulation: the intercession of the man who remained the master of the politics of illusion and the Reagans' closest confidant, Michael Deaver. On July 1, 1985, four months after the Shamrock Summit — and within days of stepping down as Reagan's deputy chief of staff — Deaver had signed up as the Canadian government's $105,000-a-year lobbyist in Washington.

Ottawa appeared to have gotten a bargain. Deaver had enlisted other free-spending governments at twice that rate, including Saudi

Arabia, Singapore, South Korea, and Mexico — $3 million worth of contracts in all before he had been in business nine months. Overnight, he had become the capital's star rainmaker, working out of a lavish Georgetown penthouse while still breezing in and out of the presidential digs on a White House pass he had somehow retained.

For a man who had so brilliantly orchestrated Reagan's image, Deaver demonstrated an uncharacteristic recklessness with his own as he flaunted that success. Still, it was his work for Ottawa on acid rain that would shortly provoke his downfall — attracting the attentions of the notoriously suspicious congressman from Dearborn, John Dingell.

Citing a front-page story in the October 27, 1985, edition of the *Washington Post*, which recounted Deaver's "unusual interest in acid rain" during the Shamrock Summit, Dingell had demanded that Congress's investigative arm, the General Accounting Office, look into his lucrative postgovernmental pursuits. Hauled before Dingell's own subcommittee on oversight and investigations, Deaver was grilled on whether he had begun his employment talks with Mulroney's office while orchestrating the Quebec City visit. At first, Canadian officials had denied any such conversation, but later Allan Gotlieb admitted that the prime minister's confidant, Fred Doucet, had raised the subject in a "light-hearted" vein.

Jokes that led to $105,000 contracts did not amuse Dingell. Soon, the inquiry expanded to focus on Deaver's role in the acid rain envoy exercise — and possible violations of the Ethics in Government Act, which barred officials from lobbying the administration for two years on any subject they had dealt with in government. A half-dozen top White House officials, including former national security adviser Robert McFarlane, testified that Deaver had pressed the envoy proposal in the weeks before the Shamrock Summit, and produced notes to prove it. Then his River Club meeting with Bill Davis, Drew Lewis, and Linda Robinson came to light. Before long, Deaver himself was calling for a special prosecutor to clear the air, which he would have occasion to regret: his responses would lead to criminal charges on five counts of perjury, and a trial that would drag on for nineteen months, leaving him a virtual social pariah in the capital.

The cornerstone of Deaver's defence was alcoholism: he had been consuming a quart of Scotch and three rolls of breath mints a day while handling the nation's business, he said, and had no idea what he was doing. At one point he told Dingell's committee that he did not even know what acid rain was, prompting Newfoundland MP George Baker to inquire: "If he doesn't know what acid rain is, what does he actually do for his $105,000?"

Ironically, he was acquitted on the one perjury count that had sparked Deavergate: his work for the Canadian government on acid rain. But for the acid rain cause itself, the Deaver connection proved a disaster. Not only had his hiring alienated many in Congress who might have looked with equanimity on the Canadian government's pleas, but it also offered an opening to the enemies of tough new emission-control measures that had just been tabled by Henry Waxman. Thomas Luken, a Democrat from Ohio, branded the legislation "the Mulroney-Deaver bill, because that is where the benefits lie." As David Hawkins of the Natural Resources Defense Council pointed out, "Opponents of acid rain controls are using the Deaver affair as an excuse to stall legislation."

After years of Hurley's efforts to position acid rain as a bipartisan and bilateral cause of almost apple-pie worthiness — a "white hat" issue as she terms it — his name gave congressional foes an excuse to talk of foreign influence peddling. In fact, many environmentalists blamed Mulroney's eagerness to ingratiate himself with the Reagans' close friend, a man who was considered almost the president's surrogate son, for undercutting her work.

If the prime minister was determined to hire a Washington lobbyist, they argued he ought to have hired one with more clout in Congress, where acid rain opponents held sway. That had been the strategy originally proposed by Jim Moorman and John Fraser — and the one pursued by the U.S. coal industry. Between 1983 and 1988 a mysterious organization called Citizens for Sensible Control of Acid Rain spent more than $5 million to block acid rain bills and contributed nearly $23 million to congressional campaigns. But that purported grassroots group turned out to be a front for a coalition of Midwest utilities and America's two largest coal producers, run out of the Washington lobbying office of Fleishman-Hillard. The same firm would later lead another battle against the green movement — on behalf of the Horsham Corporation, the Toronto gold mining giant whose board Mulroney would join after his retirement.

But Mulroney had never achieved the same success working his Irish charm on Capitol Hill. During his March 1986 Washington visit, his elation over his reception by congressional leaders had been punctured when Claiborne Pell, the patrician millionaire who chaired the pivotal Senate Foreign Relations Committee, had failed to grasp his name. "We're very lucky to have Muldoon as prime minister," Pell had emerged from their meeting to remark, "because he got into office not by American-bashing, but by saying kind words about us."

Two years later, Mulroney was still being true to that reputation on his final nostalgic visit to Reagan, wistfully paying tribute to their well-publicized friendship at a farewell White House dinner. In return, the president raised his glass to the prime minister's ability to "disagree without being disagreeable."

No progress whatsoever had been made on acid rain legislation during their shared continental tenure. Mulroney had been so embarrassed by that fact he had been obliged to stage another show of protest: a year earlier he had invited George Bush to Ottawa for what the vice president gamely told the Canadian press was "an earful."

But even after that calculated public scolding, the U.S. administration still did not bother to name an appointee to a task force implementing the acid rain envoys' report, nor had it requested the necessary budget allotment. In fact, polls showed that a majority of Canadians felt Mulroney had forged his personal relationship with the president at the expense of the country's best interests. But when reporters in Washington accused him of caving in on acid rain, the man who had won a reputation as a brilliant backroom labour negotiator shrugged. "What do you do?" he said. "Do you declare war?"

ON August 31, 1988, George Bush stood on the shores of Metropark on Lake Erie, twenty-five miles south of Detroit, in full presidential campaign mode and declared, "I am an environmentalist." For the vice president in an administration with the worst ecological record in recent memory, it was a guaranteed headline-catcher — and a surefire way for Bush to distance himself from the increasingly ambivalent legacy of Ronald Reagan. While he declined to confirm he was doing just that, his adviser Russell Train, a former EPA head, confirmed, "It's a whole new ballgame."

But some pundits noted that, whatever Bush's personal convictions on the subject, he had also recognized the political writing on the wall. All through that summer's blistering heatwave, syringes had been washing up on the beaches of New Jersey, the EPA had warned childbearing women not to eat certain species of Great Lakes fish, and an itinerant garbage barge, later found to have ties to a major New York Mafia family, had roamed the Atlantic seaboard looking for a place to dump its cargo. As Bush admitted, "1988, in a sense, is the year the Earth spoke back." Indeed, any politician who did not proclaim himself an environmentalist that year had clearly made other plans for employment.

Five months later, in his inaugural speech beneath an opaque January sky, Bush had warmed the hearts of those in the acid rain movement on both sides of the border with the line, "The time for study is over." The following summer, on his sixty-fifth birthday, he made good on his word, unveiling a series of amendments to the Clean Air Act that had the environmentalists assembled in the East Room of the White House both ecstatic and incredulous. In a move that half his presidential staff had been battling for months, Bush called for a cut of 10-million tons of sulphur dioxide a year from the tall stacks of the coal-fired industries and utilities of the Midwest — the magic number that William Reilly, his soft-spoken EPA administrator, had argued would cut acid rain damage in half by the end of the decade.

The fight had been a bitter one and, until the end, the outcome had been uncertain. On the weekend before, Bush had retreated to Camp David to mull over his decision, and even Reilly had not been sure on which side he would come down. But at 9 A.M. on the Monday of his announcement, the president had telephoned Brian Mulroney in Ottawa with the news.

What had broken the environmental logjam was a new free market spin on the greening of America. To counter industry's complaint about the cost of emission controls, a small cadre of Bush's top aides had bought into an idea that Fred Krupp and other free-marketeers at the Environmental Defense Fund in Washington had been pushing for a decade: pollution credits that could be traded among utilities on the Chicago commodities exchange like soyabeans or pork belly futures. According to the legislation, the 110 worst U.S. polluters were required immediately to reduce their sulphur dioxide emissions by certain specified amounts. But if they — or other more virtuous industries — cleaned up faster or more economically, they could sell off those unused emission credits to other culprits.

To Bush's White House counsel Boyden Gray, the wealthy scion of a tobacco fortune, that market-based environmentalism seemed inspired — another plug for neoconservative economics. As Elizabeth Barrett Brown of the Natural Resources Defense Council explains, "They saw acid rain as an opportunity to promote market systems."

The first trade that made headlines saw the notoriously dirty Tennessee Valley Authority, a government-owned utility, buy up $2.5 million in pollution credits from Wisconsin Power and Light, which was already ahead of schedule in cleaning up its act — thereby allowing the TVA to spew more than its limit of sulphur dioxide from its stacks. In the Adirondacks, environmentalists charged that most of the buying would be done by the very Ohio Valley utilities whose sulphurous vapours were already wafting eastward to kill more than three hundred of upper New York state's lakes, thus making no dint in the area's problem — or, consequently, that of Canada. Worse, the trades were both unregulated and secret, so scientists could not track the effect of the deals until it was too late. John Sheehan, a spokesman for the Adirondack Council, worried that the commodities trading scheme was "an economist's answer to an environmental problem. It doesn't ensure that these emission cuts are meaningful."

But in Toronto, Adèle Hurley joined Washington's Natural Resources Defense Council in applauding the scheme as "brilliant" — the only way Congress and the Bush White House could have been converted to the clean air cause. "I think it works," she said. "What are critics offering — ten more years of filibuster? Americans understand horse-trading."

In the small hours of an autumn night in 1990, she sat in the visitors' gallery of the U.S. Senate with a handful of American environmentalist pals, watching the signing of Bush's Clean Air Act, which aimed to halve sulphur dioxide emission levels by the year 2000. Two rows behind, the coal and utility lobbyists she had battled for nearly ten years watched in sombre silence. "I could see people I'd worked with for a decade moving back and forth on the floor of the Senate, still negotiating last-minute details," she says. Later, her gang went out for a beer on Capitol Hill to toast their victory. Back in Toronto, the coalition sent out invitations for a celebration at Casa Loma. "Who Stopped the Rain?" they read. "We did! And it's time to party."

Later, Michael Perley would add his own twist on that tagline in a dedication to his history of the movement, *Poisoned Skies*, written with journalist Ross Howard: "Who stopped acid rain?" he wrote in the flyleaf. "Answer: a combo of John Dingell, George Bush and assorted Canadian pols." He did not mention Brian Mulroney.

A year later, Hurley and Perley began closing down the coalition and deregistering at the Justice Department. "Acid rain wasn't over," Hurley admitted, "but it was over for us." In May 1991 she joined the board of her old nemesis, Ontario Hydro, and began consulting for several governments on the environmental impact of NAFTA. Then word began to trickle out of Washington: Bush, who had taken public credit for the new Clean Air Act as the major accomplishment of his presidency, was now quietly trying to gut it in bureaucratic back-rooms. In another presidential election season, pressured by an ongoing recession and grumbling business lobbyists, the environmental president had done a u-turn back towards the corporate agenda. In the long arduous process of negotiating regulations for the implementation of the act, known as "reg neg" on Capitol Hill, a secretive White House committee had managed to take some of the essential teeth out of the acid rain provisions. That committee — branded a "shadow government" by Congressman Henry Waxman — was the Council on Competitiveness, led by Vice President Dan Quayle.

Meeting behind closed doors and answerable to no one but Bush, the council had already rewritten the EPA's rules to allow industries and utilities to revise their pollution permits, unilaterally awarding themselves more emission credits without any public notice whatsoever. Waxman attacked the changes as illegal, and the Natural Resources Defense Council launched a lawsuit. But the greatest damage to the council's deregulation spree came from revelations of its own conflicts of interest. It had handed out one of its first acid rain waivers to Eli Lilly, the pharmaceutical giant based in Quayle's home state of Indiana.

The November 1992 election results — and the victory of Bill Clinton and his environmentally friendly vice president Al Gore — finally halted the Republicans' assault on their own Clean Air Bill. After years of hindering any legislative attack on acid rain, the exigencies of U.S. politics had provided the rationale for addressing the problem, then prevented those solutions from coming undone. American domestic interests had prompted action, not the bantering affections between presidents and prime ministers.

In fact, Washington environmental lawyer David Hawkins blames Mulroney's friendship with Reagan and Bush for setting the cause back by years. "He had to come back from these summits with something — anything," Hawkins says, "and it gave enormous leverage to the people on our side. They knew any fig leaf they offered him, Mulroney was prepared to go back and market as a victory."

Hawkins pauses, then recounts how he had tried out his thesis on Bush's White House aide Boyden Gray and Quayle's top adviser, William Nitze. 'Let's just say," he admits ruefully, "that I got nods on this theory."

8 Standing on Guard for Thee

MICHAEL DEAVER had chosen the site with his usual unerring instinct for the networks' needs: a little pageantry and some double-edged symbolism. To wrap up the Shamrock Summit, he had scripted a final stroll for Reagan and Mulroney on the ancient Quebec City ramparts known as the Citadelle, the nineteenth-century granite fortress high above the St. Lawrence that had been built for a war with the United States that never came.

There, against that cannon-studded backdrop, raised after the British had expelled the American invaders in the War of 1812, the two leaders signed a Memo of Understanding billed as the capstone of postwar defence cooperation. With pomp and drum rolls from the Citadelle's scarlet and busby-topped Royal 22nd Regiment — known by the tortured French translation of their name, the Van Doos — they had initialled a $1.5 billion cost-sharing agreement to raise a string of microwave radar stations, the North Warning System, across the frozen expanse of the Arctic.

Replacing the rusting, three-decades-old Distant Early Warning (DEW) Line, the updated radar grid was aimed at detecting a new generation of Soviet bombers and low-flying cruise missiles on their way over Canadian terrain to more strategically valued real estate: Washington and its intercontinental ballistic missiles seeded deep in the wheat fields of Wyoming and the Dakotas.

The TV shots of that signing ceremony were to be the last and most crucial summit visuals — a mixed message of cannons and camaraderie, of continental solidarity and fortress machismo that was merely a variation on the four-year-old White House theme: Peace through Strength. In a speech only two hours earlier, Reagan had hailed the agreement as proof of the two nations' "New Partnership." To pre-empt those who might have been unkind enough to note that Canada was, as ever, the junior partner on the team, Mulroney claimed the project as an "act of sovereignty": for the first time, Ottawa was to share 40 percent of the radar's cost in return for reaping most of the construction contracts and manning the remote sites.

But opposition critics railed against the system as a high-tech Trojan horse that would turn the Arctic into the Pentagon's new offensive playground against Moscow, ultimately enmeshing Canada in Reagan's space-based anti-missile scheme, the Strategic Defense Initiative, known as Star Wars. Days before the summit, the Liberals' arms control critic, Lloyd Axworthy, had emerged from a Commons committee briefing to worry over "a major militarization of the North. The idea that this is simply a defensive radar system is absolutely nonsense."

Only a year earlier, Trudeau had succeeded in expelling the last U.S. nuclear arms from Canadian soil. And as peace protestors marched through Quebec City with placards reading "Canadians Won't Be Cannon Fodder for U.S. Foreign Wars," one thing seemed clear: as Reagan turned up the volume of global tensions, the prospect of being drawn into his military brinkmanship filled most of his northern neighbours with fear and loathing. An accident of geography might have left the country a hapless buffer zone between the superpowers — and at the top of Washington's national security agenda — but, with the shadowy implications of the North Warning System, even many in the country's small defence community worried that Canada could become nuclear toast.

In the Commons, Liberal leader Jean Chrétien charged that, as part of the deal, Mulroney had secretly agreed to establish or upgrade a series of Arctic military bases to accommodate U.S. F–15 fighter jets during a superpower crisis — or any other time Washington saw fit. Not only would that charge turn out to be true, but Canadian officials would later admit they had gone to considerable lengths to downplay the five northern airfields, known in military parlance as Forward Operating Locations. It was not until two years later that the defence ministry would officially announce their locations, from Inuvik to the coast of Labrador, noting they had always been an "essential element" of the original Shamrock Summit blueprint. "We were pretty careful to keep the lid on that," one Canadian airforce official would reminisce nearly a decade later with a sheepish grin.

That subterfuge seemed designed to camouflage the gathering momentum of continental defence integration. In fact, after months of depicting the new radar scheme as akin to updating a rickety fence against the pit bull down the block, the benign veneer was suddenly shattered by an unlikely culprit: Caspar Weinberger. During an early-morning interview in Quebec City for *Canada A.M.*, CTV's Craig Oliver had asked the wiry U.S. defence secretary where the Pentagon planned to station its anti-cruise-missile launchers. "Some might be here," Weinberger mused, "some might be in the United States, some might be at sea." He had wrapped up the interview apparently oblivious to the shockwaves he had just unleashed, confiding to Oliver that he was glad he hadn't made any news.

Within minutes, his words were exploding over the airwaves, confirmation of Canadians' worst fears. Furious, Mulroney and his aides strode into their first summit session of the day with Reagan, CTV transcript in hand, demanding what Weinberger was up to. Privately, White House officials were miffed; this was not the first time the defence secretary had put his foot in it, and now he had upstaged their painstakingly orchestrated show.

But none of them attempted an outright denial of his assertions. Of course, Canada would be consulted before such a move, Larry Speakes rushed to say. As if that were not enough to set suspicions on edge, the Pentagon released a transcript of Weinberger's interview with the offending phrase missing — a lapse later passed off as a stenographer's oversight.

As the slights mounted, Reagan had climaxed his visit with a luncheon speech brandishing his most bellicose anti-Soviet rhetoric in recent memory. Only five days after his administration had finally opened disarmament talks in Geneva — and a week after Mikhail Gorbachev had come to power in Moscow — he chose the occasion to rhyme off Moscow's sins, including "humans being persecuted, religions banned and entire democracies crushed." Despite finding himself a guest in a country that vehemently opposed his CIA–inspired guerrilla wars, above all in Central America, Reagan had invoked them with starry-eyed lyricism. "Freedom movements are rising up from Afghanistan, to Cambodia, Angola, Ethiopia, and Nicaragua," he had intoned. Then, in a final magnanimous flourish, undeterred by that morning's flap, he invited Canada to join in Star Wars.

Clearly, it was not a speech that had been designed to reassure the nervous neighbours to the north. Despite Deaver's insistence on Reagan's need to address the Canadian people, his rhetoric had been aimed at an audience far beyond the reach of the CBC's transmitters. His target was Washington's uneasy allies in Europe and Gorbachev's new team, which had just taken over the Kremlin. Quebec City, with all its pre-cooked agreements and Irish gimmickry, had been but a quaint backdrop for a larger American agenda: to paint Reagan as the strong and well-loved leader of what Washington liked to call the free world, capable of holding together the squabbling NATO alliance against the Soviets. At a time when New Zealand had come down with a bad case of what the Pentagon termed a "nuclear allergy" — banning U.S. Navy vessels with atomic weapons from its ports — White House officials were determined to show that Canada was firmly on board the good ship Ronald Reagan.

"People here are aware that there's substantial unease about [nuclear] deterrence right now," explained Charles Doran, head of Canadian Studies at Johns Hopkins' School of Advanced International Studies in Washington, who invariably voiced administration thinking. "This can be used effectively in arms control talks — and has been by the Soviet Union. What the United States wants out of this summit is to demonstrate cohesiveness with its best ally and trading partner."

For Doran, the summit was "a celebration, a great ritual, high theatre" designed to achieve one goal, "excellent press coverage" — the same goal a classified State Department memo confirmed. Despite the administration's affections for him, Brian Mulroney was merely a supporting player in a superpower drama meant for an audience far from the icy shores of the St. Lawrence. Nor had part of that audience failed to get the message. Novosti, the official Soviet news agency, promptly issued a response. By signing the North Warning agreement, it declared, "In effect, Canada is to be an accomplice in the U.S. Star Wars plan."

IN the attic of Washington's Institute for Policy Studies where piles of declassified documents sprouted like some unruly paper garden beneath the eaves, Bill Arkin rooted among the underbrush for proof of his bad news. As Canadians protested against the possibility of getting drawn into American nuclear strategy, Arkin, a former U.S. Army intelligence analyst, cautioned that it was already too late. In a book entitled *Nuclear Battlefields: Global Links in the Arms Race* — whose publication had coincided with the Shamrock Summit — the slight, bespectacled former defence spook made it clear that the Pentagon had long considered Canada part of its war-planning.

Arkin had unearthed hundreds of secret cooperation agreements between the two countries for developing or testing potential atomic weaponry. During the course of his research, he had also stumbled upon the training manual for a California-based Strategic Air Command wing which — during a national security crisis or merely "heightened international tensions" — instructed its fourteen nuclear-armed B–52 bombers to disperse to the Canadian Forces airfield at Cold Lake, Alberta. That contingency plan was a clear contravention of Ottawa's non-nuclear policy, but a defence specialist at the Canadian Embassy in Washington had reluctantly confirmed Arkin's assertions.

Still, retired Admiral Robert Falls, a former chief of the Canadian Defence Staff, swore he had never heard of the dispersal plan or any of the other U.S. nuclear contingency arrangements for Canada in the book, declaring them "damn presumptuous." That, Arkin argued, was the point. "Canadians clearly don't have access to our war plans," he said. "It's another aspect of the way Canada is a nuclear colony of the United States."

His revelations raised an outcry in Ottawa. But in Washington no military analyst batted an eyelash at the news that Canada had long been part of U.S. strategic doctrine. Nothing illustrated that notion more clearly than the North American Aerospace Defense (NORAD) Command, the centrepiece of cross-border military cooperation, under whose wing the DEW Line had originally been built.

Conceived during the first icy frissons of the Cold War in the early 1950s, NORAD was born out of a last-ditch rationale that Queen's University military expert Nils Orvik dubbed "defence against help." At the time, Eisenhower's secretary of state John Foster Dulles had delivered an ultimatum: Canadians could either help patrol their northern airspace against Soviet bombers or the U.S. Air Force would move in and do it for them. As Ernie Regehr, research coordinator for the University of Waterloo's Project Ploughshares, put it: "Canadians erected the DEW Line not against Russians, but against American 'help.'"

Headquartered in an underground bunker in Colorado Springs, NORAD was scrupulously termed an integrated joint command. But a U.S. Air Force general was always commander-in-chief, a Canadian lieutenant-general his deputy. And for nearly three decades, each of the DEW Line's thirty-one sites across the Canadian tundra had been under the control of the U.S. Air Force, operated on a $124 million annual contract by a unit of the American multinational, ITT Corp. In fact, during the parliamentary protests over the North Warning System, Mulroney had let slip that, if a Canadian cabinet minister wanted to visit one of the DEW Line's Arctic posts, he first "had to seek American permission to go to the Canadian north."

Had there been any doubt about just who was boss, the 1962 Cuban Missile Crisis had set things straight: when John Diefenbaker balked at U.S. pressure to put Canadian forces on full wartime alert, his minister of defence, Douglas Harkness, had surreptitiously disobeyed him; the country's troops had quietly shifted into synch with their U.S. counterparts.

In that move, it became obvious with whom the Canadian military saw its interests aligned — its colleagues in the Pentagon, not its political masters in Ottawa. As Joseph Jockel, an expert on Canadian defence at Washington's Center for Strategic and International Studies, points out, the strongest pressure for keeping the country in NORAD has traditionally come from the Canadian Air Force and the top brass in Ottawa. "They see NORAD as a ticket to the big-time — access to U.S. technology and strategic planning," he says. "And the military itself gets to go to Colorado Springs and play in the biggest league of all."

During the 1960s and 1970s, the Kremlin's bomber threat declined — and so too did NORAD's clout. But by the late 1970s, with the advent of Soviet cruise missiles and a new generation of long-range Bear–H bombers — what military officials liked to call the "air-breathing threat" — the continental command suddenly found itself back at the top of the Pentagon's worry list. Pronouncing the ailing, ignored DEW Line so "porous" that Soviet intruders could slip through the gaps, NORAD officials began lobbying for new hardware. In 1979 a joint U.S.–Canadian study put its stamp of approval on the rough draft for the North Warning System.

But Trudeau, already under enormous pressure to test U.S. cruise missiles over northern Alberta — pressure to which he would finally succumb — demurred. By 1983 it became clear once again that, even if Ottawa did not agree, the Pentagon would go ahead on its own. Lest there be any doubt, a U.S. Air Force officer informed the *Wall Street Journal* that the contract for the initial thirteen long-range radars was already slated for General Electric — to whom, in fact, it was awarded.

But by then another motive was propelling Ottawa officials to argue for the North Warning System: the spectre of U.S. space-based radar systems that would render Canada's strategic trump card — its place on the map — null and void. That year, General Gérard Thériault, then chief of the Canadian Defence Staff, had warned a Commons committee that, unless the government underlined the importance of its territory to the United States, the country would find itself marginalized in allied councils of war — its influence no greater than that of an oversized Australia. For the assembled MPs, Thériault invoked what he considered a bleak prospect: "We can now foresee the day when Canadian geography will become totally irrelevant to U.S. security."

To Ernie Regehr, that plea was proof that NORAD had "helped to create a culture in Ottawa that said there's no such thing as Canadian security values — that Canadian security needs were indistinguishable from American." Soon after Thériault's testimony, a U.S. Air Force official confided to an Ottawa journalist that "Canada has agreed to help finance the new radar line so that it won't be excluded from participation in future space-based military intelligence projects." The government had announced no such policy, but already the Canadian defence establishment had been persuaded that the country could not afford to miss the Star Wars bandwagon — and that the logical first step aboard was the North Warning System.

But as the project languished on NORAD drafting tables, stalled by the 1984 Canadian election campaign, some officers admit they were not exactly disinterested in the outcome of the vote. Brian

Mulroney had ridiculed the Liberals' defence spending and called their treatment of the Canadian Forces "shabby and demoralizing," promising that, under him, the military would go "first class." When he won, cheers went up in the Department of National Defence tower on the banks of the Rideau Canal, and at Mulroney's first meeting with Reagan in Washington that month, the North Warning System was on the agenda.

Part of the urgency came from the fact that the grid was merely the northern lid of an ambitious Pentagon scheme to encircle the continent with a radar screen. Indeed, the pact that Reagan and Mulroney had signed on the Quebec ramparts, the North American Air Defence Modernization agreement, was for a grandiose $7 billion continental burglar alarm, most of which had nothing to do with Canada. Four over-the-horizon backscatter radars were to be positioned on U.S. soil — one in Alaska, three others to stand vigil over the Atlantic, Pacific, and Gulf of Mexico coasts. And a squadron of high-tech Airborne Warning and Control System planes, known as AWACS, based out of Oklahoma's Tinker Air Force Base, would patrol the perimeters.

Under the agreement, Canadians would be allowed to help staff the U.S. coastal radars and join the American AWACS crews. But it was only on Canadian soil that for the first time they would control the installations. In the Arctic, where over-the-horizon radar beams bounced off the aurora borealis, a different technology had been devised: thirteen long-range phased-array radar stations would be studded across the Far North and down the Labrador coast, manned entirely by Canadian crew; in between, thirty-nine short-range unmanned radars that resembled gigantic mechano sets would be strung along the 70th parallel to fill in the gaps and detect any cruise missiles whistling in over the polar ice floes.

Still, from the outset, the government knew that the North Warning System was only a temporary measure — a $700 million stopgap soon to be rendered obsolete by space-based surveillance technology. As a result of the Shamrock Summit agreement, in fact, both countries established an obscure committee, the Aerospace Defense Advanced Technology Working Group, whose task was to develop the very space-based radar systems that lay at the heart of Star Wars.

Despite denials by Mulroney and Joe Clark that the North Warning System had anything to do with Reagan's cherished continental "peace shield," NORAD officials had always seen the two schemes, one based on land, the other in the heavens, as complementary — or at least as logical steps in the same master anti-missile plan. The only trouble was that, for all the outcries it had provoked, Star Wars was still more rhetoric than reality — a research project whose hardware had yet to prove it could fly.

In the interim, Canadian defence officials threw themselves into the North Warning System with gusto. Budgets were allotted, contracts were let, and gigantic earth-movers began tackling the tundra. By 1987 one of the most enthusiastic boosters of the project was the man who had succeeded Thériault as the country's top gun, General Paul Manson. Two years later when he retired at the mandatory age of fifty-five, Manson would demonstrate his ongoing zeal for the North Warning System at Unisys, the giant American defence conglomerate.

In fact, his career would illustrate how Ottawa's top brass had come to imitate their Pentagon counterparts in forging an emerging military industrial community. After nearly a year at Unisys headquarters in Blue Bell, Pennsylvania, Manson took over the presidency of its newly established subsidiary, Paramax Systems Canada Inc., in Montreal, which had been awarded the contract for the system's thirty-nine short-range radars.

'M the Pentagon pipsqueak," George Bader barked across his gleaming boardroom table. He stared out through no-nonsense hornrims in a crisp white shirt devoid of designer airs, but which gave him a distinction all the same. Bader was, after all, a civilian, the principal director for European and NATO policy at the U.S. Defense Department, and, as such, he got to dress in civvies — no gold braid or chestful of commemorative glory for him. Bader always delivered his tirades against Canadian defence policies off the record — a pithy quote, no name attached. But in December 1983 Trudeau had turned on his heel outside the White House, responding to a dismissive Pentagon comment on his peace initiative with the retort that the critique came from "third-rate, third-level pipsqueaks." Since then, Bader had made a point of telling every reporter that he was the object of Trudeau's wrath; after all, by your enemies are you known.

Having rid himself of Trudeau, he had high hopes for Mulroney, who had campaigned on boosting defence spending by as much as 6 percent under the slogan "Honour the Commitment." As Bader never lost an opportunity to point out, Canada's military expenditures were the second-lowest in NATO, just ahead of Luxembourg's. For the Pentagon, that was a dangerous example not only to wary allies but to cost-conscious doves in Congress. Thus, when the Conservatives' first budget came down in November 1984 with a $154 million cut, he and his colleages were, he huffed, "horrified, dismayed, appalled."

Still, he had remained optimistic. The following year, Mulroney raised the military's allotment to a 2.75 percent increase — less than the annual 3 percent growth that Trudeau had managed in his last years in office. "We still hope for the Canadians to do the right thing," Bader noted dryly at the time. "We've been assured they have this intention of making a financial commitment in line with his campaign oratory" — he paused to make sure that a reporter did not miss his indiscretion — "oops, commitment."

Like many U.S. officials, Bader made little effort to hide his exasperation with the country's irksome anti-militarism — outcries over cruise missile testing here, suspicions over Star Wars there, and then the 1985 ruckus over the voyage of the U.S. Coast Guard's icebreaker *Polar Sea* through the Northwest Passage, which the State Department insisted was an international waterway. Every time a joint forces exercise was announced, each statement had to be vetted with excruciating care lest it ruffle Canadian sensitivities. "We are sensitive to a fault," Bader sniffed, "about Canadian sensitivities."

Behind his barbs seemed to lie genuine puzzlement: Why can't Canadians be more like us? But while others might simply think such things, Bader set out to do something about it. In December 1984, barely two months after Mulroney took office, he had dispatched a team of eleven Pentagon procurement experts on a cross-country tour to teach Canadian manufacturers how to bid for a slice of the massive $300 billion American defence pie.

First proposed by Caspar Weinberger, the idea was taken up with alacrity by his Canadian counterpart, Bob Coates, who had not yet made the fateful outing to Germany's Tiffany Cabaret, a strip club, during a NATO trip, which would cost him his job. Coates arranged for External Affairs to fund the tour to seven cities. At the peak of the biggest U.S. military build-up in peacetime history, when the Pentagon was so flush with funds that nobody had questioned a $7,600 coffee percolator, Washington was holding out the lure of $80 billion in new bidding opportunities to Canadian industry — a prospect that could also help bail the Tories out of a fix. Having campaigned on vague promises of the investment that would roll in with his new cross-border cosiness, Mulroney was now under pressure to produce. "This is where the jobs are going to come from," Coates exulted. "The possibilities are just unbelievable."

But Weinberger and Bader had other things on their minds than an altruistic employment program. As they well knew, military spending was the means to a larger goal — a form of industrial subsidy, especially in the high-tech sector, which in turn built long-term support for a muscular defence policy. For four decades, the secret of the Pentagon's budgetary invincibility was the fact that it had cultivated a vocal congressional constituency by distributing its contractual largesse evenly among the regions and states. If no such defence constituency existed in Canada — if, in fact, the peace movement constantly threatened U.S. strategic plans — the solution was clear: the creation of a Canadian military industrial complex.

The strategy was far from new: ever since Mackenzie King and Roosevelt first made their wartime pact at Ogdensberg, the country's industries had a history of cooperation with the Pentagon, spurred on by twenty-five years of accumulated Defence Production Sharing Agreements. During the Vietnam War, Canadian manufacturers had sold more than $2.5 billion of military goods to the United States — most of them, including explosives, shipped directly on to Southeast Asia with the cabinet's full knowledge. Indeed, the majority of those sales had been brokered through the government's own Canadian Commercial Corporation. In answer to a public outcry that the country was making millions out of the war, Paul Martin Sr., who was external affairs minister at the time, had pointed out that the booming weapons trade provided 140,000 jobs. "It's all very well to talk about Vietnam," he said. "But what about Canada? Canada has an economic life to live."

Still, with the country's image as peacekeeper at stake, the government's support for the weapons industry had been furtive and inconstant. With Mulroney's arrival on the scene, it swiftly became clear that one of the four pillars of what his aides liked to call "economic renewal" was to foster a thriving Canadian arms trade. Not only would Canadian defence contractors back the government's promise to update its hardware but they could also shore up Mulroney's support for Washington's security agenda. As the *Globe and Mail* forewarned in an editorial: "The more Canadian industry becomes a cog in the U.S. military machine, the less flexibility Canada will have to pursue an out-of-step foreign policy."

Not that the prospect of changing the public mindset loomed as an easy task. When the U.S. procurement team landed at Halifax's Nova Scotian Hotel, it found a traditional Canadian welcome. "Pentagon Jobs Will Kill Us," read the placards as a hundred protestors encircled the block, handing out blood-stained dollar bills featuring pictures of Mulroney and Reagan in place of the Queen. Then, before Halifax's Finest could act, the protesters marched straight into the defence seminar in the Commonwealth Room and tied themselves together in intricate webbings of twine, which somewhat complicated the arrest process. But as sixteen of them were finally carted off to jail, Cuthbert Gorham "Gif" Gifford, a former Second World War bomber pilot who had won the Distinguished Flying Cross, questioned the Pentagon's siren song. "Accepting U.S. military contracts," he warned, "creates a growing vested interest in keeping the arms race going."

Nova Scotia reporters promptly proved Gifford's point; dismissing his protest, they argued that the Maritimes needed jobs of any kind. By the time the Pentagon delegation reached Winnipeg's Holiday Inn two weeks later, Coates could breeze past a candlelight disarmament vigil and crow to the business crowd inside that the thinness of the demonstrations proved "the peace movement is in bad shape. And," he beamed, "I think that is only right and proper."

More than 2,000 businessmen had turned up at the coast-to-coast seminars to hear Colonel James Smith, one of Weinberger's aides, explain that the Pentagon wanted to "enhance the industrial mobilization base of the United States." If that phrase sounded like the usual military mouthful, most of those in his audience understood the colonel's codewords. For nearly five years, a small band within the Ottawa defence establishment and the Canadian business community had been pushing for the creation of a military common market on the continent — one that would help speed up the gradual integration of the two nations' defence policies and, perhaps ultimately, their forces.

MOBILIZATION was Bill Yost's obsession. A stocky energetic Second World War army veteran, the brigadier-general had become the senior military logistics wizard in Ottawa — a mega-trip director for every outing of Canadian troops. Over the years, he had played advance man for peacekeeping missions to Cyprus and the Sinai, and even for the Canadian truce team sent into Vietnam. Other officers might have visions of prowess on the battlefield, but Yost worried about trucks and transport ships, K-rations and stockpiles of ammunition. Still, mobilization was only part of Yost's mission; his chief preoccupation was preparation for a nuclear armageddon.

It was that war-planning which turned Yost into a champion of increasing continental defence integration. In 1969, when Trudeau had halved Canada's commitment to NATO, he had been charged with shepherding the diminished combat group from the alliance's Central Front to its new base at Lahr in southern Germany which fell under U.S. authority. For the first time, the country's traditional supply and communications lines through Britain were cut; Yost had to forge new links through the Pentagon, using American ports and military airfields. Drafting wartime contingency plans for an integrated continental supply line — later codified in an official agreement — Yost sent a fourteen-man logistics team to Fort McDill in Florida to learn the U.S. ropes; he had been gratified to find they fit right in. But he was disturbed to discover one glaring mismatch — a discrepancy in war-planning doctrines.

Ottawa had stuck with NATO's scenario for what was known as a "short war," a nuclear conflict that would last thirty days. "In that time, it would either be won or lost," he explained, "so therefore there was no need to have reserves of spare parts or aircraft beyond that. It was a come-as-you-are war, and it would all be over fast." In contrast, the Pentagon's war machine was braced for long-run hostilities. But to Yost's chagrin, there was no budging Ottawa from the short-war scenario, which, in turn, provided the government with a rationale for avoiding increased military production. "Canada really bought it," he said, "because it was cheap."

As Yost saw it, the short-war policy was to blame for the country's reluctance to create a U.S.–style defence industry, and he set out to change both mindsets. In 1980, with the blessing of many of his superiors, he resigned from the Canadian Forces and designed a job where he could have maximum effect on public opinion — ultimately overseeing federal civilian mobilization at Emergency Planning Canada, where he threw himself into doomsday arrangements. In Yost's mind was his role model, C. D. Howe, who had built a thriving wartime defence machine by commandeering both the country's raw materials and its manufacturing base. "I felt we needed plans where you could take control of everything," he said, "transport and industry too, in time of emergency."

In his new post, Yost began working closely with his American counterparts in calamity planning, an obscure White House organization known as the Federal Emergency Manpower Agency. FEMA would soon win notoriety both for its own excesses and those of the young Marine to whom it answered at the National Security Council: Lieutenant-Colonel Oliver North. Both North and FEMA's director, Louis Guiffrida, shared Yost's obsession with total control. In the event of an atomic attack — or even a perceived national security crisis such as massive political dissent — they had drafted a radical contingency plan that called for the imposition of martial law; it gave FEMA the right to appoint military commanders and to take over state and local governments and units of the National Guard. But when word leaked out about Rex–84 Bravo, which Guiffrida termed the "largest civil mobilization exercise ever undertaken," Reagan's attorney general, William French Smith, was furious.

Under a scenario called "Continuity of Government," FEMA had proposed packing the president and his cabinet into unmarked planes that would orbit the Earth, leaving the agency and a curious list of seventeen names — including Guiffrida's onetime boss Edwin Meese — to run things below. Charging that it smacked of an attempted coup, French Smith killed the contingency scheme — in which, it turned out, Brigadier-General William Yost had been intimately involved.

As Guiffrida's guest, Yost had frequently lectured at FEMA workshops, invoking C. D. Howe's example; in late 1986 he had been a keynote speaker at a seminar held in a secret bunker below a former convent outside Gettysburg, Maryland. "I used to go down to give advice," he said. "We were ahead of them in Canada." But as Yost acknowledged, Guiffrida had played his political cards unwisely. "FEMA made a power grab," he said, "and attempted to become the agency that would make all the decisions in time of war."

Still, from that shared philosophical base, Yost continued to nudge the Canadian government towards supporting an expanded military industry. Working through an assortment of defence lobbies, he hooked up with the American Defense Preparedness Association, a Washington liaison group between the Pentagon and military contractors. And in the spring of 1983 he and a handful of others inaugurated a Canadian chapter under retired Rear-Admiral Dudley Allen, the CEO of Control Data Canada Ltd., whose subsidiary, Computing Devices, produced the fire control system for the U.S. Army's M-1 Abrams battle tank. The association's members — three-quarters of them subsidiaries of U.S. military contractors — would become an increasingly vocal force in pushing Mulroney towards a more aggressive defence policy.

For an industry whose exports were largely destined for the United States, "defence preparedness" provided a handy rationale for a bigger piece of the Pentagon action. By 1987 Canadian aerospace and armaments sales were estimated at $3 billion, two-thirds of that production exported abroad. "It was a remarkable year," Canada's *Defence Review Bulletin* enthused, "the start of something big." But Allen was already counselling the industry on how to further press its case. "We must create a new business climate," he advised, "based on a set of national urgency."

IN their understated pine and antique-studded offices in Ottawa's Royal Bank tower, Tom d'Aquino and the corporate heavyweights of the Business Council on National Issues were also working to beef up the Canadian military industry — but in their own distinctively discreet fashion. In 1981 BCNI had launched one of its first blue-ribbon task forces on defence policy. Although its chairman, Peter Cameron, then head of Canadian Corporate Management, had no ties to the weapons trade, many of the other members had more than a passing interest in the fruits of a fatter military budget.

Tom Savage, chairman of ITT Canada Ltd., had the U.S. Air Force contract for operating the DEW Line; Alton Cartwright was chairman of Canadian General Electric, which, like its U.S. parent, made aircraft engines; David Race had turned his CAE Industries into a leader in tactical flight simulators; and Ron Chorlton, the head of Wajax Ltd., made aircraft hydraulic systems. Together, with three other CEOs, they jetted off for a military grand tour, dropping in on NORAD's bunker under the Colorado Rockies, NATO headquarters outside Brussels, and the Canadian Forces base at Lahr, where they donned camouflage fatigues and played soldier. In Washington, Caspar Weinberger and the U.S. Joint Chiefs of Staff also threw out the red carpet at their granite stronghold on the Potomac. "These were a bunch of gung-ho guys," recalls one fellow traveller. "The military latched on and gave us a royal good time. They thought here was a bunch of people who would give them a lot of new equipment."

The military had not misjudged its visitors. But the members of BCNI's task force were leery of coming out with a report from which they themselves would so obviously profit. "They were very cautious about being seen to promote a military industrial complex," says one former BCNI staffer. "They were worried about how they were going to get this message across without being seen to protect their own interests."

Instead, BCNI commissioned *Maclean's* columnist Peter Newman to produce a book on the subject. Inviting him along on their travels, the CEOs hoped that one of the country's best-selling authors could craft a compelling popular argument to help reshape public attitudes, which were still notoriously wary of defence spending. "The idea was to influence opinion that would influence the government," says the former council employee. "It was not to be seen to be coming from BCNI."

In late 1983 Newman produced a manuscript that sent tremors through the task force. While exhaustively researched and snappily written — and while calling for a doubling of the military budget — it took issue with one article of faith that was sacred to BCNI's membership: the testing of U.S. cruise missiles over the Canadian north. "Few of the technicalities about the cruise are understood by the general public," Newman began. "But Canadians have a way of smelling a rat."

He went on to slam Trudeau's rationale for giving in to U.S. pressure for the tests — the necessity of conforming to the country's NATO obligations — as "a blatant untruth." Other allies had declined the honour, he pointed out. Besides, the cruise missiles to be launched against the Soviets were targeted over the industrial cityscapes of France and Germany, not Arctic terrain. "By agreeing to test the weapons," he concluded, "the Trudeau administration is convinced it can get the NATO Allies, now pressuring Canada to spend some real money on *conventional* defence, off its back."

That attack was not what BCNI had bargained for. In the council's boardroom, there was consternation and a round of frantic meetings. Among those at the table was the head of Litton Systems Canada Ltd., which had the contract for the cruise guidance system — a distinction for which the company's Rexdale plant had been bombed. "The bottom line was that BCNI did not want to be associated publicly with the less-than-very-strong stand on cruise-missile testing," recalls a former council staffer. "They felt it was Canada's commitment to the U.S. and NATO at stake."

Newman later published his study under the title *True North: Not Strong and Free*, with no mention of BCNI's initial patronage. Indeed, the council took pains to distance itself from the work, but to this day d'Aquino denies that he rejected the writer's report. "Did we ask Peter Newman to do some work for us which we did not use?" he said. "Yes. But that happens all the time."

Still, BCNI was left with three years of assembled research and no one to make its case. Finally, d'Aquino commissioned a known quantity, retired Brigadier-General George Bell, the founder of the Canadian Institute for Strategic Studies in Toronto, who had acted as the task force's technical adviser. Published in September 1984, the month Mulroney came to power, and entitled *Capabilities versus Commitments*, his report came to the not-surprising conclusion that, "Overall, Canada's military capabilities and preparedness are inadequate." To remedy the situation, BCNI recommended a massive boost in troop numbers and a stunning 80 percent real increase in defence spending over the next decade.

Faced with a recession and a military budget that already stood at $11 billion — larger than any other department or federal outlay except for the service of the national debt — Mulroney was to prove slow in acting on that advice. But he was quick to follow up on one item dear to the hearts of both BCNI and Bill Yost. Although it was scarcely noticed at the time, during the Shamrock Summit he and Reagan had devoted more verbiage to the need to "strengthen our North American defence industrial base" than they did to the much-ballyhooed North Warning System.

Later that year in its official *Handbook for Industry*, the Pentagon listed 139 Canadian firms in the "American defense industrial base." To pave the way for more military production and harmonizing of equipment, the Mulroney government also set up a Defence Industrial Preparedness Task Force under a chairman whose thoughts on the subject were reassuringly familiar: BCNI's Peter Cameron.

As Cameron's appointment made clear, Canada's burgeoning military industrial community was already increasingly cosy. From his presidential suite at Paramax — which would be blessed with millions of dollars in controversial subcontracts for the country's new patrol frigates and EH101 helicopters — Paul Manson would hail the "family spirit" uniting the Canadian military and the defence industry. But others were less sanguine about the trend. More top officers were following the American example and flocking to defence contractors' payrolls, but, at the time, without any Washington-style conflict-of-interest guidelines. In his article "The Steady Drummer," Ottawa foreign affairs analyst Edgar Dosman underlined "an urgent need to set certain ground rules for DND–business relations."

Dosman also worried over the growing politicization of the procurement process. "It has become more sophisticated," he said, "more 'Americanized.'" Mulroney had been quick to adopt the White House practice of doling out defence plums where he could reap the most political benefit. In one of the stormiest examples, he transferred the CF–18 maintenance contract from Bristol Aerospace in Winnipeg to Montreal's Canadair, infuriating Manitobans, not least among them his own health and welfare minister, Jake Epp.

In June 1987 Cameron's task force released its first report, which urged Canada and the United States to set up a defence common market — "an unhampered flow of defence goods between the two nations in which all national economic boundaries are eliminated." Rejecting "the state-centred perspective" — a euphemism for nationalism — the report hailed "a continental approach to North American security." If those phrases had become common wisdom in the corridors of the Department of National Defence, at the height of the free trade debate they were nothing if not inflammatory. As Dosman put it, "National Defence, in its own way, is also cheering on free trade."

Hastily, the department swept the paper under the rug, dismissing it as a preliminary draft and hanging the blame on a woman staffer. Five months later — and weeks after the trade pact had been sewn up in Washington — a toned-down version appeared, still urging "total integration" of the two defence industries, but on a more gradual "evolutionary" basis. At the root of its thesis lay Yost's argument that it was time to throw out NATO's short-war doctrine: "Canada must prepare for a variety of peacetime, crisis and wartime contingencies," the report urged, "including a single, prolonged conventional conflict."

By then, Tom d'Aquino and his band of corporate defence warriors were growing impatient with Mulroney's cautious approach. In 1987 a second BCNI task force agitated for a 4–6 percent annual real increase in defence spending until the end of the millennium and the creation of a continental defence industrial base. Its report gave short shrift to investing in peacekeeping, the country's one area of expertise, noting that "other defense priorities take precedence."

Only four days later, on June 5, 1987, Perrin Beatty produced the first Canadian White Paper on defence in sixteen years, entitled *Challenge and Commitment*, which echoed exactly those sentiments. Scarcely mentioning peacekeeping, it devoted six pages to the need for building a continental military industry and acquiring billions in new war toys. As one defence industry newsletter exulted, "This man is our champion!" At the top of Beatty's wish list was a $7 billion fleet of nuclear-powered submarines to safeguard Arctic sovereignty — a reaction to the *Polar Sea*. But that mission made the subs less than popular at the Pentagon: George Bader made no attempt to hide his lack of enthusiasm for a fleet aimed at fending off the U.S. Navy.

Defence analysts had hoped Beatty would make hard policy choices, focusing the country's efforts on a handful of tasks instead of leaving the military stretched thin, trying to fulfil an array of missions from NATO to NORAD with token troop commitments. But Bader and the Pentagon had vociferously opposed any attempt to pull Canada's symbolic NATO presence out of Europe, and Beatty was nothing if not a fan of the American Way; in fact, some scholars had been unkind enough to note that his glossy White Paper, sprinkled with colour photos, seemed patterned on the Pentagon's annual report, *Soviet Military Power*.

At York University, David Langille, an economic historian who had spent years tracking BCNI, noticed that the White Paper bore a striking similarity to the council's defence task force report. Intrigued, Langille filed Access to Information requests, which yielded him Beatty's correspondence. In notes to BCNI, he found that the minister enjoyed such a cosy consultation with d'Aquino over the review that BCNI appeared to have delayed its own report to avoid embarrassing the government with their similarities.

But despite that backstage choreography, Beatty's White Paper died the cruelest of policy deaths: it promptly became irrelevant. As the Berlin Wall tumbled, brick by souvenir brick, half a century of strategic conventional wisdom was being called into question. Beatty's blinkered views, which had so ardently aped the Pentagon's, were suddenly an anachronism. "It all proved a little untimely," conceded a former Canadian defence attaché in Washington. "When it was being put together of course we were still talking about evil empires and there was all the NATO pressure to build up — which meant U.S. pressure."

But suddenly even the Pentagon's budget arguments were coming unhinged. Congress had already begun slashing defence funding in terms that Corporate America could understand, calling for a "peace dividend." Ironically, Mulroney seemed the last to catch on to that shareholders' package. After the 1988 election, as U.S. aerospace assembly lines were gearing down, he embarked on a belated hardware shopping binge. Over the next four years, as if to make up for lost time, he ordered the army 1,200 new Light Armoured Vehicles and dispensed contracts for a $1.1 billion low-level air defence system to protect Canadian airfields — only eighteen months before withdrawing all Canadian troops from Lahr. But his most provocative purchase was $5 billion worth of the world's most expensive shipborne helicopters, the infamous EH101s that would later become a pivotal election issue, cancelled by the Liberals. Clearly, the influence of the country's military industrial community had taken hold. As Peter Langille, author of *Changing the Guard*, noted, "Canada is definitely the last country to reap any peace dividend."

Nor did that dizzying spending help the country's balance of trade. In 1988–89 the largest single supplier to the Canadian government was the U.S. Navy, which won $312.1 million in contracts — many of them for weapons systems on the new patrol frigates. Close behind, in sixth place, was the U.S. Army, which had snared 287 government orders worth $92.6 million. A year earlier, Canada had the distinction of ranking as Washington's second largest military customer within NATO, snapping up an estimated $1.3 billion in equipment. The American government, not homegrown industry, it turned out, was the biggest beneficiary of the government's new defence policy.

Even in 1994 when brutal cutbacks began under the Liberals, the commitment to hardware shopping continued. As George Bader and Caspar Weinberger had foreseen, the military had succeeded in building itself a Canadian constituency — one far more impassioned about weaponry than manpower or national sovereignty.

Despite the refurbishment frenzy, the country's military turned out to be equipped for the wrong kind of war. In a chaotic new world order where peacekeeping was suddenly urgently required, the defence establishment, which had traditionally scorned that task as sissy stuff, found its blue berets overbooked and woefully outfitted. Around the globe, regional and ethnic conflagrations were raging uncontrolled — conflicts far more bloody and intractable than any of the old East-West nuclear wargaming. But they called for transport planes and desert savvy, not CF–18 fighter-jets and continental radar screens.

Then, just as security scholars were writing a requiem for the decade-long defence boom, a fellow afficionado of arms catalogues appeared on the horizon to offer a brief boost to business: on the first weekend of August 1990, Saddam Hussein's tanks lumbered across the Kuwait border.

A S the world sat glued to CNN watching 100,000 U.S. Marines pour into Saudi Arabia, Brian and Mila Mulroney dropped by George Bush's family compound outside Kennebunkport, Maine, for their annual sleepover at the summer White House. No sooner had a presidential chopper deposited the prime minister on the estate's tennis court than he strode out with Bush to meet the press in front of a modest cedar-shake guard cottage. Against that backdrop, designed to conceal the patrician comforts of the actual presidential digs up the lane, Mulroney hailed Operation Desert Shield with such rhetorical zeal that the *Cleveland Plain Dealer* promptly poked fun at him.

When word leaked out that, during a fishing trip on the president's Cigarette boat *Fidelity*, Mulroney had hooked his host in the earlobe, the paper refused to buy the official explanation that the culprit was Bush's son Jeb. Not only had news cameras caught the gaffe, but Mulroney himself appeared to confirm the deed, protesting to reporters, "It was not a hostile act." For the *Plain Dealer*, the incident was an occasion to comment not on the prime minister's casting skills but on his eagerness to clamber aboard the Persian Gulf war wagon. At a time when many Americans themselves were still wary of Bush's sabre-rattling, the editorial punned, "The visitor from Ottawa has adopted the U.S. position hook, line and sinker."

Indeed, that was precisely the cause of consternation back home. Days after Bush had branded Saddam Hussein "worse than Hitler," Mulroney had called a nationally televised news conference to denounce him as "a criminal of historic significance" and to declare that Canada was sending two destroyers and a supply ship to the Middle East. Breaking with fifty years of tradition, he had committed Canadian troops to a foreign conflict without seeking Parliament's approval — a move that Mackenzie King had not dared at the outbreak of the Second World War. Chrétien called it "absolutely unacceptable" not to recall the House: "What is happening is extremely dangerous, and Canadians are being kept in the dark."

Even Mulroney betrayed concerns about how the history books might view his lapse. He announced that the HMCS *Athabaskan* and *Terra Nova* and their crew of 800 would not technically be on active duty until they arrived in the Gulf in early October, by which time Parliament would have reconvened. But even then the government would never offer a formal war resolution for debate. When the House finally voted on January 22, a week after the U.S. bombing raids began, it was on a vaguely worded motion in "support of the United Nations in ending the aggression by Iraq against Kuwait."

Mulroney's aides boasted that he had been among the first whom Bush had called to rally multinational backing for a counterstrike; it was the prime minister, they claimed, who had persuaded him to launch the American bombing campaign under the flag cover of the United Nations. But U.S. histories of the war make no mention of his role. And once Bush had decided to resuscitate the U.N. for his purposes, he had every reason to curry Ottawa's favour: at the time, Canada had a seat on the Security Council.

When Parliament opened on September 24, Mulroney had delivered an impassioned rationale for throwing the ill-prepared Canadian military into the fray at an estimated cost of $600 million. "Canadians have never looked for a free ride," he thundered, "and we are not going to start today." In fact, as it turned out, like many in the American administration, including members of Bush's own family, some Canadians were looking for business. The secretive

Kuwait Investment Office, a government agency, was holding an estimated $1 billion in Canadian stocks, real estate, and mining investments at the time, including a small stake in Gordon Investment Corporation, the equally secretive Toronto brokerage that was favoured by many of the government's friends and supporters. For years, the Kuwait Investment Office and Prince Nawaf, a half-brother of both Saudi Arabia's King Fahd and its defence minister, Prince Sultan, had been shareholders in Peter Munk's Horsham Corporation, whose board Mulroney would join after his retirement.

At the time the Gulf War broke out, the government itself was trying to gain a toehold in the Middle Eastern arms bazaar. In 1986 Joe Clark had gone to Riyadh looking for a share of the Saudi munificence that had pumped billions into the U.S., British, and French economies. Although Canadian defence contractors already supplied many of the components in the Pentagon's wares sold to the kingdom, including the M–1 tank, Mulroney's ardour in supporting Operation Desert Storm would soon pay greater dividends. General Motors' diesel division in London, Ontario, finally clinched a contract it had been courting for years: an order for at least 1,117 Light Armoured Vehicles, which put Canada in eighth spot on the 1991 global arms hit parade. In fact, four months after the war's end, the government would be obliged to change a section of the Criminal Code to accommodate that sale: under the previous provisions, companies had been forbidden from exporting automatic weapons — a key feature of the Light Armoured Vehicles.

Astonishingly, in March 1991, when Bush visited Ottawa, Mulroney had issued a plea for an end to all arms sales to the Middle East — a notion that horrified the Canadian defence industry. Bush refused to comment and took a wide berth of the proposal. But later, prime ministerial aides would explain that, at the time, Mulroney had been lobbying for a job as U.N. secretary general.

Still, when Mulroney had committed Canadian troops to the Persian Gulf, he knew he was walking a political tightrope. Polls showed that he had public backing for his initial rush to join the multinational embargo against Iraq — indeed, the strongest support for an initiative that he had enjoyed in years — but those sentiments did not run deep. Even after a two-month Kuwaiti-financed public relations campaign that had vastly inflated the Iraqi threat, Allan Gregg's focus groups revealed that voters flatly rejected all the fancy talk of upholding international law; the main reason Mulroney had thrown the country's lot into the Gulf, they said, was "to go along with the U.S."

Even among the Canadian military, Mulroney's first troop commitment was greeted with less than enthusiasm. At Maritime Command in Halifax, there was, according to one former official, "a little furore": both destroyers were equipped to hunt submarines — one particular threat that Saddam Hussein lacked — not dodge missiles and mines. In Washington, the Canadian defence attaché, Major-General George Kells, scrambled to borrow missing parts and weaponry from the U.S. Navy to refit the ships. So hastily did that rearmament take place that both vessels were still conducting weapons tests on their way to the Red Sea. "This was all done by phone — no traditional paperwork," chuckled an official two years later. "To be honest, some of the paperwork is still catching up."

Barely a month later — in response to increased pressure from Secretary of State James Baker — Mulroney threw in more firepower. He ordered a squadron of CF–18 fighters and 450 support personnel from the NATO airbase at Baden-Soellingen to provide air cover for the destroyers — a purely defensive mission, he emphasized. But they too were far from battle-ready. As an internal defence department review later revealed, at one point Ottawa's high command considered pulling the jets out of the Gulf because of failures in their electronic warfare equipment.

Nor was the squadron's welcome from the U.S. Air Force overwhelming. During one of Mulroney's phone calls with Bush, he had appealed for a parking place for the eighteen planes, and the Pentagon had guaranteed room in Saudi Arabia. But when the Canadian air commander arrived, he found the base already stacked wing to wing with other allied fighters. The CF–18s ended up consigned to the dusty outpost of Doha in Qatar — dubbed Canada Dry One — because, as one general put it, "There was no room for them at the inn."

Still, as the U.S. political and military machine hurled itself ineluctably towards war, the Chief of the Defence Staff, General John de Chastelain, sent another Canadian Forces unit, a signals squadron, and six more CF–18s to the Middle East. By mid-January when the fighting began, there were more than 1,800 Canadian military personnel at assorted posts in the Gulf. But as Mulroney recalled Parliament for an emergency session hours before bombing began, support was already eroding. Anti-war protestors heckled him and chained themselves to the Parliament Buildings, in the process damaging the Peace Tower. In the Commons, Chrétien showed his exasperation with the prime minister's obfuscation over strategic plans. "The government does not have the moral authority to lead our country into war," he erupted. But that night Canadians found themselves in their first shooting war in nearly forty years, bit players in a nightly made-for-TV drama that briefly pre-empted sitcoms as the networks' most compelling fare — and whose popularity would prove just as evanescent.

Two hours after the U.S. bombing raids began, Mulroney announced he had authorized de Chastelain to put the country's forces on an offensive footing. For many, that changed role shattered the smug image of Canadians as Boy Scouts abroad, neutral and non-belligerent peacekeepers. But in fact the decision had already been made by the cabinet's tiny war committee more than four days earlier.

On New Year's Eve, Mulroney's associate minister of defence, Mary Collins, a vivacious Vancouver MP, had arrived in Bahrain at Canadian naval headquarters for a whirlwind tour of the Gulf. Flying on to Qatar, she found the Canadian air contingent less than content with its role, ordered to fly racetrack patrols over the country's three ships, far from the action. "They felt: What good were they doing just sitting there?" she says. And by week's end, American Air Force officials were making the same plea: one general argued that the Canadian pilots were humiliated by the tameness of their mission. "Those air force guys felt just awful about it," he said. "I mean, tears would come to their eyes."

General Charles ("Chuck") Horner, the chief of all allied air power and the architect of the U.S. bombing campaign, had been personally moved by their plight. A former bomber pilot who had flown more than seventy missions over North Vietnam, Horner had spent weeks trying to convince the Canadian commanding officer, Admiral Kenneth Summers, to let the squadron join the allied bombing campaign — but to no avail. Tensions between the two were palpable, and Horner did little to hide his scorn. But finally he did what so many in the U.S. military had learned to do: he took the political route.

When Mary Collins arrived at Horner's air command headquarters in Riyadh, he had a word with her. Stressing allied solidarity, he hammered away at strategic efficiency and praised the Canadian flight record. To his delight, he found a receptive ear, boasting later that it had taken a woman — and a politician at that — to see reason. "They thought to be effective, we had to do more," she says. "That was the really tricky issue."

Two days later, Collins flew back to Ottawa overnight and walked straight into an early-morning war cabinet meeting with Mulroney and half-a-dozen select ministers. "That was where it had to be resolved," she says, "The question was: How far were we going to go?" Daily, opposition critics were demanding whether Canadian troops would become Iraqi cannon fodder, and Mulroney was increasingly nervous over the political ramifications of acquiescing to the U.S. request. Even within the war cabinet, there was dissent; after all, throwing Canadian forces into the bombing campaign meant putting them under American command. But finally he gave the go-ahead.

At Canada Dry One, Canadian pilots whooped with glee. But their enthusiasm was reined in by the need to refit their CF–18s for bombing duties. Despite the historic milestone of Mulroney's offensive order, most were unable to join the U.S. bombing spree until its final days. By then the chief remaining target was the panicked retreating Republican Guard, whose charred convoys were discovered strewn across the desert in a spectacle that sickened even the swaggering U.S. commander-in-chief, Norman Schwarzkopf. By the end of those sorties, the air war had claimed the lives of an estimated 9,000 Iraqi troops and 13,000 civilians.

To this day, Horner has nothing but words of praise for the integration of Canadian flyers under his command. "It was superb," he says. "The problem that I always have — and many U.S. Air Force guys have — is we tend to take Canadians for granted. It's the fact that our two nations are so much alike. I realize those are fighting words for Canadians, but the trouble is you could switch the uniforms and no one would know the difference!"

If the two nations' forces were not yet quite as interchangeable as Horner might wish, the fact remained that, during the Persian Gulf War, an American general had gone over the head of the Canadian commander to literally call the shots. Within eighteen months, that general, the burly and gregarious Chuck Horner, would arrive in Colorado Springs as the new commander-in-chief of NORAD, the crown jewel of bilateral defence cooperation, whose future was suddenly in question.

DEEP in the bowels of Cheyenne Mountain, in a vast self-sufficient bunker beneath 1,750 feet of Colorado granite meant to defy a Soviet nuclear attack, an intruder had surfaced on the radar screens of NORAD's operations centre. On the monitors lining the small darkened room, an ominous blip signalled that a suspect aircraft was threatening to invade the continent's airspace. Hunched over computers that digested data from a dizzying array of radars, space-based satellites, and aerostat blimps floating above the Mexican border, NORAD's duty team tracked the plane as it headed up the western coast of Mexico with telltale slowness.

Thousands of miles away, an EC–3 Sentry AWACS spy plane with Canadian crewmen aboard had picked up the aircraft's trail on its own radar. Within minutes, an order had squawked over the loudspeakers of a U.S. Southern Command hangar in Panama: "Scramble the Eagles!" Instantly, two of NORAD's F–15 fighter jets, sitting on five-minute alert around the clock, had roared off the runway. Despite the fact that each was armed with a 20-mm internal gun mount and Sidewinder and Sparrow missiles, the pilots were under strict orders not to fire. Their mission was merely to get a look at the suspect plane — "ident" in military parlance — to make out its tail markings and whether its windows were blacked out, all clues to the twin-engine turboprops preferred by Colombia's cocaine cartels.

If that assignment sounded simple enough, it was not, thanks to the techno-marvels of the world's finest war-fighting machines. Getting close enough for a covert glimpse of a Piper Cub plodding northward at 220 knots an hour could demand awkward aerial acrobatics for an F–15 pilot with an average speed of Mach 2.5. Nor, when it came time to collaring the smuggler, could any of NORAD's personnel take part. Under U.S. and Canadian law, the military was required to leave the shootouts and arrests to law enforcement agencies. Such were the paradoxes since NORAD's multibillion-dollar might had been enlisted in George Bush's war on drugs.

Launching an AWACS to track a cocaine smuggler's flight path cost US$2,833 an hour. And dispatching one of NORAD's CF–18s to track an airborne suspect out of the Canadian Forces base at Bagotville, Quebec, could rack up an hourly bill of $7,686. The sheer asymmetry of the battle had prompted critics to demand why the combined bilateral firepower of NORAD was needed to play the hemisphere's narcocop. "If you ask, 'What kind of aircraft do we need for drug interdiction?'" David Cox, a Queen's University military expert, had observed, "I'm pretty sure the answer is that it's not necessary to use a $25 million CF-18 to track a Piper Cub. NORAD is basically looking for self-employment."

Indeed, with the collapse of the Soviet Union, an increasing number of analysts both inside and outside the military had begun questioning the very existence of the $8 billion continental command whose sole *raison d'être* had been to detect and deter attacks from an enemy that no longer existed. Four years after the Shamrock Summit, the Cold War's end had turned the entire North American Air Defence Modernization scheme into a $7 billion white elephant.

Quietly, with none of the fanfare that had marked the scheme's unveiling, the Pentagon had mothballed most of its major components. Out went the notion of a continental burglar alarm: the over-the-horizon backscatter radar slated for Alaska was cancelled, and another designated to guard the Pacific coast was put into cold storage at Mountain Home Air Force Base in Idaho. Only the Atlantic coastal radar outside Moscow, Maine, survived, switched on eight hours a day — a national security system on bankers' hours.

As for the North Warning System, once the symbol of Canada's new continental defence partnership — all that survived of the former grand design was a skeletal radar grid so porous that it made the old DEW Line seem a paragon of security. After considerable debate, the thirteen long-range microwave radar stations had been installed across the Arctic, some on former DEW Line sites, manned by crews of ten to fifteen civilians employed by Frontec Logistics Corp., a division of Edmonton's Atco.

But by 1991 the system's thirty-nine unmanned short-wave radars were still two years behind schedule on Paramax's assembly line: their prototypes, which had been tested in Alaska two years earlier, had failed to function. As one officer summed up the delay: "It was not necessarily wholesale deception, but let's just say that they probably thought the technology was readier than it was." NORAD's high command tried to cancel the contract, but Paramax's penalty clause locked in payment. Gradually, over three years, the radars were hauled to their sites and left in what the military called "warm storage" — installed but not activated.

Still, to Canadian officials, the most infuriating aspect of the dismantled scheme was the one they had tried hardest to keep secret: the five Forwarding Operating Locations — airfields with six hangars, dormitories for up to 200 troops, and runways long enough to accommodate U.S. fighter jets — each with a pricetag of more than $50 million. Mulroney had won the construction contracts for Canadian firms in return for picking up half the costs — a provision that officials had pitched at the time as an economic coup. But the Canadian defence department budgeted on a five-year basis, while the Pentagon was subject to the annual mood swings of Congress. By 1989 Ottawa had awarded the contracts and spent most of the money, agreeing to reimbursement later. Then the U.S. Senate Appropriations Committee cut the project's funding.

Already, Canadian officials had seen the writing on the wall and had cancelled one of the airfields, slated for Kuujjuaq in Quebec. Press reports suggested it was scrubbed because Innu protest groups had demanded an environmental impact study — a cover story that made one NORAD official smile. "It was money — raw dollars," he says. "Canada was getting further and further in the red."

But it was too late to stop work on the four remaining airfields. "We were so far along that not to complete them would have cost Canada more," says Major-General James O'Blenis, NORAD's second most senior Canadian official. "We were left holding the bag."

By the most conservative estimates, that bag amounted to $60 million. Discreetly, Mulroney's government had protested being bilked, first through the military, finally resorting to diplomatic channels. But as of the winter of 1994, Washington had resolutely refused to pay its outstanding tab. Still, so sensitive was the subject to the defence establishment's relationship with the United States that a Canadian reporter inquiring about the embarrassment was quietly informed that her access to information from the embassy in Washington might be cut off if she pressed the subject further. By that time it had become clear that any reimbursement would be in the form of services, not cash.

The most striking aspect of the default was the extent to which the Conservative government had tried to conceal an issue that might raise fundamental questions about a defence policy so closely linked to the whims of Washington. Just as General Thériault had predicted, with Canadian geography no longer essential to U.S. national security, the country had fallen off the Pentagon's radar screens. In Washington, Canada was fast becoming a strategic irrelevance.

That fate was all the more disturbing to officials who sensed a threat to the very command that guaranteed Ottawa a seat at the Pentagon planning tables — and a ticket to the latest in U.S. technology. When Lieutenant-General Robert Morton arrived in Colorado Springs as NORAD's deputy commander-in-chief in the fall of 1989, he realized the Cold War's end was bad news for the air defence business. "It ran the caution flag up about how long the NORAD agreement would survive," he recalls, "without the spark of Soviet military might and fear."

Morton promptly launched an internal mission review in the hopes of outflanking the budget-cutters in both countries. Then on September 5, 1989, George Bush came to the rescue with his drug war. If some defence officials harrumphed at the prospect of glorified police work, for NORAD's high command the new aerial surveillance mission was, says Morton, "a shot in the arm." Or, as one retired general put it, "When something like the drug role comes along, you grab onto it like a drowning man onto a buoy."

But pursuing drug smugglers was an item on the American national security agenda; Canada's role as deputy sheriff was an afterthought. When NORAD got its marching orders, "It was very much a 'U.S. Eyes Only' type of thing," one general recalls. "No foreign sharing." In the integrated command, that meant either Ottawa would have to be allowed in on the act or NORAD would be forced to bow out of the mission. Among Canadian officers, there were fears that they would be blamed for further marginalizing NORAD or, worse, dealing it a death blow.

The State Department formally requested Ottawa's approval. And, to the astonishment of officials familiar with the pace of federal decision-making, that approval shot back within forty-eight hours. Without seeking Parliament's assent, Mulroney secretively signed the country on for a sidekick's role in carrying out American domestic security policy. Suddenly, Canadian taxpayers were helping foot the bill for the U.S. drug war.

Just as he would twice commit Canadian troops to U.S.–led U.N. missions abroad without consulting the Commons — first in the Persian Gulf, then Somalia — Mulroney had modified a pillar of the nation's defence policy with no public debate. In fact, NORAD would chase aerial drug mules for two years before its new role would be formally spelled out in a six-paragraph Memo of Understanding tacked onto the agreement's renewal in April 1991.

Nor was that the only diplomatic hitch. When the State Department obtained permission for NORAD's counter-drug flights over Latin American nations, it had neglected to mention that there might be Canadians on board. But when External officials set out to rectify the oversight, their American counterparts begged them not to stir up the sensitivities of Latin governments. Astonishingly, Mulroney agreed, leaving Washington to negotiate overflight clearance for Canadian troops with foreign capitals.

Five years after the Pentagon's high-tech drug war began, a National Security Council review would conclude that, despite spending $1.1 billion a year, its efforts had failed to stem the flood of cocaine into the United States. Other critics saw NORAD's drug patrols over South and Central America as the first thin edge of a military wedge designed to enforce a new Pax Americana over the hemisphere. Michael Klare, a Massachusetts defence scholar, had already predicted that, freed from its obsession with the Soviet Union, "America's war machine of the 1990s will face south, across the Rio Grande, rather than east across the plains of Europe."

To some sceptics, it seemed more than coincidental that Bush had launched his crusade against Latin drug lords at the very moment his National Security Council was beginning trade negotiations with Mexico. In strategic circles, hemispheric defence was fast becoming the new fashion. In the fall of 1991, dozens of security experts gathered at Washington's National Defense University to ponder how they could put military muscle behind NAFTA and Bush's economic agenda for Latin America. Sobered by the stakes in the just-finished Persian Gulf War, some panelists called for hemispheric self-sufficiency in oil, with troops ensuring continental supply lines and U.S. access to strategic mineral reserves.

At a time when Washington was defining national security not in terms of military might but economic advantage, Canadian commanders in Colorado Springs worried that the White House might turn NORAD into NAFTA's military equivalent — in the process, diluting Canada's clout. With a knowing eye for the political winds, Chuck Horner did not rule out the notion of a trilateral command in Colorado Springs. "There's no doubt in my mind that five years from now NORAD might include Mexico," he said. "It's a political thing, not a military thing. But militarily, it's do-able."

Still, Horner had seized on another prospect as the best hope for salvaging his command's future. And in the spring of 1993, the day after Mulroney named Kim Campbell his last defence minister, she found Horner sitting in her office. He wanted her blessing for a controversial new NORAD role: Ballistic Missile Defense — or BMD, as it was known in Pentagonspeak — a system of ground-based, and eventually space-based, anti-missile batteries designed to safeguard the continent from nuclear attacks by rogue dictators like Saddam Hussein.

For his presentation, Horner's most powerful weapon was an image etched in memory from nightly newscasts during the Gulf War: Iraq's SCUDs arching over Dharhan and Tel Aviv, their fiery trails suddenly exploding in silent collision with U.S. Patriot missiles. Half a world away, NORAD's supercomputers deep inside Cheyenne Mountain had choreographed those Middle Eastern fireworks. U.S. satellites along the equator had monitored each SCUD launch, feeding the data on the missile's path back to NORAD's Cray II; two minutes later, electronic commands to the Patriot batteries in Saudi Arabia and Israel had repositioned them for interception.

Those images had packed a powerful visual — and political — wallop. Within months of the war, Congress had passed the Ballistic Missile Defense Act, which committed the Pentagon to a "theatre" defence against short- to medium-range missiles, designed to protect American troops stationed abroad, by 1995. Suddenly, military scholars were discussing continental anti-missile shields — a concept with a decidedly familiar ring. If the BMD scenario sounded remarkably like Ronald Reagan's old Star Wars script, it was, in fact, a variation on the theme. His Strategic Defense Initiative (SDI) had envisioned an umbrella of space-based missiles to shield the continent from a massive Soviet atomic attack. But the Pentagon had revised the costly and contentious design to focus on a largely ground-based anti-missile system that could protect an allied consortium against nuclear blackmail threats from Third World despots. Bush's title for that international insurance scheme was the chummy Global Protection Against Limited Strikes — G-PALS.

The name change signalled that defence officials saw Star Wars as a public relations — not a technical or conceptual — disaster. As NORAD's General Timothy Gill confirmed, "It was not marketed very well with our allies — especially in Canada." In fact, few Canadians knew that, ever since the Quebec City summit, the federal government had been engaged in one phase of BMD development, even out-funding Washington on research for space-based radar. After all the hoopla announcing the North Warning System, one of the few aspects of the $700 million plan that had survived was an offshoot linked to Reagan's old Star Wars scheme.

In 1992, with notable fanfare, both Congress and the U.S. Defense Department had announced the demise of SDI — an obituary that was to prove somewhat premature. At the Pentagon, the SDI office — and much of the organization itself — appeared curiously intact, the plaque on the door merely changed to Ballistic Missile Defense Office. In fact, Washington's Center for Defense Information had received a package with a transparent new address sticker reading "BMDO" pasted over the still perceptible old return address, "SDIO." That thinly concealed attempt at creating a new identity for Reagan's discredited scheme prompted Tennessee Senator Jim Sasser to quip that Star Wars had gone under the FBI's Witness Protection Program. But NORAD's deputy commander-in-chief, Canadian Lieutenant-General Brian Smith, had argued that the rechristening was essential: "The political advice we got was, 'You're still carrying around all this baggage with the same name, so get rid of it.'"

For Horner, Ballistic Missile Defense was the key to NORAD's survival, and selling it was simply a question of judicious public relations. "It needs to be done very carefully," he said. "It must be presented to the public very intelligently." But BMD had also become the hottest new subject in strategic planning, the object of intense turf warfare among the U.S. services. If NORAD was to win the new BMD mission over its chief rival, the newly created U.S. Strategic Command, it would need Ottawa's approval. "Command and control of ballistic defence so far has excluded NORAD because of the assumption that Canada was against it," Smith explained. "But the architecture is being developed now so it could be a NORAD mission — if Canada would let it be."

Recalling the Canadian outcry against Star Wars at the Shamrock Summit, NORAD's brass had despaired. But in 1991, when Bush canvassed allied leaders about enrolling in G-PALS, Mulroney had stunned his own military with a response of carefully crafted neutrality. "He didn't sign up," Smith noted. "He just said, 'Interesting initiative, George. We're willing to pursue it further.' In fact, in diplomatic terms it was rather an encouraging reply: it didn't close any doors."

Once again, without a hint of public debate, Mulroney had hitched the country to the U.S. strategic agenda. Paradoxically, he had done so at a time when there had never been less pressure to pursue that course. With the implosion of the Soviet empire, Canadian solidarity was no longer required for strategic or even territorial reasons. For the first time in postwar history, Ottawa could disregard Washington's national security agenda with impunity. "For the first time," confirmed Washington security analyst Joseph Jockel, "Canada is free to make its own defence policy."

But would Ottawa seize that historic opportunity? Jockel laughed in reply: "No, it'll probably muddle along." Indeed, even under the Liberals' 1995 defence White Paper, the government would choose to stay the continental course — still content to play Washington's junior partner.

9

Showbiz Inc.

"**L**OW KEY**"** is a phrase that Nicholas Veliotes likes to use as a verb, as in "We have low-keyed it." Tall and intense, his face weathered by years in the Middle Eastern sun, the American book industry's chief lobbyist strides through Washington, anonymous and unnoticed — unlike his celebrated counterpart from the movie business, Jack Valenti, better known on Capitol Hill as Mr. Hollywood. "We have different styles," Veliotes shrugs, as he slips into a restaurant chosen more for its convenience than its social cachet — and where not a head has swivelled at his arrival. "We're not big into glitz."

Where Valenti has launched his diatribes against the Canadian government's attempts to introduce a national film policy in high-wattage news conferences and public harangues, Veliotes has pressed his case in the discreet hush of embassies and ministerial backrooms — but with equal effect. He is credited with the virtual gutting of the Mulroney government's Baie Comeau book publishing policy, the last vestige of the vaunted regulatory bulwark once promised as proof of the Conservatives' commitment to safeguarding Canadian culture. As president of the Association of American Publishers, Veliotes was also a pivotal silent player during the final tense hours of the free trade talks, lobbying against Ottawa's insistence that Canadian cultural industries be exempted from the provisions of the pact. That exemption, he points out, U.S. publishers and film-makers "reluctantly acquiesced to . . . but we've never approved or accepted." Indeed, if Veliotes has left the rhetorical pyrotechnics to Valenti, he has been no less active behind the scenes in seeing that the Canadian cultural exemption remains, as he puts it, "quarantined" from other nations and trade agreements.

But then, pulling global strings comes naturally to a career diplomat who spent most of his thirty years in the U.S. foreign service on the front lines of the Cold War struggle for hearts and minds. In 1981, after overseeing American interests in the strategic hot spots of Laos, India, and Jordan, he was named Reagan's first assistant secretary of state for Near Eastern affairs — a hardliner whom his boss, Al Haig, had personally pegged to keep a vigil on the tinder box of the Middle East. Two years later, with Haig out of the White House, Veliotes had been dispatched to Egypt as ambassador, or what the *Washington Post* termed "America's tough cop."

It was in Cairo that he had a singular brush with indiscretion — one that was to shed light on his particular brand of diplomacy. In October 1985, as the Egyptian government let three Palestinian terrorists who had hijacked the Mediterranean cruise ship *Achille Lauro* escape on an Egyptair flight, Veliotes was overheard on an open ship-to-shore radio screaming at top Cairo officials to "prosecute those sons of bitches." When he resigned abruptly from the foreign service three months later, friends blamed that broadcast outburst for hastening the end of a brilliant career. But if the State Department objected to his shoot-from-the-hip style, it was precisely what caught the attention of the U.S. publishers' association, which was looking for its own tough global cop to patrol the cultural marketplace.

For many, Veliotes's background illustrated the enormity of the strategic stakes in question as the Canadian cultural community struggled to protect an industry considered vital to the country's independence, and even its ultimate survival. In a world where trade sanctions have superseded tanks and troops as the new instruments of international leverage, his appointment provided a telling glimpse into that uneasy terrain where one country's notion of sovereignty collides with another's concept of national security. For while Canadians talk of culture in terms of national identity and consciousness, Veliotes and his colleagues speak of export statistics and legal precedents in a multibillion-dollar business considered crucial to the U.S. balance of payments. As Hollywood's legendary Samuel Goldwyn once summed up the U.S. view of the cultural debate: "Nobody ever called it show art; it's show business."

In 1989 American entertainment exports generated a $4.5 billion trade surplus for Washington — second only to those of the defence industry. No U.S. sector was leading the march into world markets with more determination and chutzpah — raising Euro-Disneylands outside Paris, churning out Hindi versions of *Jurassic Park*, and cloning fifteen versions of *Wheel of Fortune* around the world, even shipping each local Vanna White look-alike to California for advanced lessons in the fine art of letter-turning.

That global drive was not propelled by any international altruism. As the cost of movie-making skyrocketed, studios could seldom break even from North American box-office take — a so-called domestic market in which Canada was routinely lumped. As much as 60 percent of some blockbusters had to be recouped by sales abroad. Of $11.9 billion in film revenues in 1989, 38 percent came from foreign markets. Those figures helped explain why Jack Valenti, the mercurial silver fox who headed the Motion Picture Association of America, occupied one of thirty-five seats on the White House private sector trade advisory panel.

In that $850,000 post, he carried the banner for an industry in which a handful of massive communications conglomerates controlled film and TV studios, record companies, and the continent's largest book and periodical publishers. And within those empires, each division remained acutely alert to the implications of any regulatory battles engaging the other provinces. When a policy jolted the publishing industry, Valenti's studio bosses studied the aftershocks for a precedent that might affect their own box-office receipts — all the more so when the threat came from Canada, the world's leading market for both American films and books.

While Canadians might lament that nearly three out of every four titles in the country's bookstores were American, U.S. publishers considered that space on the country's shelves critical to their profit margins. For some leading houses, more than one-third of revenues depended on overseas sales. Of $1.64 billion in foreign exports by the U.S. book industry in 1992, nearly half went to Canada — a $700 million market nearly twice the size of second-place Britain.

Nor was it any secret that those exports had an impact far beyond the bottom line. As Harvard foreign policy expert Joseph Nye told a forum on global popular culture: "A country that stands astride popular channels of communication has more opportunities to get its message across and to affect the preferences of others." For years, U.S. policy-makers had taken pride in the role that smuggled bluejeans and rock 'n' roll LPs had played in loosening the grip of the Soviet *diktaturat*. "American popular music, like American popular culture generally," declared neoconservative ideologue Irving Kristol, "has a wonderfully corrosive effect on all totalitarian and strongly authoritarian regimes."

But communism was not alone in its vulnerability to the siren song of U.S. mass entertainment, as France's culture minister Jack Lang and other Europeans were already worrying in 1982. At a UNESCO conference in Mexico City, Lang had infuriated the Reagan administration by calling for a crusade against "a certain invasion of fabricated images and standardized music" that "level national cultures and want to impose a uniform way of life on the entire planet." Thundering that "culture is not owned by one power," he had exhorted an audience of Third World officials to resist the U.S. entertainment industry steamroller. "Our destiny?" he had demanded. "Is it to become the vassals of an immense empire of profit?"

In the executive suites of America's entertainment conglomerates, those were fighting words — above all as the United States felt the growing economic muscle of Europe and Japan. As Washington's *National Journal* noted in an article entitled "Tinseltown's Trade War": "The export of American culture is a way to preserve U.S. influence in the world at a time when the U.S. role in economic and security issues has been waning."

Veliotes insists that notion had never occurred to him when two members of the publishers' search committee approached him with a job offer in late 1985. One of them was Lawrence Levinson, who headed the Washington lobbying office of Gulf + Western Industries, Inc., the parent of publishing colossus Simon and Schuster. Like Valenti, Levinson was a veteran of Lyndon Johnson's White House and the most powerful member of the association — "our 800-lb. gorilla," as one colleague called him. As he made clear, he had a particular corporate problem that required Veliotes's diplomatic skills.

In December 1984, the same month that Brian Mulroney had proclaimed Canada open for business, Gulf + Western had bought out New Jersey–based Prentice Hall, overnight becoming the largest U.S. publishing house. Now its takeover of Prentice Hall's Canadian subsidiary was subject to scrutiny from Investment Canada, the Tories' updated — and decidedly upbeat — version of Trudeau's Foreign Investment Review Agency. Not only was the review considered an effrontery in the forty-second-floor executive suite of Gulf + Western headquarters, but in New York's financial circles the case was also being eyed as a test of just how open Mulroney's regime would, in fact, prove for American business.

For Veliotes, the publishers' offer came as a surprise. "I said, 'I'm not sure I know much about it,'" he recalls. "And they said, 'Yes, you do, because we want someone effective dealing with the international community.'"

N July 6, 1985, Mulroney's communications minister, Marcel Masse, strode out of a cabinet committee meeting in Baie Comeau and straight towards a thicket of waiting microphones. In rushing to announce his new policy on foreign ownership in publishing, former aides confide that — having finally wrestled approval from a cabinet philosophically opposed to exactly the sort of free market curbs he was proposing — Masse was not going to risk giving anyone time for second thoughts. "I was definitely predisposed to a more activist cultural policy," he admits, "so right from the beginning, some people were afraid of me in Ottawa — in cabinet and everywhere."

In a government of messianic free-marketeers who scorned the arts, only a maverick would have dared to unveil a nationalistic publishing policy beneath a citation from French writer Albert Camus: "Without culture, and the relative freedom it presumes, society, even when perfect, is no more than a jungle." A loner even in the Quebec caucus, where he was one of the most influential figures, Masse's role models came not from Washington but from Paris. He had been a student there when France's legendary culture minister André Malraux raised museums and legal battlements to enshrine that country's artistic heritage. For a Quebecker coming of age on the crest of French-Canadian nationalism, Malraux's mission had seemed perfectly logical — as did the denunciations of American cultural imperialism by his successor, Jack Lang.

When Masse arrived in Ottawa in the fall of 1984, he was stunned to discover that — unlike in France or Quebec — there were few federal dikes to fend off the encroaching tides of U.S. mass-market entertainment. "Look at the result," he would rage years later as he prepared to pack up his emptied office on Parliament Hill. "In cultural terms, we are the most colonized country in the West in the last fifty years."

Masse concluded that only drastic action would wipe out what he calls the skeleton in the arts community's closet: after fifteen years of funnelling millions into culture — making Canada second in state support for the arts among twenty-four industrialized nations — the country's artists still claimed a lower share of their own markets than those anywhere else. "That was the secret nobody wanted to talk about," he says. "Even the artists."

But Masse, a former Lavalin marketing executive, had analysed the structural reasons for that failure and made them part of his sales pitch to cabinet. Rather than throw more money at culture, he argued, why not change the rules of the ownership and distribution game, guaranteeing Canadian artists a niche in their own market-place? By giving cultural industries a bigger share of revenue, the government could wean them off the grants that were anathema to die-hard Tory disciples of Reaganomics. But he also had another rationale — one designed to take the wind out of the sails of his fiercest opponent, Finance Minister Michael Wilson. In order to sell the free trade deal to a reluctant public, Masse pointed out, the Conservatives would have to show themselves stout defenders of national sovereignty. What better way to do that than to raise supportive dikes around Canadian culture, which — along with the country's social programs — formed what Masse termed the two "bookends" to keep Mulroney's free trade policy in place?

It was pure chance, Masse says, that, as one of those two bookends, he chose to tackle a publishing policy first. Political urgency forced his hand: on both sides of the border, the industry was awaiting the government's verdict on Gulf + Western's takeover of Prentice Hall Canada. Under what had become known as his Baie Comeau policy, such indirect acquisitions required the new U.S. owner to sell 51 percent of the subsidiary's shares to a Canadian firm within two years — a policy that Masse clearly meant to apply to Prentice Hall. But Gulf + Western's lawyers argued that the rules could not be applied retroactively, and for months the government had dithered over the politically charged decision. Even the cabinet was split on the issue. Still, Masse admits that, in pressing forward with his policy, he had no inkling of the forces he had provoked, above all south of the border. "They didn't mind if I said, 'Give the arts more money,'" he says. "But talking about structure — film policy, publishing policy, the market — that's when I became a dangerous person. That's when I began to have problems."

The first problems came from his own department. As he found his directives countermanded or ignored, he came to suspect his top civil servant, Deputy Minister DeMontigny Marchand, then on loan from External Affairs, of trying to sabotage the guidelines. At a tense staff gathering at Quebec's Château Montebello, he finally confronted Marchand, who protested his innocence. But later that day, Masse announced his replacement by Alain Gourd, a department staffer whose family owned a private Quebec broadcasting network, Radio Nord, and whose cousin had been a Quebec member of parliament for the Liberal party until 1984. As it happened, Gourd was not at the meeting to hear news of his promotion. He was closeted with Sinclair Stevens, the minister in charge of Investment Canada, who had suddenly found himself under siege by Gulf + Western's top guns.

Swooping in on the corporate jet were Donald Oresman, the conglomerate's veteran counsel, and Richard Snyder, the rapier-tongued president of Simon and Schuster, which contributed nearly a quarter of Gulf + Western's $4.2 billion revenues — second only to its Paramount film division. Small-boned and nattily dressed, Snyder was a publishing legend — the executive who had signed up two *Washington Post* reporters, Carl Bernstein and Bob Woodward, for what became their Watergate blockbuster, *All the President's Men*. A man of mercurial moods, Snyder would later be characterized by the *New York Times* as a brilliant dealmaker whose fans praised his toughness and uncanny intuition, but whose enemies bemoaned "the tyrannical and ruthless braggadocio of a man who will not be crossed."

For Stevens, an arch-conservative who considered himself a friend to both business and the United States, Snyder's manner came as a shock. "He was rude, he was belligerent, he was patronizing," Stevens recalls. "He said, in effect, 'The nerve of a pipsqueak politician like you! We bought a conglomerate, and why the government of Canada feels it can intervene to say that a little tentacle hanging in Canada was reviewable — well, we want it understood that we won't have our rights trifled with up here.'"

Stevens tried to explain why Canadian cultural policies were issues of sovereignty, while Investment Canada had just approved an oil company takeover without a moment's hesitation. But he met with threats. Gulf + Western could close down Prentice Hall Canada and simply walk away, Snyder warned. "It struck me," Stevens says, "that they had sent in their heavies to beat me up."

Instead, Snyder's dressing-down had the opposite effect. Masse suddenly found himself with an unlikely ally who began to suspect that bigger issues were at stake than Prentice Hall's $30 million a year in Canadian sales. "The numbers were no big deal," Stevens says. "I was puzzled why, at the State Department level and certainly at that corporate level, there seemed to be almost an obsession with getting their own way." While Snyder had never spelled out fears that the case could set a precedent for other countries — not to mention other Gulf + Western film and cable TV holdings — Stevens finally got the message. But he also got another message as well.

"I came to the conclusion that it's the way Americans market their whole society to the world," he says. "If you control print, video and movies, you in effect get to show the world what good culture is all about: the clothes they want to wear, the food they want to eat. It's a tremendous marketing tool for your whole way of life."

IN the first week of December 1985, a year after he had declared the country open for business, Brian Mulroney chose a curious forum to dismiss concerns that he might sign away Canadian culture as part of the U.S. free trade talks: a speech to Americans — and not merely any Americans, at that. Invited to the University of Chicago as the star of *Time* magazine's Distinguished Speakers series, he directed his remarks to an audience that included not only 1,000 college students but former U.S. ambassador Paul Robinson and the top executives of Time Inc., the media giant that had been waging a war against the Canadian government's cultural policies for a decade. Accorded the pomp and police escort of a U.S. president and introduced with fanfare by *Time*'s editor-in-chief Henry Grunwald, Mulroney made a point of assuring his listeners, including an Ottawa press gallery contingent, that Canada's "unique cultural identity" was "not at issue" in the free trade negotiations. "You will have to understand that what we call cultural sovereignty is as vital to our national life as political sovereignty," he said. "In the United States you cast the net of national security over more areas than we; in Canada, we cast the net of cultural sovereignty more widely than you."

But to many who pondered his text, those reassurances seemed expressly vague — so vague that they figured only as an afterthought in the *Globe and Mail* report of his speech. Most of Mulroney's address had been devoted to promoting the notion of the trade deal itself, complete with reminiscences about his own formative bilateral cultural experience — singing "Dearie" for Chicago's Colonel Robert McCormick for $50, which he termed the first "foreign aid project." Invited by Grunwald to repeat the performance, the prime minister was halfway to the microphone before second thoughts prevailed.

Still, the Canadian cultural community was less than reassured by the fact that Mulroney had chosen to make his point as the guest of a corporation that had an undisputed axe to grind with Ottawa. In 1976, in an attempt to foster an indigenous magazine and broadcast industry, Pierre Trudeau had defied two decades of pressure from *Time* founder Henry Luce and introduced Bill C-58, which denied tax deductions on advertising in non-Canadian periodicals or broadcasting outlets.

As its Ottawa lobbyist, *Time* had already hired Tom d'Aquino, who would later take over the Business Council on National Issues. Warning of the legislation to come, d'Aquino had bounded into Grunwald's office to announce the latest in Canadianspeak: "Henry, I've got news for you," he reported. "You're in the cultural industries business." He loved to recount his client's stupefied response. "I most certainly am NOT!" Grunwald had sputtered. But *Time* was not without other ripostes. In retaliation for the bill, Congress swiftly struck back with its own tax law barring writeoffs for any association that held a conference in Canada — a blow to the tourist industry.

U.S. broadcasters too were irate over a measure that they charged had wiped out $25 million in potential advertising profits on border stations. Championing their cause was Walter Annenberg, the multimillionaire owner of *TV Guide*, who also happened to be one of Ronald Reagan's best friends. So close were they that every New

Year's Eve the Reagans repaired to Annenberg's palatial Palm Springs estate for a weekend with assorted glitterati, including Frank Sinatra. And Annenberg's wife, Leonore, had served as the president's first protocol chief. Not that the media mogul had always been accustomed to such high-toned company. In 1939 he had been indicted by a federal grand jury for tax evasion with his father, Moses, who ran an illegal gambling wire service. In return for getting the charges against his son dropped, Moses Annenberg had pleaded guilty, forking over $9.5 million in back taxes and spending two years in a Pennsylvania penitentiary. It was while his father was in jail that Walter Annenberg had taken over the family business, which included the *Philadelphia Inquirer*, the *Daily Racing Form*, and two skin magazines, one of which had been banned by the Canadian government. Later, he had acquired *TV Guide*, *Seventeen*, and a half-dozen radio and TV stations.

Less than a year after Reagan's arrival in the White House, Annenberg had chosen the pages of *TV Guide* to sound off against what he called "Trudeau's crusade to 'Canadianize' his country's culture and economy at the expense of the United States." In a three-page editorial entitled "Canada's Unfairness Doctrine," he launched a scattershot attack on Bill C-58 and a litany of other Republican pet peeves, from broadcast quotas to the year-old National Energy Policy. In case congressmen missed his thoughts, Annenberg took out a full-page ad in the *Washington Post* to repeat his diatribe, calling for retaliation against specific targets — Canadian banks and cable TV companies, which were then on an expansion spree in the United States.

Within a week, his outburst was echoed by Reagan's U.S. trade representative, Bill Brock, who would soon begin plotting a free trade strategy with d'Aquino and Rowland Frazee, chairman of the Royal Bank — one of the Canadian financial institutions most vulnerable to Annenberg's threats. Brock presented legislation to Congress which was an exact replica of the Canadian measure, forbidding U.S. advertisers from deducting the cost of ads on Canadian TV stations. As that border broadcasting war heated up over the next four years, Brock personally spearheaded the administration's assault, urging a Senate committee to take even more drastic action against Bill C-58 — "a serious abrasion between the two countries . . . We simply can't allow it to fester."

A year later, he applied more muscle — commissioning a report to Congress from the showbiz and media heavyweights who wielded enormous clout in U.S. election campaigns. To orchestrate it, he turned to the leader of the services subcommittee on his private-sector trade advisory group: Jim Robinson, the chairman of American Express, who was no disinterested bystander in the media wars. In 1979 American Express had sunk $175 million into what became known as Warner-Amex Cable, a subsidiary then headed by Drew Lewis and his top aide, Robinson's wife, Linda.

To undertake the two-year study of the communications industry for Brock, Robinson in turn tapped Thomas Wyman, then the chairman of CBS, who could hardly be expected to gaze upon the landscape with neutrality. Nor could the twenty-six multinationals Wyman polled, among them *Time*, *Reader's Digest*, American Express, Warner Communications, the American Association of Advertising Agencies, and the National Association of Broadcasters — in short, a hit parade of those nursing the biggest grudges against the Canadian government.

In September 1984, the month Mulroney came to power, Wyman handed over his report, whose title summed up its wide-ranging gripes: *Trade Barriers to U.S. Motion Picture and Television, Pre-recorded Entertainment, Publishing and Advertising Industries*. In fact, the slim thirty-three-page document was not a study at all, but a survey of those nations and practices that U.S. industry executives deemed the worst stumbling blocks to their global ambitions — with no corroborating evidence required to back up their complaints. In that litany, no nation seemed a more frequent target than Canada, which was pronounced "a particularly troublesome area." The country was accused of hindering American commerce in a dozen different ways, from Bill C-58 and Canadian content regulations on the airwaves to unfair subsidies from agencies like the Canada Council and the CBC, the *bête noir* of U.S. broadcasters.

In retrospect, what seems most remarkable about the report is that, by the end of Mulroney's nine years in power, most of those cultural institutions would find themselves under siege, crippled by constant budget cuts or threatened with legislated oblivion. As Wyman's exercise made clear, the U.S. assault on Canadian cultural policies was no arcane sideshow by the entertainment industry, but a central plotline that galvanized some of the most influential players in the free trade drama, from banks to broadcasters, on both sides of the border.

Before the Shamrock Summit, many of Wyman's grievances were at the top of Reagan's agenda. And with only weeks to go before Air Force One touched down in Quebec City, Henry Grunwald was under the impression that Bill C-58 had a prominent place on the president's cue cards. But despite *Time*'s lavish attention to the festivities — devoting its second Canadian cover to Mulroney in six months — the prime minister's aides had to beg off resolving the magazine's woes. Any solace for *Time* would have devastated the country's private broadcasters, including Mulroney's most generous financial supporters, the Bassetts, and their backers the Eatons, of CTV's Toronto flagship Baton Broadcasting. "It took a real scramble to get that off the rails," recalls one bemused ministerial aide. "Essentially, Mulroney's cronies outweighed Reagan's."

Still, as the prime minister was to discover, no one waxed more emotional on the subject of Canadian cultural policy than the president. "It's the only thing the Old Man really cares about," one White House domestic policy adviser confided. "You'll think he's dozing through a cabinet meeting and suddenly he'll sit up and deliver a lecture on how the Canadians are trying to screw up the film business." For Reagan, it was not simply a question of an ex-actor's nostalgia. In much the same way that Brian Mulroney was the candidate from Big Steel, Ronald Reagan was the candidate from Hollywood Inc., handpicked by his studio bosses to head the Screen Actors Guild, then groomed for a political career, first as governor of California, then finally as commander-in-chief. Indeed, no one had been more responsible for his astonishing ascension to power than the trio of men who had built the forbidding smoked-glass highrise on the fringes of Los Angeles known as the Black Tower — the headquarters of MCA Inc.

Founded in Chicago in 1924, the Music Corporation of America was the brainchild of Jules Stein, an ophthamologist who spied headier profits in booking bands for the South Side nightclubs controlled by Al Capone and other mobsters. Having signed up most of the stars of the jazz age from Benny Goodman to Tommy Dorsey, Stein set his sights on the idols of the silver screen. In 1937 he sent two of his lieutenants, Taft Schreiber and a former casino publicist named Lew Wasserman, to Hollywood, where they built MCA into the biggest movie agency. By 1946 the corporation had such a stranglehold on film talent that a federal anti-trust judge investigating its practices dubbed MCA "the Octopus."

By the early 1950s its tentacles even reached onto the sound-stages of the budding television industry. MCA itself began churning out a series of hits, among them *Ozzie and Harriet*, *Dragnet*, and *Alfred Hitchcock Presents*, even though those productions violated a longstanding agreement with the powerful Screen Actors Guild prohibiting agencies from production. Pressure built on MCA to choose between its two ventures. Then, suddenly, in 1952 the pressure disappeared. That year, Reagan, an MCA client who had become guild president, granted the company a blanket waiver — a waiver that would prove unique; no other talent agency would ever succeed in winning similar dispensation. But it helped turn MCA into Hollywood's leading production house, giving it the wherewithal later to buy up faltering Decca Records, the parent of Universal Pictures, at firesale prices. A year after winning the exemption, in what critics charged was a *quid pro quo* — although another justice department investigation failed to prove it — MCA launched a new weekly TV series, *General Electric Theatre*, whose host and program supervisor was Ronald Reagan.

The actor whose movie career had so recently appeared to be in a slump was suddenly being groomed for greater things. As GE's public spokesman, Reagan toured the country delivering what became known as The Speech, a patriotic anti-communist crowd-pleaser that won him the affections of the ultra-conservative California tycoons who became known as his Kitchen Cabinet. Handpicking him as their standard-bearer for governor in 1966, they teamed up with Jules Stein to mastermind his victory. MCA's Taft Schreiber became Reagan's campaign manager, having already arranged a financial cushion for his political bid: along with Reagan's lawyer, William French Smith, he had negotiated the sale of the actor's Malibu ranchland to Twentieth Century Fox — the foundation for the president's later wealth.

Once in the governor's mansion, Reagan did not forget his bene-factors. He promptly pushed legislation through that gave the studios huge tax breaks on their film libraries. The measure proved a particular boon to MCA, which had not only acquired Universal's archives but had just paid $10 million cash for Paramount's pre-1948 prints, including Bob Hope and Bing Crosby's road movies.

Meanwhile, the same year that Reagan arrived in the statehouse, Lew Wasserman, his former agent and Stein's heir apparent, had also taken on a more prominent political role. Assuming the chairmanship of the Association of Motion Picture and Television Producers, he set up a new Washington office to lobby for the studios' interests. To head it, Wasserman chose the Texan who had become his key contact in the White House, a peppery sometime LBJ speechwriter and backroom player named Jack Valenti. Often accused of catering to MCA's interests before those of other studios, Valenti would spend the next three decades known among film cognoscenti as Lew's man. As former Canadian movie-house mogul Garth Drabinsky, a onetime MCA partner, confirmed, "I don't think Valenti's closer to anyone than Wasserman."

MCA's sudden interest in politics appeared to coincide with its fear of further federal anti-trust suits, not party loyalty. As the corporation steadily extended its reach, Wasserman cultivated Lyndon Johnson and the Democrats while Stein and Schreiber toiled in the Republican vineyards. But with Stein's death a few months after Reagan won the White House in 1981, Wasserman effortlessly crossed those party lines, once again offering a guiding hand to his former client's career.

No sooner had Reagan arrived in the Oval Office than he launched a series of measures that did not fail to delight the Black Tower — effectively deregulating the entertainment industry, stripping the Federal Communications Commission of much of its authority, and eviscerating the Justice Department's anti-trust division. Ironically, in 1983 that deregulation mania produced an unanticipated result, threatening to hand over the studios' traditional syndication royalties to the TV networks. But neoconservative ideology proved no match for old ties. Soon after Lew Wasserman stepped into the breach, Reagan overruled his own administration's free market fervour.

That incident helped burnish the legend of the man already so feared that *Vanity Fair* would dub him "Hollywood's Godfather." Not only did Wasserman enjoy an open line to the Oval Office, but he schmoozed regularly with such Capitol Hill barons as the Senate Finance Committee's chairman, Lloyd Bentsen, and California's junior Republican senator (later governor) Pete Wilson, a vociferous opponent of Canadian cultural policies. No one else in Hollywood could raise as much money for the perpetually yawning campaign coffers of congressmen, who scrambled to take his calls. And on MCA's board, Wasserman was careful to place both a respected Republican, former Tennessee senator Howard Baker, who would later become Reagan's chief of staff, and ex-Democratic National

Committee chairman Robert Strauss, the party's garrulous back-stage fixer.

But nothing so neatly summed up his position as the Ronald Reagan Presidential Library — Wasserman's pet project high in the hills north of the American dream factory. There, inside the Spanish-tiled museum for which he had raised millions, display after display, including most of Reagan's movie-era stills and an introductory film biography, carried the copyright not of Reagan but of Lew Wasserman.

Certainly, when Thomas Wyman set out on his review of foreign trade barriers to the entertainment industry, it was no accident that he chose to consult MCA. Like Gulf + Western, the onetime Octopus had evolved into a $2-billion-a-year leviathan whose movies and TV series had helped gild Wasserman with a Midas myth, from Steven Spielberg's *E.T.* to *Miami Vice* and *Murder, She Wrote*. Through its recording arm, the company not only had distribution rights for Berry Gordy's Motown label but also a multimillion-dollar concert business that would later team up with Molson's to become the largest rock promoter in Canada, complete with its own amphitheatre at Ontario Place. In addition to its theme parks and Universal's blockbuster studio tour, MCA had extended its reach into publishing, snatching up G. B. Putnam and Berkeley Books.

By 1985, those holdings gave Wasserman more than a passing interest when Gulf + Western ran up against the Canadian government's publishing policy. While the two corporations might be rivals in many fields, Wasserman and Charles Bludhorn, Gulf + Western's founder, had become partners in both the USA Network, a pay-TV cable channel, and Cinema International Corporation, a joint overseas distribution arm that reaped enormous profits from the sale of their films abroad. But perhaps the most eloquent testimony to their convergent corporate interests lay in another pooling of resources: as its Washington lawyer-lobbyist on the Prentice Hall case, Gulf + Western chose none other than Lew Wasserman's close friend — and MCA's director — Robert Strauss.

ON August 6, 1985, barely a month after Marcel Masse unveiled his Baie Comeau policy, Ambassador Allan Gotlieb wrote Sinclair Stevens a four-page letter on the subject of Prentice Hall Canada. In it, he so forcefully argued Gulf + Western's case that some infuriated Canadian officials later leaked the confidential missive to the press. Masse himself was apoplectic. As one of the minister's former aides recalls, "Masse felt Gotlieb had forgotten who he was working for."

Pointing out that the embassy was "in the midst of developing a major campaign in the United States to convince the investment community that Canada is an attractive destination for U.S. investment," the ambassador bemoaned the fact that the Baie Comeau policy "could not have come at a more unfortunate time" and was "likely to damage that initiative." Nothing less than the credibility of Mulroney's government hung on the decision, he warned. "The message is clear: the weight of at least some parts of the media will be directed at discrediting the Government position that foreign investment is welcome in Canada." But Gotlieb's most compelling argument was the threat that he passed on from his friend Robert Strauss: unless Gulf + Western got its way with Prentice Hall, Strauss had warned, it would adopt a "scorched earth response." Just in case Stevens missed the point, Gotlieb noted that, "While hyperbole is to be expected in this town, there is no more astute observer here than Bob Strauss." What the letter neglected to mention was that Strauss was now Gulf + Western's hired gun.

While neither Strauss nor Gotlieb had spelled out just what form that scorched earth riposte might take, Masse alleges that he may have had a taste of the flames. A month later, he received a panicked call from his Quebec riding secretary to say that RCMP officers had shown up with a warrant to search his campaign records. As allegations of fundraising irregularities were leaked to the press, Masse went to Mulroney and resigned his portfolio until his name was cleared. "I said, 'If it's like that,'" Masse recalls pointedly, "'I won't sit in cabinet with a knife in my back.'"

Was he suggesting that the abortive investigation of his campaign finances which sidelined him for three months that fall was linked to his Baie Comeau initiative? Masse shrugs. That same month, he points out, a reporter from Newfoundland at the *Globe and Mail* received a tip from a longtime source to look into Sinclair Stevens's financial affairs — a tip that would eventually lead to a conflict of interest scandal and force Stevens from office eight months later. "You can draw your own conclusion," Masse says. "Sinc Stevens's problems started a few weeks after mine."

By the time Masse returned to his Communications ministry

three months later, he had, as one former aide put it, "lost that fight. While he was out of cabinet, the rhetoric had been cranked up. They went around behind his back." By then Gulf + Western had also hired former Newfoundland premier Frank Moores, who had meta-morphosed into Ottawa's best-connected lobbyist.

At the same time, Mulroney heard from another of his key fundraisers who was pleading Gulf + Western's cause. John Tory Sr., president of Thomson Corp. Ltd., owners of the *Globe and Mail* and a vast continental media empire, wrote to the Prime Minister's Office pointing out that any scorched earth response might well singe his company. In a letter and in meetings with Charley McMillan, Tory cautioned that a "poorly thought out, counterproductive and discriminatory" decision against Gulf + Western "could lead to retal-iation against Canadian owners of U.S. publishing businesses."

As it turned out, Tory had good reason to be nervous. On Capitol Hill, where Paramount Pictures had funnelled at least $165,000 to campaign coffers over the previous three years, the corporation's pleas had also moved a congressman and two influential senators to write to Mulroney with personal appeals. Gulf + Western chairman Martin Davis, who had taken over after Bludhorn's death, had writ-ten to Secretary of State George Shultz, Commerce Secretary Malcolm Baldrige, and U.S. Trade Representative Clayton Yeutter demanding their intervention in his case. And only a month before Tory's worried plea to the prime minister, Shultz had pressed the matter at his regular quarterly meeting with Joe Clark in Washington. During that session, the State Department had released

a list of fifty American publishing firms that Canadians had bought over the previous decade — thirty-three of them newspapers acquired by Thomson Corp., making it the largest foreign publisher in the United States. Those purchases had also helped contribute to a balance sheet which, by 1992, drew 59 percent of its $5 billion revenues from south of the border. That fact had clearly not escaped the notice of Gulf + Western officials, who, according to a Shultz aide, had considerately provided the State Department with the Canadian acquisitions list.

But Tory had even more solid reasons for believing these were no idle threats. While most Canadians thought of the Thomson empire in terms of smalltown newspapers whose managers tended to count paperclips and break out in hives at the thought of unions, Thomson Information Publishing Group, a division headquartered in Stamford,

Connecticut, also ranked as one of the largest U.S. book publishers. Its titles, from *Jane's International Defense Review* and *Accounting Principles* to *The Physicians' Desk Reference*, might not be household words or rate a place on the bestseller lists. But with $880 million in sales in 1985, the company commanded sufficient sway to rate a perennial seat on the board of the Association of American Publishers — the Washington lobby that would soon hire Nicholas Veliotes.

In the fall of 1985, Thomson's representative on the AAP board, James Lisy, had a ringside seat as the association plotted its strategies to battle Masse's Baie Comeau policy. The campaign was being orchestrated by Lawrence Levinson of Gulf + Western, but he had no trouble finding allies on the board with their own complaints against Ottawa, including the representatives from the book divisions of *Time* and *Reader's Digest*. If John Tory was alerting Mulroney to a possible congressional backlash against Canadian interests in the United States, he had an insider's knowledge of the plot. Once again, it appeared to be payback time, as talk of retaliatory legislation hung in the air.

By February 1986 U.S. pressures had escalated to such a point that Michael Wilson accused Marcel Masse of sabotaging the upcoming free trade talks. To make matters worse, just when the minister of communications was scheduled to meet with Gulf + Western's Donald Oresman in Toronto, he found himself stranded in one of the worst blizzards of the winter. Finally, weeks later, over a teleconference call from Stevens's Ottawa office, with Wilson sitting vigilantly on the sidelines, Masse wound up the government's deal with Gulf + Western. On March 12, 1986, just six days before Mulroney was due in Washington for a summit with Reagan, a chastened Marcel Masse and Sinclair Stevens took their seats before a bank of Ottawa TV cameras and declared that Investment Canada had approved the takeover of Prentice Hall, making Gulf + Western the biggest presence in Canadian publishing.

"It wasn't a defeat," insists one of Masse's top aides, a career civil servant who did not share his minister's cultural zeal. "It was a compromise. We knew what the traffic would bear. If we had applied the Baie Comeau policy retroactively, it would have poisoned the air."

IN the summer of 1985 — the summer that Allan Gotlieb had dispatched his scorched earth warning on the Prentice Hall case — Jeremy Kinsman was seconded to Ottawa from his post as the ambassador's longtime protégé and lieutenant. In Washington he had cultivated the Democrats and liberal media while Gotlieb worked the Republican administration. But suddenly Kinsman found himself rerouted from a coveted arms control portfolio at External Affairs and sponsored by Gotlieb for another job considered equally crucial to national security: assistant deputy minister in the Department of Communications, where he became the point man on the controversial cultural brief as the free trade negotiations were getting underway. In that assignment, the dashing and Byronic diplomat would once again prove adept at wooing the media and the cultural community — a constituency that was leading the fight against free trade.

If Ottawa had felt obliged to let Gulf + Western have its way with Prentice Hall, Kinsman argued, it had struck a blow for cultural nationalism and the Baie Comeau policy on a second front: overshadowed in all the uproar was the fact that, in approving the conglomerate's takeover of another Toronto textbook publisher, Ginn Canada, the government had obtained a promise that within two years Gulf + Western would sell 51 percent of its shares to a Canadian firm. Kinsman had portrayed the deal as a brilliant commercial coup — the repatriation of a leading educational publisher. "Ginn — that was the one we wanted," he crowed triumphantly. "That was the key company."

But nearly a decade later, the Ginn case would still be sending shockwaves through the country's political and cultural communities — an object lesson in disastrous deal-making, riddled with secret subtexts and sabotaged with covert oral side agreements. As one publishing analyst had warned *Maclean's* at the time, Ottawa had absolutely no legal means of enforcing Gulf + Western's obligation to sell majority control of Ginn. In the conglomerate's $2 billion empire, which included Madison Square Garden and the New York Rangers and Knicks, that obligation amounted to scarcely a hiccup, but an irksome hiccup all the same. It swiftly became clear that the company had no intention of complying. Two Canadian publishers made overtures to buy the Ginn shares supposedly up for grabs, but both Malcom Lester and Robert Fitzhenry found themselves rebuffed. As a secret government briefing memo would later note, in a model of understatement, "There was some doubt about Gulf + Western's good faith in pursuing its commitment to divest control." In March 1988, when the two-year deadline was up, the conglomerate informed the government that, having received no acceptable offers, it had carried out its part of the deal; Gulf + Western intended to hold on to its full 100 percent interest in Ginn.

Lest there be any objections, a new wrinkle had crept into the transaction. Nicholas Veliotes had managed to arrange for the insertion of a virtually unnoticed clause in the free trade agreement — one that seemed designed to anticipate the Ginn case. According to that provision, if Ottawa required the forced divestiture of a U.S. business in the cultural sector as part of an indirect takeover, the government itself would have to offer to buy out the American owner "at fair open market value." Veliotes boasted that he had called the government's bluff: if Ottawa insisted on making American corporations sell their holdings, then it would have to take the rap for what he liked to brand expropriation. "That was the sop put in there for the intellectual property community," he exults, using the lofty term he favours for the U.S. communications industry. "It put the Canadian government in the loop of buying that property and then peddling it. It ruined perfectly good Canadian companies."

Accordingly, on March 11, 1988, Robert de Cotret, by then in charge of the Canada Development Investment Corporation, the crown corporation charged with handling the Conservatives' privatization drive, announced that the CDIC had offered to buy the controlling interest in Ginn from Gulf + Western. The price at the time was estimated at $6 million, less than two-thirds of what the government would ultimately pay. But oddly, as a secret briefing memo would later point out, the CDIC's board — then chaired by longtime Ontario Tory Darcy McKeough — decided that the terms of the agreement were not "commercially sound." In fact, the negotiations would drag on for more than another year before the deal was finally sewn up — a year during which Mulroney was fighting for his political survival in a tense re-election campaign centred entirely on the free trade pact. It was a year when any hint of cultural concessions on the Conservatives' part would have spelled political suicide. But as soon as the campaign was over, Mulroney named his close friend, Montreal lawyer David Angus, the Tories' chief bagman, to the CDIC board.

From the first of its prolonged negotiations with the CDIC, Gulf + Western had insisted on including a curious clause in the sale agreement: should the government's Baie Comeau policy change to eliminate the forced divestiture provision — and should Ginn still be in the CDIC's hands — Gulf + Western would automatically have the right to buy back the company for the same price it had received. According to the briefing memo, the government had initially rejected the clause. But Gulf + Western had continued to raise the proviso and had even written it into draft versions of the contract. At the end of the year, it was still the subject of heated debate. In a December 29, 1988, memo to his acting communications minister, Jeremy Kinsman noted that "Everyone agrees now that buy-back provision is not on . . . The political arguments you advance . . . rule out any such trade-off."

But suddenly, a week later, with the free trade agreement finally in effect on January 1, Oresman flew to Ottawa to announce that the only stumbling block left to closing the Ginn sale was the buy-back provision. Astonishingly, this time around, the government gave him the nod. The contentious issue reportedly never went before cabinet, but de Cotret promptly okayed it. Apparently on the strength of that political approval, Paul Labbé, the head of Investment Canada, called Oresman in New York to announce that their deal was on. According to the government's secret briefing memo, there was only one stipulation: "It was further agreed that this right would not form part of the purchase and sale contract between CDIC and Paramount." In other words, there was to be nothing in writing.

The deal would drag on for months. In February 1989, when George Bush made his first whirlwind trip to Ottawa as president, promising action on acid rain, his briefing notes show that his secretary of state, James Baker, suggested, "We should see if we can get something for it." Whether the two issues were linked remains unclear. But Bush had more than the usual reasons for taking an interest in Gulf + Western's woes. Among its directors was one of his closest friends, his former Texas business partner J. Hugh Liedtke, the chairman of Pennzoil, who had just helped orchestrate Bush's inaugural gala only weeks earlier.

Three months later, the government announced that the CDIC had purchased Ginn along with another small textbook publisher called GLC. But it took another four months before the final price was nailed down. At one point that spring, Labbé had even ended up in an epistolary slanging match with Oresman, complaining about Gulf + Western's "excessive" foot-dragging on the sale. Finally, in September 1989, they agreed on a pricetag for Ginn, but it would be another full year before they settled their squabble over the worth of GLC — eventually obliging Gulf + Western to refund $100,000 in overpayments to the Canadian government. By then, the combined bill for the two firms had soared to $10.3 million. And under the extraordinary terms of the deal, Mulroney's government had some-how managed to pay that inflated price for 51 percent of Ginn without acquiring effective control of the company. Gulf + Western retained veto power over every major decision — including the sale of the CDIC's share to a new Canadian partner.

In announcing the terms, Mulroney's minister of privatizations, John McDermid, waved off objections, declaring that the govern-ment had no intention of staying in the publishing business for long. But it soon became apparent that Gulf + Western was in no hurry to wrap up the arrangement. The final closing required the CDIC to resolve some outstanding details — among them the renegotiation of distribution rights for Ginn's titles with Gulf + Western's other publishing subsidiaries. But the New York office managed to drag out that apparently simple process for another three years. According to the government's secret briefing memo, in April 1992 the CDIC had sent an executed agreement to Gulf + Western to finalize the sale, only to find it was never returned. "This distribu-torship agreement needed to be settled before CDIC could market the Ginn business," the memo explained. "It remained the major unresolved issue that continued throughout the period of time that CDIC held its interest in Ginn."

That unfinished business provided a convenient hurdle whenever a Canadian company expressed interest in buying the government's shares of Ginn. During those three years, twenty-five Canadians tried to bid on that controlling interest — some, like Ron Besse of Canada Publishing, Avie Bennett of McClelland & Stewart, and Anna Porter of Key Porter Books, with more sincerity than others. But according to the briefing memo, the "CDIC responded to inquiries by indicating that it was not in a position to market the interest until all of the commercial issues with Gulf + Western had been resolved." Clearly, it was a case of contractual Catch-22: the government could not sell its share until the details were ironed out, but as long as those details remained outstanding, the CDIC was obliged to hold on to control of Ginn. And that, after all, was one of the necessary conditions for Donald Oresman's verbal buy-back provision to kick in.

Another condition would arrive in January 1992 when Perrin Beatty, Mulroney's newly appointed communications minister, suddenly announced an updated publishing policy — eliminating Baie Comeau's forced divestiture rules. In December 1991 — a full month before Beatty unveiled his new policy — Oresman wrote to the CDIC's new president, Ward Pitfield, reminding him that Ginn's unwritten buy-back agreement would be triggered if the government changed its publishing guidelines. Since the cabinet had approved Beatty's proposal only days before, his timing seemed more than fortuitous. Clearly, somebody within Ottawa's inner circles had been whispering in Oresman's ear at Gulf + Western, by then known as Paramount Communications Inc.

Still, even after Beatty's announcement, which provoked only mild protests from the battered Canadian publishing industry, both sides waited for a decent interval before activating their secret understanding. In May 1992 the Finance Department asked for a legal opinion from a Justice Department lawyer named Mark Jewett, who assured the government that verbal agreements such as Paramount's were enforceable. Jewett went so far as to warn that if the CDIC offered its shares to anyone else, the government could be leaving itself open to a lawsuit. Other legal experts have since disagreed with that verdict, but the CDIC appeared content to bow to his judgment. In November 1992 Ward Pitfield quietly opened negotiations to sell Ginn back to Paramount for $10.3 million — the same amount that the government had paid three years earlier.

In return, Beatty demanded some gesture of consolation — "performance undertakings" to promote Canadian authors and books, which his officials negotiated with Paramount's Canadian managers. But according to the briefing memo, "These were rejected by Paramount's headquarters in New York." In the end, the government settled for crumbs — a series of undertakings that were "not considered entirely satisfactory," but deemed "likely the best set possible under the circumstances." Given those remarkable efforts not to whip up a fuss with either Paramount or the White House by defending the country's interests, one publishing industry assessment of the deal could only conclude that there had been "a quiet understanding from the outset." In other words, the fix had been in all along.

If so, the only thing it had required was patience. And Donald Oresman, Paramount's veteran strategist, was no stranger to that quality. It was the art of the deal that had always fascinated him, he claimed, as much as the outcome itself. After all, Oresman was a devoted birdwatcher who kept a pair of binoculars handy in his corner aerie high above New York's Central Park. There, occasionally, his patience was rewarded when a peregrine falcon swooped by his forty-second-storey windows, pouncing on lesser prey.

AT a 1986 Washington dinner party thrown by Richard Rivers, a partner in Robert Strauss's law firm who specialized in Canadian trade woes, one guest was recounting a recent ordeal at the Canadian ambassador's residence. That guest was Deirdre Murphy, whose husband, Peter, was then the chief U.S. free trade negotiator. To an attentive cluster of Canadians and Americans, she related how Allan Gotlieb and his wife had invited some of the capital's movers and shakers to dinner and a gala screening of Denys Arcand's *The Decline of the American Empire*, which had just been hailed as the toast of the Cannes Film Festival. But as the sexual romp had unrolled on the screen, Deirdre Murphy had recoiled in horror. Glancing around the screening room at such older officials as Federal Reserve chairman Paul Volcker and his wife, she was astonished that the Gotliebs would subject them to such fare. "I mean," she sputtered, "it was just soft porn!"

If misperceptions haunted the free trade negotiations, none were to prove quite as glaring as those around the issue that Canadians liked to call culture and Americans referred to as the entertainment industry. Mulroney and his officials repeatedly insisted that culture was not on the table. But on the opening day of the talks in Ottawa, when Peter Murphy strode by a media stakeout and declared that everything was on the table, he knew he was pressing a hot button that would come in handy throughout the negotiations. "It became such an issue for Canadians, I thought: Why should we just throw it away?" he said later. Besides, he and his deputy, Bill Merkin, were feeling the heat from Jack Valenti. "He was," said Murphy, "always on our back."

In the fall of 1985, when reports began filtering out of Ottawa that Marcel Masse was following up his publishing policy with a task force on the Canadian film industry, Valenti had gone ballistic. For the studios, any legislation represented a high-stakes threat — a precedent that risked spreading to other, more populous movie-going nations in Europe or Asia. "The contagion effect," Valenti had dubbed it. But no measure posed a greater peril to box-office health than the reforms that Masse was contemplating to give Canadians a greater share of the distribution action. At his Washington offices, where each of the six major movie-makers contributed an estimated $5 million a year to watch over their global interests, Valenti shot into action.

For decades, Hollywood had been fighting off Canadian attempts to foster a national film industry with an assortment of legislative remedies. As early as 1920, the prospect of being frozen out of the country had provoked Paramount's legendary chief, Adolf Zukor, to forge a partnership with a Toronto cinema owner named Nathan Nathanson to set up a string of local movie houses. To this day, their venture, Famous Players, remains the country's largest theatre chain — still a wholly owned subsidiary of Paramount Pictures. Later, Trudeau had attempted to tackle a national film policy, complete with screen quotas for Canadian movies. He went so far as to send a delegation across the country to promote it among the provinces. But in 1971 one of his ministers returned from meetings with the U.S. studios and helped squelch the measure: Jean Chrétien, then president of the Treasury Board, reported that Washington was rattling the sabres of retaliation.

More than a decade later, Trudeau's communications minister, Francis Fox, made another stab at the problem. In a comprehensive task force report, which became known as his Red Book, Fox called for a new round of measures to nurture an indigenous film industry. Waylaid by a personal scandal, Fox never got to implement his report, but in 1984 Masse inherited the Red Book and seized on it as a model. Still, the movie business would prove so complex that the free trade negotiations were already underway before the minister and his aides had worked out a distribution formula for their new film policy. Then suddenly, in late 1986, before Masse's bill could take shape, he was transferred out of the portfolio.

Flora MacDonald, his successor, vowed her determination to follow up on the film legislation, and the cultural community had no reason to doubt her claim. A longtime Red Tory, MacDonald had already won her stripes as a cultural nationalist, breaking ranks with the party in 1976 to support Bill C-58. On Valentine's Day in February 1987, as the free trade talks became increasingly stalemated, she invited a select gathering of Canadian film-makers to the ballroom of Toronto's Sutton Place Hotel: with Jeremy Kinsman at her side, she announced a new film bill that would establish a licensing system for distributors "within weeks."

Under its terms, the major U.S. studios would only be able to distribute in Canada those movies which they had produced or financed, or for which they had won worldwide rights. For the rest, largely independent or foreign productions like Australia's blockbuster *Crocodile Dundee*, distribution rights would finally be opened up to bidding by Canadian companies. In the packed hotel ballroom, the crowd went wild, erupting in rapturous applause, hoots ricocheting under the chandeliers. Jaded movie-makers leaped to their feet in a standing ovation, and Toronto producer Danny Weinzweig, who had worked with Kinsman on the proposal, had tears in his eyes. For Weinzweig, who had started in the film business at sixteen, it was the realization of a lifelong dream.

Amid the euphoria, one film executive had refused to rise from his seat, and not merely because of his unwieldy girth: Harold Greenberg, the streetwise chairman of Montreal's Astral Inc., sat at MacDonald's table, refusing to join the hurrahs. Once known as the chief booster of a national film industry, Greenberg had financed some of the country's best homegrown productions, including the movie version of Mordecai Richler's bestseller, *The Apprenticeship of Duddy Kravitz*. But since 1983, Astral had become the biggest wholesaler of U.S. home videos in Canada. And its bread and butter came chiefly from distributing such American series as *L.A. Law* to Canadian cable and pay-TV channels, including its own First Choice (later renamed the Movie Network). That joint venture with Twentieth Century Fox and Columbia Pictures Television was worth millions to the Montreal firm that Greenberg had built from a string of photo labs. If his heart lay in the cultural nationalist camp, Harold Greenberg's bottom line was totally dependent on Hollywood. "I listen to this and I think it's utopia," he said, recalling MacDonald's film policy. "But it'll never work. The Americans can never live with it."

Over the next decade, Greenberg would straddle those conflicting loyalties, frequently pegged to argue Canada's case against Valenti in public debates, yet privately carrying the studios' colours in Ottawa. During one 1992 faceoff at the National Association of Television Programming Executives in New Orleans, he would laboriously try to explain why culture was important to Canadians, while Valenti retorted to delighted applause, "I didn't realize that Astral was a cultural corporation, Harold; I always thought it was a commercial operation."

At the time of MacDonald's announcement, Mulroney had already appointed Greenberg to the government's private sector trade advisory group — one of a handful of CEOs from Canadian cultural industries who, without exception, boasted publishing or broadcast interests in the United States and favoured a continental free trade pact. His support for free trade was hardly a surprise: Greenberg's partners in Astral were the Edper/Brascan/Hees group, whose chief overseer at Brascan, Trevor Eyton, an Astral director, was leading the business advisory team cheering on the trade negotiations.

But as Greenberg had predicted, Flora MacDonald's film policy failed to materialize within weeks. Jeremy Kinsman, who had become MacDonald's closest confidant and aide, decided to learn from what he saw as Marcel Masse's missteps with the Baie Comeau policy: he made a pilgrimage to Los Angeles in an attempt to explain the government's motives behind the film bill and to allay the studios' fears. For Kinsman, it was an illuminating experience — and one that left him shaken. "Valenti had provided his members with a lot of anti-Canadian material — clips and speeches," Greenberg said. "He told them what was happening in Canada was really anti-Americanism and it would be detrimental to the studios."

At the Walt Disney Company, then president Frank Wells did not even deign to receive Kinsman in his office. Instead, they met in the cafeteria, where he flipped his chair around at the table, straddling it as if he might take flight momentarily. "I shouldn't even be meeting with you guys considering what you're trying to do to us up there," he announced as his opening salvo. As another participant recalls, "He was thoroughly pissed and he let us know that right off the top. It was a very hard-nosed session — no frills and no niceties."

At Fox, Greenberg's chief U.S. partner, Kinsman made the Canadian case to a senior vice president of marketing, who remained equally unmoved. Ironically, his warmest reception came from

Paramount, where then studio chief Frank Mancuso invited Kinsman to lunch in his executive dining room. A native of Buffalo, Mancuso had once worked in Paramount's Toronto office and showed more understanding of Ottawa's plight. But he, too, made clear his vehement opposition to any Canadian film bill. "They agreed that a country has to define itself to itself — that Mickey Mouse and Clint Eastwood just don't do it for a country like us," Kinsman recalls. "They were fascinated by it and they had a lot of sympathy for us, but our solutions hurt them."

Kinsman never did call on Lew Wasserman — an omission that was no oversight. For months, the government had been negotiating with the man considered the most powerful in Hollywood through his Canadian lieutenant, Garth Drabinsky. In early 1986, as the free trade negotiations were just getting underway, MCA had acquired an initial 30 percent share — later increased to 49 percent — of Drabinsky's Cineplex-Odeon theatre chain. That $159 million investment not only had given the Black Tower a guaranteed outlet for Universal releases, but overnight had turned MCA into a major player in the U.S. movie exhibition business from which the studios had long been barred by Washington's anti-trust legislation. Under Reagan's laissez-faire regime, some corporations were gingerly testing those restrictions by acquiring cinemas. But by buying into Cineplex, MCA had taken a safer and typically more circuitous route — one less likely to provoke congressional regulatory hawks. With Drabinsky as its flamboyant front man, MCA helped finance Cineplex's dizzying expansion drive across the United States, devouring circuits from Maryland to California to become the continent's second-largest movie chain.

Refurbishing cavernous and decrepit old movie houses into multiplexes with plush marble foyers and trendy capuccino bars, Drabinsky is credited with helping to save the film business from the onslaught of the home video with both panache and a canny gift for self-promotion. Canadian journalists loved to chronicle how he opened each new theatre with a star-studded gala reminiscent of a Hollywood première. But if the Toronto press accorded him the lion's share of the publicity, the *Financial Post*'s Rod McQueen turned up at one U.S. ribbon-cutting only to discover Drabinsky playing a minor supporting role to the real star of the show: his mentor, MCA president Sid Sheinberg, who was Wasserman's second-in-command. Still, so firmly ensconced in MCA's affections did Drabinsky seem at the time that Kinsman had no compunction about using him as a conduit to Hollywood's most influential studio.

There was only one problem with that calculation. As Drabinsky admits, he was never in favour of Masse's film policy. Like Greenberg, the Cineplex supremo was straddling both sides of the fence: playing token Canadian in Hollywood, while representing his U.S. partners' interests north of the border. As a theatre owner and sometime film producer, he argued for tax incentives to stimulate Canadian productions, not screen quotas or distribution arrangements that would put a dent in his — and MCA's — profits. "I thought we should be shoring up the Canadian companies' balance sheets at the beginning of the process," he says. "After the fact was absurd when the U.S. guys were putting up all the money and doing all the advertising and taking all the risks. To come in then and say, 'We want a piece of the action,' was nonsense."

The uneasiness of Drabinsky's position became clear during the free trade talks when both sides leaned on him to work out a deal. On one hand, he had Valenti calling him "all the time — and I mean all the time. He was paid a lot to care." On the other, Drabinsky found himself on the line with Simon Reisman, the chief Canadian negotiator, who was making an even more extraordinary plea — asking him to help rein in not only Jack Valenti but the cultural nationalists at the Department of Communications whose film policy was threatening to sink the trade deal. "Simon Reisman called me because he was frustrated," Drabinsky acknowledges. "He was very supportive of my position and wanted my support in Ottawa."

Reisman's deputy, Gordon Ritchie, says that his boss was never in favour of the cultural exemption in the trade talks — indeed, that the two of them were frequently at loggerheads over the issue. Only Mulroney's need to sell the pact to the public by appearing to protect Canadian culture kept the exemption in play. In his numerous talks with the prime minister on the subject, Drabinsky never got the impression that Mulroney had any interest other than that political calculation. "I don't think Brian was a big cultural nationalist at all," he says.

In Los Angeles, where the consulate had organized a day-long seminar on free trade, Drabinsky agreed to explain the Canadian position to the Canadian-California Chamber of Commerce. But in his rambling discourse, he dismissed "some rather extreme Canadian demands," damning them as propaganda organized by a vocal

few, while offering a novel rationale for Washington's indul
not scuttling the trade agreement. "If for sentimental
Canada has to be downright pampered in this area," he argued, "the
price would be miniscule when compared to everything at stake."
Still, nowhere in his eleven-page text did he once endorse Ottawa's
film policy.

On the American negotiating team, Peter Murphy also had hopes
that Drabinsky could break the cultural impasse in Washington's
favour. Word came down from the White House that Reagan's pal
Lew Wasserman was trying to prevail on his Cineplex partner to
wrest a compromise from Ottawa on its contentious film policy —
a development that Drabinsky insists he cannot recall. "Lew tried
to lean on him," insisted Murphy. "He was supposed to be the guy
who could find a deal for us. But Lew couldn't control him." Soon
afterward, in fact, tensions began developing between Drabinsky
and MCA which eventually led to his humiliating ouster from his
own company.

But long before that, Wasserman had another intercessor on hand
to take up the studios' cause. In April 1987 Ronald Reagan arrived
in Ottawa for his annual spring summit with the man he liked to
call "North America's other Irishman." With his TelePrompTer set
up beneath the august carved oak of the Commons Chamber, Reagan
delivered a parliamentary discourse on free trade and acid rain. But
behind closed doors, the subject at the top of his agenda was outrage
over the planned Canadian film policy. According to one former top
ministerial official, "To Mulroney's credit, he defended it."

As Marcel Masse had already discovered, Mulroney shared at
least one characteristic with Reagan: a minister could often win his
sympathy with a catchy phrase or anecdote. When Masse told
Mulroney that Canadian films had only 3 percent of the country's
screen time, the prime minister had been fascinated by that paltry
figure. "What impressed the PM was that 3 percent," Masse recalls.
"So when the film policy came up and Ronald Reagan read his cue
cards, Mulroney said, 'What if the Russians had 97 percent of the
screen time in the United States and Hollywood had 3 percent?
Wouldn't you at least try to react?'"

As Mulroney had calculated, the Russian reference was enough to
snare Reagan's attention. The president even agreed to give the
matter further consideration. But as soon as Air Force One lifted off
from Uplands Air Force base, other U.S. interests quickly stepped in.

Later that month, Jack Valenti arrived at Flora MacDonald's office for what promptly turned into a showdown.

Before the meeting, MacDonald had been apprehensive. For months, aides had regaled her with tales of Valenti's legendary clout, and even Kinsman had been charmed by the suave Texan who had gone out of his way to introduce Kinsman's daughter to Michael Caine during the Montreal Film Festival. "I'd heard all this great build-up about this man who could talk the ear off a brass monkey — how he could persuade anybody to do anything," MacDonald admits. "Well, I almost laughed when he walked in. He came up to my shoulder. I had to look down at this little man. I must say, it was a great psychological boost."

For twenty minutes, Valenti delivered a lecture that set her seething with its condescension. If she wanted to create an indigenous film industry, he argued, she ought to levy a 10 percent tax on every movie ticket sold, and any money left over from showing Canadian films could be ploughed back into making more of them. But U.S. culture was now global culture, and Canadians would just have to face up to that reality, he proclaimed, scoffing at the notion of etching a national identity on celluloid. "What you're doing is making a leap of faith," he said.

"Mr. Valenti," MacDonald replied, "What you don't understand is that from its beginning, Canada was a leap of faith. If the Fathers of Confederation took your dictates, we'd never have had a country." For the next twenty minutes, MacDonald delivered her own none-too-short course on Canadian history, while both their aides sat back in stunned silence. If she never succeeded in winning him over, she at least felt a certain satisfaction in making him squirm. After Valenti had marched out, Kinsman turned to her to quip, "We really should have sold admission to that."

But outside the elevators, Valenti conducted his own impromptu press conference, denouncing the government's temerity as just another commercial ploy to keep some of Hollywood's profits for itself. Nor did he let up the pressure. In fact, he continued to raise such a fuss during the trade negotiations that on at least one occasion his old Texas crony James Baker called and told him to cool it. Soon Peter Murphy and his negotiating team noticed that Valenti was nowhere in sight, not even flexing his influence from his privileged perch on the government's trade advisory committee. "No, no, that's beneath him," Murphy would later crack. "He goes right to the top. He likes to cut his own deals."

Six months later, during the final all-night negotiating crunch of the trade talks in Washington, Valenti appeared, in fact, to have done just that. In a subsequent memo to Baker which was leaked to a Washington trade newsletter after the conclusion of the pact, a U.S. bureaucrat noted that Mulroney's government had "promised to solve Jack Valenti's problem on film distribution within the next two weeks." In an interview later, Murphy acknowledged that Baker had worked out a secret deal with Valenti apart from the actual text — one which, like the Ginn agreement, seems never to have been put in writing. "That's the one area that was most seriously done by the White House people," Murphy said. "Baker handled it. You never could tell what he was up to. There's probably nothing written. But Valenti got what he wanted. In the end, he wrote this letter to Baker saying the agreement, *as discussed*, is acceptable to the association."

Thus, Mulroney and his free trade team could emerge from the talks crowing that culture had not been on the table; like other elements of the deal, Canadian film policy appears to have been quietly taken care of at another table far from public sight. "It was just an agreement between Baker and Valenti," Murphy said, "but Mulroney had to go along with it. Everything that was signed was signed at the very top."

Soon afterward, the Conservative government suddenly began renegotiating the terms of Flora MacDonald's proposed film bill, which still had not been tabled. As the Canadian delegate to those sessions, the Prime Minister's Office dispatched Glen Shortliffe, then deputy clerk of the Privy Council. From the American side, the State Department nominated an unusual but hardly disinterested duo: Gulf + Western's Donald Oresman and his colleague Arthur Barron, president of the conglomerate's Entertainment Group. As one incredulous ministerial aide marvelled, "Paramount rewrote our film policy."

Those negotiations would drag on over most of the next year, long after the free trade agreement had been signed by Reagan and Mulroney in January 1988. It was not until later that spring, in fact, that the last session wrapped up in a Montreal hotel room, producing a compromise bill which was such a pale imitation of MacDonald's initial version that an outraged civil servant leaked the original to the NDP. Still, Daniel Weinzweig and others in the film community were prepared to embrace even those watered-down provisions when MacDonald finally presented them to the House of Commons in June. But a month later, Mulroney called an election, and Canada's long-awaited film legislation expired on the order paper, never to be resuscitated.

To the arts community, it was all a cruel government plot — a charade meant to take the wind out of free trade opponents' sails by conveying the appearance of protecting Canadian cultural sovereignty while, in fact, taking no concrete action. But to MacDonald, those accusations stung worse than Jack Valenti's taunts — all the more so when, in the election, she lost her own seat. To this day, she still speaks bitterly of the country's ungrateful cultural nationalists on whose behalf she had tried so valiantly to fight.

But as events unrolled like some Saturday serial over the years to come, they only served to fuel her critics' suspicions. For as it turned out, Canadian culture had not been left quite as sacrosanct in the free trade agreement as Mulroney had advertised. In fact, Peter Murphy and Bill Merkin had swaggered out of the final weekend talks with the opposite impression. As Merkin admitted later, "We thought we had pulled something over on the Canadians."

Not only had Valenti's side deal shot down Ottawa's proposed film legislation, but the agreement itself effectively barred any future government from ever again introducing measures to safeguard the country's cultural independence. While the much-publicized first paragraph of the clause acknowledged Canada's exemption on the subject of culture, the second paragraph began with the politically charged phrase "notwithstanding" and went on to undercut the preceding assertion: in unmistakable terms, it spelled out Washington's right to retaliate for harm to American entertainment industries if Ottawa brought in any new cultural legislation whatsoever. "We thought we had very good language in there," Merkin said.

So too, it seemed, did Derek Burney, the prime minister's chief of staff, who had flown into the U.S. capital to wrap up the deal with Baker. As Merkin recalled, "Just as the ministers were about to sign, Derek looked at the culture section and said, 'This is bad.' And Baker said, 'I'm not going to change it at this late date.'" Indeed, the U.S. team had proceeded to sell wary congressmen on the pact by brandishing the assurance that Washington could quite legally lash back at any new Canadian cultural presumptions.

Five years later — five years without a single piece of new Canadian cultural legislation making it to cabinet — Peter Murphy would take undisguised satisfaction in the straitjacket that he and Baker had succeeded in imposing on his unwitting counterparts. "The Canadians, in a sense, didn't get it," he said. "Because the way the agreement is written, if there's a problem, the U.S. will take action — and it doesn't have to show injury." Murphy could not resist a triumphant grin. "The retaliatory possibilities are huge."

"I was accused of being a Paramount lackey," Nicholas Veliotes chuckles pointedly over his plate of pasta arrabiata. "I say, 'Oh, if only it were so.'"

Despite that coyness, Veliotes had devoted considerable energy to Paramount's concerns in Canada, and from the first he had not bothered to mask his sentiments about Canadian cultural policies, no matter how far removed some of them might seem from his publishing portfolio. "How can you say Canadian culture is being protected," he scoffs, "when you're pirating TV programs and putting in your own commercials? You're both watching the same crap." Later in the conversation, he will refer to Canadians "stealing TV signals." And when the subject of Marcel Masse's Baie Comeau policy comes up, he refuses to discuss it in anything but Washington's preferred terms. "That wasn't a culture issue," he snaps. "That was a bread issue."

Indeed, in the complex bilateral minuet played out around the Ginn sale — a slow dance of deception which turned on the clause that Veliotes had managed to insert into the free trade agreement — some diplomats detected a byzantine design that bore traces of his choreography. But if he was, in fact, at work behind the scenes, he would not remain there for long.

On November 30, 1990, as the long-drawn-out Ginn deal hung in limbo, Veliotes abruptly surfaced in person at the Canadian Embassy in Washington, provoked by a new round of nationalistic rumblings up in what Ronald Reagan had termed "North America's attic." The previous year Marcel Masse had returned to the Department of Communications for the third time, a changed man, more determined than ever to create a new cultural infrastructure for the country. From his exile in the Energy Department, he had watched with growing fury as other cabinet colleagues chipped away at the arts battlements he had raised. When Robert de Cotret had allowed Britain's Penguin Publishing to take over the Canadian subsidiary of New American Library, Masse had not bothered to hide his rage. On his Department of Energy letterhead, he had blasted de Cotret for "abandoning" his Baie Comeau guidelines, then promptly sent copies to all the country's publishers — thereby guaranteeing that the letter would find its way into the press.

But now Masse had a radical new plan — a sweeping cultural blueprint that would roll all his past efforts into one complex, tamper-proof package. Chief among the provisions of that omnibus culture bill was a scheme to put all foreign takeovers of cultural industries out of the reach of de Cotret and Investment Canada. Instead, he proposed handing them over to a new Cultural Investment Review Agency that would be run by the Canadian Radio-television and Telecommunications Commission (CRTC), the independent agency that already had a mandate to police broadcasting ownership and content requirements.

Michael Wilson had fired off a brusque two-page letter to Masse that might have been dictated by Veliotes himself, damning the plan as "contentious and costly." According to one exaggerated scare scenario that Investment Canada had drawn up, the government buy-out provisions that Veliotes had insinuated into the free trade pact could oblige Ottawa to spend as much as $45 million a year purchasing publishing branch plants it had forced U.S. owners to sell. Pointing out that the proposal "runs counter to the government's open-for-business philosophy," Wilson warned that it "could pose a continuing irritant to our relations with the United States."

As if on cue, three congressmen submitted bills to retaliate against Canadian-owned communications and cable companies with holdings in the United States. And from his formidable perch as chairman of the House Energy and Commerce Committee, Michigan's John Dingell, already the scourge of Canadian acid rain activists, submitted a blistering tirade against Masse and his Baie Comeau "expropriation" policy to the U.S. Trade Representative's Office — a tirade that turned out to be on behalf of Gulf + Western. "By tolerating the Canadian example, do we not encourage similar actions by other governments?" Dingell thundered.

But what had finally set off the alarms in Veliotes's Washington office were reports that Masse planned to toughen up the publishing rules, giving Canadians even greater control of book distribution. "It's worse!" Veliotes protested to Derek Burney, who by then had been rewarded with the ambassadorship to Washington. "Unacceptable!" For their meeting, he had brought along only one member of the AAP board, Paramount's Lawrence Levinson, who underlined the corporation's distress. "Most of our revenue is derived from distribution," he argued. "If you cut the heart and soul out, we are left with shells."

Two months after warning Burney that the Baie Comeau policy remained a "major irritant" in Canada–U.S. relations, Veliotes flew to Ottawa. At a welcoming lunch thrown by Bush's new ambassador, Edward Ney, he met a handful of officials from External Affairs who had never approved of Masse's publishing scheme — and who, he says, helped him plan his strategy. For a round of meetings that included lunch with Masse's deputy Alain Gourd, Veliotes once again had a Paramount representative in tow: Gerry Doucet, who had taken over the corporation's lobbying account when his partner Frank Moores retired. In Veliotes's notes on that encounter, which he supplied to the Canadian government, the former ambassador used a phrase whose force only a diplomat might grasp: if Masse's new cultural review agency demanded forced divestiture of any kind, he warned Gourd, it would be "unfortunate."

A month later, back at the Canadian Embassy in Washington with Paramount's Lawrence Levinson, it became clear just what he had meant. At a time when Ottawa was trying to prepare a public argument for joining the NAFTA negotiations, Levinson made a thinly veiled threat to arrange for the denunciation of the government's policies in Congress. The embassy's Roy Norton pointed out the risk of that tactic. "Nobody needs to make threats," Norton said. "We pointed out that in so doing it wouldn't be helpful, that nothing was served by making a big stink about what Canada was contemplating." In his report on the lunch, Norton added that Levinson had thought it over and "subsequently confirmed that his counsel to the U.S. publishing industry had been to take a very low profile vis-à-vis Canadian policies."

That low profile would soon pay off. A month after Veliotes's visit to the embassy, Masse was transferred out of the communications portfolio for the last time and replaced by the more accommodating Perrin Beatty. All that fall, Masse had been trying to move his omnibus culture bill forward, only to discover that he could not even get it on the cabinet agenda. Not only were the free market zealots at the finance department and the Privy Council Office blocking it, but his aides suspected that so were some of his own bureaucrats.

In September 1990, soon after his plans had begun to take shape, Alain Gourd had secretively flown to Washington to alert Derek Burney. On the return trip, Gourd had also stopped in Toronto to brief Thomson president John Tory. A year later, after Masse's grand cultural dreams had come to nought, Mulroney would promote Gourd to one of the top posts in the federal civil service, deputy clerk of the Privy Council and associate secretary to the cabinet.

Masse had cared passionately about his former culture portfolio. But others had not failed to notice that it had been handed over to him whenever free trade negotiations loomed on the horizon and nationalists needed some reassurance about Mulroney's continental drift, then yanked away again before he could actually enact any lasting legislation. Even his Baie Comeau policy had remained just that — a policy, never a law. And less than a year after his final departure from the ministry, Perrin Beatty's revised publishing guidelines had taken the last teeth out of the measure.

Some reports had credited Veliotes with that victory, but he shrugged off the accolade. Still, sitting in a Washington restaurant later beneath a wilting summer sun, a Canadian reporter asked Veliotes if, in fact, there had been secret promises made to him outside the free trade agreement that the government would quietly, in its own time, do away with Baie Comeau's provisions. "I wasn't told that," he says, then pauses with a cryptic smile, toying with his pasta. "I was told the Canadian government was reviewing the policies — all of them. I said, 'In the course of your review, please keep our concerns in mind.'"

In fact, one reason Masse had finally thrown in the towel on his grandiose dream of creating an overarching Canadian cultural policy was that he had accidentally stumbled upon the clues that his own government had already bargained away any such possibility. One afternoon, he had received a phone call from Paul Audley, a trusted aide charged with drafting the legislation, inviting him to an urgent private dinner the following night. Audley had just returned from a meeting at Investment Canada, where he had learned alarming news: in the midst of briefing the agency's Gordon Dewhirst on Masse's plans, Dewhirst had informed him that the whole scheme was out of the question because it violated undertakings already given to Washington by Mulroney's government.

"What undertakings?" Audley had demanded. Had there been some under-the-table agreement? But Dewhirst had promptly clammed up. When Audley relayed the conversation to his boss, Masse seemed both astounded and disturbed. But shortly after he began making his own inquiries on the subject, the minister seemed to lose heart in his portfolio. Years later, he still refuses to admit that he discovered another secret deal with the White House. "I don't believe in secret deals," Masse says, "but I do believe there are people who are deeply convinced it's not in the interests of Canada to have a cultural policy — bureaucrats and ministers."

One of those whose support for his cultural schemes abruptly withered after the free trade deal was none other than Brian Mulroney. Despite repeated entreaties both by letter and in person, Masse found his new omnibus bill studiously ignored by the prime minister and his staff. Had Mulroney lost interest? Masse never received a satisfactory explanation. But surprisingly for a politician who had never shown more than a perfunctory interest in the arts — a man whom Harold Greenberg had once characterized as "not into the Canadian cultural scene, and never was" — Mulroney would suddenly acquire ties to the entertainment industry after his exit from office. A year after his retirement, as he amassed a string of lucrative corporate directorships, even the most jaded trackers of his post–prime ministerial activities were stunned when Greenberg, an avowed Liberal, suddenly made a surprise announcement. Fresh from negotiating a joint development venture with the USA Network — the cable-TV partnership formed by Wasserman's MCA and Paramount — Greenberg named Mila Mulroney a director of Astral Inc., which remained one of Hollywood's chief television distribution arms north of the border. As it turned out, that year Astral also decided for the first time to pay its board members $12,000 a year, plus $500 for each meeting they attended.

PRESIDING over a White House luncheon honouring the ten distinguished winners of the National Medal of the Arts in the summer of 1991, George Bush had suddenly jumped up from his seat next to violinist Isaac Stern. "All right, you artists," he declared.

"Now I want you to meet some real artists!" With that, the dining-room doors swung open to reveal baseball legends Joe DiMaggio and Ted Williams, who had just arrived to accompany Bush to an All-Star game with Brian Mulroney that night in Toronto's SkyDome.

If that presidential fanfare had been meant as a joke, most of the American arts community did not take it that way. In fact, to many it seemed to sum up the Bush administration's attitude to culture at a time when the Republican and religious right wing had just unleashed a full frontal assault on its various incarnations, both high and low. Leading the attack on some vaguely defined American "cultural elite" — which somehow seemed to include the producers of Murphy Brown — had been Bush's vice president, Dan Quayle. But close on his heels was the Senate's ultra-conservative avenger, Jesse Helms, excoriating the National Endowment for the Arts (NEA) for handing out taxpayers' dollars to a photography exhibit that featured the explicit photos of Robert Mapplethorpe. From an attack on pornography, his wrath had ripened into an all-encompassing demand to close down the NEA, the only U.S. federal funding agency for the arts.

But in the midst of that high emotion, one of the most affecting cases for government funding of culture came from the pen of Joe David Bellamy, the director of the endowment's literature program. Decrying the fact that "the United States already gives less for the arts than many civilized nations," he spent most of his argument lauding the Canadian example — in particular, the Canada Council. Comparing the council's 1987 arts budget of $110 million with the endowment's total allotment of $176 million for a nation ten times the size, Bellamy cited Margaret Atwood and Alice Munro as the best evidence to support government patronage of the arts.

"The Canadians care about building a cultural identity and having a national memory," he wrote. "As we approach the end of the twentieth century, and the end of the millennium, I think we should look with great alarm at the condition of American culture and American literature, because market forces are putting it out of business. Literature is in an especially precarious condition because it is the last of the arts to realize that it cannot pay its own way in the marketplace. Do we want our legacy as a nation to be Terminator 2 and Wayne's World?"

Ironically, as Bellamy was penning that paean of praise to Canadian culture, Mulroney's government was swiftly dismantling its life support systems. The Canada Council, under its unlikely new chairman Allan Gotlieb, suffered a succession of draconian budget cuts before being handed the announcement of its effective emasculation in a proposed merger with the Social Sciences and Humanities Research Council of Canada.

Within the government, bureaucrats had begun to mutter openly about putting the National Film Board out of its misery, transforming the agency that had collected ten Oscars into a minor service bureau. And after overseeing a prolonged budgetary assault on the CBC, slashing the corporation's annual expropriation from $900 million to $793 million in the Tories' first five years in power alone, a handful of Mulroney's friends and former aides were clambering for the "semi-privatization" of the public network. Heralding the advent of the 500-channel universe, most of whose profits seemed destined for the pockets of a few Conservative supporters, they seemed happy to fan the mounting doubts over the future of the single institution that had served to bind together the vast and sparsely populated land — a network that Flora MacDonald had once hailed as "the central instrument of the government's cultural policy."

Leading that charge was Hugh Segal, an ebullient backroom Tory operative who had once offered Canadian corporate leaders three-day tours through the upper echelons of the Reagan administration, including meetings with Vice President George Bush and other high-ranking officials, for $2,950 a head. Known as the Happy Warrior, Segal had been drafted by his old boss William Davis as one of Mulroney's last chiefs of staff when the prime minister's popularity was plunging towards an all-time nadir. Finally departing after an abortive attempt to snatch the party leadership from Kim Campbell, Segal had joined Gluskin/Sheff, a flamboyant Bay Street investment firm from whose offices he conducted his CBC campaign. He envisaged turning over a third of the CBC's ownership to pension funds and other large investors — an attempt, as he put it, to "bring some private capital to the table in a way that respects the imperatives of public broadcasting."

Fittingly, at the time of that CBC debate, the firm's principals, financiers Ira Gluskin and Gerry Sheff, were in the throes of demonstrating the cultural miracles that private capital could work — arranging to sponsor a Toronto showing of the Barnes Collection, an exhibit of paintings amassed by the late Philadelphia industrialist

Alfred Barnes, who had exemplified the role of the philanthropist in the arts. In the course of negotiating for those rights, Gluskin and Sheff had prevailed upon one of America's most celebrated living examples of the species: Ronald Reagan's billionaire friend Walter Annenberg. After interceding with the Barnes board on Toronto's behalf, Annenberg and his wife, Leonore, had turned up for Gluskin/ Sheff's glittering pre-opening party for 1,700 at the Art Gallery of Ontario. There, among the Renoirs and the Matisses, not to mention the champagne and the caviar, they rubbed shoulders with many of the prominent figures whose interests had also collided with Canadian cultural policies, including publishing magnate Ken Thomson and his lawyer John Tory Sr. Among the crowd, too, was Gerry Sheff's companion Helga Stephenson, who would soon be named the chairman of Canadian Paramount's new parent, Viacom Canada — in tandem with its new president, former pollster Allan Gregg. In such a heady black-tie gathering of the Canadian elite, Annenberg would have had no trouble locating kindred spirits who opposed the legislative barricades once raised to defend the country's cultural sovereignty.

But by 1994, many of those targets of Annenberg's ire were already vanishing. No film or publishing policy stipulating Canadian ownership requirements remained on the legislative books. As the federal and provincial governments drastically cut back grants to the arts, the country's cultural organizations were increasingly forced to follow the American model and rely on private and corporate benefactors. Many, including the National Ballet, had even turned to U.S. philanthropies such as the Ford Foundation, on whose board, ironically, sat former CBS chairman Thomas Wyman.

Not that the U.S. showbiz leviathan had been mollified by those victories. During congressional hearings into the North American Free Trade Agreement, Jack Valenti had once again denounced the Canadian cultural exemption as ominous — the agreement's "fatal flaw" — warning that if the Europeans brandished it as a precedent during the GATT negotiations, he would "bring out every Patriot missile, every F–16 in our armory, leading whatever legions we can find." Despite that florid bellicosity, the Europeans, led by France's Jack Lang, refused to be cowed by his threats, declaring their own film and broadcast policies off-limits to Hollywood's relentless appetites. Indeed, those other nations had taken inspiration from their perception of Canada's determination. It was only at home that determination seemed seriously in doubt — and with guᵥ reason.

In Washington, the chief officials in the Bush administration let it be known that they regarded the Canadian cultural exemption as a temporary aberration. At another congressional NAFTA hearing, Bush's trade representative, Carla Hills, testified that, even if Ottawa had once again taken what she termed an "abrogation" on the cultural issue, "We don't recognize it." Following her to the witness table, Jim Robinson, who had not yet been dethroned as chairman of American Express — or as head of the U.S. Business Roundtable's trade committee — also lamented culture as the only sector where American industry had fallen short in the negotiations. But outside the hearing room, he made it clear that the fight was far from over. "It's obviously important in Canada now," he said. "But often with issues like that, with the passage of time, things change: you begin to think of it as a trade issue rather than an element of national sovereignty."

As he spoke, the debate north of the border was already shifting. Desperate to justify its existence and continued federal funding, the Canadian cultural community was arguing its case in terms of box-office receipts and the number of jobs it provided — borrowing the vocabulary of the marketplace. Increasingly, the arts were being addressed as a commodity — one that the country could perhaps no longer afford.

To Marcel Masse, that development seemed entirely predictable. In a cavernous office overlooking Parliament Hill during the dying days of the Mulroney regime, he shook his head in frustration. "This country will disappear if we are more and more like the Americans," he said. "Why should we have different political institutions if we're exactly like them? If we don't have a cultural identity, we have no reason to exist."

Then he asked a reporter if she knew how to cook a frog. If you put the creature into a pot of boiling water, he pointed out, the frog would jump. "But if you take fresh cool water and put the frog in, it feels at ease. Then you turn on the stove. As it gets warmer, the frog thinks it's a wonderful society — and in the end, the frog is cooked."

In the fading afternoon light, Masse smiled a bitter smile. "If we had a cultural policy, the frog would have jumped," he said. "Slowly and slowly, we've Americanized ourselves — and in the end we're going to end up cooked."

10 Let's Make a Deal

HE SAT UNEASILY at the front window table of a Washington fern bar, unnoticed amid the lunchtime crowd. The familiar freckled face was ashen, the gangly frame gaunt under a tweed jacket, and even the unruly thatch that had won him his nickname, Carrot Top, had faded to dark autumnal straw. His movements were slow and deliberate, like a man who feels any sudden motion might rock his fragile equilibrium, and his voice struggled with exhaustion from weeks of chemotherapy. At forty-five, Peter Murphy was waging his final, and he knew futile, battle with brain cancer — a battle that dwarfed any of the verbal and psychological warfare he had once waged with Simon Reisman as America's chief free trade negotiator.

Now, in the fall of 1993, the obscure technocrat whose name had become a household word in Canada — the personification of *Them* to the south — looked back on those two turbulent years oppposite Reisman's rages and calculated pyrotechnics with the perspective of a man fighting for his life. "I almost died when I was in the hospital," he said quietly. "It's an amazingly clarifying experience."

From that vantage point, Murphy refused to badmouth his mercurial foe — a courtesy Reisman had not returned. In an interview with journalist Linda McQuaig shortly after the agreement was signed, Reisman had raged on about Murphy's youth, his inexperience, his lack of a mandate — in short, the humiliating lack of stature of the man that Washington had named to do battle with him.

But it was that very stature gap which summed up the Canadian-American free trade minuet. To the Mulroney regime, the free trade talks had become the government's *raison d'être*, its chief, indeed its only, economic policy; as one External Affairs official repeatedly told a *Maclean's* reporter, "Remember, there is no Plan B." To the Reagan administration, the negotiations were an obscure sideshow to the real goal — getting a new round of the General Agreement on Tariffs and Trade negotiations on track which would include measures that some of America's most vocal transnationals were demanding in their new global push. If the Canadian talks produced an agreement that set some precedents for the coming GATT tussle, so much the better. But there was no interest in getting a deal at any price — an agreement that might create loopholes through which some other uppity nation like France or Brazil might squeeze.

No, the purpose of sitting down with Ottawa was to teach the other nations of the world a lesson, as Treasury Secretary James Baker confessed in *The International Economy* only weeks after having cut the deal. Under the title "The Geopolitical Implications of the U.S.–Canada Trade Pact," Baker emphasized that the agreement was a "lever" against those countries which were dragging their heels on GATT. "Other nations are forced to recognize that the United States will find ways to expand trade — with or without them," he wrote. "If all nations are not ready, we will begin with those that are and build on that success." Or, as Peter Murphy put it, "If this puts pressure on the Europeans, well, why not use it?"

To Baker, agitating on several fronts showed "hard-nosed Yankee-trader realism." Besides, as he noted, it was cheaper and more efficient to pick off one country at a time. Not that the White House was wasting any money on its Canadian gamble: Murphy, his deputy Bill Merkin, and a single secretary had been deposited in a cubbyhole on the cramped top floor of the Winder Building, the trade offices across 17th Street from the White House, just like any other cogs in the vast Washington bureaucracy.

In Ottawa, the government had rented an entire floor of the Metropolitan Life Tower for its lavish Trade Negotiations Office, newly panelled and decorated with expensive leather swivel chairs.

There, at a consulting fee of $1,000 a day, Reisman presided over a staff of one hundred, including — to her shock — Sylvia Ostry, the deputy minister of international trade. Washington might be saving its big guns for the GATT talks, the chief preoccupation of Clayton Yeutter, who had replaced Brock as the U.S. trade representative, but in Canada, Mulroney betrayed the fact that his overriding obsession was snagging a deal with the Americans by limiting Ostry to multilateral negotiations, then forcing her to answer to Reisman, who was outside the bureaucratic pecking order.

Ever since they came to power, the Tories had been trying to dump Ostry, a perceived Liberal and avowed multilateralist, who had become a respected international economist during her stint as chief statistician at the Organization for Economic Cooperation and Development in Paris. She had been subjected to a humiliating grilling on minutiae by finance committee chairman Don Blenkarn. Then Trade Minister James Kelleher, a former Sault Ste. Marie corporate lawyer who was a true believer in a U.S. deal, had tried to sideline her. As it happened, Ostry and Reisman were old friends. "Simon, I don't know whether I can stomach this," Ostry had confessed, to which Reisman had signalled that while she was to report to him in theory, she need not do so in fact. Already, the feisty Reisman was confounding his political masters.

If Ostry was kept on a short leash, he was answerable only to the prime minister. To many of External's trade warriors who had laboured so long and deftly to get the talks on the agenda, Reisman's appointment had been a source of private chagrin. Suddenly they found that the old warhorse from the 1965 Auto Pact negotiations had insinuated himself into Mulroney's favour with a bravura fifteen-page missive setting out his own aggressive battle plan and branding anyone who opposed the negotiations a wimp.

Some such as Kelleher had been less than enthusiastic about Reisman, but it was precisely that bluster which had dictated Mulroney's choice. "The prime minister was very concerned that the people of Canada didn't feel we could stand up to the United States," Kelleher said. "He saw in Simon a real bantam rooster who would make sure people saw we were going to put up a good fight. It was more for the optics than the substance."

For all his tough talk and tempestuousness, Reisman was a continental pragmatist who never did believe in the cultural exemption he found himself so vigorously defending. He, too, wanted the country open for business. Among the boards he sat on at the time were those of two Canadian multinationals with increasing U.S. interests, Bombardier and George Weston Ltd., the Toronto-based grocery and paper-making giant that ranked as one of the continent's biggest food wholesalers; both directorships he would keep throughout the negotiations.

But at the time Mulroney named him to the job, Reisman was also an adviser to an audacious $100 billion water export scheme that epitomized the worst fears of free trade opponents, who saw the talks as a U.S. ploy to colonize Canadian resources. Known as the Great Recycling and Northern Development (GRAND) Canal, the megaproject called for building dikes between Hudson and James Bays, creating a massive freshwater lake whose waters could then be pumped south through a complex network of canals, locks, and even the Great Lakes to the parched boomtowns of Arizona and California. In *Power from the North*, Reisman's old friend, Quebec premier Robert Bourassa, had enthusiastically touted the proposal, as had former U.S. defence secretary James Schlesinger; in the book's preface, Schlesinger had even used it to argue for the necessity of a continental energy policy.

But the scheme had another high-profile booster: Brian Mulroney. Among the four major engineering firms involved in the consortium was one the prime minister knew well: Bechtel Canada Ltd., whose American chairman, Stephen Bechtel, then shared a seat with him on the board of M. A. Hanna. Even after his election, Mulroney had told *Fortune* magazine that he favoured water exports to the United States.

In 1985, already installed as chief trade negotiator, Reisman had argued that the GRAND Canal project "could provide the key to a free trade agreement." When word leaked out about his water interests, ecologists saw red; Keith Penner, a Liberal MP from the James Bay area, lambasted the project as "an environmental Frankenstein." All through the free trade negotiations, the government would repeatedly deny that water was on the table, later insisting that references in the final text applied only to exports of the fancy stuff yuppies bought by the bottle. But that point remains in dispute. And environmentalists' suspicions were fed by the fact that, after the furore, Reisman had pointedly refused to recant. From his lofty new chief negotiator's digs, he released a statement that managed to be both equivocal and provocative, but one with which his opponents could hardly take issue. "In my judgement," he said, "water will be the most critical area of Canada–US relations over the next 100 years."

Still, none of Reisman's critics could quibble with his qualifications for the job. That was all the more reason for Derek Burney and his fellow free-marketeers at External to feel crushed when, three months after Reisman's posting, the White House named Peter Murphy. "It was a bit disappointing," Burney admitted. "We put forward this icon who wanted to rewrite the history of the world, this gladiator; they put forward a middle-level bureaucrat."

For Reisman and the rest of the Canadian team, who saw the trade talks as a romantic venture, a heroic chance to take on the Goliath to the south, that was the insult. Peter Murphy was so clearly a nobody. Worse, he was a *sick* nobody who might not be able to take the grind of the most important foreign policy negotiations in Canadian history. It had been Murphy's health that had brought him home from the GATT talks at Geneva, where he had been the chief U.S. textile negotiator, a rising star in USTR's cocky young trade cohort. Suddenly, in Switzerland, he had been convulsed with seizures. He lost the feeling in his legs, and couldn't sit up, put two fingers together, or write his name. Doctors had diagnosed it as a lesion on the brain. He had recuperated over the next six months, and then found himself assigned to the Canadian talks.

Murphy's condition was no secret to Mulroney or his government, although they never let on to the Canadian public. In the spring of 1986 the launch of the negotiations had to be put off after he received a definitive diagnosis — he had a malignant brain tumour — and through most of the talks he was heavily medicated. His mentor, Bill Brock's deputy Mike Smith, had thought he was doing Murphy a favour with the no-sweat assignment, but neither of them had counted on the volcanic Reisman. "He made my life miserable," Murphy said, but not without the trace of a wry smile. "And the harder I worked, the more it dragged on me."

Reisman had made only the meagrest attempts to hide his scorn for the young whippersnapper with whom he had been paired. But from the first he had correctly sized up the situation: Murphy did, indeed, have no real mandate to strike a deal. That was the point. "Peter's basic premise was that Canada is viewed in Washington as a bunch of whiners," said his deputy, Bill Merkin. "They always want a special deal. We felt, no matter what, at the end of the day, they would escalate this to the White House. So Peter's view was: I'm not going to give anything away now, before the political deal."

As Merkin admitted, for the next two years Murphy's strategy was to stall until the White House and the Prime Minister's Office moved in. He was, as Reisman's deputy Gordon Ritchie finally concluded after a year at the table, "a hollow man," which meant that, for more than two years, the negotiations were a hollow exercise. While daily melodrama was being whipped up in the Canadian media over each alleged twist and turning, nothing substantive was happening. "Remember, that for two years, we basically made no concessions," Merkin said. "There was not a lot to inform people about."

In fact, the only thing that worried Murphy and Merkin was that someone would inadvertently dislodge that stalemate: Ronald Reagan. While they laboured in the trenches laying the foundations for his continental vision, they fretted he might be in a brocade armchair in the Oval Office with Brian Mulroney, bantering away some key provision. Whenever the two leaders met, the U.S. team alerted the National Security Council to keep a tight rein on the commander-in-chief. "We were nervous about him negotiating with the prime minister because we knew the prime minister was up to speed," Merkin said. "We were afraid Reagan would sit there and nod, and give away something."

THROUGHOUT the long standoff, a frustrated Reisman would periodically taunt Murphy, "If you can't handle this, then we'll get somebody else." But Reisman's mistake was to underestimate his opponent's grit. Murphy may have been a textile negotiator in Geneva, where he was used to getting his way with Third World regimes, but that experience was worth pondering. What the Canadian team forgot was how charged those negotiations were in Congress, especially with the Southern barons of the Senate. South Carolina's octogenarian Strom Thurmond and North Carolina's Jesse Helms routinely crushed young technocrats who failed to protect their states' textile mills from the increasingly threatening sweatshops of Thailand and Taiwan. Peter Murphy had always understood exactly whom he had to please: the industries whose lobbyists and multimillion-dollar political action committees increasingly called the electoral tune both in the White House and in Congress, where any final agreement had to be ratified.

When he started the Canadian negotiations, he had received no specific instructions on most issues from the trade office. For marching orders, he went to the administration's handpicked club of corporate heavyweights: a blue-ribbon private sector panel known as the Advisory Committee on Trade Negotiations (ACTN). An umbrella group of Fortune 500 executives, its membership came largely from the Big Three automakers and the energy, defence, and communications industries; in turn, the ACTN presided over dozens of specialized industry subcommittees. "When I started the negotiations, I had no idea what the U.S. position was," Murphy said, "so I had to go into this circular discussion till I found out what the industry wanted. We had forty-four different industry guys and we had to see them all."

At the top of his list was Ed Pratt, a tough-talking ex-Marine from Georgia whom Reagan had personally appointed to head the ACTN after his generosity in the 1980 elections and whom he counted as a friend. But Pratt's connections were not merely political. As chairman of Pfizer Inc., he was also president of the Pharmaceutical Manufacturers Association (PMA), the voice of the $75 billion brand name drug industry. Known as "John Wayne" Pratt among certain Canadian officials, he liked to announce to new acquaintances that he knew how to kill a man with a single blow, nor was anyone inclined to question that claim. "When you went to an international meeting, you always knew who was from Pfizer," says an industry insider. "They all had Marine haircuts and were very aggressive."

Pratt had brought that particular boot-camp spirit to the PMA, which never hesitated to flex its muscles to protect an industry that already ranked as America's most profitable. Mainly centred in New Jersey, the drug companies had won the state its nickname as the nation's medicine chest and would give New Jersey's celebrity senator Bill Bradley, a former basketball star, more than a passing interest in the Canadian free trade agreement. But Bradley was not alone in jumping when the phone rang from the PMA. Its Washington lobbying office had an annual budget bigger than that of some municipalities — $31 million in 1992, of which $4 million was handed out to the campaign coffers of accommodating congressmen.

But Pratt had a special beef with Canada. In 1969 Trudeau had brought in legislation that undercut the U.S. companies' exclusive licence agreement. Lambasted by the PMA as compulsory licensing, the amendment had made it feasible for Canadian firms to copy brand name drugs for sale under generic labels, provided they paid a 4 percent royalty fee. The measure had accomplished what it set out to do, spawning an indigenous industry that had carved out 3 percent of the $4 billion Canadian prescription drug market. It had also made the country's drug costs the lowest in the world. According to a report by University of Toronto economist Harry Eastman, the amendments had saved Canadian consumers $211 million in 1983 alone.

But for Pratt, the legislation was an abomination, which he liked to portray as an infuriating precedent for Third World countries like India and Brazil with their massive pirate drug mills. Worse, it provided ammunition for the industry's enemies back home. Whenever Arkansas senator David Pryor attacked the pharmaceutical giants for preying on senior citizens or blocking national health insurance, he would invariably brandish the example of Canada, where costs of the same prescription drugs averaged 32 percent lower.

The PMA had managed to get the country placed on the administration's Section 301 watch list of unfair trading nations. And although its overriding aim was to see long-term patent protection enshrined in any new GATT deal, the association was determined to smash the Canadian legislation. Pratt's friend Bill Brock had tried pressuring his Liberal counterpart, Gerry Regan, to no avail. But with Mulroney's election, the State Department had detected "prospects for remedial action," as a briefing memo reported, in the new government's "free enterprise orientation."

Brock had introduced Pratt to Jim Kelleher as an adviser, somebody who could help him along the thorny free trade trail based on the U.S. model. "When Bill Brock said to me, 'Jimmy, how are you gonna bring in the private sector to these negotiations?'" Kelleher recalls, "I said, 'Geez, I don't know.' He said, 'Jimmy, you can't do an agreement like this without the private sector.'" In fact, he claims many corporate chiefs initially distrusted his overtures. "They thought I was using them," Kelleher laughed. "I had a son-of-a-bitch of a time. I had to promise to come to their meetings and every damn thing. And of course, the bureaucrats were madder 'n hell. They saw it as a diminution of their power."

Undaunted, Kelleher flew to New York, where Pratt showed him how the U.S. legislation and system worked, then sent a team of his own advisers to Ottawa to help the minister "Canadianize it," as he put it. The result was the prestigious International Trade Advisory Committee, later headed by Mulroney's friend Trevor Eyton of Brascan, and the Sectoral Advisory Groups on International Trade, which would include many of the government's favourite corporate boosters as well as union representatives — most of whom boycotted the meetings.

During that process, Pratt and Kelleher discovered they spoke the same language. Both had homes on Florida's Gulf Coast, near Fort Myers, where they promptly went quail hunting together and became doubles tennis partners at the exclusive Gasparilla Island club — pastimes they share to this day. Kelleher scoffed at the notion that the PMA chief was trying to curry his favour over the drug question. "If he was, he's still at it," Kelleher said. In fact, by July 1986 Mulroney had transferred him out of the trade portfolio, naming him attorney general and charging him with a "clean up" of the Canadian Security and Intelligence Service. But Kelleher admits he probably introduced Pratt to the prime minister, who gave him a sympathetic ear.

Still, Pratt's ace card was Ronald Reagan, whom he had succeeded in whipping into a state of indignation on his industry's behalf. He had talked Reagan into bringing up the pharmaceutical issue during the president's first meeting with Mulroney as opposition leader in June 1984. And clearly, by the time he took office, Mulroney understood its import to the White House. Six weeks before the Shamrock Summit in March 1985, his top aide Fred Doucet had called a meeting with the ministries involved. "He said, 'Brian wants this for when he meets with Reagan,'" recalled Russ Wunker, who by then was executive assistant to Health and Welfare Minister Jake Epp. "I got the impression they thought this was something that could be done in six to eight weeks." In fact, the issue would prove such a political hot potato that it would take nearly another three years to resolve. But when the Quebec City summit rolled around, Pratt's ire rated third place on Reagan's agenda.

After a talk with Pratt, Peter Murphy had no doubt about his marching orders on the pharmaceutical question: his job was to wangle an intellectual property clause encompassing patent protection in the free trade negotiations. Then suddenly, without warning in early 1986, he was told not to bother: the drug-makers were doing a side deal with the Canadian government at the highest level. "They got some kind of settlement," he said, still visibly irked at the memory of being sandbagged. "Was it an under-the-table deal? All I know is that as long as it was going on, I didn't have access to it and we had no possibility of negotiating it." For Murphy, a former ambassador to GATT, any political deal was rife with the potential to make trouble for future U.S. negotiations in Geneva. Still, a mid-level bureaucrat did not quibble with Ed Pratt or the PMA. "They just like doing things themselves," he shrugged.

In Ottawa, federal bureaucrats soon got the same message: the government immediately moved to bring in a new pharmaceutical bill to undo Trudeau's. "It was clear to us inside all along," says one former ministerial staffer. "It was Mulroney. He gave the orders, absolutely, unequivocally. If there's one thing I fault the government for, it was their willingness to do anything to please the Americans." He recalls top aides turning up at meetings to argue that "Brian needs . . ." and "Brian wants . . ." Pratt flew up to Ottawa at least once in the Pfizer corporate jet. And in March 1986, as Murphy and Reisman began their first exploratory meeting in Ottawa, he was among the guests at Reagan's state dinner for Mulroney.

But if Pratt was the powerhouse of the multinational drug indus-try in Washington, its point man in Ottawa was John Zabriskie, the tall, ambitious head of the local subsidiary of Merck & Co., the world's largest drug-maker, based in the New Jersey town of White House Station. Known for his toughness and smarts, Zabriskie was already an executive on the rise within the company, and after winning a new Canadian patent law he would be rewarded with the presidency of its American division. In fact, Merck Frosst Canada had a special stake in the legislative landscape: with a handful of the most profitable patents on the market — including the high-blood-pressure medication Vasotec — the company had the most to lose from generic copies of all the U.S. brand name manufacturers in the country.

Merck's plant outside Montreal had become the showcase of an industry that had traditionally been centred in Quebec, where it still had a reputation for its influence in provincial politics. "In Quebec, you won't find a politician or a cabinet minister who doesn't have somebody in the family working for Squibb or Smith Kline and Beecham," one pharmaceutical executive pointed out. "We were, and still are, a very important part of Quebec culture."

That importance had not escaped the notice of Mulroney, who had campaigned in Montreal during the 1984 election with a promise of restoring patent protection to the drug companies, hailing them as the research engine of the future. Seven years later, with his own popularity plummeting, the prime minister and a phalanx of cabinet ministers would preside at the ribbon-cutting for Merck's new $70 million biomedical research centre outside Montreal before a cheering crowd of 4,000 — to whom he joked that they might well constitute the better part of his supporters in the country.

To lobby on Merck's and the multinationals' behalf, Zabriskie had turned to Frank Moores's firm, Government Consultants International, where the account was being handled by both Moores and his partner Gerry Doucet, the brother of the prime minister's senior adviser, Fred. For many of those involved, the deal seemed sewn up soon after the Shamrock Summit, and all that remained was the announcement. Mulroney's communications director, Bill Fox, repeatedly called Russ Wunker to alert him of a press conference within days. "But it didn't go anywhere for the longest time," Wunker recalled. "I used to joke with Fox, if I had $5 for every time he told me there was going to be an announcement, I'd be a rich man."

Mulroney had found himself in political heavy weather, with two cabinet ministers under investigation and a sudden revolt by the country's grey panthers. After his decision to de-index old-age pensions, he was caught on national television being berated by a livid senior citizen named Solange Denis. "You lied to us!" she cried. "You made us vote for you, and then goodbye Charlie Brown." That exchange was equally terrifying to Michel Côté, the minister of consumer and corporate affairs, who was charged with bringing down the pharmaceutical bill — a measure sure to raise drug costs for pensioners and provincial health insurance plans. Côté watched the TV encounter in Edmonton, where he was trying to win the province's approval for the bill. "Côté went ashen," says a former aide. "Then someone made it worse by saying, 'This could happen to you.'"

By April 1986, a month before Murphy and Reisman kicked off their negotiations, Côté's legislation still had not materialized. To Murphy's new boss, Clayton Yeutter, this was clearly the betrayal of an understanding. "Even our patience ultimately begins to wear thin," he rumbled menacingly. Within days, Mulroney seemed to be offering an apology as he conceded that the country had acted "as a scavenger in the area of intellectual property."

But a succession of retaliatory U.S. tariffs on Canadian exports made the prospective pharmaceutical bill a PR nightmare for Mulroney. In June, Vice President George Bush dropped by Vancouver and Ottawa to smooth the troubled trade waters, but he also found time to push the pharmaceutical agenda. In fact, Bush had some personal acquaintance with the issue: in 1977, after leaving the CIA, he had joined the board of one of America's largest drug companies — Eli Lilly of Indianapolis — and received 1,500 shares, which he placed in a blind trust when he became vice president.

Later as president, Bush's administration would continue to enjoy close ties with Lilly, not least of all through Indianapolis's native son Dan Quayle, his vice president. Quayle's uncle had set up Lilly's first lobbying office in Washington, and his family was also a substantial Lilly shareholder. Bush's aide, Mitch Daniels, before joining the administration, had overseen the company's lobbying efforts as Lilly's vice president for corporate affairs, and would return to that post later. Not surprisingly, under Bush's presidency, the drug-makers' leading demand, intellectual property rights, shot to the top of the U.S. agenda during the NAFTA negotiations.

The vice president's June 1986 visit to Ottawa seemed to have a persuasive effect: by the end of that month, Michel Côté finally tabled the Tories' year-old drug bill — although not so anyone would notice. Trying to slip it onto the order paper in the dying hours of that spring's Parliament, Côté ended up outwitting himself: the measure languished on a Commons commissionaire's reception desk, untabled, while the House recessed.

In the next cabinet shuffle, a new, more enthusiastic minister replaced Côté: the following November, just as Murphy was getting down to the serious phase of the free trade negotitations, Harvie André introduced Bill C-22, giving the multinationals a seven- to ten-year monopoly on their wares. Admitting the government had been under "enormous pressure" from the U.S. drug companies, he stoutly denied that the measure had any link to the free trade talks. Even then, the Americans were not satisfied. One senior U.S. trade official declared the bill "barely acceptable": the brand name makers had been demanding the same seventeen- to twenty-year patent protection they had in the United States.

That victory would take another five years and a second bill, one of Mulroney's last pieces of legislation while in office. His government would claim the updated legislation was required to fall into line with the upcoming GATT treaty, but some industry experts still question that legal opinion. "It was 100 percent Mulroney's idea and doing," said one former aide. "Each draft of the bill was sent to his office and his first comment was, 'Did Mike see this?' meaning Mike Tarnow." By then, Tarnow had replaced Zabriskie as head of Merck Frosst Canada. Already it was clear Bill C-22 had not brought discernible benefits to the majority of Canadians beyond the brand name makers' commitment to spend 5 percent more on research: within three years of its passage, the cost of prescription drugs in the country had almost doubled to $1.9 billion, wreaking havoc with provincial budgets.

But that ongoing pharmaceutical battle would prove a boon to some of Mulroney's friends. Among them was Bill Fox, who left government in 1987 to set up his own Ottawa lobbying business. There — and later when he joined other denizens of the Tory backrooms in Earnscliffe Strategy Group — Fox would sign up three major American drug-makers as clients, including the Canadian subsidiary of Ed Pratt's Pfizer Inc.

Jim Kelleher, too, would end up with ties to the U.S. brand name drug-makers. In 1990, two years after his defeat at the hands of Sault unions that could not forgive him for the free trade deal, he joined the Toronto law firm of Gowling, Strathy and Henderson, which had developed the largest intellectual property practice on the continent. Its founding partner Gordon Henderson had represented Merck in its successful suit against the Canadian generic firm Apotex, but as Kelleher put it, "I don't think there's a drug firm in the world we don't act for."

During the 1992 constitutional referendum, before Mulroney's second drug bill was introduced, the Pharmaceutical Manufacturers Association of Canada, the U.S. firms' Ottawa front, would also donate $214,000 of prepaid airtime to the government's Yes campaign — the largest single donation of any individual or corporation. The brand name industry had originally booked the airtime for its advertising war against its generic rivals — a campaign that had featured a blindfolded man attempting to make his way across a street in heavy traffic beneath the slogan "Knowledge is power."

As the free trade talks progressed, that image of a blindfolded citizen seemed a bitterly ironic commentary on the state of the Canadian public. For, contrary to Harvie André's vehement assertions that Bill C-22 had nothing to do with the free trade talks, it had almost sunk the deal. After a stormy passage in the House of Commons, the legislation had run aground in the Liberal-controlled Senate, where it sat in a seven-month filibuster. During the last tense days hammering out the final trade agreement in Washington, the White House had threatened to throw the whole thing overboard unless Ottawa rammed through the pharmaceutical bill.

That pressure came directly from Ed Pratt, whose corporate advisory committee was pivotal to winning approval of the deal in Congress. "He was breathing down our necks," Murphy said. "He was banging around on the Hill, and he would call me directly. He was there the whole time, even though he knew we weren't going to pick up intellectual property in the agreement."

The pact finally went ahead without the drug bill. But when Liberal senators relented three weeks later, the government broke out a celebratory round of drinks in a panelled antechamber. "I didn't realize it would take so blooming long," Harvie André sighed. But until the very end, Mulroney, André, and other ministers kept up their pretence that the drug bill had no connection to the trade talks. It was the young Turks in Clayton Yeutter's office who let the pharmaceutical cat out of the bag. In their initial October 4, 1987, summary of the deal for Reagan's cabinet, they acknowledged an agreement for the "effective protection of pharmaceuticals in Canada by liberalizing compulsory licensing provisions." By the time an updated version of the text was released to the press days later, that admission had disappeared. But both Murphy and Merkin confirm the link.

What was significant about the Mulroney government's denials was that they signalled the extent to which subterfuge had become its official *modus operandi* in Canada–U.S. relations. Even before Murphy and Reisman had hit centre stage, the prime minister and his inner circle were cutting secret side deals with powerful American interests. The pharmaceutical bill was only the most obvious. Many of the clues to other confidential arrangements would emerge accidentally, or years later, long after the election that would hand Brian Mulroney a second term in office. Then he would move on to implementing the next phase of Reagan's continental imperative.

In January 1989 a brief bureaucratic notice in the *Canada Gazette*, the government's legislative bulletin, provided the next piece of evidence: two months earlier, it announced, the cabinet had awarded a Schedule-B banking licence to American Express, whose chairman, James Robinson III — better known around the PMO as "Jimmy Three-Sticks" — had founded the U.S. coalition that finessed the trade pact through Congress. The government had selected a curious day to go about that banking business, but a day that could not have been better chosen for secrecy: on November 21, 1988, most politicians and reporters were at the polls, preoccupied with the outcome of a federal election that had turned into a referendum on the free trade pact. As journalist Linda McQuaig noted in *The Quick and the Dead*, "It seemed like an odd day for cabinet ministers to be sitting around tidying up housecleaning matters; after all, they could have been out of a job the next day."

The fact they were not was due in no small measure to David Culver, the chairman of Alcan and a longtime friend of Robinson's, who had served on the American Express board since 1980. In July 1987, shortly after Robinson dispatched his executive vice president Harry Freeman to set up the American Coalition for Trade Expansion with Canada in Washington, Culver had followed suit with a Canadian version. He and a handful of other members from Tom d'Aquino's Business Council on National Issues formed the Alliance for Trade and Job Opportunities, which operated out of Alcan's head office in Montreal. Its co-chairmen were former Alberta premier Peter Lougheed and Donald Macdonald, whose royal commission had paved the way for Mulroney's trade initiative — and who had his own links to the American Express machine: in 1956 he had been Freeman's classmate at Harvard Law School.

During the cliffhanger 1988 election, Culver's alliance devoted $2.3 million to ads promoting the free trade deal — almost as much as the Conservative Party itself, which was limited by law to spending no more than $8 million for the whole campaign. Thus, thanks to a fluke that the Canadian Elections Act had not foreseen — a single-issue vote — the coalition's drum-beating for free trade provided Mulroney with $2.3 million extra in radio and TV spots during the final weeks of his tight re-election race.

Two months later, when news leaked out about Amex's banking licence — giving the corporation access to Canada's huge and profitable automatic teller network, despite the fact that it failed to meet legal requirements — the Canadian Bankers Association leaped to an obvious conclusion. "This was done because Robinson supported free trade," fumed Toronto Dominion chairman Robert Korthals, who was later criticized for his outburst. "This was the deal that I guess the Prime Minister made with him, and it would appear that he didn't think of the implications of this policy-on-the-run-for-my-friend approach."

But Mulroney seemed to understand those implications all too well. Why else the secrecy? According to Harry Freeman, American Express's bid for Canadian banking status had begun in 1985, soon after the prime minister's election, and had been quietly approved in principle by the finance ministry a year later, just as the free trade negotiations were coming to a crunch. But for three years, that bid had been kept under wraps.

Critics charged that the licence was a reward to Amex for promoting the free trade pact in Washington. But as Freeman noted, selling the Canadian agreement to Congress was "a slam dunk. There was no organized opposition," he said. "The AFL–CIO shrugged their shoulders. A lot of people said, 'A free trade agreement with Canada? I thought we already had one!'"

In fact, others argued that the gratitude was the other way around. Certainly, the surreptitious manner in which Mulroney's government had awarded those considerations to U.S. multinationals raised questions: To what else had Canadian voters been blindfolded?

IN the fall of 1985, Mulroney's pal Robert Bourassa was making his own last bid for re-election, but the two kept in constant touch by phone. At one campaign stop in the northern Quebec outpost of Chibougamau, Bourassa confessed to the *Toronto Star's* Bob McKenzie that he'd just warned the prime minister of the risks inherent in his roll of the dice: a free trade agreement could unleash "an internal dynamic" whose momentum was unstoppable. "Free trade leads to a customs union, which supposes common external tariffs," Bourassa said. "And that leads us to a common market.

And from there, it's on to a monetary union and a sort of political union."

But those risks were far from the minds of Derek Burney and his aide Michael Hart two months earlier as they boarded Mike Smith's sailboat at Annapolis, outside Washington, on a cloudless July weekend. The pair had come on a secretive mission to probe the deputy U.S. trade representative for clues on whether they could get any kind of acceptable deal at all. Over beer, they skimmed the waters of Chesapeake Bay, plumbing the Americans' will.

Smith insisted that the White House would settle only for a guarantee that there would never again be barriers to U.S. investment or ownership, especially of Canadian resource companies, as there had been under Trudeau's Foreign Investment Review Agency. "That was our bottom line," says Bill Merkin, who served as Smith's first mate. Burney made clear that Ottawa needed protection from U.S. trade reprisals — the endless countervail and dumping cases that were plaguing Canadian industries and costing them millions in lawyers' and lobbying fees. As Burney tells it, he got the assurances he was seeking. But as Merkin recalled, that was, perhaps, a misunderstanding — only the first of many that ran through the two-year bargaining process like a leitmotif. "Mike was very careful what he said," Merkin explained. "And my guess is Derek came away thinking, 'Well, they didn't say no.' But we knew it was almost a political untouchable. We never had any authority to give them that."

Jim Kelleher had gone ahead and drawn up the legislative authorization to begin negotiations, winning cabinet approval, when, as he said, "the prime minister told me to go fishing." In the spring of 1986 the U.S. Senate finance committee put the White House on notice that it might vote down the so-called fast-track authority for negotiating with Ottawa, which would prevent Congress from meddling with the final terms of the settlement. The revolt was led by the committee chair, Bob Packwood, and three other lumber state senators, who were under pressure with an election looming to rein in Canadian softwood imports. But the committee mainly wanted more say in crafting a tougher U.S. trade policy at a time it felt ignored by the White House. At 8 A.M. Yeutter had woken up Kelleher with the bad news. As the minister protested, Canada had been "sideswiped" by a domestic squabble between Reagan and Congress.

At the White House, frantic political horse-trading began. This was not the example that James Baker had intended to make of Canada. Reagan himself was recruited to get on the line with Packwood, but in the end the committee deadlock hung on a single swing vote — that of Senator Spark Matsunaga of Hawaii, a state that had no bone to pick with Ottawa. The White House promised him a multimillion-dollar federal project for Hawaii. "It cost them a lot of money," said Kelleher, who has a photo in his Senate office of Mulroney taking the call from the White House notifying him of Matsunaga's capitulation. "Brian is slapping me on the back and Charley McMillan is there grabbing my hand," he said. "We were all just whooping it up."

The next crisis broke a month later, as Peter Murphy kicked off the talks with Reisman in Ottawa, where some wag had hung a photograph in the negotiation boardroom showing a small boy dwarfed by an elephant. While Bill Fox's media machine was depicting the week as a landmark in Canadian–U.S. relations, Washington's International Trade Commission announced a 35 percent duty on Canadian cedar shakes and shingles which threatened to cost 4,000 British Columbia jobs. Mulroney seemed genuinely stunned, denouncing the move as "bizarre, appalling, and unacceptable" — uncharacteristically strong language for him. He promptly fired off a letter to Reagan expressing his "profound disappointment." Tom Niles, the new U.S. ambassador, had tried to talk him out of sending it, but Niles's advice came too late; the embassy chauffeur was already hand-delivering the protest to the White House.

"The timing could not have been more offensive," said Myer Rashish, the former State Department official who had nurtured Reagan's North American accord. "It plays to every Canadian paranoia: it conveys to the Canadians that the United States takes them as second-class citizens."

But was that, in fact, the idea? In a cable to the State Department, Niles had reported that the Canadian government, "as expected, is showing signs of panic." Nor had the White House stepped in to put off the announcement as it would do countless times later. A top official had called Murphy and Merkin in Ottawa the day beforehand to warn them of the bombshell on its way. Merkin laughed at the recollection: "We packed up and got out of town."

That blow put Reisman's team on the defensive from the first week — a typical negotiating ploy. But as American trade sanctions piled up over the next year and free-marketeers muttered about the spectre of a trade war, a frenzy built on the Canadian side to wrest some sort of deal from Washington. Reisman and Gotlieb argued that this was precisely the sort of harassment a trade pact would prevent. Already, the dynamic that Bourassa had warned of was in play. A policy that had originated with Reagan was becoming a do-or-die scenario for Mulroney.

More than a year after the negotiations began, anxious leaks filtered out of Reisman's camp that there were still "big rocks to move" and "bullets to bite." In truth, he had been unable to force Murphy to reveal the U.S. positions on most key issues. "We knew the exquisite close press attention in Canada could be used to our advantage," Merkin said. "Peter would say something and suddenly Simon would have to defend a non-issue, basically taking us away from substantive issues, which we didn't want to deal with."

In the Canadian media, Murphy's every utterance was front-page fare; fellow U.S. trade negotiators were stunned to find their shy, laconic colleague besieged by the press the moment he stepped off the plane in Ottawa. "It was like travelling with a rock star," marvelled USTR official Alan Holmer. But in Washington no one was paying attention — not even Clayton Yeutter, who was wrapped up with the Japanese negotiating semiconductor chip quotas. "We'd hold briefings for Congress and nobody would show up," Merkin recalled. "There was nobody looking over our shoulder, so we could play Negotiation 101 with Simon and drive him crazy."

Never a master communicator, the impenetrable Murphy would purposely mumble or obfuscate. "He'd make them guess what he was getting at," Merkin said. When it came to Ottawa's entreaties for an exemption from U.S. trade complaints, he would refuse to commit anything to paper. That, Merkin admitted, was the unaddressed hurdle at the heart of the talks: "We were dancing around the issue big-time."

Nor were he and Murphy sharing their strategy with the State Department, which they did not trust. "They wanted an agreement, and they'd just give it away," Murphy scoffed. He also avoided briefing Niles. "We didn't want our ambassador up there mucking around in it," he said, "so we didn't keep him as plugged in as we could have."

By the summer of 1987, Ontario's premier David Peterson, who had fought the talks, was railing that he could not find out if Reisman's two-decade-old Auto Pact, which had helped build the provincial automotive industry, was on the table. Reisman himself had told a Cleveland legal symposium that the safeguards ought to be phased out, and Peterson had good reason to fret. That spring a new figure had appeared on the rarefied bilateral landscape: Fred Jones Hall, an Oklahoma auto-parts heir who had suddenly been named head of the State Department's Canada desk.

A political appointee, Hall was the godson of Holmes Tuttle, the California multimillionaire who was one of the leaders of Reagan's Kitchen Cabinet. More than half a century earlier, Tuttle and Hall's grandfather, Fred Jones, had started out working side by side at a Ford plant in Oklahoma for 5 cents an hour. Tuttle had headed for California, where he bought a used car lot — the first step to a vast fortune that made him the state's biggest auto dealer; Jones had stayed in Oklahoma, founded Braniff Air Lines, and set up an automotive parts business. But the two had remained close — so close that Tuttle had often talked of a patronage appointment for his godson. But it was not until early 1987, when the Iran-Contra affair had left Reagan's presidency adrift and political appointees were bailing out of the administration at an alarming rate, that Fred Jones Hall received his urgent summons from Tuttle. "He said, 'Now is the time to serve your country,'" Hall recounted.

At the time he was appointed, U.S. officials were intent on watering down the Auto Pact — above all, the provision that required American manufacturers to assemble one car or truck in Canada for every one they exported. Such an erosion would threaten Ontario's industrial base, where the auto industry provided a third of all manufacturing jobs. But before Hall had time to pack up for Washington, he was dispatched to Ottawa to accompany Reagan on his first visit to the capital in six years. There, where he watched in disbelief as the NDP's Svend Robinson booed the president on the floor of the Commons, the main topic on the agenda was how to salvage the foundering trade talks.

Hall admitted he might have preferred an ambassadorship, but that would have required divesting himself of his corporate holdings, including Fred Jones Manufacturing Co., his grandfather's Oklahoma auto-parts empire and eleven car dealerships. Instead, he stayed in close touch with his business while keeping an eye on the Canadian talks. Newly married and expensively tailored, sporting gold and enamel cufflinks in the shape of cars, Hall cut a solitary figure in the U.S. capital. He confessed he knew only two people when he arrived: the president and George Shultz. As for his Canadian dossier, his knowledge was equally limited but precise: in addition to the auto industry, he knew the oil business. Nearly a decade earlier, Trudeau's National Energy Program had provoked him to sell his family's Alberta oil exploration company to Imperial Oil — a sale that still rankled.

Over lunch at a tony Washington watering hole where rattlesnake was featured on the menu, Hall left the inescapable impression that his assignment was not only to oversee a trade agreement that could affect the family business; it was also to keep an eye out for the interests of other members in the California Kitchen Cabinet, notably those of Hollywood. He made it clear there was one issue, above all others, that the president cared about: the country's cultural exemption, which would leave a contentious proposed film policy intact. "Does he ever!" Hall declared. "It may be only a question of a million dollars, but it could have the effect of a hydrogen bomb on the trade talks."

In the end, the fireworks came from another source: on a September day in Washington, a month before congressional fast-track negotiating authority ran out, Simon Reisman stormed out of the Winder Building, declaring the talks were off. Murphy and Merkin had been expecting the walkout and were relieved when at last it came. "I thought, 'Thank God,'" Murphy sighed. "'Somebody else can do this.'"

As he suspected, the Canadian exit had been planned. A day earlier, Reisman's deputy, Gordon Ritchie, had flown to Ottawa to secure Mulroney's permission. And Merkin smirked when, as the Canadian team left, Ritchie handed out a press release in both official languages. "Which meant they had to have prepared it before," he said. "We knew they'd be back."

But the standoff dragged on. Mulroney needed some protective mechanism from U.S. trade sanctions; after all, he had sold the negotiations to the Canadian public on that basis. The White House was adamant on securing the unrestricted right to invest in Canada, but for Mulroney that was a political hot potato. A month earlier, Allan Gregg's polls had shown that 72 percent of Canadians wanted to keep some restrictions on foreign investment. At last, it was time for the politicians to move in for a settlement. In the Prime Minister's Office, Derek Burney took over the negotiations, elated that Treasury Secretary James Baker was finally on the case.

"You knew when you got James Baker on a file," Burney said, "that it was something the President wanted done."

In Washington, the prospect of facing James A. Baker III across a negotiating table did not always produce the same warm fuzzies. A brusque Houston blueblood with eyes the colour of flint, Baker had demonstrated such ruthlessness at taking care of White House political business that he had earned the distrust of many on the Republican Party's right wing, who accused him of routinely sacrificing ideology to expediency. But Baker had also shown extraordinary skill in schmoozing the press through a conflict-of-interest scandal that would have sunk any other cabinet official.

In early 1989 the *Washington Post* had discovered that, throughout his tenure at Treasury, Baker had retained direct control over huge personal share blocks in a handful of American corporations that might have been affected by his portfolio — including the holding company of New York's Chemical Bank. Indeed, if there were two issues that Baker knew cold, they were investment and financial services. "It cost Canada dearly," Merkin said. "He put his foot down on both those issues and those were the two areas where Canada gave."

But there was another issue that, as a crack Houston corporate lawyer, James Baker knew just as well: energy — the centrepiece of the negotiations for many in corporate America. When Baker reluctantly agreed to sell his Chemical Bank stock, he revealed he had also held shares in Exxon, Amoco, and Texaco during the free trade talks, where he managed to nail down a major eleventh-hour concession from the Mulroney government on Canadian oil and gas reserves.

At the beginning of the negotiations, Murphy and Merkin believed they had squeezed all the energy concessions possible from Ottawa. But the Big Six U.S. oil companies were pushing for unrestricted access to the country's supplies. They had even attempted to secure their own side deal through a colleague deemed to have unassailable Canadian connections: Drew Lewis, the former acid rain envoy who had become chairman of Union Pacific Corp., which controlled huge continental oilfields.

But on the final bleak, rainy autumn weekend of the negotiations, as the clock ticked towards the witching hour when the fast-track deadline expired, Saturday midnight October 3, Baker managed to get energy provisions on the table again: to the astonishment of Murphy and Merkin, he had won the assurance that, in a crisis,

Washington would have call on Canadian oil and gas reserves, with no greater limits on energy exports to the United States than those imposed on the country's own citizens. "Baker worked out the numbers," Murphy marvelled. "God only knows if we'd have an agreement without it, because it was an important issue — a selling point in Congress." At last, Ronald Reagan had won his continental energy policy, the catalyst for his North American vision.

Inside the august stone fortress of the U.S. Treasury Building, the fractious Canadian delegation had swelled to an unruly size. In addition to Derek Burney, Trade Minister Pat Carney and Finance Minister Michael Wilson had flown in, as well as Wilson's deputy, Stanley Hartt; Allan Gotlieb had showed up from the embassy, but as Gordon Ritchie would vehemently insist, he "was there as a courtesy, not a decision-taker." Ritchie was later scathing in his assessment of the "overly accommodating Gotlieb," whom he accused of wanting to cede to the Americans on several key points. Indeed, so numerous and ample were the egos present that many are still fighting to this day over what happened and how. Another participant would later dispute Ritchie's version of events. "Nonsense," he cracked, "Gotlieb was a very valuable part of the team. Simon had to have someone to yell at."

Shortly after midnight, Baker and Burney emerged before the sodden media, which had been camped outside the Treasury Building in the rain all night. Both sides claimed victory, although there was no immediate way to judge those assertions: the technocrats would still be working out the finer points of the agreement long after the next morning's press conference signalling the deal was done. Over the weeks to come, the draft text would continue to change, with clauses evaporating at the first whiff of controversy. But a leaked U.S. briefing paper for Baker and Yeutter offered the clearest assessment of Washington's perspective: "Essentially," it said, "in the text, we got everything we wanted."

The White House took greatest pride in the clause it had considered the dealbreaker — investment. "We could not end the life of Investment Canada, their screening agency," the paper conceded, "but we greatly circumscribed the scope of its activities by limiting them to [the] review of only large acquisitions . . . The real achievement of the agreement is that henceforth the vast majority of new U.S. investments in Canada will occur with no interference by the Canadian government."

Indeed, foreign control of the country's economy — already the highest of any industrialized nation — would increase after the deal closed in 1988. Before the negotiations, 50 percent of Canadian manufacturing, 45 percent of the oil business, and 40 percent of the mining and smelting industries were owned by those outside the country — a figure already reduced under Trudeau from previous highs. After the agreement, foreign ownership would jump in forestry, pulp and paper-making, and mining, but most of all in the chemical sector.

The U.S. briefing paper also provided the first hint of secret promises that Ottawa had made to deal with U.S. gripes over its pharmaceutical and film policies. Mulroney and his fellow minister would heatedly deny any such deals, despite the overwhelming evidence of subsequent events to confirm them. Indeed, over the next year, as free trade critics mobilized and the 1988 election drew nigh, the government grew increasingly zealous in defending its version of the pact. Opponents were ridiculed as dinosaurs, clinging to a retrograde view of the country and lacking the machismo to move forward. Even supporters found their positions closely monitored for heresy. In 1988 Pat Carney discovered that all her personal files on the negotiations, which she had donated to the National Archives, had been shredded. According to the Archives' evaluation, that was no mean task: "30 feet of docketed correspondence and five cubic feet of departmental memoranda." "They were destroyed on purpose," she charged. Although no culprit was found, Carney was adamant. "They wouldn't have been destroyed without someone's authority." Three years later, the Privy Council Office finally arranged to pay her $20,000 in compensation. But as she pointed out, no money would make up the loss: future historians would be unable "to make complete judgments because they won't have much of the material."

In Ottawa, civil servants who proved ardent evangelists for the free trade agreement found their careers flourishing at External Affairs and other bureaucracies. Two key trade officials received ambassadorships. Lest anyone miss that message, Sylvia Ostry was made an example of what could happen to someone who did not prove a sufficiently enthusiastic cheerleader. As the chief organizer for the 1988 economic summit of industrialized nations that Mulroney hosted in Toronto five months before the election — a gathering Ronald Reagan would hail as an "open-for-business summit" — she was instructed to win an endorsement for the free trade deal in the final communiqué. After an all-night negotiating session at the Metro Convention Centre, she had wrung a statement from her reluctant European counterparts that the leaders "welcomed" the pact. Limping back to her hotel room at dawn, she had just stepped into her bath when she received an irate phone call from Derek Burney summoning her to a meeting of the Canadian team.

There, Burney had administered a blistering rebuke that left many witnesses aghast: the prime minister, he raged, was furious at her failure to secure a more forceful plug on the day the free trade debate was beginning in the House of Commons. Ostry was obliged to reconvene her fellow sherpas in the convention centre basement until she finally wrested the demanded endorsement from them. That afternoon at the leaders' wrap-up press conference, after frenzied behind-the-scenes lobbying, Mulroney beamed from the stage over his semantic victory: a single word, the adverb "strongly," had been added to the clause welcoming his free trade agreement.

On the sidelines, Ostry's foreign counterparts whispered their sympathy. But the next day, *Toronto Star* columnist Carol Goar reported that "several Mulroney aides admitted, when pressed, that they considered Ostry arrogant, imperious and not worthy of her own vaunted self-image."

In July 1988, a month after the summit, at the kind of genteel self-congratulatory ceremony the White House had become so expert at staging, Reagan officially sent the pact to Congress, hailing it as "the cornerstone for the North American accord, that new era of growth, opportunity and friendship on our continent." On his left, grinning and applauding, stood Clayton Yeutter, who had blurted out an indiscretion after the pact was initialled which recalled Robert Bourassa's warning. "The Canadians don't understand what they have signed," he gloated to a *Toronto Star* reporter. "In twenty years, they will be sucked into the U.S. economy."

BILL Merkin stared into a network news camera. Two years after the free trade agreement was in place, he was trying to explain why yet another U.S. Commerce Department trade complaint had been launched against a Canadian industry. If Canadians thought the pact would spare them from American trade complaints, Merkin shrugged, there had been a "misperception." The scorn in his voice was veiled, but unmistakable: if Ottawa's negotiating team had never really caught on to the game, that was their misfortune. Indeed, Merkin would repeatedly underline that his Canadian counterparts were, to some extent, snookered.

Mulroney and his officials had crowed over their victory in securing a binding dispute-settlement process from Washington which would put an end to the country's interminable cross-border trade battles. "The crowning jewel" of the pact, Kelleher had termed it. But Merkin would insist that did not mean countervail and dumping actions were over. "Canada wanted somehow to be exempt from U.S. trade law, but they never got that and they knew they didn't get it," he said. The problem, he suggested, was that, in the heat of the 1988 election campaign, "The agreement was oversold."

Not only did U.S. trade retaliation not end, but three years after the pact went into effect on January 1, 1989, the number of cases increased to such a point that Simon Reisman declared, "The Americans are bastards." Gordon Ritchie accused Washington of breaching both the spirit and "in some cases even the letter itself" of the agreement. In January 1992 External Affairs Minister Barbara McDougall flew to the U.S. capital to protest, threatening retaliation. And even the new ambassador to the United States, Derek Burney, a true believer, was decrying the "harassments" and urging Canadian industries to start launching their own dumping and countervail cases against the Americans. Meanwhile, the disputes piled up legal and lobbying fees.

Over a decade, as one complaint after another was launched against Canadian softwood lumber producers, they had hired a dizzying array of U.S. lobbyists: at one point, the forestry coalition had two rival consultants on its payroll — former Democratic presidential candidate Walter Mondale and the man who had been the architect of his defeat, Reagan's campaign strategist Ed Rollins. Later, it would hire the firm of Robinson, Lake, Lerer and Montgomery — whose principal partners were Jim Lake, a former campaign aide for both Reagan and Bush, and Linda Robinson, the wife of the chairman of American Express. The softwood lumber industry estimated it had spent $20 million on U.S. lobbyists to repeatedly fight a case that it finally won in 1994.

Indeed, Mulroney had originally touted the free trade initiative as the engine that would create "jobs, jobs, jobs." But by March 1991 435,000 had been lost in twenty months, and a year later unemployment was at 11.2 percent, the highest in seven-and-a-half years. Part of the blame was laid on a general continental recession. But three years after the final deal was cut, 65 percent of the manufacturing jobs that had vanished in Ontario were from permanent plant closings. Ritchie argued that the agreement should never have been expected to create employment; Mulroney's promises were "a specious claim made in the heat of an election campaign."

The free trade agreement did provide a jobs program in one sector: the trade consultant industry. Most of those involved in the negotiations ended up thriving as advisers in the ongoing disputes. Ritchie himself would set up shop in Ottawa, representing Canadian softwood lumber producers, as well as Stelco and the corporation that had led the election pitch for the agreement, Alcan. Simon Reisman, too, would return to the consulting business, hired by the multinational grocery business, Beatrice Foods, and Ranger Oil, where he would become chairman as the company began exploration in the United States, Peru, and the Gulf of Mexico.

In Washington, Clayton Yeutter, who had once strong-armed the Japanese into concessions on computer chips, raised eyebrows by joining the board of a company that had directly benefited from his forcefulness, Texas Instruments. And in October 1988 his deputy trade representative, Mike Smith, packed in thirty years in government service to set up a trade consulting practice at the Steptoe and Johnson law firm, which would reap huge profits from Mexico during the NAFTA negotiations.

That year, Bill Merkin also left government to join Washington's Strategic Policy Inc., which promptly landed a contract from one of the most beleaguered Canadian industries: the country's breweries. From February 1990 until July 1993, his firm would earn $1,159,991 from the Brewers Association of Canada, the Brewers of Ontario, and John Labatt.

Only Peter Murphy did not make any money from the Canadian free trade negotiations. After leaving government, he joined the Washington lobby firm of Cassidy and Associates as vice president of international affairs, but was soon too sick to play rainmaker. On October 20, 1994, six years after he had wrapped up the agreement with Ottawa, he died.

That pact had drastically changed Canada's course, and nobody knew it better than Murphy. Sitting in a Chevy Chase restaurant a year before his death, he acknowledged the parallels between the U.S. aims in the Canadian trade talks and those with Mexico, which were kicking up a controversy in Congress at the time. During the NAFTA debate, Canadians would read with a certain smugness that Washington's real designs on Mexico were not economic but political: to "lock in" the free market reforms of President Carlos Salinas de Gortari against the whims of any future nationalistic successor. If the notion had a faintly imperialistic ring, it might also have had a disquieting resonance. For, as a 1989 State Department briefing note for George Bush would reveal, the trade agreement with Ottawa had been aimed at those same considerations: "to prevent a return to inward-looking, nationalistic policies of the 1970s, especially in energy, investment, banking and services."

Canada, too, had been locked into a neoconservative economic destiny. And, as Murphy confirmed, that had been the ultimate aim all along. "We didn't enter the agreement over tariffs," he said. "The Canadian agreement is a political one — to make sure you don't go back to those policies like the National Energy Policy."

No matter what measures Mulroney might take to placate Reagan or Bush, they would never be enough to reassure Washington that another Pierre Trudeau would not come along and try to re-Canadianize the country. "It wasn't that Mulroney aggressively needed prodding," Murphy said. "It was a future prime minister we were worried about."

11 Partying to Win

THWACK, **THUMP**. It was the sound of one hand slapping. Canadian Press reporter Juliet O'Neill and a cluster of photographers planted on the Canadian ambassador's driveway snapped to attention. They had been gossiping among themselves during a lull in the parade of limousines disgorging the famous and powerful who had come to pay tribute to Brian Mulroney on his March 1986 state visit to Washington. Then, on the porch outside the front door, the scarlet-sheathed arm of the ambassador's wife, Sondra Gotlieb, had suddenly been raised. O'Neill watched in disbelief as it struck out at the pale, powdered cheek of Connie Gibson Connor, the embassy's social secretary. Flesh met flesh in a forehand, then a backhand.

Thwack, thump. The sound rent the stillness of the balmy spring evening air. There was some added tympani: the skittering of an amethyst and pearl earring down the porch steps and the swift tattoo of Connor's evening sandals as she, too, fled down the stairs and around the mansion towards the back servants' entrance. But the next morning, as wire service terminals clattered out O'Neill's story, which a fearful deskman had spiked the night before, there were those in the stunned U.S. and Canadian capitals who detected another sound: the death knell for a high-profile Canadian foreign policy that had transformed Sondra and Allan Gotlieb into diplomatic superstars, anointed by *Vanity Fair* and the *Wall Street Journal* as the hottest couple on Embassy Row.

Not only had the Gotliebs succeeded in scaling such dizzying heights on Washington's treacherous social slopes that one-third of the cabinet could be seen at their parties, but they had shored up their celebrity by providing a rare glimpse of the capital's inner workings through Sondra's twice-monthly columns in the *Washington Post.* In satires that took the form of fictional letters to a friend named Beverly back home, she had chronicled the comedy of manners being played out in the city's most rarefied social circles. In the process, she had assured her husband and herself leading roles in the ongoing plot of that insular universe on the Potomac which she had christened Powertown.

But therein lay the paradox on which the Gotliebs suddenly found themselves impaled. Had they not crafted such social and media stardom for themselves, Sondra's gaffe might have passed unnoticed instead of rating headlines around the globe as what the *Post* termed the Slap Flap. Nor could the scandal be dismissed only as a portent of the Gotliebs' own social demise. For in Sondra's columns and Allan's speeches, both had taken pains to make clear that they had deliberately used the city's social scene as the chief instrument to win attention for Canada's concerns from its most vital ally and trading partner.

Gotlieb had devised that strategy in the days of Pierre Trudeau, conferring on it the earnest title Public Diplomacy. But in her *Post* satires, his wife had given it another name — a name far better suited to Mulroney's glitz and Gucci style: Partying to Win. Whatever its label, it turned out to be a foreign policy tool tailor-made for the irrepressible social animal who had succeeded Trudeau at 24 Sussex Drive.

No one valued the fruits of the Gotliebs' labours in the social vineyards more than Mulroney. And when the prime minister arrived at their Rock Creek Drive residence on that fateful evening of March 19, he was already in high spirits, basking in the afterglow of a guest spot on NBC's *Today Show* and the most lavish welcome showered on any Canadian leader in recent memory. For the boy from Baie Comeau, this, his first full-dress visit to the U.S. capital, had been the stuff of dreams come true. Sitting beside Reagan on the White House lawn while the Marine Corps band serenaded his presence and cannons boomed a nineteen-gun salute, he had been unable to contain his awe. Leaning over to the president, he whispered, "That's a gorgeous sight."

Even ABC's Sam Donaldson had been unable to rain on his parade: noisily demanding to know why the two leaders had broken with tradition to remain sitting during the ceremonies, Donaldson had forced the White House to reveal the elaborate measures required to mask Mulroney's balance problem. But the press ignored that revelation in favour of officials rhapsodizing over his chummy relationship with Reagan.

At the White House state dinner the previous night, even the *Washington Post*'s veteran social chroniclers had marvelled that "It was 'Ron' and 'Nancy' and 'Brian' and 'Mila' by the time the toasts rolled around." Still, one of its reporters could not resist recording Mulroney's "knowing grin" as he apologized later for his first-name breach of protocol. Not that he could be blamed for wanting to show off before a glittering crowd that included the Agha Khan, Fiat chairman Gianni Agnelli, and *National Review* publisher William Buckley Jr., whose brother-in-law Austin Taylor was chairman of Toronto's McLeod, Young and Weir. Mulroney had even invited his old friends Paul Desmarais and Ross Johnson along to share his moment of glory. Now, capping his visit, was this final black-tie dinner at the Gotliebs' residence, where he was to play host to Vice President George Bush.

The only problem was that the guest of honour had another engagement that night, a speech in Philadelphia, which the embassy was reluctant to acknowledge lest it appear Mulroney rated second place on Bush's dance card. The vice president had only agreed to drop by the ambassador's residence later for coffee, but dinner had been held for him all the same. By the time Bush's limousine pulled up at 9:30 P.M., the cocktail hour had dragged on for nearly two hours and, in a city where the movers and shakers made it a point to be home in bed by 10:30 P.M., tempers were fraying. It was near the end of those two hours that Sondra Gotlieb stepped onto her front porch with Connie Connor, supposedly to ask about the presence of another White House official. In fact, she was on the lookout for signs of Bush when she delivered the blow that would immortalize her in Canadian-American relations as "the slugger."

Still, the slap had occurred outside the party, witnessed only by an accidental few. Inside the residence, most guests remained blithely unaware of the incident until they picked up the next morning's paper. At the chintz-decked tables in a huge dining tent that had been raised in the ambassadorial garden, the Americans' relief at finding a Canadian leader so accommodating was thick enough to cut with a knife. As Mulroney at last made his toast to Bush over the Manitoba golden caviar and the Ontario Château des Charmes, lawyer Robert Strauss had leaned across the table to grin at his friend James Baker with a proprietary air: "He does well, doesn't he?"

In fact, Mulroney had done so well he was furious when it became clear that Sondra Gotlieb had upstaged his triumph — a triumph he would never manage to duplicate. For hours after the dinner, as his forty-seventh birthday dawned with a sudden funereal air, he had paced his suite in the Madison Hotel, raging at the injustice as Bill Fox and Fred Doucet tried to plot damage control before they knew the full extent of the damage. The next morning, Bruce Phillips, the former CTV newsman whom Mulroney had rewarded with a patronage posting as Gotlieb's press counsellor, had released a terse statement claiming "an incident of a purely personal character" had occurred, but was "immediately regretted, an apology extended and at once accepted, and the issue was immediately resolved."

But the Slap Flap would remain headline-fodder for weeks. And two months later, the *Post*'s influential Style section, which had boosted the Gotliebs to prominence, raised the question of the awkward social cloud that had descended over the embassy. "A Big Chill for Canada?" its headline inquired.

In Ottawa, the External Affairs' rumour mill was already writing obituaries for Gotlieb's diplomatic career, without remorse. In his years heading the foreign ministry, he had won respect, but seldom affection. Still, to many at External the most intriguing question was not what fate would befall the ambassador, but what would become of his vaunted strategy for dealing with Washington. What would happen to Partying to Win now that the Gotliebs' own party seemed to be over?

IN Sondra Gotlieb's prescient comic novel, *First Lady, Last Lady*, her heroine, Nini Pike, had berated her husband for accepting a diplomatic post. "Why on earth would you want to become the ambassador?" she'd asked. "Give Washington to the Belnaps . . . Stephen and Moira can play bridge with the congressmen and run after the senators. That's what ambassadors do. All prestige and no power. High-class lobbyists. Let Moira give the tea parties and burst into tears when the cabinet wives don't show up."

A few months after the book was published in 1981, when Allan Gotlieb's appointment to Washington was announced, Nini Pike's query had echoed through Ottawa: Why on earth would he want to be ambassador? As one of the country's most senior mandarins, he had held some of the most important deputy ministries in the federal government. For the previous five years, as undersecretary of state for external affairs, he had exercised more power than any ambassador could dream of, nominally running the country's foreign policy for his political masters.

The Washington posting was a chance to put his own convictions into action. After Richard Nixon had slapped an across-the-board surcharge on all U.S. imports, Trudeau's attempt to lessen the country's dependence on Washington had led to the Third Option — an attempt to strengthen ties and trade with Europe. But it had also led to an outbreak of economic nationalism, climaxing in the Foreign Investment Review Agency and the National Energy Policy, which had provoked a reaction from Reagan's new army of free-marketeers that was growing uglier by the day. By 1981 Canadian relations had sunk to their lowest level since 1965, when Lyndon Johnson picked Lester Pearson up by the collar after an anti-Vietnam War speech in Philadelphia, thundering, "You pissed on my rug!"

Gotlieb felt Trudeau's lack of concern about his relations with Washington was a disastrous mistake. From his days heading the department's U.S. desk, he firmly believed that relationship remained the indisputable fulcrum on which the country's fate turned. In a 1991 lecture to the External Affairs department, Gotlieb would spell out that belief, referring again to the three policy options that former trade minister Mitchell Sharp had once presented to Trudeau: "It seems that history at this time has dictated the inevitability of the second option," he asserted, "closer economic integration with the United States."

As a graduate of Harvard Law School and a don who had read international law at Oxford, Gotlieb had analysed Canada's foreign policy with the same rigour he had once brought to parsing clauses in cod war agreements. His conclusion was that Ottawa's traditional quiet diplomacy was no longer working in Washington. In the wake of the Vietnam War and Nixon's Watergate scandal, he pointed out that the influence of the presidency, and indeed the entire U.S. executive branch, had been weakened. As Congress eagerly moved into that vacuum to make foreign and trade policy, Canada was increasingly running afoul of Capitol Hill and U.S. industries with the financial wherewithal to turn senators into their champions.

He argued that Ottawa could no longer rely on making its case discreetly through the bureaucratic back channels of the State Department. In a city where, unlike Ottawa, the centres of power were dispersed and the White House and Congress increasingly at odds, Gotlieb called for a new brand of diplomacy. He proposed sending the country's emissaries to roam the halls of Congress, making its case to cabinet and cultivating U.S. groups whose interests coincided with those of Ottawa. According to his prescription Canada ought to work the system, just like any lobbyist for Exxon or General Motors.

But unlike the influence-peddlers whose natty presence in one corridor of the Capitol had won it the nickname Gucci Gulch, the Canadian government could not rally any votes to pressure key congressmen. Thus, while Washington's most adroit lobbyists had traditionally kept their names out of the press, Gotlieb advocated a strong media and social presence to provide the embassy with compensating leverage.

For Ottawa's staid foreign policy establishment, it was an audacious strategy. But Trudeau, who had never favoured a low profile in his own political life, had bought it. When the architect of the scheme promptly proposed himself to carry it out, the prime minister had waved Gotlieb off to Washington, confident that Public Diplomacy was in the best possible hands.

At the time his posting was announced, it had provoked some raised eyebrows. In Ottawa, Gotlieb had been regarded as an owlish technocrat, brilliant and ambitious but often brusque, unlikely to cut the social mustard on Embassy Row. But what few of his critics understood was his telling passion for nineteenth-century French artist James Tissot, who had once been dismissed as a superficial society painter. Gotlieb's personal store of Tissot drawings — which ranked as the world's largest private collection — would stud the walls of the ambassador's residence, giving its endless black-tie evenings the echoes of another era's opulence and jaded *mondanité*. It scarcely seems surprising that the devotee of an artist who had once epitomized continental society would plunge into Washington's black-tie circuit with such gusto. Or that Sondra Gotlieb would later write in *Vanity Fair*, "Parties are the single most useful activity an embassy can engage in to promote its country's interests."

Later, Tom Axworthy, one of Trudeau's top advisers, would admit that none of the prime minister's confidants had realized just what Gotlieb meant when he talked about lobbying on Washington's social circuit. After all, as he was dispatched to the Congress of Vienna, hadn't Talleyrand told Louis XVIII, "I have more need for casseroles than written instructions"?

Washington's history had been littered with foreign envoys who had made a splash in the small town on the Potomac with their grace, their pomp, or their tables — from Lord Harlech's Kennedy family connections that had bathed the British Embassy in the reflected glow of Camelot to the caviar extravaganzas thrown by the Shah of Iran's envoy, Ardeshir Zahedi. Jimmy Carter's four-year effort to de-imperialize the presidency with a tide of down-home beer and peanuts had temporarily dimmed the chandeliers. But when Ronald and Nancy Reagan swept into Washington in a flurry of limousines, designer furs, and Hollywood friends, the tuxedo had come out of mothballs again as a political tool. Partying to Win was a tactic made to measure for the court of Ronald Reagan.

But Gotlieb was advocating no ordinary diplomatic foray onto the cocktail-and-canapés circuit. Instead of seeing the social scene as yet another Washington power centre to lobby, he had concluded that it was "the key to all their centres of power," as he told journalist Elaine Dewar. "It became clear to me that where Washington comes together is in the evenings, socially."

There were only two flaws in his scheme. One was that, by increasing the country's visibility, there could be a downside as well, ensuring that every misstep would be noted. The other had been summed up by a veteran Ottawa technocrat in one word:

Sondra. "As soon as you understood how much depended on her," that official pointed out, "you knew you had a highly unstable, volatile instrument of policy. Everybody knew she was unpredictable."

In fact, as respected CBC radio journalist Elizabeth Gray was only too well aware, the embassy Slap Flap was not Sondra Gotlieb's first. Years earlier, at a party in Ottawa, she had suddenly, inexplicably, struck her friend Gray across the face.

AS Sondra Gotlieb liked to tell it, her social celebrity just happened — like one of her inevitable mishaps. She had never been in Washington before she arrived as the ambassador's wife, and the Gotliebs' only previous diplomatic posting had been years earlier in Geneva, when Allan was just starting out his career. There, she had distinguished herself first by failing to pick up the after-dinner signal that the ladies were to leave the table when the port was served, then by blundering into the men's washroom, where Allan and his confrères caught her washing her hands in the urinal.

When the Gotliebs threw their first big Washington dinner for Mark MacGuigan, then Trudeau's external affairs minister, it had a certain quality of Geneva redux. A blinding snowstorm had blown guests onto the doorstep of their Rock Creek Drive mansion early, when Allan was still upstairs on the phone. Sondra had descended the mahogany staircase only to realize she didn't recognize a single face other than MacGuigan's. When she sighted a man who cut an appealing figure admiring her husband's collection of art nouveau boxes, she sidled up to him and confessed that she didn't know any of her guests; would he introduce her?

Ben Bradlee, the dashing and outspoken executive editor of the *Washington Post*, found it such a novel approach that he delightedly obliged. He and his wife, Sally Quinn, a former *Post* Style section star, watched in amusement as Sondra greeted one of her invitees. "Hi, I'm the hostess. Who are you?" she extended her hand. "I'm Caspar Weinberger," the startled secretary of defence replied — a response Gotlieb later immortalized in her column.

The next day, Bradlee sent a Style reporter around to Rock Creek Drive to profile the offbeat new ambassador's wife. Sondra Gotlieb lived up to his advance billing. She told the *Post*'s Stephanie

Mansfield how, at eighteen, when she was flunking out of university back home in Winnipeg, her parents had virtually arranged her marriage to Allan, then an Oxford don, whom she had known only ten days before the wedding. She recounted her Geneva misadventures in vivid detail, and made no attempt to hide her befuddlement about Washington protocol and her ineptitude with servants. And then there was the time in a Los Angeles hotel when she met California governor Jerry Brown in her bathrobe.

The day after the profile appeared on the trendy front page of the Style section, the *Today Show* asked her to appear as a guest. More importantly, the *Post* editorial board invited Allan Gotlieb to drop by for a talk. Within weeks, the *New York Times*, too, had recorded the new stand-up comedy act on Embassy Row: Allan, the earnest, bespectacled straight man; Sondra butting in to observe, "For some reason, people's eyes glaze over when you say Canada. Maybe we should invade South Dakota or something."

Overnight, the Gotliebs were off and running on the capital's social circuit, propelled by her daffy media persona. "Washington likes originals," notes a former embassy staffer. "And people were curious about Sondra, so they invited the Gotliebs out. That *Washington Post* story catapulted them right into the middle of the social scene and positioned them in a way that would have taken months to achieve by normal diplomatic channels. After that, they had it made."

In retrospect, some long-time students of capital society speculate that the Gotliebs had taken to heart one of the key tips in gossip columnist Diana McLellan's witty 1982 book, *Ear on Washington*: cultivate an image. To many, the image that Sondra Gotlieb presented was one with a noble tradition in the capital, personified by the late, irrepressible Alice Roosevelt Longworth, Teddy's daughter, who kept a cushion beside her with the needlepoint invitation: "If you don't have anything nice to say, sit by me."

But when Canadian journalist Elaine Dewar showed up to interview the ambassador's wife, she had found a slightly different persona — or personae. "Sondra would try one mode on and when it didn't work on me, she would slip into another," Dewar recalls. "She kept trying on roles to see what I would react to." Years later, when another reporter asked Gotlieb how, as a well-travelled diplomat's wife, the author of gourmet cookbooks and award-winning satirical fiction, she could have left the U.S. media with the image of such an unsophisticated scatterbrain, she explained that just before leaving Ottawa she had made a cross-country tour promoting *First Lady, Last Lady*. "I was still thinking in terms of a book tour," she said. "I thought, 'You've got to give them an angle.'"

Indeed, former embassy officials remember the Gotliebs' social celebrity as no accident. As soon as the new ambassador arrived in Washington, press counsellor Patrick Gossage had been charged with getting them ink, not to mention the cream of the city's vast media contingent for their guest lists. Gotlieb had carefully targeted a nucleus of opinion-makers: Joseph Kraft, James Reston, David Brinkley, and *Washington Post* publisher Katharine Graham — all of whom Sondra would later characterize in her column as "the famous press rather than the working press."

Gossage and his team had courted key names in the media with the same determination that other embassy staffers blitzed congressmen over hog tariffs. Gotlieb had emphasized repeatedly that the Serious Media, as Sondra put it, was even more critical to Public Diplomacy than the politicians on Capitol Hill. No matter what party was in power, the opinion-makers remained. "They have constancy," he had explained to Dewar. "Everything you say about their power is an understatement."

Soon after his arrival, Gotlieb had asked Undersecretary of State Myer Rashish, whom he had already met during Reagan's first ill-fated summit with Trudeau, to introduce him to columnist William Safire. Later that year, when Rashish was ousted from the State Department by his mercurial boss, Al Haig, he found himself dropped from the Gotliebs' guest lists — while his longtime friend Safire become a regular presence at their table.

In seducing the press, the Gotliebs enjoyed two strokes of luck. One was that many of the U.S. media's rising stars at the time happened to be Canadians. When Peter Jennings was named ABC's chief anchorman, the Gotliebs threw a party in his honour that attracted some of the most stellar names in the Fourth Estate. Soon Barbara Walters and the *New Yorker*'s Elizabeth Drew were turning up at their soirées, and the Gotliebs were the recipients of one of the capital's most coveted symbols of chic: an invitation to drop by Katharine Graham's summer house on Martha's Vineyard.

Their other good fortune was that, when they arrived in town, virtually the only couple they knew — through their friend, *Toronto Star* columnist Richard Gwyn — had been a major media catch: influential political analyst Joseph Kraft and his artist wife. In Polly Kraft, whose social panache had burnished her husband's career, the Gotliebs had found a well-connected guide who took Sondra in hand, enlightening her about the distinction between A and B guest lists. More importantly, Kraft introduced her to the grande dames who, with the press and lobbyists, made up what Gotlieb termed the city's "permanent village." As Diana McLellan summed up their status: "They're as in as you can be when you're out of power." Elaine Dewar recalls that, talking about the city's legendary Georgetown hostesses, the ambassador had rhymed off their names "as if he was talking about the pope."

Not long after the Gotliebs' arrival, two of those hostesses became regulars at the embassy's Rock Creek salon: Evangeline Bruce, the wealthy widow of former super-ambassador David K. Bruce, and Susan Mary Alsop, the ex-wife of columnist Joseph Alsop, who wrote social chronicles for Town and Country and other elite glossies. As Alsop noted of the Gotliebs' gatherings, "You know when you go there, you will meet people who are crucial."

But despite those heady social successes, by early 1982 the ambassador still found that the leading powers in the Reagan administration were not returning his calls. His frustration mounted as he watched Sondra, drawn into a network of ladies' lunches by Polly Kraft, routinely breaking bread with the wives of administration officials he couldn't get on the phone. One day when she came home from yet another afternoon with cabinet wives, he finally proposed a ploy: Why not throw a dinner for one of them? As Sondra would later explain in one of her columns: "In Washington . . . if you want people to come to your party, you have to make it in honour of somebody very well known."

The name Gotlieb proposed showed his canny reading of access in the Reagan era: Jean French Smith, wife of William French Smith, the attorney general who had been Reagan's personal lawyer in California and had helped set up the trusts that held the president's wealth. As one social scribe put it, "They were the key couple in the first Reagan term. If Adolf Hitler came to town and the Smiths took him under their wing, he'd have it made."

Sondra would later claim that she balked at her husband's suggestion. "I thought, 'Gee, that's pushy.' I had a really Canadian attitude." But the next afternoon, she took a deep breath and dialed Jean French Smith's number at the Jefferson Hotel. Her hands, she recalled, were shaking. "To call somebody up and say you'd like to give a dinner in her honour when you're not even sure if she'll remember you," she said, "that takes chutzpah." She paused before adding what, in retrospect, became obvious: "Except in Washington." As Hope Ridings Miller, a former social editor of the *Washington Post*, observed, "It's a city where, if you have enough nerve to invite people, they think you're in a position to ask them."

Jean French Smith was, in fact, delighted by the offer and produced a list of her friends to invite, including other cabinet members and the troika then running the White House — James Baker, Michael Deaver, and Edwin Meese. That guest list provided the wings on which the Gotliebs soared in the inner circles of the Reagan administration. "It all took off from there," Sondra acknowledged. "It may sound like a pretty cynical approach, but we discovered parties were a way to get yourself known and accepted. It's a way for your husband to get his views across."

Over wine and their signature Manitoba golden caviar, Gotlieb discreetly pleaded Ottawa's case on the issues of the day — not strong-arming, just some gentle nudges. He found, as Sondra put it, "Over drinks people will tell you things that they won't tell you at the office." Afterward, Gotlieb would zealously follow up on his contacts: those who had accepted his hospitality were not inclined to refuse his phone calls. Once he had gained entrée, he was skilful and dogged at marshalling his arguments on behalf of Ottawa's latest woes. A former U.S. Commerce Department official remembers that at one point in Reagan's first term, Gotlieb had paid six calls on his boss, Malcolm Baldrige — a frequent dinner guest — while the Japanese ambassador, whose country was under constant attack for its ballooning trade surplus, had come calling only once.

At the White House, the ambassador had first cultivated Edwin Meese, Reagan's top aide since their days in the California statehouse. In early 1985, when Meese was named attorney general, Gotlieb had transferred his attentions to Michael Deaver, who would soon become an even closer friend and collaborator.

By that time, the Gotliebs' parties had taken on a dynamic of their own. According to embassy sources, the ambassador had calculated that to remain a player on the social circuit, his dinners had to offer some advantage to his guests. In a city where information is a commodity revered second only to power, he had set out to create a venue for its exchange with himself as a key broker.

"Gossip is power because you may learn something useful," he told the *Washingtonian* magazine. "People pay a fortune for intelligence and you can pick up some solid intelligence on the cocktail circuit."

To keep the A-list coming to Rock Creek Drive, he mobilized his staff to think up constant inducements: Alfred Sung fashion shows with lunch, dinners with Margot Kidder or Donald Sutherland, and a soirée with Edmonton Oilers' superstar Wayne Gretzky, to which the ambassador — who had to be briefed on Gretzky's exact accomplishments — had invited George Shultz and Federal Reserve chief Paul Volcker, both diehard hockey fans.

Still, the biggest attraction remained Sondra Gotlieb. Her "Dear Beverly" letters, which the *Post* began publishing in November 1983, had cemented her celebrity. Later she insisted that, like everything else in her life, they started out accidentally. After coming up with the idea for a book based on a series of letters home recounting Washington's arcane social rites, she had mentioned it to Meg Greenfield, the *Post* editorial-page editor, over lunch at the Jockey Club. Overnight, her epistolary career was born. "It was sheer coincidence," she said.

Former embassy staffers recall much debate within the chancery over whether the column would have merits as a policy tool. When the ambassador decided she should go ahead, as long as it did not touch directly on U.S. politics, he took an active role in its composition and personally vetted every final draft. Like some anthropologist turning a scholarly eye on distant and exotic tribal rituals, Sondra Gotlieb dissected a universe where, she wrote Beverly, dinner guests had to keep in mind that they're "sitting next to a job, not a person," and hostesses were obliged to put their invitees at round tables "so that no one feels below the salt." In her sly vision, Powerful Jobs, Serious Media, World Famous Socialites, and Most Expensive Lobbyists schemed their way through Georgetown's salons, while she and her husband, Mr. Ambassador, the bemused outsiders, stumbled through the capital's quaint folkways.

Winking at Washington's tendency to dismiss spouses of the powerful as mere appendages, Gotlieb had dubbed herself Wife Of. But, in fact, she had written herself a more complex part: the role of Bumbling Innocent Abroad who, in her guilelessness, sees everything clearly. It was a satirist's role in the tradition of Mark Twain — the hayseed who shrewdly lampoons the mores of sophisticated society — but it would later backfire on her. When the Slap revealed she was not an unwitting innocent at all, but a player who had come to care too much about the game, her former fans reacted as if they had been duped. "It's a great irony," said Rashish, "that after five years of being the toast of the town, all that anybody is going to remember is the slap."

As the column catapulted its author to stardom, Mr. Ambassador was candid about the extent to which his wife's celebrity paid off for him. Everywhere he went, he found himself greeted by Sondra's faithful readers. When he led former Alberta premier Peter Lougheed to an appointment with North Carolina senator Jesse Helms, Lougheed became increasingly agitated as Helm's attention drifted away from his careful exposition of the merits of bilateral free trade. Suddenly, the senator interrupted the premier to blurt out to Gotlieb, "Are you really Husband Of?" A few months later, Helms, who was notorious for shunning the dinner circuit, turned up at Rock Creek Drive.

From the first, the columns had been controversial in Canada. One MP rose in the Commons to protest the propriety of a diplomat's wife poking fun at the social shenanigans in her host country. Others objected on the grounds that they perpetuated the country-cousin image Canadians had long suspected Americans had of them. But there was no doubt they served as a drawing card for the Gotliebs' dinners, which became an increasing embassy preoccupation.

The ambassador's staff understood that what mattered was not only that the Powerful Jobs showed up, but that their presence was also duly noted in the *Post*'s social columns. To that end, Patrick Gossage courted the Style section's assignment editors and constantly fed social columnist Chuck Conconi the most stellar names from each gathering. Those guest lists virtually never included other members of the diplomatic corps, whom Nancy Reagan had already signalled she had no time for by cancelling their traditional White House festivities. And even top Canadian Embassy officials were often invited only when there was a last-minute cancellation to fill. Recalls one former diplomat, "The Gotliebs measured their success in direct proportion to how many influential Americans they could get to come to dinner."

As it turned out, so too did others — not least among them the new residents at 24 Sussex Drive. When Brian Mulroney had made his first official visit to Washington as opposition leader in June

1984, he had counted the Gotliebs' dinner for him as the highlight of his trip. In his honour, they had mustered the most coveted Powerful Jobs on their computerized A-list, no ragtag assembly of what Sondra called "Used-To-Be-Close-Tos" — as in close to power. And Mulroney knew the difference. "Brian was just delighted," says his press secretary Bill Fox. "He was an avaricious consumer of U.S. news and he knew who all the players were. You could mention the name of some obscure K Street lawyer and he'd say, 'Oh, yeah, didn't he run Mondale's campaign?' He's always been a very social person."

But Mulroney had also been delighted by another aspect of that evening: the ambassador's effusive toast to his political prospects. Even those Canadian journalists who had been invited on the condition they not report on the event were taken aback by the fulsome tribute, which suggested that Mulroney was a shoo-in as the next resident of 24 Sussex Drive. The gesture had been all the more startling considering that, back in Ottawa, everyone had been under the impression that Gotlieb was a Liberal. There, reports were circulating that, in the event of a Tory win, he figured on their diplomatic hit list. Those rumours may, in fact, explain his excess of zeal. "He was seen as a bit of a Grit," Fox says, "so I think if anything he may have gone half a step further to show he had no favouritism."

Certainly, that trip had spawned Mulroney's affections for Gotlieb, whom he had never before met. But some cynics saw a blockbuster gala the ambassador threw within days of the Conservatives' election as a calculated reminder of their social leverage in the U.S. capital. Its ostensible purpose, to celebrate the upcoming marriage of the State Department's Richard Burt to White House social secretary Gahl Hodges, struck some observers as odd, since the wedding was not for another four months. If Burt was a rising star at State, he also had a reputation for betraying scorn at Canada's concerns, greeting embassy officials with a sardonic "So how's your acid rain?" But that dinner dance, which attracted Caspar Weinberger and George Shultz, is credited with helping to prolong Gotlieb's term in Washington. When Mulroney flew into town a week later for his first prime ministerial visit, one of his key announcements was that the ambassador would be continuing at his post.

But another factor also strengthened the unlikely alliance between them. "You can't discount the influence Allan had on

Brian's U.S. policy," Fox says. "They were the champions of free trade." Gotlieb was passionate on the subject. On the front lines of the tariff wars between Ottawa and Washington, he had become convinced of the need for insurance against the ongoing attacks by U.S. industry that left the country constantly vulnerable. At his dinner table, the Powerful Jobs from the Reagan administration who became his friends all sang from the same neoconservative hymnal as well, extolling the joys of the free market.

Already, Gotlieb had been working with Ed Lumley and a group of Trudeau's officials towards a sectoral agreement. But in Mulroney, he finally had a prime minister who shared his obsession with the United States and was determined to nail down a comprehensive free trade pact that would change the course of the country's history. Both saw the chief hurdle as a public relations, not a policy, problem — how to sell it to the wary Canadian public.

But in Ottawa, Gotlieb had a rival for Mulroney's ear on U.S. relations: Derek Burney, the longtime free trade enthusiast who had taken over External's American desk and had his own pipeline to the White House. There never would be any love lost between them. But Burney had ingratiated himself early with Fox, Charley McMillan, and the prime minister's other gatekeepers who preferred his meat-and-potatoes style to Gotlieb's sometimes haughty intellectualism. Burney had even turned up at the embassy and delivered a lecture to the assembled staff on how he would be running the relationship with Washington out of Ottawa. "Gotlieb had to sit there and listen to that," recalls one former official who was present at the time. "You can't imagine his face."

In early 1985, just as Burney and officials from both countries were arranging to slip the starting signal for free trade negotiations onto the Shamrock Summit agenda, panic seized the ambassador's office: word had leaked out that Michael Deaver, Gotlieb's key White House contact, would soon leave to go into business for himself. But later Gotlieb had returned from a summit planning session with a sigh of relief. Deaver, he announced, had agreed to stay on until after the Quebec City show, in the process assuring Gotlieb's own future.

Soon after the Shamrock Summit, the ambassador and his wife had thrown one of the first farewell parties to honour Deaver's departure from the White House. And the embassy's public relations machine made sure that the *Post*'s social columns were informed how, after dinner, Magic Mike had indulged his favourite pastime, tickling the ivories of the Gotliebs' baby grand — a legacy of his college days as a cocktail pianist.

Those who had watched Deaver and Gotlieb work together saw a natural symbiosis — the one an expert on style, the other on substance, but both with a canny appreciation for strategy, subterfuge, and the subtle nuances of power. They also shared an insatiable appetite for gossip. Certainly, no one in Washington who knew them registered surprise when, two months after the Shamrock Summit — and six days after leaving government — Deaver had begun negotiating a contract as Canada's $105,000-a-year lobbyist.

Despite Gotlieb's pitch for the embassy's own lobbying role in Washington, he had already shown that he was not averse to turning to the hired guns of Gucci Gulch.

THE address on his silver-embossed stationery read simply, "The Power House, Washington, D.C." — nothing more. For those in the market for a little reputation refurbishment, that was sufficient; after all, anyone who required further information obviously did not deserve the services of Robert Keith Gray, the dean of the capital's lobbyists.

A suave, steely haired Nebraskan, Gray had once served as an aide to President Dwight Eisenhower. But in 1961 he had joined the public relations firm Hill & Knowlton Inc. to set up its first Washington office. Begun over three decades earlier in Cleveland by John Hill, the former editor of a steel trade paper who had a horror of unions and government meddling in business, the company had always specialized in corporate accounts, among them the city's main rolling mills. In Washington, Gray had pioneered the notion of a full-service firm that combined PR and government relations, the polite term for lobbying. Over the next two decades, he had built Hill & Knowlton into the capital's leading agency — one with wide-ranging foreign and intelligence ties. Gray had teamed up with South Korea's controversial lobbyist Tongsun Park, who would later be the focus of the capital's Koreagate scandal, and had rented office space to renegade CIA agent Edwin Wilson, who would be convicted for hiring out his services to Libya.

But such awkward alliances left no tarnish on Gray. After serving as deputy to Reagan's 1980 campaign chairman William Casey, he had overseen the Inaugural blowout that set the lavish, limo-and-mink style of the Reagan years. Then he quit Hill & Knowlton to capitalize on those connections, setting up his own Gray and Company in the ancient Georgetown hydro station that provided his arch address. Among the accounts he took with him was the American Iron and Steel Institute, one of John Hill's first clients, which still counted among its members M. A. Hanna.

Gray and Company became Washington's biggest lobbying firm, with $9 million in annual billings. Not only did Gray charge by the hour, but he also introduced the notion of a retainer, which guaranteed merely that a client would get his phone calls returned — now standard lobbying practice. Over the years Gray would set the style for lobbyists around the world as the billion-dollar business of buying access increasingly captured the political process.

As early as the 1960s, Gray saw the importance of working Washington's social scene, occasionally logging three parties in one night and boasting that he wore out two tuxedos a year. Not that all his clients would have been welcomed in the Georgetown salons he favoured. On Gray and Company's roster were Baby Doc Duvalier, South Korea's controversial Reverend Sun Myung Moon, and the soon-to-be-notorious Bank of Credit and Commerce International (BCCI), better known by its clients at the CIA as the Bank of Crooks and Criminals International. Gray himself held a seat on the board of BCCI's Washington front, First American Bank.

His firm's shadowy international division showed a predilection for boosting those freedom fighters favoured by Reagan and his friend William Casey — with whom Gray claimed he checked out every client. He had long represented the government of Saudi Arabia, which, by the fall of 1984, was secretly financing the Contras with $1-million-a-month payments. And one of the early organizers of Contra support, Oliver North's right-hand man Rob Owen, had briefly been on the payroll of Gray's international division, which was headed by a former CIA official. Another of Gray's longtime clients was Saudi arms dealer Adnan Khashoggi, frequently a commercial cutout for his country's royals.

Certainly, Gray's connections were unquestionable in November 1984, two months after Mulroney's election, when Allan Gotlieb turned to his services. The ambassador had been sold on the idea by one of the stars Gray had hired to help snare new business, Joan Braden, a veteran capital wit whose dinner parties regularly featured Henry Kissinger and former defence secretary Robert McNamara.

At Gray and Company, the Canadian government contract was considered a real catch — or, as journalist Susan Trento later wrote in her book *The Power House*, "a fat cow account to milk." In her own memoir *Enough Rope*, Braden acknowledged that "the Canadian account was a bottom line account. Everybody who could fancy the slightest reason for piling on piled on." Braden remembered asking Gray, "Why were six people from the press department attending a conference in Ottawa? Why not two people or one person?" But her complaints, she said, only earned her treatment as "a goddamn woman who happens to know the ambassador socially and thinks she knows public relations."

That fall, Gray had trumpeted his formation of a new communications group to serve Canadian businesses in the United States and, in a bilingual press release, he had quoted himself on the subject. Declaring that he had done so "in recognition that Canada–U.S. relations are entering a new period of close, government-to-government cooperation," he announced that the division would be headed by Peter Segall, a Montreal-born lawyer-lobbyist with ties to the Bronfmans.

Segall had set up the Canadian Business Roundtable to monitor congressional and regulatory developments that might sideswipe corporations north of the border. He arranged for Gotlieb to speak to the group in Montreal, only to discover that the ambassador's plane was snowbound in Boston. But the indefatigable ambassador had agreed to deliver his address from an airport pay phone. As the executives listened to his trade spiel over a speaker phone, they were startled to hear the line go silent in mid-rhetorical flight. Suddenly an operator's voice intruded: "Deposit four more quarters, please."

But the government's fling with Robert Gray ran into more than heavy weather. In 1985 the *New York Times* ran a story on a press release it had received from Gray and Company touting one of the Canadian Embassy's social events: in it, the firm had not only misspelled the name of the reporter with whom it was trying to curry favour; it had also managed to mangle Gotlieb's name and the name of his guest of honour. As snickers rippled through Washington's salons, the embassy had quietly cancelled its contract.

Meanwhile, Gotlieb had already hired the services of another impeccably well-connected lobbyist, Robert Strauss, the Democrats' genial Mr. Fix-It. Although he had served as Jimmy Carter's trade representative and special envoy to the Middle East, Strauss also enjoyed ties to the Reagan White House. Not only was he on the board of MCA, one of his longtime clients, but he was so trusted by MCA chairman Lew Wasserman that he would represent both sides when Japan's Matsushita Electrical Industrial Company bought out MCA — in the process pocketing an $8 million fee.

In politics, too, Strauss was expert at working both sides of the street. When the Iran-Contra scandal threatened to swamp the White House, Nancy Reagan would invite him around for advice. And his Texas roots had made him such a pal of James Baker, George Bush, and their mutual friends in the oil business that Bush would later name him ambassador to Moscow. Kremlinologists would bridle at the appointment of a backroom political broker who spoke no Russian and knew no Soviet history at the very moment the rival superpower was disintegrating. But as the Soviet Union crumbled, Strauss would serve as corporate America's envoy to that ripe new market, assuring that U.S. interests won drilling rights in the republics' vast oil fields and tapped into the hunger for U.S. rock music and movies.

Strauss already had a pipeline to Mikhail Gorbachev, once the Kremlin's agricultural boss, through his longtime political pal Dwayne Andreas, chairman of agro-conglomerate Archer Daniels Midland, one of the chief exporters of U.S. grain to the Soviet Union. Besides acting for the firm in Washington, since 1981 Strauss had served on its board, where, during an eighteen-month period alone, his director's fees had earned him $156,972. Andreas's influence, too, crossed party lines: once known as the chief backer of Democratic presidential hopeful Hubert Humphrey, he had also been investigated during the Watergate scandal for his overenthusiastic contributions to Richard Nixon. And by the 1980s he had become one of the main backers of Kansas senator Bob Dole, who was Archer Daniels Midland's leading defender in Congress. Andreas, Dole, and Strauss even shared neighbouring co-ops at the Seaview Hotel, which Andreas had founded in Florida's Bal Harbor — and where the Gotliebs had been guests.

But Gotlieb's hiring of Strauss also proved an embarrassment. During the uproar provoked by the leak of his 1985 letter to

Sinclair Stevens, passing on Strauss's warnings of a "scorched earth response" in the Gulf + Western/Prentice Hall case, critics had been outraged to discover the letter failed to mention that Strauss appeared to have a curious conflict of loyalties in the case. Not only was he Gulf + Western's lobbyist at the time, but until only seven weeks earlier — from January 1, 1984, until June 15, 1985 — the Canadian government had been paying him and his law firm, Akin, Gump, Strauss, Hauer & Feld, $10,000 a month as its own voice in Washington.

Not that the controversy had soured Gotlieb's relations with Strauss. On the contrary, at the time of the Slap Flap, the wise-cracking dealmaker had every reason to beam through the Canadian Embassy dinner for Mulroney. Only a week before the prime minister's arrival in Washington, Investment Canada had finally given its long-delayed assent to the takeover of Prentice Hall by his client. In return, Strauss would prove a staunch friend to both Gotlieb and the Mulroney government: two months after the Slap, as a social pall descended over the Gotliebs, Strauss arranged a small but chic dinner party in their honour at the home of Katharine Graham. And later, as the free trade negotiations broke off at the eleventh hour, he penned an influential plea for the op-ed page of the New York Times entitled "Keep Talking with Canada on Trade."

After the leak of Gotlieb's letter, Ottawa would never again employ Strauss's services directly. But others in his firm would carve out a thriving practice in Canadian trade and regulatory woes: at various times, its client list would include the Quebec government, the Bank of Nova Scotia, Molson Breweries, and Gordon Investment Corp., a subsidiary of Toronto's Gordon Capital. Richard Rivers, who handled many of those cases, would also serve as counsel to the private sector advisory panel on financial services headed by American Express chairman Jim Robinson.

Another Akin Gump partner, Vernon Jordan, claimed indirect ties to Mulroney through the prime minister's friend Ross Johnson, on whose board Jordan served at RJR Nabisco. Indeed, in 1993, that complex web of political and corporate IOUs would seem to converge when, four months after Mulroney stepped down from office, the first of his lucrative corporate rewards came from Bob Strauss's old pal, Dwayne Andreas.

But it was Deaver's lobbying contract that would cause Gotlieb — and the country — the most grief. Parading his success on the cover of *Time* scarcely ten months after he left the White House, Deaver had become the symbol of everything that was wrong in Ronald Reagan's Washington, where critics charged that democracy was for sale to the highest bidder. Setting up Michael K. Deaver and Associates in a penthouse on Georgetown harbour, where he employed the White House decorator, he continued to arbitrate Nancy Reagan's staff rebellions and orchestrated the president's fireside summit in Geneva with Gorbachev. As one presidential staffer had sniped, "He took the White House with him."

But Deaver also flaunted his access. "There have been lobbyists in Washington for as long as there have been lobbies," *Time*'s Evan Thomas observed. "But never before have they been so numerous or quite so brazen. What used to be . . . a somewhat shady and disreputable trade has burst into the open with a determined show of respectability. For many, public service has become a mere internship for a lucrative career as a hired gun for special interests."

The *Washington Post* zeroed in on Deaver's foreign accounts, including the Canadian government, charging that he and other former administration officials were "being paid millions of dollars . . . to help those clients block or counter administration initiatives." But thanks to Michigan's implacable acid rain foe, John Dingell, Deaver's activities on behalf of Ottawa won him more ink than any of the other ethics violations on which he was eventually charged. Suddenly, Canada had found itself Exhibit A in the case against foreign influence peddling — synonymous with political sleaze.

Even before Deavergate had turned into a criminal case, the controversy had made embassy officials so nervous that press counsellor Bruce Phillips called *Maclean's*, unsolicited, when he got wind of a story brewing, to announce that Deaver was "not a lobbyist" for the government. Despite a contract on file at the Foreign Agents registry of the Justice Department listing his possible "political activities" for the embassy, Phillips insisted that Deaver offered only advice. "We do our own lobbying," he yelled into the phone.

The embassy had good reason for its unease. After years of successive governments complaining they could never get noticed in Washington, Deavergate prompted many MPs to blame Gotlieb's lobbying theories for bringing on unwanted attention. Only months after the ambassador had proudly recounted to the *Toronto Star*'s

Val Sears his "bold, innovative, perhaps sometimes even radical steps in the implementation of our policies toward the United States," his words had come back to haunt him. With Public Diplomacy, Sears worried that Canada was "behaving exactly like a U.S. lobby for oil, airlines or the right to carry a gun." Suddenly, the citizenry back home seemed nostalgic for its bland international Boy Scout image. It had been all very well to gussy up the country's reputation, but, as Myer Rashish pointed out, "Now Canada is just like the rest of the girls."

In the midst of the Deaver investigations, Sondra Gotlieb's Slap Flap seemed to signal the death of Partying to Win. Indeed, the Gotliebs would never again entertain with the same chutzpah or hoopla. As the chandeliers dimmed on Rock Creek Drive, they would shun the spotlight they had once so ardently sought.

In both capitals, critics began to question just how much political profit the Gotliebs had reaped from playing the social card. When their dinners and their reputations were still flourishing, the ambassador had credited his warm relations in high places with winning Canada exemptions from the Reagan administration's potentially disastrous tariffs on steel and copper. "My success is the absence of harm," he had said at the time. But when harm came the country's way in a cruelly coincidental series of trade sanctions following the slap, all of his socializing had been unable to ward off the blows.

While he was dining regularly with the administration's stars, he had failed to pick up signals that members of the Senate finance committee felt such resentment over their exclusion from Reagan's trade policy that they were preparing to hold hostage the fast-track authority for the Canadian free trade talks. In fact, one Senate aide pointed out that Gotlieb had fanned the resentment in Congress. "People here were left with the impression that Canada felt it had the exec in its pocket," he said, "so why worry?"

But as events soon showed, Gotlieb couldn't count on the administration's favour either. Reagan himself had signed the order for a devastating tariff on Canadian shakes and shingles the week the free trade negotiations began — another swipe of stunning political insensitivity that had caught the ambassador off guard. He had never cultivated the lower-level White House officials who might have alerted the administration to the uproar such a measure might cause in Canada. Quipped one domestic trade adviser: "I'm not grand enough to be invited to the Gotliebs."

California congressman Henry Waxman, the country's chief ally in the House of Representatives on acid rain, was stunned when the embassy ignored his pleas not to endorse the ineffectual acid rain envoys' report, then dismissed him later as just another congressman. "I felt quite abandoned by the embassy," Waxman told the *Toronto Star*.

There had been indications early on in the Gotliebs' tenure that all the partying was not necessarily bringing the concrete results they sought. When Trudeau had launched his Peace Initiative, many of those who tried hardest to sabotage it were the same individuals who had been supping on fiddleheads and Maple Surprise at the ambassador's residence. "All the people who had been at the trough turned out to be the ones who took the biggest swipes," said Gossage. "All the goodwill and visibility we had so painstakingly constructed really only yielded results in the margins when real issues were at stake."

Some analysts would later point out that the Canadian government may have harboured unrealistic expectations of just how much could be accomplished by Public Diplomacy. While a higher social profile produced introductions and access, there was a danger in mistaking attention for effectiveness. Certainly, no ambassador in Canadian history had ever snared such laudatory press or a spotlight on such national issues as acid rain. And Gotlieb was instrumental in convincing Katharine Graham to establish the *Washington Post*'s first Canadian bureau. But if the ambassador and his wife had won friends, their parties and personal relations could not influence policy when Canadian concerns ran counter to American domestic interests.

Even the Serious Press proved predictably ungrateful. William Safire had led the media attack against Deaver for his own reasons: he blamed the imagemeister for moderating Reagan's stance towards Moscow. And Ben Bradlee's regular presence at the Gotliebs' table failed to prevent the *Post* from recording their fall from grace in vivid detail.

In fact, the person least surprised at suddenly finding herself on the social outs seemed to be the chronicler of Powertown's ruthless rites herself. As Sondra Gotlieb had written in one of her letters to Beverly, "This is a town where status shifts so swiftly that a euphoric Powerful Job who never had time to return his phone calls can easily turn into a decompressing Used-To-Be-Close-To whose telephone never rings."

Once, during their social heyday, the Gotliebs' confidants had predicted with a knowing air that, as soon as the ambassador's term was up, he would join Deaver's public relations firm. But as the lobbyist's gilt-edged clientele vanished at the first whiff of his taint, that possibility had been foreclosed. Still, the External Affairs' obituaries for the ambassador proved decidedly premature. He would stay on in Washington for nearly three more years, replaced by his rival Derek Burney only after the free trade pact was wrapped up and sealed with the electorate's apparent approval.

For much of that time, Gotlieb would be enmeshed in yet another diplomatic controversy, fighting efforts by Whitney North Seymour, the special prosecutor investigating the Deaver case, to force him to testify. After balking at Seymour's request, the ambassador had relented and supplied written answers to some of his questions. But his responses had provided the foundation for one of the criminal counts of perjury that the special prosecutor had promptly brought against Deaver under the Ethics in Government Act. Pleading diplomatic immunity, Gotlieb had no trouble enlisting Mulroney's help in trying to quash Seymour's subsequent court order, which could have compelled him to testify about conversations involving the prime minister's closest aides. Besides, he pointed out, such a waiver could set a dangerous precedent for diplomats in both countries.

But Seymour had argued that, by submitting his written answers, Gotlieb had already waived his immunity. In May 1987 the special prosecutor had taken an unprecedented measure: he dispatched an FBI agent to serve subpoenas on Sondra and Allan Gotlieb at the chancery; embassy officials and RCMP guards refused to accept them. Ottawa delivered a written protest to the State Department charging a violation of international law. Seymour countered with a ten-page motion filed in Federal District court to compel Gotlieb's testimony; accusing the Canadian government of "duplicitous behaviour," he argued that the ambassador's sworn account was essential to establish Deaver's perjury. "Once the door is open," he wrote, "restrictions cannot be imposed on the proper use of the information supplied." A month later, a federal district judge disagreed, ruling that Gotlieb could not be compelled to appear in an American court proceeding.

Seymour was furious, all the more so the following December when Deaver was convicted on three of five counts of perjury — but not the one based on his testimony about his involvement with the Canadian government. In his final report to Congress, the special prosecutor had stated his thoughts on that verdict. "Whatever the merits on the legal issue of waiver," he wrote, "the result of Gotlieb's refusal to testify was clear: it was the major factor in Deaver's acquittal on Count Four of the perjury indictment."

A year later when the Gotliebs finally left Washington only days before Ronald Reagan packed up for California, Deaver did not show up for their farewell cocktail party. Nor did the new secretary of state, James Baker, who nevertheless paid absent tribute to Gotlieb as "the most outstanding ambassador this city has seen in a long, long while. He's an insider, he's well informed and he knows how to work the system." What Baker did not add was that the ambassador also knew the system's unspoken rules. Gotlieb left Washington with a distinction summed up by the title of a biography on former CIA director Richard Helms, one of his frequent dinner guests: he had been *The Man Who Kept the Secrets.*

AFTER a six-month decompression as a visiting professor of Canadian studies at Harvard, Allan Gotlieb moved to Toronto in mid-1989, where he and Sondra found a Rosedale mansion within commuting distance of his office at the venerable law firm Stikeman Elliott. The firm counted among its Montreal partners David Angus, Mulroney's chief party fundraiser, but Gotlieb himself would never actually practise law from his spacious corner office: despite a string of prestigious legal degrees, he had never sat for the Ontario bar exams. Instead, he became a consultant. The diplomat who had so ardently promoted the notion of Canadian government lobbying abroad returned home to metamorphose into a lobbyist himself.

But that pastime did not appear to interfere with a string of corporate directorships rolling in. For a man who had never been in business, the list was impressive. There emerged a common thread: the companies that sought out his presence on their boards had either led the free trade lobby in Canada (like Alcan), were close to the government (like Conrad Black's Hollinger Inc.), or were fighting

Canadian policies and exports (like the Connecticut-based forestry giant Champion International and New York–based publisher Macmillan Inc.).

Macmillan had been acquired by British mogul Robert Maxwell, a client of Robert Gray's and a man with ties to Israeli intelligence. Maxwell's mysterious 1992 drowning death would later expose his empire as a financial shell, but at the time of Gotlieb's appointment the firm was expanding its Canadian subsidiaries, Maxwell Macmillan and Maxwell Communications of Canada. As an Anglo-American company, Maxwell Macmillan was at odds with the indigenous Canadian publishing industry, which had been pushing for a federal policy to shore up its feeble market slice. According to those who worked with him as ambassador, Gotlieb had vehemently opposed that view, siding instead with his friend Bob Strauss and Hollywood's Washington lobbyist Jack Valenti, who were fighting Canadian cultural policies of any variety. As Toronto cinema tycoon Garth Drabinsky, who often dealt with Gotlieb on the issue, later recalled, "Allan was very big on free trade in culture."

Given Gotlieb's vehemence over Gulf + Western's right to take over Prentice Hall Canada in 1985, it seemed fitting that an American publisher would consider him in tune with the sentiments of its boardroom. What did not seem fitting to many in the Canadian cultural community was the patronage plum that Gotlieb won from Mulroney: the chairmanship of the Canada Council. To most, it seemed a deliberate act of revenge — naming the man who had promoted the free trade pact in the United States to head a body that doled out grants to those very artists who most vociferously had opposed it. Indeed, in announcing the appointment, Mulroney had made clear it was a reward for services rendered: he thanked Gotlieb "for his very significant contribution to the successful negotiation of the Canada–U.S. trade agreement and its recent approval by the U.S. Congress."

But artists almost unanimously saw the posting as a hostile act. "The appointment could quite easily be viewed as a move by the Tories to get rid of the Canada Council," Margaret Atwood warned, "to make the Americans feel good." Novelist Timothy Findley wrote the *Globe and Mail* to voice "alarm and dismay." He pondered "whether Mr. Gotlieb is being brought in as the Great Dismantler to preside over the 'harmonization' of Canadian culture." Branding the choice "an astonishing symbolic gesture of contempt," Findley saw in it yet another sign of the government's "gross insensitivity to the concerns of the cultural community."

In the *Canadian Forum*, writer Heather Robertson sounded the same alarms, counting up Gotlieb's post-diplomatic rewards and questioning his loyalty to an arts agency that helped to determine the economic fate of Canadian publishers, when he sat on the board of one of their American rivals. Robertson's dissent was not the sort of press that Gotlieb had grown accustomed to receiving in Washington. He promptly took a page from another of his corporate benefactors, Conrad Black: he sued Robertson and the *Ottawa Citizen*, which had reprinted her article (although he did not bother to drop a writ against the penniless *Canadian Forum*), demanding $325,000 in damages.

Instead of chilling further comment as Black's lawsuits so often did, Gotlieb elicited more outrage. Even the council's writers' advisory committee demanded his resignation until he had settled or dropped his lawsuit. "The chairman of the Canada Council should be seen as someone who supports writers," said committee member June Callwood, "who might even be on the side of free speech."

Eventually Gotlieb withdrew both suits, but bitterness in the cultural community remained. Later, artists would point out that, for all his political clout, he had been unable to stave off the budgetary axe aimed at the council: during his term, from 1989 until 1993, its parliamentary grants had fallen from $73 million to $66 million in real terms. Nor were suspicions allayed in 1992 when Mulroney's government announced plans to merge the venerable arts agency with the Social Sciences and Humanities Research Council, leaving Gotlieb at the helm of both. The move was defeated only when a handful of Tory senators, led by Mulroney's onetime confidant Finlay MacDonald, staged a last-minute revolt.

But fuelling fears that such an amalgamation had been part of Gotlieb's mandate all along was a "confidential annex" to the order-in-council approving his appointment which concealed his pay. Four years and a court case later, Ottawa researcher Ken Rubin won the release of documents that showed Gotlieb received between $450 and $600 for each day he spent on council business. His predecessor, internationally known contralto Maureen Forrester, had received only $325.

But Gotlieb's biggest post-ambassadorial plum was also the most appropriate to his new status as a hired gun: he was named to the board of New York's Burson-Marsteller Inc., International, the world's largest public relations and lobbying firm. As part of that package, he became chairman of Burson-Marsteller Canada Ltd. and head of its Ottawa-based government relations division, Executive Consultants Ltd. At the time, the corporation was beginning its whopping $18 million contract with the government of Mexico to promote the passage of NAFTA in Parliament and Congress.

Gotlieb joined the lobbying game just as Ottawa was aping the Washington model of access-for-sale. Led by Frank Moores and Gerry Doucet, a new era of middlemen were selling their connection to friends in high places. Between 1984 and 1989, the year Gotlieb moved back to Canada, lobbying had mushroomed into a $200-million-a-year industry that even some Conservatives admitted needed reining in. But unlike in Washington, the registration requirements, which did not materialize until 1988, remained weak, and there never would be an outcry over foreign influence peddling. The only foreign influence of any note was that of Corporate America, which had distributed its largesse so evenly among the country's legal and lobbying firms that politicians of every persuasion had a stake in preserving the status quo.

As head of Executive Consultants, Gotlieb registered one client, Markborough Properties Inc., the real estate arm of the Thomson publishing empire, which had vigorously opposed the Baie Comeau publishing policy. But his file at the federal Lobbyists Registry in Hull also contained another entry for his work at Stikeman Elliott: in that capacity, Gotlieb had become the Ottawa point man for the Horsham Corporation, the holding company controlled by Canadian gold tycoon Peter Munk.

12 The Canadian Connection

FOR ALLAN GOTLIEB, 1986 had not been a very good year. After the ignominy of the Slap Flap and the ongoing legal tussles over Deavergate, Washington's most headline-conscious ambassador had taken to ducking the media, above all the Canadian press corps that he felt had delighted in chronicling his woes. But by late fall he had decided to face that unruly lot: in November the invitations went out for his annual year-end media briefing over breakfast at the chancery. The occasion offered an opportunity to display his prodigious intellect, not to mention his insider gossip, and it invariably won him clips on the networks back home, desperate for forecasts of the year ahead. But after the invitations had been issued, the forecasts for the year ahead in Washington had abruptly changed. On November 25, after weeks of frantic document-shredding by Ollie North at the White House, Gotlieb's friend Ed Meese had stunned the world by calling a press conference to reveal the sketchy outlines of the Iran-Contra scandal.

Overnight, Reagan's Teflon presidency had plunged into a crisis of credibility that shook its very foundations. The president who had so stoutly vowed he would never do business with Iran or bargain with terrorists for U.S. hostages had secretly done both. Worse, in absolute defiance of Congress, the profits from those sales had been rerouted to his favourite freedom fighters vainly flailing at the Sandinista regime in Managua. Already, critics were brandishing the dread word *impeachment*, invoking the spectre of the Watergate scandal that had catapulted postwar America into its first national identity crisis. "There's no question the president is weakened," Gotlieb would worry over breakfast, pondering the fate of the free trade talks. "It's a one-issue town."

For weeks, Canadian reporters too had been transfixed by that issue, scrambling to keep up with revelations that were unfolding like the plotline from some over-ambitious thriller writer — one with a taste for improbable international intrigue who had tried to cram too much into a first novel. At times, it seemed that scarcely a nation had *not* been involved in one side of the deal or the other. If Israel had fronted most of the arms shipments to Iran, it soon became clear that military hardware had been discreetly making its way to Teheran from virtually every European country. Even those nations bereft of weapons or gunpowder plants had been happy to facilitate the complex offshore financing. Meanwhile, as congressional funding for the Contras ran out, South Korea, Taiwan, and even tiny Brunei had been solicited by top U.S. officials to cough up multimillion-dollar contributions. But no country had proved more generous to the CIA's ragtag band of Central American guerrillas than Saudi Arabia, which had secretly donated $32 million after Reagan made a personal pitch to King Fahd. In return for receiving a fleet of AWACS spy planes, the stoutly anti-communist House of Saud had been bankrolling U.S. covert operations around the globe, from Afghanistan to Angola, almost from the moment Reagan took office.

Still, to most Canadian journalists, the byzantine, off-the-books affair had seemed a distant and alien event, typical of the Reaganauts with their compulsion for privatizing everything, even foreign policy. But as they straggled into the chancery's sombre pan-elled library on Massachusetts Avenue for coffee and eggs, the U.S. scandal had suddenly hit home. Nights earlier, one of its most flamboyant stars, Saudi arms dealer Adnan Khashoggi, had turned up on Barbara Walters's show to take the heat for his role in the U.S. arms sales to Iran. Fresh from damage-control consultations with his friend Robert Gray, Khashoggi had gone on camera and dropped a phrase that sent shockwaves through Parliament Hill. As the inter-view unrolled aboard his luxury-fitted DC–8, with its extravagant chamois and gold lamé living room, its gilt bathroom fixtures, and king-sized bed topped by a genuine sable spread, he slipped in a pointed aside: his Iranian deals had been made possible, he said, by last-minute bridge financing from Canadian and Cayman investors.

His offhand admission had been meant to contain a revelation that appeared in the *Wall Street Journal* on the very morning the Canadian press corps had shown up for breakfast with Gotlieb. From Salt Lake City, where Khashoggi had bailed out of his grandiose new $500 million U.S. headquarters complex, the *Journal*'s John Fialka reported that a pair of mysterious Canadian investors had stepped in to commandeer the arms dealer's dwindling Utah assets to collect on an outstanding debt. According to the story, Ernie Miller, the owner of a seedy suburban Toronto motel, and his accountant, Don Fraser, who had decamped to the tax haven of the Cayman Islands, had taken over Khashoggi's Triad America Corporation when they became convinced they were being stiffed for part of the millions they had lent him over the previous year. In typical circumlocutory fashion, Khashoggi suggested that part of the sum had been used as interim financing for his arms shipments to Iran — a fact Justice Minister Ray Hnatyshyn reported to the Commons that he had confirmed by phone with Meese. But when the ayatollah's weapons inspectors balked at paying for those outdated and overpriced U.S.–made TOW missles, Fraser and Miller had been left with a serious dent in their offshore accounts.

In Washington, the story had been accepted as just another bizarre twist in a tale that already defied credulity. But it raised more eyebrows in Toronto, where no one in the financial establishment had heard of Khashoggi's benefactors. When the media circus descended on Miller's Black Hawk Motor Inn, wedged between car lots in suburban Richmond Hill, the exercise proved no more enlightening. A burly real estate developer known for his colourful way with words and his penchant for eschewing socks, Miller had fled into hiding behind the gates of his heavily guarded mansion nearby. But as the TV lights ambushed his sleepy Indian desk clerk, they exposed a seedy bikers' hangout with a pool table in the lobby, strippers bumping and grinding in the bleak basement bar, and cigarette burns studding the bedspreads upstairs, where the rooms were rented for $35 a night to itinerant construction workers and those on the downside of their luck. Even to the most cynical eye, the Black Hawk seemed an unlikely source for a bridge loan to a jet-setting Saudi arms dealer who had just been dubbed by a biographer *The Richest Man in the World.*

Soon Miller and Fraser's trail grew cold. But in Washington, "the Canadians," as they quickly became known by the capital's Iran-Contra afficionados, promptly came in for a round of unusually bad press. From behind the closed doors of the Senate intelligence committee, word trickled out that a Khashoggi aide named Roy Furmark, who operated out of an unmarked Madison Avenue office with an unlisted phone number, had shown up in beard and trenchcoat to testify that the Canadians were to blame for Meese's decision to expose the clandestine arms deals. In fact, a Lebanese paper, *Al Shiraa*, fed by the irate Iranians, had already broken the news. But according to a flurry of declassified CIA memos, in early October Khashoggi had sent Furmark to warn their old friend, William Casey, the director of Central Intelligence, that unless the Canadians got the $10 million they were owed from the botched arms shipment, they were threatening to blow the whistle to their Democratic friends in Congress. Casey had offered Furmark a ride back to New York on his plane, then tapped Charles Allen, one of his top covert experts, to check out the story. It seemed an odd assignment considering that the CIA had already electronically tracked every weapons transfer and financial transaction in such detail that the agency knew precisely how much the armsbrokers had overcharged. Still, even if Allen's memoranda were concocted as a cover story, no one disputed his conclusion. "We have a festering sore on our hands," he reported to Casey.

Meeting Furmark in a Manhattan steakhouse for a debriefing, Allen had taken notes on the stationery of the Roosevelt Hotel in a cramped personal shorthand. According to those jottings, while arranging a May 1985 shipment of TOW anti-tank missiles to Iran, Khashoggi had found himself in financial straits, forced to borrow $15 million from two obscure sources. The first $5 million had come from a secretive Syrian trader named Oussama Lababedi, headquartered on the French Riviera, whose Western Bancorporation owned four Houston banks and would soon declare bankruptcy. For the remaining $10 million, Khashoggi had turned to "a number of Canadian financiers." Furmark had initially declined to name them, but as he warned Allen, "the Canadian entrepreneurs, who have investments in oil, gold, mining, and real estate, reportedly are aggressive, tough-minded individuals who have influential contacts in Washington."

By then, he claimed, they were also extremely unhappy campers. While Lababedi had been repaid, they had been fobbed off with a mere $1.1 million of their promised $11 million payday. Not only did they know that the Israeli government and top aides to Prime Minister Shimon Peres were up to their necks in the clandestine Iranian deal, but they also realized the same cast was running the Contra resupply show. They had surmised their profits had been rerouted to the jungles of Central America, and Furmark warned the CIA not to underestimate their threats to expose the operation.

Over the following months, declassified documents would trickle into congressional hearings detailing Khashoggi's complex loans from Vertex Finances, S.A., where Fraser listed himself as president. Headquartered at Euro Bank, a Cayman Islands institution he had set up on the second floor of a lowrise in Georgetown, the pastel capital, Vertex was just one of dozens of companies Fraser ran out of the bank's luxury suite located a convenient fifteen-minute drive from his high-security manor house on the island's unfashionable north coast. Miller was a regular visitor to Euro Bank's offices, and Khashoggi too had dropped by with his top aides for a meeting in its spacious boardroom. As dozens of documents showed, the trio had extensive financial ties that predated the explosive $10 million loan.

But at his press breakfast in December 1986, Allan Gotlieb left the distinct impression that the subject made him uneasy. Indeed, he seemed at pains to show that he had only the sketchiest grasp of its details. "I don't have the names of the Canadians involved," he said. At the other end of the conference table, his top political officer, Paul Heinbecker, the former head of External's U.S. desk, sat with the *Wall Street Journal's* story on Fraser and Miller beside his place mat, their names carefully underlined. But Gotlieb seemed impatient to cut short any further questions on the subject. "I don't want to get into the details anymore," he scowled. He insisted he was "absolutely unaware" of any Canadian government involvement. "There was no such activity," he said carefully, "to my knowledge."

Since both the Iran and the Contra operations had been run out of Reagan's National Security Council, some reporters expressed astonishment that the White House had not informed its friends in the Prime Minister's Office that Canadians — in fact, if Furmark's report was to be believed, rogue Canadians — were involved. "We are seeking information ourselves about that," Gotlieb intoned. "I do not believe Ottawa was aware." He himself had learned of the Canadian connection only days earlier in the press, he insisted. When a reporter with CIA friends asked why an embassy car had been sighted at the agency around that time, the ambassador dismissed it as nothing unusual. "Oh, we're out there every two days," he said.

As writer Jim Littleton had demonstrated in *Target Nation*, Canadian intelligence had a long history of cooperation with the CIA. During the Second World War, a Canadian had been used as a liaison between the British and the U.S. spy services: Sir William Stephenson, better known by his code-name Intrepid. And on more than one occasion, Washington had found it convenient to take advantage of the neighbourly soil north of the 49th parallel for tasks that might risk political embarrassment on home ground. At the time the Iran-Contra scandal broke, nine Canadians were suing the CIA for the psychological devastation wrought on them during the 1950s by brain-washing experiments at Montreal's Allen Memorial Institute, which had been funded by the agency and the Canadian government. The suit had been dragging on for years, and the group's lawyer, a Washington civil rights veteran named Joe Rauh, had repeatedly voiced his frustration at Ottawa's reticence to fight for the rights of its own citizens. Seven months before the Iran-Contra scandal broke, Rauh had written Mulroney protesting that, in six years, "the Canadian government has not volunteered a single document or a single piece of information that would further the case. On the contrary, at this very moment Canadian officials are withholding from us a great number of documents vital to our case because the CIA has told Canada to suppress those materials."

Now, as the Iran-Contra scandal washed over the U.S. capital, Gotlieb appeared equally reluctant to betray excessive interest in the Canadian Connection. But after Furmark's confidential testimony to the Senate intelligence committee, he had, in fact, ducked out a back door and headed straight for a debriefing with embassy officials. "We had reason to believe he was going to call us," Gotlieb admitted. His terms seemed uncharacteristically vague for a diplomat of acute linguistic precision. Repeatedly, he mispronounced Furmark's name in imaginative variations. "Furmart," he called him at one point; "Furbank," at another. "The idea occurred to some people," he said, "it would be interesting to know what he would be saying."

In fact, if some people such as the prime minister harboured the slightest curiosity about Furmark and his allegations, they need not have waited on his confidential session with the Washington embassy staff. Brian Mulroney had a much more direct pipeline to Khashoggi's elusive message-carrier: his longtime crony Frank Moores, who was ensconced as Ottawa's most controversial hired gun just a few blocks from Parliament Hill. Moores had known Furmark since well before 1972, when he had ousted Joey Smallwood as premier of Newfoundland and taken over the province's partnership in a contentious oil refinery rising in the remote outpost of Come By Chance. In those days, Furmark was already a familiar figure in the corridors of power in St. John's, the point man for his boss, a brash New York oil adventurer named John Shaheen, who had dreamed up the disastrous $200 million refinery scheme and who, a decade later, would serve as one of the catalysts for Reagan's secret arms deal with Iran.

THE idea was an audacious one, but then audacious ideas were nothing new to John Shaheen. Wiry and dapper, the grandson of Lebanese immigrants to Chicago, he had such a gift for the improbable pitch that his friend and former lawyer, Richard Nixon, had once dubbed him "the world's greatest salesman." As director of the special operations branch of Washington's Office of Strategic Services during the Second World War, Shaheen had headed up the OSS shop of dirty tricks with such flair that he was rewarded with a Silver Star and the Legion of Merit. One project, code-named Javaman, had constructed a remote-controlled speedboat bomb aimed at torpedoing enemy shipping. If the kamikaze motor boat never did make it into the North Atlantic fray, it did succeed in terrorizing the inhabitants of Myrtle Beach. On a test run off the North Carolina coast, it sank a derelict freighter with such a blast that it shattered seaside windows and forced residents out of their houses, screaming that the Germans had invaded.

Even after the war when he turned his brainstorming to profit, Shaheen was never averse to kicking up a ruckus — first, taking on the life insurance establishment with airport vending machines to dispense pre-flight policies, then challenging the forces of Big Oil. In 1948 he had tried to set up the first independent refinery in Puerto Rico. And two decades later, after offering to take over the timber rights for a Newfoundland pulp mill, he talked Joey Smallwood into teaming up with him to realize his dream — raising a monster refinery in an impoverished fishing port on Placentia Bay. Perched on one of the few natural deep-water harbours along the northeastern seaboard which could accommodate giant tankers without an environmental fuss, the Come By Chance facility was slated to process 100,000 barrels a day, mainly of Saudi crude.

As Furmark, his chief financial officer saw it, Shaheen's genius was to pull off the deal without risking a cent of his own. To fund it, he had drafted the British government, which had guaranteed the $120 million first mortgage through its export agency, as well as Japan's Ataka Corporation, then one of Tokyo's top ten trading companies. The provincial government, run by Smallwood as his private fiefdom, had guaranteed a $30 million construction bond issue and advanced another $5 million in cash for bridge financing. But that generosity had provoked such an uproar in the legislature that two Liberals quit Smallwood's ranks and stormed across the aisle: John Crosbie, who would soon formally convert to the Conservative Party, and Clyde Wells, later to become premier himself. Their misgivings about Come By Chance were to prove well founded. According to Furmark, Shaheen had cannily deduced that, by going into business with governments, he could not lose: when the crunch came, they would be obliged to bail him out. That calculation would ultimately leave Newfoundland taxpayers $45 million out of pocket.

But four years before that debacle, the controversy had helped hasten Smallwood's political demise. On October 10, 1973, when Shaheen finally unveiled his refinery before 3,000 guests imported for the occasion, standing beside him on the dais was the province's first Tory premier, Frank Moores, who had just manoeuvred Smallwood out of office. Like everything Shaheen touched, the ceremony was an extravagant affair. Representing the London investors, British MP Winston Churchill attempted to deliver the keynote address, only to find himself drowned out by the ill-timed fly-past of a Vulcan bomber from the air base at Goose Bay. No sooner had he finished than the crowd, shivering through five-degree weather and icy gusts that threatened to lift the enormous circus tent out onto the North Atlantic, descended on a lavish 400-metre-long banquet table groaning under shrimp, suckling pigs, and roast sides of beef. Some guests were sighted beating a hasty retreat with lobsters tucked in their pockets.

THE CANADIAN CONNECTION 265

But amid the hoopla, the greatest excitement had arrived with the gleaming white *Queen Elizabeth 2*, the pride of the Cunard line, at the end of the 1,140-metre tanker wharf. Shaheen had chartered the luxury liner at a cost of $97,000 a day to ferry a cast of 1,000 international dignitaries from New York to witness his moment of glory in the desolate outport. Among those gamely trooping down the gangplank was a short, balding figure whose name frequently made the world's society columns, but failed to rate a mention in the St. John's *Evening Telegram*: Adnan Khashoggi. The Saudi arms broker had cemented a friendship with Shaheen during a 1966 oil deal, but they were also united by another bond — their longtime ties to the embattled president, Richard Nixon. As the Watergate scandal threatened to swamp Nixon, neither had wavered in his support, either moral or financial. Indeed, only nine months before the Come By Chance ceremony, Shaheen's $100,000 campaign contribution had won him a VIP box at the Kennedy Center for Nixon's second inaugural gala, where he hosted Khashoggi and his stunning wife, Soraya, as his guests of honour.

There, they had rubbed shoulders with one of Shaheen's best buddies from the OSS, William Casey, who had long performed what Furmark termed the oilman's "special" legal work. By then, Casey had additional prestige: Nixon had just named him undersecretary of state for economic affairs, overseeing the mounting oil crisis. From the moment they met, Shaheen and Casey had recognized each other as kindred spirits who savoured their wartime derring-do, taking risks that had shocked the plodding patrician types in the service, whom Casey mocked as "the white shoe boys." They seldom missed the regular OSS old boy reunions, where Shaheen was in charge of the awards committee, and they kept in touch with other comrades who had signed on with its postwar successor, the CIA. On such occasions, Shaheen usually bought several tables, inviting his trusty aide Roy Furmark, who had spent years doggedly flying from their Park Avenue offices to St. John's every Monday morning to supervise the building of Come By Chance. Thus, as the Iran-Contra affair unfolded, there was a family feeling in the air — a sense of old roots and arrangements that defied cursory congressional scrutiny. On the windswept wharf at Come By Chance, a circle of interests had been knit that would endure and strengthen over the years, despite the roller-coaster course of individual fortunes.

Even before the refinery ceremony had wrapped up, the first political storm clouds had rolled in for Khashoggi. A week earlier, his monarch, King Faisal, had financed the surprise salvos of the Yom Kippur war against Israel. Aboard the QE 2 en route to Newfoundland, Khashoggi and his Lebanese publisher friends had been elated at Egypt's initial victories. But by the time the ship hove into the outport, the tide was turning and Nixon was being pressured to begin an airlift of arms to Israel. In the liner's wireroom, an urgent cable arrived from Riyadh, summoning Khashoggi to resume his duties as the kingdom's backstage emissary to the United States.

For a deal-maker routinely dismissed as a flashy hedonist, it was not an unaccustomed role. Years earlier, David Kimche, a top official of the Israeli secret service, had approached him as a conduit to the Saudi royal family, and for fifteen years the man whom Mossad code-named The Eagle had bridged the chasm between Jerusalem and Riyadh. Jetting around the world in sybaritic splendour, partying with film stars and playgirls aboard his luxury yacht, Khashoggi had the perfect cover as a secret agent: his flamboyance. He would also demonstrate his capacity for unflinching loyalty. In 1976, three years after the Come By Chance unveiling, he would become a fugitive from U.S. justice, providing an alibi for two Saudi generals in the Lockheed bribery scandals being investigated by the Securities and Exchange Commission. Khashoggi declared that he had pocketed the payoffs himself, in order to save the generals — and presumably their royal patrons — embarrassment.

By then, Shaheen too had fallen on troubled times. His refinery had been forced into bankruptcy by Morgan Stanley, the New York merchant bank hired to probe the deal by his disgruntled Japanese investors. Never fully operative, plagued by labour and design glitches, and capable of producing only low-grade oil, it had racked up $600 million in debt less than three years after its spectacular kickoff. During that time, it had somehow managed to miss out on the astronomical prices provoked by the postwar Arab oil embargo. Some critics claimed that it had been an elaborate scam from the start. But in an affidavit in the provincial supreme court, an embittered Shaheen raged that he had been the victim of "a plot so perfidious, so Machiavellian" to undo him and his upstart oil company — orchestrated through Morgan Stanley by the seven sisters of Big Oil — that it dwarfed any previous corporate malfeasance.

The refinery scandal, in turn, almost sank Frank Moores's 1975 re-election bid. But as he fought for his political life, even importing Nixon's pollster, Robert Teeter, his cash-strapped campaign received a discreet contribution hand-delivered from Shaheen's Park Avenue headquarters by an intermediary. Later that year, safely back in power, Moores would rise at the federal Tory leadership convention and nominate his good friend Brian Mulroney. When that gesture ended in defeat and Mulroney took over the presidency of Iron Ore, Newfoundland's largest employer, he frequently flew into St. John's on the corporate jet, staying the night at the premier's residence all through those years when the Come By Chance fallout was threatening Moores's regime.

Even after Moores left St. John's for Montreal in 1979 to help launch Mulroney's Conservative leadership bid, he and Shaheen stayed in touch. For the maverick oilman, winning back his refinery had become an obsession. And in the fall of 1980, shortly after a bankruptcy trustee had ordered him to repay the province $46 million, Shaheen's youngest son, Bradford, made a $71 million cash offer to repurchase Come By Chance. That overture turned out to be financed by an Iranian named Cyrus Hashemi, who would resurface six years later in the Iran-Contra affair.

In the spring of 1985 Hashemi had approached Shaheen with a scheme to sell U.S. anti-tank missiles to Iran in order to win the release of a half-dozen American hostages being held by Iranian-backed terrorists in Lebanon. But he also had another motive for playing backstreet matchmaker: in return, Hashemi wanted the U.S. Justice Department to drop charges against him for an earlier attempt at selling arms to Teheran. Shaheen had relayed the overture to Bill Casey, who was haunted by the ayatollah's outlaw regime. Before long, Hashemi was introducing his Iranian contact to Adnan Khashoggi, and the arms dealer was winging his way to Hamburg along with his old Israeli spymaster, David Kimche, to hammer out the details of the weapons transfer. By that time, Kimche had won the clandestine blessing of Robert McFarlane, Reagan's national security adviser, to negotiate the banned sale of U.S.–made spare parts to the Iranian airforce. As they worked out the nuts and bolts of that high-stakes gamble, one of the key players at those meetings in the summer and fall of 1985 was Roy Furmark, Shaheen's Brooklyn-born former aide who had enlisted in Khashoggi's service.

Meanwhile, at the very moment that Shaheen and his circle were orchestrating the clandestine Iranian arms deal, he was in constant

contact with Frank Moores — plotting once more to ransom his
refinery, this time from the clutches of Petro-Canada. In early 1985
Toronto Sun reporter Bob Fife got wind that an Israeli company, Dor
Chemicals, had put in a bid on the benighted facility in order to sub-
vert the Arab oil embargo. But no sooner had he begun to make
inquiries on the subject than he got a call from Moores, by then the
capital's most ubiquitous lobbyist. Toiling on behalf of Shaheen's
Peninsular Oil Refining, a rival bidder, Moores proved surprisingly
well informed: he provided Fife with a detailed list of all five offers
in the secret government tender. During a phone interview in New
York, Shaheen too had exuded cockiness. One reason, he confided to
Fife, was that Mulroney had just named John Lundrigan, Moores's
former business partner and minister of industrial development, as
a political appointee to the board of Petro-Canada Ltd. As it turned
out, their confidence was not misplaced. In July 1985 Shaheen did
indeed win the Come By Chance tender, but four months later
Peninsular withdrew its offer when he died of cancer.

Those cross-border ties might have qualified merely as another
intriguing coincidence in the Iran-Contra affair were it not for
another twist. In October 1984, a month after Mulroney's Conservative landslide, Adnan Khashoggi had begun spending an
unaccustomed amount of time in Canada.

ON the fringes of the runway at Ottawa's Uplands Airport, the
cameras were already in place. But overshadowing Richard Pyman's
video crew from Toronto, which had been hired to shoot a modest
souvenir tape, was the world-weary U.S. TV team from *Lifestyles of
the Rich and Famous*, set to celebrate the *modus vivendi* of a certain Saudi arms dealer in all its outrageous excess. As the wheels of
Khashoggi's DC–8 touched down outside the capital on an October
morning in 1984, his trip to Canada had taken on all the trappings
of a state visit. Not only had the organizers insisted that he be
addressed as the "Honourable" Adnan Khashoggi — a title reserved
for Privy Council members — but in the middle of the previous
night they had routed an RCMP officer from his bed with a panicked
request for a security clearance that would allow his palatial private
jet to land at the military airfield.

Waiting on the tarmac to greet him was Saudi ambassador Ziad

Shawaf, an old schoolfriend who whisked him off in an official limousine for a private confab to which the rest of his party was pointedly not invited. When Khashoggi reappeared, the remainder of his capital stopover was spent on business rounds: visiting the Canadian Development Investment Corporation, touring high-tech Mitel Corporation, and conferring with the brass of Petro-Canada, where he was received by its chairman, Wilbert Hopper.

Originally, Khashoggi had been scheduled to see Mulroney. He had his heart set on meeting the new prime minister, since he already knew Pierre Trudeau, whom he had hosted three years earlier at his luxury Kenyan game ranch. According to a tentative itinerary telexed to his Paris apartment by his Toronto advance man, Timothy Khan, he had even been slated for a 5 P.M. appointment on the last day of his stay. Mulroney was "very excited at the opportunity of meeting with Mr. Khashoggi," Khan reported, "and has also asked his senior Cabinet ministers to prepare for the visit on October the 22nd." A month later, it was unclear what had happened to that prime ministerial enthusiasm. Khan claimed that Mulroney had been forced to cancel because of pressing commitments, and, certainly, no public record of their meeting has emerged. But if he thought better of being seen hobnobbing with Khashoggi, that prospect had not put off some of his wealthiest Bay Street supporters or Ontario premier William Davis, one of Mulroney's regular telephone confidants.

Night had fallen by the time Khashoggi's flying road show moved on to Toronto, landing in freezing rain and fog at the private Innotech Aviation terminal, where Davis had rolled out the red carpet. There, huddled patiently inside the cramped lounge waiting to greet him was Frank Miller, the provincial minister of trade and industry, and a handful of leading business lights, including Christopher Trump, then vice president of corporate affairs for Spar Aerospace. Khashoggi's aides had requested a telegenic honour guard of scarlet-clad Mounties to salute his arrival, but he had to make do with an Ontario Provincial Police motorcycle escort, waiting, sodden, in the rain, to lead his nine-limousine cavalcade downtown with lights flashing and sirens screaming. Miller's ministry had agreed to pick up the $9,000 tab for the limos, including an 8-metre stretch Lincoln for the man whose aides called him the Chief. And at the King Edward Hotel, an entire floor had been reserved for Khashoggi and his twenty-member entourage, complete with a chiropracter, burly barber, and masseur, as well as Max Helzel, a former Lockheed vice president he had known since the bribery scandal days, whom he introduced as his aerospace consultant. His agenda, overseen by Miller's ministry, was crammed with official lunches and dinners. As Timothy Khan had exulted by telex, the Ontario government was "going first class."

The next morning when the limo caravan pulled up at Queen's Park, dwarfing the premier's official car, Davis and three cabinet ministers received Khashoggi in the oak-panelled Council Chamber, where the pair exchanged gifts as if he were, indeed, a visiting potentate. Presented with the usual soapstone carving, the arms dealer produced elaborate mother-of-pearl inlaid boxes for Davis and Miller, each cradling a gleaming golden dagger on a bed of green velvet. As they took their places at the cabinet table, Miller seemed intent on impressing his guest that this was no Third World backwater. "We're modest, sir," Davis interjected, "but this is where the action is."

That seemed to be precisely what Khashoggi had calculated. Over the next three days, with the government's official blessing, his motorcade would criss-cross the city, alighting at the country's leading banks, brokerage houses, and a half-dozen corporations that leaned towards military and high-tech wares. He looked over de Havilland Aircraft, which Mulroney had just put on the privatization block; stopped by Spar's showcase facility, where the company was bidding on contracts for the planned Arabsat; and toured the province's Urban Transport Development Corporation, which made heavy trucks for the military. In the boardroom of Bell Canada, he was received by vice president Leonard Lugsdin like a long-lost uncle, which in a way he was: in 1978 when Bell won its $2.6 billion contract to install a new Saudi phone system, Lugsdin had personally leased an entire Riyadh subdivision for the company's crews from Khashoggi's younger brother Adil. Since then, the Saudi wheeler-dealer had offered to act as the company's agent in other developing countries, most recently in India. But as Bell's filings with the Securities and Exchange Commission in Washington revealed, its agent in the Saudi deal had been Prince Mohammed, whose father, King Fahd, had once sent him to London to learn the ways of the world under the arms dealer's wing.

Before Khashoggi's arrival, the *Toronto Sun* had bannered his net worth as $5 billion. And terming his trip a "goodwill mission," vaguely muttering about investment possibilities using the royal "we," he found himself embraced by Toronto's financial establishment with star-struck fervour. When he expressed a whim to see a Saudi exhibit at the Royal Ontario Museum on his way into town from Spar's Weston plant, the museum's chairman, Conservative lawyer Eddie Goodman, gave new meaning to his nickname "Fast Eddie": hurling himself across town on forty-five minutes notice, he was waiting on the ROM's front steps when Khashoggi's stretch Lincoln pulled up. Nor did eighty of the country's top CEOs utter a peep of protest when Khashoggi kept them cooling their heels over cocktails for two hours at a $20,000 black-tie gala that Miller threw in his honour at Windows, the Four Seasons' rooftop restaurant. Some, like Jean de Grandpré, the Bell chairman, had flown in from Montreal for the occasion. But when the guest of honour finally made his entrance with a panache that Hollywood might have envied, all was forgiven. The crowd offered a standing ovation to the squat Saudi and his Amazonian second wife, Lamia, who towered over him with a gigantic diamond-encrusted sapphire nestling in her décolletage.

If his hosts had visions of petrodollars dancing in their heads, Khashoggi seemed to be eyeing them with reciprocal thoughts. Wherever he went, from the Bank of Montreal to the thirty-third-floor boardroom of brokerage McLeod Young Weir, he trotted out flowcharts to illustrate a complex counter-trade deal he was pitching. With pointer in hand, he would whip through its multiple barter arrangements, intended to move commodities through a succession of Third World nations including the Sudan, where he and the Saudi monetary agency had already invested millions. But his rapid-fire exposition invariably left listeners bewildered. At one conference table, a veteran numbers-cruncher who routinely juggled dozens of deals at a time was struggling to follow his drift when he had an epiphany. No wonder he was having trouble keeping up with Khashoggi's labyrinthian counter-trade scheme, he thought: that was the point of it all, its beauty and sheer genius. At the end of the day, he concluded, no one would be able to retrace the transactions or where the money had gone. "There was something else happening," he marvelled later. "And one of the steps always involved arms."

Still, at some stops, Khashoggi's hosts were left mystified as to the motive for his visit. And many, like Bell's Leonard Lugsdin, were puzzled at the man he had chosen to organize the trip. Timothy

Khan turned out to be a self-promoting law-school-dropout-turned-suit-salesman who was working out of his parents' Mississauga basement. But by the time Khashoggi showed up at the Bell board-room, Khan had been relegated to the background. Another familiar figure had materialized to take over the lead role: Peter Munk, the arms broker's longtime business associate, who had just moved back to Toronto after a twelve-year self-imposed exile in London. Clearly, Khashoggi had chosen to use Khan as his front man rather than Munk, the Hungarian-born entrepreneur who remained tainted by the 1967 collapse of Clairtone, his high-profile hi-fi venture.

Once hailed as a Canadian wunderkind, Munk and his partner David Gilmour had talked the Nova Scotia government into invest-ing in a plant whose fate bore an eerie resemblance to that of John Shaheen's refinery: when Halifax pulled the plug, horrified at the mounting losses, provincial taypayers were left on the hook for $20 million.

Munk and Gilmour had fled to London to start over as resort tycoons with a tract of ragged coastline on the rainy side of Fiji. In England they had joined forces first with swashbuckling Big Jim Slater of Slater-Walker Securities, whose own empire would soon collapse. Then at a society dinner, Gilmour met Khashoggi, who leaped at the chance to invest $12 million in their Southern Pacific Properties. The trio went on to buy up the Australian Travelodge chain amid a storm of controversy, then drafted a grandiose blue-print for a luxury resort outside Cairo, complete with a golf course designed by Robert Trent Jones, at the foot of the pyramids. The Egyptian government had finally vetoed that contentious greening of the desert, provoking a lawsuit that was still dragging on when Khashoggi arrived in Toronto.

He himself had turned his interests to a series of small U.S.–based oil companies with a tendency to shift their assets and change their names, ultimately earning him a blistering report by the California bankruptcy trustee for one of them, Oasis Petroleum. In 1981, the year Reagan came to power, Khashoggi and his partners in Oasis had bought 1.3 million shares in BRG Resources, which became Barrick Petroleum Corporation, registered in Delaware. When Peter Munk moved back to Toronto, the vehicle on which he chose to rebuild his shattered financial reputation was a Canadian affiliate of the same name. Born out of the amalgamation of two obscure companies and a share swap that amounted to a reverse takeover, his rechristened

Barrick Resources Corporation was promptly listed on the Toronto Stock Exchange with a modest $35 million capitalization.

But on Bay Street, where one leading powerbroker pronounced him a leopard — as in leopards don't change their spots — Munk was still regarded warily. Khashoggi was intent on boosting his prospects — and not incidentally those of Barrick, which had just gone into the gold mining business. With fanfare and TV cameras in tow, he toured the stock exchange, where he made a show of buying 10,000 Barrick shares, then trading at $1.39. But he seemed miffed when a reporter demanded how he would finance the purchase. "Margin," he had snapped. When pressed for further details, it became clear he was risking only $5,560 for his $13,900 symbolic investment. Not that he could be blamed for the caution of his gamble. According to reports at the time, Adnan Khashoggi and his brother Essam already controlled nearly half of the company's shares through Horsham Securities and their offshore Triad International Corporation.

But they were not the only Saudis with a stake in Munk's new Canadian incarnation. Through a holding company called Killarney Ltd., another sizeable chunk was held by Prince Nawaf bin Abdul Aziz, the half-brother of both the late King Faisal and his successor, King Fahd. In 1983 Barrick officials had also bragged of yet another shareholder with connections to the kingdom: Faisal's brother-in-law and top adviser, Kamal Adham. Nearly a decade later, when Adham's name emerged in a U.S. fraud indictment for his role in the notorious Bank of Credit and Commerce International (BCCI) — costing him a $100 million fine — he would be identified in terms that Barrick had neglected to publicize: as the former head of the CIA–sponsored Saudi intelligence service.

Thus the corporation that, in 1993, would offer Brian Mulroney his most generous post-retirement rewards had begun its existence a decade earlier funded largely by the Saudi royal family and its key agents. At the time Khashoggi landed in Toronto, the House of Saud had a uniquely close relationship with the Reagan administration. Just three months earlier, in July 1984, King Fahd had begun under-writing the top item on Reagan's covert foreign policy agenda, making the first of his secret contributions to the Contras' account in the Cayman Islands.

After Khashoggi's PR plug for Barrick, Munk threw a black-tie bash at his Rosedale mansion for some of the city's Conservative elite, including James Marshall Tory, the senior partner of the law firm Davis would later join. On a previous night, developer Robert Campeau, still the toast of the leveraged buy-out set, had hosted a soirée for Liberal luminaries featuring Pierre Trudeau and Ottawa-born singer Paul Anka, who had become part of Khashoggi's circle in Las Vegas. But with Mulroney newly installed in Ottawa, it was Munk's Tory festivities that found their way into Zena Cherry's society column in the *Globe and Mail*. Shortly after his arrival, one of the first Toronto tycoons Khashoggi met with privately was Mulroney's ally Trevor Eyton, the chairman of Brascan, who would later win a place on Barrick's board. And as he wound up his trip, he was fêted on a day-long jaunt to Muskoka by some of the prime minister's other key financial backers. Flying up to Lake Joseph on a government float plane with Lieutenant Governor John Black Aird, he was hosted for lunch at the Sherwood Inn. There he was scheduled to break bread with Conrad and Montegu Black and cable czar Ted Rogers. But in the end, only real estate tycoon Joe Barnicke, department store heir John Craig Eaton, and Douglas Bassett, the scion of the Baton broadcasting empire, showed up. Afterward, Bassett whisked the arms dealer off to his retreat on Lake Rosseau aboard an antique mahogany launch called *The Rascal*.

Although none of the participants could later recall a single investment or contract that resulted from his four-day sojourn, those slim pickings did nothing to discourage Khashoggi or his hosts. Within months, his top aide and friends had invested an estimated $5.9 million in Timothy Khan's Toronto company, Akhana International Consulting Corporation, which took offices just down the hall from a corner suite leased to the newly retired William Davis for his toils as Mulroney's acid rain envoy. Later, when Davis vacated his digs, Khan moved in. Swanning around town in expensive suits from Khashoggi's New York tailor, Bijan, and an assortment of Jaguars and Rolls Royces, he introduced himself as the Chief's personal representative and talked of million-dollar killings on the Vancouver stock exchange and offshore companies in Jersey or the Caymans. With the wife of Khashoggi's right-hand man, he was a frequent visitor to the offices of Gordon Capital, where they were entertained by its head, Jimmy Connacher.

But Khan's main task seemed to be promoting the arms dealer's presence in Toronto. He sponsored an Akhana car in a minor 1986 Molson Indy race, and during Frank Miller's campaign to succeed

Davis for the provincial leadership he took tables at two fundraisers and donated buttons proclaiming "It's Miller Time!" — a U.S. beer slogan. But in 1985 his major political contributions went to Mulroney's federal party coffers. The PC Canada Fund reported receiving $3,435.80 from Khan, Akhana, and a company called A.K. Holdings Ltd., which he claimed was part of Khashoggi's empire.

Meanwhile, Khan jetted about the world as yet another member of Khashoggi's amazing airborne entourage, popping up at his fiftieth birthday extravaganza in Marbella or at conferences of Reagan's ultra-conservative supporters in Washington. In the spring of 1986 Spar's Christopher Trump was shocked to receive a missive from him announcing that he had just returned from a White House briefing on Central America. "The time has come for all Canadians to stop thinking of Nicaragua as an American problem," he urged. By then, Khashoggi himself had already written Reagan offering to help out the Contra cause.

Nearly a year after Khashoggi's first Toronto trip, Timothy Khan sent out invitations for a reprise gala at the King Edward Hotel. This time, even Mulroney's friend Peter Pocklington had flown in from Edmonton for the black-tie gathering. Once again, the Chief kept the cream of Bay Street waiting two hours, dashing in from the airport to catch seven of the eight dinner courses, then reboarding his DC–8 for the return flight to Washington after midnight. Leaving his oldest son, Mohamed, behind to check out aircraft plants in Montreal, Khashoggi made clear he had pressing business in the U.S. capital. In fact, his first $5 million arms delivery to Teheran had taken place a month earlier.

A separate shipment of aircraft engine parts from Montreal's Pratt and Whitney had been okayed for export to Iran by External Affairs officials the same month. The $3.7 million order for those parts, which could be used in the Iranians' Bell Cobra Helicopter gunships, had originally been vetoed by External's Joe Clark. But when the application was resubmitted a few months later, claiming the parts were for the helicopter's civilian twin, department officials had rubber-stamped it, according to a government spokesman, without bothering to inform Clark. The first shipment would not take place until more than a year later. During that period, one of Pratt and Whitney's frequent visitors was Reagan's former secretary of state Al Haig, a director of its U.S. parent company and a man who claimed William Davis among his friends. As the Iran-Contra investigation would later reveal, Haig had okayed the first secret Israeli shipment of U.S. military spare parts to Teheran while he was still in the White House.

For Khashoggi, his overtures to Iran were part of a sweeping peace proposal he had been trying to sell Washington, spelled out in careful detail in a forty-seven-page strategy paper that he liked to call his Marshall plan for the Middle East. In 1983 he had first presented it to William Clark, Reagan's national security adviser, whose confirmation hearings had demonstrated that he had a somewhat hazy grasp of geopolitics. But he had more luck with Clark's successor, Robert McFarlane, who would oversee the arms sales to Iran. Despite later White House attempts to ridicule the plan, much of the administration's strategy seemed to be based on his script. Indeed, he had hired one of McFarlane's deputies, Chuck Tyson, a former Reagan campaign aide with close personal ties to the president, to run his Madrid marketing office. In Khashoggi's lexicon, "marketing" was the euphemism used for brokering arms sales, and Madrid would soon become a major transfer point for weapons destined for Iran. Tyson insists he was involved in other kinds of marketing. But in retrospect it seemed noteworthy that he had been one of three American national security specialists who had accompanied the Chief to Toronto in 1984.

Later, when the Iran-Contra scandal broke, the leading lights of Corporate Canada would rush to distance themselves from the Saudi wheeler-dealer they had once courted. After all, among Charles Allen's briefing notes from Roy Furmark there was mention of a $1 million "counter-trade" deal he and Khashoggi had been working on at the time. And Frank Miller would wince to recall his remonstrance to a reporter who questioned his welcome for a kingpin of the global arms bazaar. "Ontario businesses deal in arms, too," Miller had scolded at the time. "Let's not throw the first stone when we're in glass houses." But in retrospect what seemed most disconcerting was the souvenir video that Timothy Khan had sent him to immortalize the trip. At the end of the tape, the announcer had used a prophetic phrase: Khashoggi's Toronto hosts, he declared, "were unanimous in their desire to . . . develop and expand the Canadian connection."

THE CIA's Charles Allen was a meticulous note-taker, and during his frequent meetings with Roy Furmark in the fall of 1986 he proved true to form. But what seemed unusual about his notes on the unravelling Iranian arms deal — declassified during the congressional hearings — was that one particular report was not released with the rest until long after the media glare had faded from the investigations. As it revealed, the Canadian connection to the Iran-Contra affair was not purely Canadian at all. Don Fraser and Ernie Miller had financed Khashoggi along with the most unlikely character in a decidedly unlikely international cast: an Indian guru named Sri Chandra Swamiji Maharaj, better known to his followers as Swamiji. "The swami was bankrolling Khashoggi all along," confirmed Timothy Khan. "He was paying for the planes, the yachts, the parties — everything."

Celebrated by the *National Enquirer* as Liz Taylor's guru, the burly holy man was not your usual Indian saint. Ever since he had emerged in New Delhi during the 1970s as the protégé of one of Indira Gandhi's top cabinet ministers, Narasimha Rao — later to succeed her assassinated son Rajiv as prime minister — he had eschewed the spiritual needs of the masses for those of politicians, millionaires, and movie stars. His most famous devotee was the ruler who merited the title once attributed to Khashoggi as the world's richest man: the boyish and fabulously wealthy young Sultan of Brunei. According to some in Khashoggi's circle, it was to reforge his frayed friendship with the sultan, another of his disgruntled former lenders, that the arms broker had sought out the swami's services.

To make the introduction, Khashoggi's aides had called on Steve Martindale, a former Mormon lawyer and lobbyist for Robert Gray, who was known as one of Washington's most artful social mountaineers. But Martindale was not without his own Canadian connections. During the Trudeau years, the former aide to Nelson Rockefeller had become friends with U.S. ambassador Tom Enders and his socialite wife, Gaetana, flying up to Ottawa for sporadic visits. Later, one of his acquaintances from those days, Margaret Trudeau, had hired him as her agent when she was peddling *Beyond Reason*, her kiss-and-tell memoirs of sex, drugs, and rock 'n' roll in the post-Pierre fast lane. After the Iran-Contra scandal broke, when a Canadian reporter called to interview Martindale about his role, he confided that he had first checked out her bona fides with another longtime friend from Ottawa who had taken up residence in Washington, Sondra Gotlieb. He insisted he held no grudges over Gotlieb's caricature of him in her *Washington Post* column as "Sonny Goldstone, Social Asset and Gilded Bachelor," a jaded figure forever offering tips on how to clamber up the capital's slippery social inclines.

As Martindale told it, he had found himself tragically duped by a cast of jet-setting con men who had used his services, then left him in the dark. "It was like being the doorman at a whorehouse," he lamented, "and not knowing what was going on inside." In 1984 the swami had cultivated him as a well-connected Republican who could arrange introductions to the Reagan crowd, and he had duly obliged. Setting up meetings and photo ops with top congressmen including Maine's Republican senator William Cohen, later a member of the Iran-Contra panel, he had squired the white-robed guru around Capitol Hill. Martindale made many of the introductions that, as Furmark later warned the CIA, Miller and Fraser threatened to use to spill the beans about the covert arms deals. But long before Martindale came on the scene, the swami had wangled his own ties to a handful of Democrats. One of them, California's congressman Mervyn Dymally, had become so enchanted that he had pilgrimaged to Toronto for an audience at the Black Hawk Inn, and had even received a loan from Miller, which he disclosed on his 1981 House financial declaration.

On September 2, 1985, when Martindale got a call from one of Khashoggi's aides pleading for a meeting, the guru was ensconced behind the electronic gates of Miller's mansion in Gormley, north of Toronto, where his host chauffeured him about in a white Rolls Royce with licence plates that read Luxmi, the Hindu goddess of wealth. But Khashoggi was undeterred by the swami's demand that the rendezvous take place on Canadian turf. With his DC–8 on loan to President Mobutu Sese Seko of Zaire, he was obliged to venture aboard his first commercial flight in fifteen years, winging his way from Paris to New York via the Concorde, then chartering a private jet to Toronto with Martindale. But unlike his other heavily hyped trips to the city, this time his arrival was determinedly low profile. He stayed only four hours. Still, in that time, the Moslem arms dealer and the Hindu holy man forged a friendship that would outlast congressional investigations and their mutual scrapes with the law.

Three days later, the swami had moved into Khashoggi's opulent Olympic Towers penthouse in New York, where he became a regular in the flying carpet show. Together, chanting mantras, they made an unforgettable sight as they flew off to visit Mobutu, freshly deposed Haitian dictator Jean-Claude Duvalier, and the Philippines' disconsolate ousted strongman Ferdinand Marcos, who lay dying in Hawaii — all three then flush with purloined wealth. The month Khashoggi met the swami, he made his first arms transfer to Iran. And by the end of the year, Miller and Fraser's Cayman Islands corporation had funnelled its initial loans his way. The first for $6 million had been made on the basis of a handshake, as Khashoggi's astounded aide Emanuel Floor discovered when he was called in to document another for $8 million — this one in exchange for an option on shares in Triad America, the company that controlled the Khashoggis' troubled Salt Lake International Center. Those funds had come from Vertex's predecessor company, Sarsvati, named after the Hindu goddess of knowledge.

By the spring of 1986 Sarsvati's largesse to Khashoggi totalled $21 million. But his Salt Lake development was still in dire straits and he told Floor he needed another $10 million for "a joint venture" to facilitate certain "international marketing." Finally in March 1986, he and Floor flew to the Cayman Islands to consolidate the Sarsvati loans under one lump sum from Vertex and to clinch two new deals with Miller and Fraser. Over the following days, as Floor and Fraser negotiated the terms of the transactions in Euro Bank's offices, Miller had become confused over the intricate financial web. Khashoggi had finally stepped in to explain the money cycle, sketching out a circular transaction on Floor's yellow legal pad: one box, representing the arms sales, was marked "Iran," and another, to which a portion of the profits was slated, was labelled simply "BCCI." According to Floor, another Fraser-run company was to bail out Triad's Salt Lake City development with $9 million in exchange for shares, while the $10 million for the arms deal was secured with separate collateral: Khashoggi's interest in Peter Munk's Barrick, which by then had been renamed American Barrick Resources Corporation.

Those negotiations offered Khashoggi his first business dealings with Don Fraser, who counted among his friends another character in the tangled Iran-Contra cast. Before he left Toronto in late 1978, Fraser had served as campaign chairman for a Tory firebrand who had also been his lawyer: John Gamble, the ultra-conservative MP who, in 1983, would lead the Dump Clark movement that opened the way for Mulroney's Tory leadership bid. Three years later, John Morrison and Gordon Jackson, two of Gamble's backstage lieutenants who had helped orchestrate that putsch, would turn up on the part-time payroll of one of Ernie Miller's companies.

As the Iran-Contra scandal washed over that tiny interlocked circle, Gamble emerged as the lawyer and spokesman for both Fraser and Miller. With his usual flair for making headlines, he gamely admitted to being a director of Vertex Finances in the Cayman Islands, as well as an Ontario affiliate called Vertex Investments Ltd. But he too had his own ties to the band of self-appointed patriots running Reagan's off-the-books foreign policy. In 1984, shortly after he lost his parliamentary seat, he had taken up an offer from John Singlaub, the retired general and CIA official who was remaking the North American chapter of the World Anti-Communist League. Over the next two years, as Singlaub tapped into WACL's global network, including its founding Asian governments in South Korea and Taiwan, to raise funds for the Contras, Gamble headed its Canadian branch and took turns with him as the continental chairman. At one key September 1985 conference in Dallas, where the guests included Contra leaders Adolfo Calero and Enrique Bermúdez, the plucky Markham right-winger had been one of the featured speakers.

On at least three occasions, Singlaub himself had flown to Toronto to drum up support for the Contras after their congressional funding was cut off. During a November 1986 conference organized by WACL's subsidiary, the Anti-Bolshevic Bloc of Nations (ABN), at the city's downtown Holiday Inn, he had arranged for the appearance of Mario Calero, Adolfo's brother, as well as assorted other freedom fighters. Inside the front cover of that program, the list of VIP patrons had featured six of Mulroney's most rightwardly inclined MPs: Ontario's Patrick Boyer, John Oostrom, and Andrew Witer; Alberta's David Kilgour and Alex Kindy; and Donald Blenkarn, the Mississauga member who was chairman of the Commons influential finance committee. Some of the Tories in attendance denied any knowledge of the Contra fundraising efforts, but Blenkarn and Witer admitted meeting Singlaub more than once on the subject, while insisting they had never coughed up contributions themselves.

Amid the wreckage left by Ed Meese's Iran-Contra revelations, Gamble had also been obliged to come up with explanations for two bravura deals Fraser had launched on the Vancouver Stock Exchange, using Khashoggi's drawing power to push the prices to a level reflected in one company's name — Skyhigh. In fact, that resource shell company was used to buy one of Khashoggi's few remaining viable U.S. assets, Edgington Oil — a subsidiary of Triad Energy — and apparently to spirit it out of the clutches of his American creditors. In the summer of 1986, as Khashoggi was named vice president of Skyhigh Resources and Timothy Khan joined the board, its price was indeed soaring when Fraser launched a second play. This time, his shell was called Tangent Oil and Gas Ltd., where one major shareholder turned out to be their fellow financier in the Iranian arms deal, Oussama Lababedi. But just as both stocks were peaking on a wave of headlines and chutzpah, the Iran-Contra revelations stopped them cold with a cease-trading order, precipitating their crash. Six months later Fraser would launch another VSE stock called Caribbean Resources, on whose board he would be joined by Frank Moores's old friend John Lundrigan.

By that time, Miller and Fraser had denied any involvement in the arms deal; the money they had lent Khashoggi, Fraser said, was for his Salt Lake City ventures. Even Khashoggi had suddenly seen fit to recant his confessions to Barbara Walters. In a carefully staged interview with the *New York Times* in Paris, where he was avoiding testimony to the congressional hearings, he and Roy Furmark recounted an entirely new version of events, insisting that they had been playing "games within games" with William Casey when they came up with the tale of the Canadians' threats. But months later, the CIA would release the first of Charles Allen's notes, confirming Khashoggi's original story, and Special Prosecutor Lawrence Walsh would put his stamp on that version of events. Later, it would turn out that Khashoggi was anxious to conceal the involvement of the jet-setting swami who was still travelling in his slipstream. That concern was shared by others, including the Indian government, whose charismatic new leader, Rajiv Gandhi, had become close to Mulroney during Commonwealth conferences.

Indeed it was not until two years after the Iran-Contra investigations that word leaked out about the swami's existence. Months after a *Maclean's* reporter had published those revelations, she received an unsolicited call offering an introduction to the guru. But when she flew to Toronto for the appointed rendezvous in a hotel not far from Miller's house, the holy man was nowhere in sight. In his place was the caller, a rotund public relations agent named George D. McLean, who claimed to have met the swami in 1983 on a trip to the Far East. An admitted expert in damage control, he claimed he was consulting for Miller's computer firm while acting *pro bono* for his friend, the guru.

But McLean had a colourful personal history which raised questions as to just how high the Iran-Contra affair reached. In November 1985 he had become the managing director of a storefront operation in the Caribbean tax haven of St. Kitts, called First Trust Corporation Ltd. Four years later a Toronto lawyer, Donovan Blakeman, whom he had recruited to the board, would plead guilty to laundering $16 million in profits for a continental drug ring — nearly $3 million of it through McLean's trust company. Among First Trust's documents at the time was a list of five names that McLean had presented as character references: one of them was Patrick MacAdam, Mulroney's former college mate who had been appointed his liaison with the Conservative caucus. Indeed, McLean had registered MacAdam's address as the Prime Minister's Office.

McLean boasted an even lengthier tie to the man whom MacAdam had helped out on Mulroney's 1983 leadership bid: Frank Moores. During the early 1970s, when Moores was premier of Newfoundland, McLean had been denounced on the floor of the Provincial Legislature for reaping an inordinate number of the government's fattest public relations contracts. He had worked in both of Moores's provincial election campaigns and, as another veteran Tory operative characterized him, "He was Frank's alter ego. Whenever you saw George McLean, you knew Frank Moores was not far behind." In fact, one of the highlights of McLean's eventful career was choreographing the 1973 ceremony to launch John Shaheen's star-crossed refinery at Come By Chance which had woven together so many disparate skeins in the Canadian connection.

WHEN Adnan Khashoggi dropped the bombshell that Canadians had served as bridge financiers for his Iranian arms deal, the media promptly showed up on the doorstep of Peter Munk's brick bunker in Toronto's trendy Yorkville district. For Munk, the timing could not have been more unfortunate. His gold-mining fortunes had just begun to flourish in Utah and Nevada and, with his stylish British wife, Melanie, he was once again lionized on the city's black-tie circuit. A few unpleasant legal matters remained under investigation in Britain and a lawsuit loomed in a remote rural court outside Salt Lake City, but he would eventually triumph in both matters. And scarcely anyone ever brought up references to his Clairtone past. Then, suddenly, he found himself in the nightly newscasts again, trying to explain his decade-and-a-half friendship with the star middleman in the Iranian arms deal.

Munk hastened to point out that Adnan Khashoggi was not on his board; Barrick's director was his mild-mannered brother Essam. Some reporters appeared to buy that explanation but anyone with a nodding acquaintance of the Khashoggis' impenetrable financial affairs chuckled at that hair-splitting. Ever since Adnan Khashoggi's troubles with the U.S. Justice Department and his sensational $2 million U.S. divorce from Soraya, his American front man had been his artistic younger brother who lived on an estate outside Santa Barbara, where he had built his horses a swimming pool and consulted the Chief constantly on major financial decisions. In fact, months earlier, when Ernie Miller and Don Fraser had taken over Triad's Salt Lake City operation, Khashoggi had ordered Essam off the board at their request.

On November 26, the day after Ed Meese's revelations, an obscure subsidiary of Munk's American Barrick Resources suddenly announced a shareholders' meeting at a Montreal airport hotel to vote on an urgent restructuring plan. According to a notice issued at the time, United Siscoe Mines would do a stock swap and buy up all the outstanding Barrick shares owned by Horsham Securities in a reverse takeover that would make Siscoe the corporation's holding company. Along with that fancy footwork would come a new name, the Horsham Corporation. But the most startling aspect of the scheme was that Munk was creating a new class of multiple voting shares, to be held only by himself. Despite a minor stake in Horsham's equity, they would suddenly give him majority voting rights. Patriotism was brandished as the reason for the rejigging, keeping the corporation in Canadian hands. But in fact, according to the new breakdown, the Khashoggis' two holding companies would still retain more than a quarter of the stock, while Prince Nawaf remained the second-largest shareholder. Designated as Horsham's new president was Tariq Kadri, the Khashoggis' longtime lawyer, and an officer in their Salt Lake City development.

As the Reagan administration floundered under the Iran-Contra revelations and Khashoggi's frenetic deal-making came under increasing scrutiny, that shareholders' meeting was abruptly cancelled. Six months later, a brand new restructuring of American Barrick took place along the same lines, this time with no trace of Tariq Kadri or the Khashoggi brothers, who were declared out of the picture. In fact, their Barrick shares had been transferred to a Panama corporation named Coliton. But a year later, as his business thrived, Munk heaped scorn on Khashoggi's business acumen, announcing to a journalist: "I don't see Adnan anymore." What he neglected to mention was that he had picked up the pieces of his Saudi friend's U.S. empire, wiring money to the families of those arrested in an abortive Iranian arms deal and hiring the out-of-work Emanuel Floor to promote his Utah mine.

But Khashoggi's name was no longer convenient to drop. All through the congressional investigations into his covert arms deals, he was forced to avoid the United States as his holdings collapsed like a house of cards and creditors foreclosed on his yacht, his planes, and his other luxury toys. Finally, he was paraded back into the country in shackles. He had been arrested in Switzerland for having allegedly abetted Imelda Marcos in smuggling her assets out of Manila. Humiliated publicly, he sat through the long months of a trial where Timothy Khan testified against him. But there was no sign of Miller or Fraser, and no mention of the high-flying swami who had spent so much time with Khashoggi and Marcos. After his acquittal, his lawyer announced that King Fahd was picking up his multimillion-dollar legal bills. And within weeks, he made a surprise reappearance at the opening-night Tex Mex festivities of George Bush's July 1990 economic summit in Houston: billeted at the same hotel as Margaret Thatcher, he was the guest and brand new business partner of a leading Republic fundraiser named Jerry Dale Allen, who claimed to be a close friend and former associate of the president's son Neil.

By then, the Canadian connection had become just another quirky footnote in a scandal that seemed so hopelessly tangled it had confounded a dogged special prosecutor and ultimately achieved the apotheosis of spin control: it made the public's eyes glaze over. No small measure of that containment was credited to Mulroney's government, which, from the first, had shown a marked reluctance to expose any of the tantalizing trails that had led north of the border. When a Contra resupply plane had been shot down over Nicaragua in the fall of 1986, first implicating the Reagan administration — and specifically Bush's vice presidential staff — it turned out to have been a used Cariboo bought in Rouyn-Noranda, Quebec. But in the Commons, the government shrugged off the NDP's questions. When the congressional hearings revealed that, in setting out to fill the Contras' weapons shopping list, retired Major-General Richard Secord had gone straight to a Montreal arms broker named Emmanuel Weigensberg — whose Trans World Arms Inc. was well known to the State Department's Munitions Control Branch — the government announced that it had looked into the matter and that no laws had been broken. In fact, despite Adolfo Calero's complaints to a congressional hearing about Weigensberg's $2.3 million shipment as "the slow boat from China," the Pentagon appears to have had no qualms about Weigensberg's reliability. In 1994, after the collapse of the Soviet Union, the Montreal weapons broker was surreptitiously negotiating to buy S–300 missiles, the Russian equivalent of the Patriot, in the Republic of Belarus, on behalf of the U.S. Defense Intelligence Agency.

Indeed, if at times there seemed to be Canadian fingerprints all over both ends of the Iran-Contra arms deals, they were given short shrift on Parliament Hill. But considering that many of them led straight to the fringes of Mulroney's own party, it seemed passing strange that the government professed to know so little about the details. With the first astonishing revelations, Joe Clark rose to declare that the government had not colluded with Washington in the secret arms shipments to the Contras and that Reagan had not put any pressure on Mulroney to take part. Then Deputy Prime Minister Don Mazankowski announced that he had run into a "stone wall" when he tried to get information out of Washington about the scandal. But by December 15, Justice Minister Ray Hnatyshyn proclaimed a victory: Meese's staffers had agreed to cooperate with the RCMP to find out if the Criminal Code had been transgressed. Still, it was not until nearly six months later that Solicitor General James Kelleher announced that the Mounties had found no evidence of Canadian wrongdoing and had called off their probe. No report was released and a request for a parliamentary investigation was quickly scotched. "External Affairs is strangely silent on this," charged Vancouver New Democrat Ian Waddell. "I think the Canadian government would like to wash their hands of it."

In the end, the scandal left Peter Munk unscathed as he floated on a floodtide of adulatory press clippings and staggering profits, expanding into Latin America and Berlin, taking over Lac Minerals and the Bronfmans' discounted Trizec real estate holdings. Not only was he one of the country's highest-paid CEOs, but he had hired Allan Gotlieb as his Ottawa lobbyist. In the fall of 1992 he won an official stamp on his social resuscitation: an Order of Canada, whose citation lauded him as a "successful entrepreneur . . . committed to improving the standard of living for others." Then in November of that year he demonstrated that commitment, naming Brian Mulroney — under whose regime he had thrived — to both his boards. To those Conservatives who had blamed Mulroney's down-fall on his irredeemable attraction to glitz, it seemed singularly appropriate that he had found a berth in the service of the world's most profitable gold company. Critics who had tracked his government's propensity for secret deals found irony in the fact that he had crafted a political after-life with a company tied to the Reagan/ Bush administration's most devastating scandal. When Munk announced that former president George Bush had joined Mulroney on Barrick Gold's international advisory board, another circle seemed complete.

Initially, the press had focused on Mulroney's staggering stock options, which were calculated to be worth $1.5 million; after all, the Barrick board appointment brought him only $12,000 a year, plus $600 for each meeting, and as a Horsham director he received a mere $15,000 annual fee. But a year later, without touching his share possibilities, he had raked in an astonishing remuneration: $141,000 from Barrick and $120,375 from Horsham for "advisory services" — a total of nearly $300,000. Munk credited him with making the introductions to Paul Desmarais and with putting together their joint gold mining venture in China. There, Desmarais's Power Corporation had formed a consortium with Hydro-Québec and Ontario Hydro to sell millions in dam-building and energy infrastructure services to a country where investors had traditionally met difficulties in getting paid for their mega-deals in cash. But he had also joined forces in a separate company with Munk to extract and export tons of Beijing's gold reserves. It seemed a perfect match — a symbiosis that might have emerged straight from one of Adnan Khashoggi's circular quick-sketches to illustrate the notion of counter-trade.

13 Spin Control

ON THE GLEAMING WHITE MARBLE PLAZA of the
new Canadian embassy on Pennsylvania Avenue, Washington's
social set had gathered for the inauguration of a building meant to
symbolize the country's new pride of place on the continental landscape. Planted halfway between the White House and Capitol Hill,
its angular prow thrusting towards the National Gallery across the
street, Arthur Erickson's $90 million neoclassical colossus was the
only foreign presence allowed on the thoroughfare known as
America's Main Street. "Of course," former defence secretary James
Schlesinger hastened to reassure the astonished Ottawa press corps,
"the Canadians, since they've joined the free trade agreement, are
no longer foreign."

On every side, monuments rose in testimony to America's muscular patriotism. And in the ambassador's sixth-floor office where
wrap-around glass framed the sunset-gilded cupola of the U.S.
Capitol, even jaded senators were snapping shots of each other with
their Instamatics against that familiar backdrop. Indeed, the building elicited rave reviews from Americans less for its adventurous
architectural collage than for the perspective it offered on their own
treasured iconography.

But at the top of the embassy's sweeping front staircase, TV star

Al Waxman recoiled in horror to see that one of Canada's own rare national symbols had been desecrated. "Hey, somebody shot holes through our flag," he protested, staring up at the giant maple leaf banner tethered sideways inside an open-air rotunda and scarred with random slashes. Waxman's wife, Sara, a cookbook writer, swiftly grasped that aerodynamics, not crime, was at play. "It's like when you cut slits in the top of a piecrust," she explained. But in May 1989, five months after the implementation of the still-contentious free trade agreement, that gesture of expedience provided an unfortunate image for an occasion intended as a metaphor for Canadian-American relations.

For Brian Mulroney, who had flown in from Ottawa to officiate at the unveiling, the ceremony was already more modest than he had once planned. In 1985, in the afterglow of the Shamrock Summit, he had asked his friend Ross Johnson to chair a blue-ribbon committee to raise $4 million for an opening gala to be filmed by director Norman Jewison as a U.S. television special. The committee had never materialized, except on Johnson's corporate curriculum vitae, and the gala plans had gone by the wayside when Johnson's high-stakes leveraged buyout of RJR Nabisco backfired on him. Only three months earlier, he had resigned from the company, pilloried in the press as a symbol of corporate greed run amok and what New York investment guru Felix Rohatyn termed Ronald Reagan's "casino society."

At the embassy opening, Johnson was conspicuous by his absence, as was Nabisco's donation — Haida artist Bill Reid's stunning bronze *Spirit Canoe*, destined for the terrace reflecting pool. The massive work would not arrive for another two years, gathering dust in a New York foundry as Nabisco Canada balked at a pricetag that had soared from $300,000 to $1.5 million — despite the fact that the company had won a $1 million tax deduction on its gift from Mulroney's government.

But the toned-down embassy inauguration seemed more in keeping with the new folksy, no-frills era of the patrician who had recently taken over the White House: George Bush. In a curious gesture of deference to his presidency, Mulroney had chosen a tie in its signature colour — a shade the First Lady had declared "Bush Blue" — which perfectly matched the embassy ribbon he was cutting. Even in unveiling the building that stood for Canadian autonomy on U.S. soil, the prime minister had chosen to pay homage to American political symbolism.

"Canadians dare in the way that this building dares," Mulroney declared as he did the honours. But amid all the tributes to continental togetherness, it was Secretary of State James Baker who honed in on the awkward heart of the bilateral relationship — the differences between the two nations. Nothing had more starkly underlined those differences than the bitter two-year free trade fight, which, only six months earlier, had threatened to cost Mulroney his job. The arts and academic communities had led the assault, warning that the pact would sound the death knell for Canadian culture, social institutions, and values. And only a multi-million-dollar corporate advertising campaign and some deft fear-mongering in the final days before the vote had saved him. "We respect those differences," Baker had intoned, "even as we continue to enjoy one of the most successful international partnerships in the history of the world."

But with NAFTA already quietly taking shape on the administration's drawing boards, Baker had no taste for another cliff-hanger north of the border which could threaten Washington's leadership in the new economic world order. As Bush's envoy to Ottawa, he had pegged a man with his own ideas about those bilateral differences — and the skills to help wipe them out. Sleek, silver-haired, moving among the embassy crowd with elegant assurance in his trademark bow-tie, Edward Noonan Ney cut a striking figure — one that might have stepped straight out of a Chivas Regal ad. For nearly four decades, he had been in the business of changing minds, selling dreams and perceptions along with breakfast cereal and soap.

As the former chairman and CEO of Young and Rubicam, the world's largest advertising agency, he had also co-chaired the elite Madison Avenue team that had lulled Americans into re-electing Ronald Reagan in 1984 with misty patriotic images proclaiming "It's morning again in America." But more recently, to pull off Bush's election, Ney had demonstrated his capacity for playing rough. The campaign had profited from an emotionally charged TV spot that had come to symbolize the moral bankruptcy of negative campaigning: a subtly racist commercial of a black convict named Willie Horton who had raped a white woman while on the lam from a prison furlough granted by the Democratic nominee, Massachusetts governor Michael Dukakis. Ney would try to distance himself from the ad, emphasizing it was the handiwork of an independent group. But anyone who understood Washington's conservative geography knew that group had long worked intimately with the Republican administration; nor would the advertisement have run without the benediction of Ney's oversight team. Indeed, reviewing the campaign later with a *Maclean's* journalist, Ney admitted he and fellow strategist Roger Ailes had seized on two themes to tarnish Dukakis's squeaky clean image — one of them the pollution in the governor's own front yard. "We had two things going in," Ney said. "We had Boston Harbor and prison furloughs."

As his reward, Ney had won the political appointment to Ottawa. At the news, the capital's hostesses had fretted that he and his chic second wife, Judy, would not find life on the Rideau up to snuff after Manhattan, where their next-door neighbour was Henry Kissinger. But the Neys were not unfamiliar with the Canadian political scene: they had been frequent dinner guests of the Gotliebs in Washington, and in Ottawa they quickly became part of Brian and Mila Mulroney's inner circle, with its own ties to the Fifth Avenue and Palm Beach crowds.

At sixty-four, long known as the Cary Grant of advertising, Ney shared at least one quality with Mulroney, taking such pains with his sartorial presentation that friends loved to recount how he once flew off to Britain declaring that one could no longer get a decent suit made in New York. It was only when he spoke that Ney struck a note at odds with his finely crafted elegance. His voice was a rasp, rising at will from the seduction of a foggy whisper to the edge of steel upon sandpaper when he had a point to make.

Ney spoke of everything, including foreign affairs, in an adman's terms — positioning the message and controlling its spin. In an address to Canadian advertising executives soon after his arrival, he had advised them to promote the nation like a brand name recognition campaign, prompting a sardonic headline in *Marketing* magazine: "Be Patriotic — Sell Your Country as a Brand to Survive Competition." But in that speech, Ney signalled the stakes that Washington already saw at play on the tumultuous global Monopoly board — stakes to which most Canadians were still oblivious. At the time, only a handful of academics and national security planners were promoting a world divided into regional trading blocs and the urgency of creating a U.S. zone of influence in the hemisphere. But Ney was already warning that in the wake of the Soviet empire's collapse, warfare "will not be fought among military alliances, but among trading partners. It will not be waged with missiles and tanks, but with marketing strategies."

He did not mention that national differences could pose an inconvenient hurdle to the creation of such a regional trading zone. But even as he spoke, many of those differences were fast disappearing — and he would do his part in helping to eliminate the rest.

I N 1988, the year before Ed Ney's ambassadorial appointment, he had been awarded his industry's highest honour, induction into the U.S. Advertising Hall of Fame. For many of his peers, he was the consummate adman whose career summed up the evolution of the business of persuasion, and he loved to regale friends with tales of the rough-and-tumble universe he joined straight out of the navy, when account executives would come to fisticuffs over campaigns in the agency corridors and everyone kept a glass of milk on his desk to combat ulcers. An account executive himself, never on the creative side, Ney had moved to Young and Rubicam in 1951 and stayed there for the next thirty-eight years, helping to transform it into the world's top agency, with billings of $5.3 billion and a client list that included Ford, Colgate-Palmolive, and General Foods. During the 1960s, as head of its international division, he regularly toured its Canadian subsidiary, which still boasts the branch plant accounts for many of those multinationals.

In 1970, emerging from a corporate coup as president, Ney led the agency into a new era when the whims of wild-eyed creative directors were replaced with sophisticated consumer research. As advertising became the pervasive postwar cultural influence, marketing techniques had already become more subtle and insidious — an evolution immortalized in Vance Packard's *Hidden Persuaders*. Campaigns were no longer merely about hyping a product or even a politician, but about playing on moods and myth, social class and fantasy, with computerized targeting systems known as VALS — for values and lifestyles — that divided the populace into precise categories from "emulators" (go-go yuppies) to "experientials" (menopausal New Age types). In fact, Young and Rubicam's research subsidiary, Consumer Insights, became so adroit at playing on the emotional pulse of the populace that Hallmark Cards dropped the agency when it deemed a new client, telephone giant AT&T, was getting the same sort of heartstring-tugging campaign.

But if the sell was increasingly soft, the competition for accounts was fierce. In February 1990 Young and Rubicam pleaded guilty on a charge of conspiring to bribe foreign officials and paid a $500,000 fine for a kickback scheme that had begun in 1981, when the agency won the Jamaica Tourist Board account the year after Edward Seaga's pro-Washington government came to power with U.S. help. Later, after Ney arrived in Ottawa, the case would continue to haunt him when Jamaica's former minister of tourism, Anthony Abrahams, named him in a Connecticut civil suit seeking $10 million in damages arising from the investigation.

Certainly, as the 1980s dawned, the advertising game was playing for increasingly high stakes. And as clients extended their global reach, U.S. ad agencies followed suit, merging into ever-more enormous transnational incarnations. At Young and Rubicam, Ney had embarked on his own acquisitions spree, buying up Burson-Marsteller, the world's leading public relations agency; Wunderman, Ricotta and Kline, the largest direct mail operation; and Sudler and Hennessey, the top health care agency. He also presided over two of the industry's biggest international joint ventures in France and Japan, and, at the time of his diplomatic appointment, had moved on to become chairman of another subsidiary he created, Paine Webber–Young and Rubicam Ventures, which offered advice on the wave of corporate mergers and acquisitions then sweeping the continent.

By the time Ney landed in Ottawa, that takeover wave had already hit the Canadian advertising industry, beginning its swift Americanization. In 1988 New York's Interpublic Group had swallowed two of the country's largest and most venerable agencies, MacLaren and Foster Advertising, whose parent holding company, Sherwood Communications, had first brought Richard Wirthlin to Toronto. Seven years later, only a single Canadian-owned firm, Montreal's Cossette-Communications-Marketing, would remain among the country's top ten agencies — with Young and Rubicam Canada in third spot. As part of that evolution, the number of TV and radio commercials produced in Canada would drop by 25 percent — a toll that riled nationalists like Jerry Goodis, who had once been vice chairman of MacLaren. "The shots are called not from Toronto or Montreal," he said, "but from London or New York." As advertising lineage continued to plummet, Toronto media buyer

Patrick Walshe blamed it on "the North Americanization of business. It's the death of the Canadian ad agency."

That centralized buying also had the potential to determine the
fate of the country's media, where advertising routinely dictated
what TV shows lived or died and had replaced subscriptions as the
lifeblood of newspapers and magazines. With buying increasingly
done out of headquarters for multinationals like Coca Cola and IBM,
which preferred uniform global campaigns, nations found it increasingly difficult to define their own distinctions. "Advertising is at
least as important as culture for a country to see itself," lamented
Reet McGovern of Toronto's Paul Grissom and Associates. "And
we're losing those images of what it's like to be Canadian."

For the multinationals, Canada represented a $10 billion billing
jackpot, with the government's own $91 million in contracts the
plumpest prize. For decades, Ottawa had required any agency bidding on its accounts to be 100 percent Canadian-owned. But in the
same month that Mulroney was presiding over the embassy ribbon-
cutting in Washington, the government's Advertising Management
Group, which answered to Conservative Senator Lowell Murray,
had quietly changed those rules, permitting any firms with up to
49 percent foreign ownership to land a federal contract. Some agencies, such as McCann-Erickson Advertising, which had been taken
over by New York's Interpublic Group, promptly recreated sham
Canadian divisions to take advantage of the provisions: a year after
buying out Foster, it set up a tiny new 51 percent Canadian subsidiary on a separate floor of its building and dusted off the name
Foster Advertising Ltd. to bid on government work. Ottawa insisted
that the changes had been required by government-procurement
provisions in the free trade agreement, which, in theory, had opened
federal contracts in both capitals to bidding from companies of
either nation. But to William Bremner, the chairman of Vickers and
Benson at the time, the clause smacked of a rigged deck. "There
isn't a rabbit's chance in hell that Canadians would get U.S. government business," he said.

In fact, critics predicted that the steady Americanization of the
Canadian industry could also colour the country's political process.
In Europe, scholars had blamed the invasion of multinational mega-
agencies for helping to discredit the once thriving political model
of social democracy in favour of the free market faith that had
swept Thatcher's Britain and Reagan's America. As NDP political

consultant Robin Sears had pointed out during the 1988 election campaign, "Paid media" — advertising — "have become the most important political tool in North American politics."

When it came to public policy, no one knew better than Ed Ney the power that advertising could wield. He had discovered its possibilities back in 1962 when Norman Cousins, the editor of *Saturday Review*, had asked him for a cross-country campaign to sell a contentious international agreement to Congress: their efforts had ultimately won approval for John F. Kennedy's controversial nuclear test ban treaty with the Soviet Union. Two decades later, Reagan had appointed Ney to his Board for International Broadcasting, chaired by media mogul Malcolm Forbes, which ensured that Radio Free Europe and Radio Liberty carried out their mandate "with regard to U.S. foreign policy objectives." As the ambassador boasted to a conference of the Canadian Advertising Association, that programming was later credited with helping to bring down the Berlin Wall. "Is this simply a pretension, believing that marketing people can really contribute to the political well-being of their nations and beyond?" he had demanded his audience. "I think not."

Shortly after taking up his diplomatic duties, Ney made it clear that he meant to carry out that sense of mission. In an interview with *Saturday Night* writer Charlotte Gray, he declared that he intended to draw on his marketing expertise for his new assignment. "I come from a service industry," he said. "The guys in the State Department can deal with hard numbers and niggling problems about shakes and shingles. We in the embassy can contribute to the spirit of the relationship, through culture, education and that kinda stuff."

Like any soft sell, it sounded benign. But it was precisely in "culture, education and that kinda stuff" where the differences between the two nations were most pronounced — and had proven the greatest stumbling blocks to seamless continental integration. The Canadian cultural exemption in the free trade agreement still rankled in Washington as a precedent that threatened U.S. economic security around the globe — all the more so with NAFTA and GATT negotiations looming ahead. But in few places had it provoked higher emotions than in the executive suite of *Time* magazine — a prized Young and Rubicam client. In fact, the agency had handled the *Time* account for so long that Ney's friend Richard Munro, Time Inc.'s former chairman, would joke it had been "forever — since the beginning, if you'll pardon the expression, of time."

Bill C-58, the 1976 measure introduced by Trudeau in an attempt to shore up a national media industry, had hit *Time* and *Reader's Digest* the hardest. But while *Reader's Digest* had made a commitment to produce a Canadian edition — a commitment it kept until 1993 — *Time* had shut down its sizeable Montreal editorial operation and stalked out of the country in a huff. Tom d'Aquino, the magazine's Ottawa lobbyist at the time, would later claim credit for that decision, recounting a conversation with editor-in-chief Henry Grunwald. "I said, 'Henry, accept Bill C-58,'" he recalled. "'It's a fact of life — you may do very well.'" As he would take delight in pointing out, "In fact, they've done better. The cost of running an operation in Canada is not small. But if you have a product that people want, that they think they need, and if you eliminate the cost of production . . ." Tom d'Aquino left the rest unsaid. But by cutting its advertising rates in half, *Time* easily compensated for its clients' lost writeoffs. Today, with only a single Canadian correspondent in Ottawa — and virtually no Canadian editorial content — *Time's* Canadian edition is one of the most profitable in its international stable, with a reported $22 million a year in revenue.

Still that windfall had not placated Grunwald or Richard Munro, who saw the legislation as a direct affront not only to *Time* but to its myriad sister publications. And no one had been more keenly aware of the bill's impact than their advertising guru Edward Ney, who developed a first-hand resentment of Canada's cultural policies. Because of its role in the *Time* case, Young and Rubicam had been the only ad agency included on Thomas Wyman's 1983 trade advisory committee which took a swipe at Ottawa's barriers to the U.S. communications industry. Nor was Ney unaware of the grievances other entertainment conglomerates were still nursing against Canadian legislative barriers. He counted Jack Valenti among his friends, and *Time* had been a partner in the USA Cable Network with Gulf + Western and Lew Wasserman's MCA — the two corporations leading the attack against Ottawa's efforts to bolster sovereignty in the film and publishing industries. When Ney talked about cultural activism in his new job, it was a sure bet he didn't mean showing up at a few symphony concerts.

AS Edward Ney saw it, it was all a vicious plot — a virtual Canadian conspiracy to discredit the free trade agreement. In an interview with Ottawa writer Lawrence Martin, he raged against "a deliberate strategic decision by a group of think tanks, others (that is, the media) and political parties to portray the FTA as a failure." That outburst took Martin aback. "If I was a Canadian and saw the media every day," Ney stormed, "I'd have said, 'Geez, they're a terrible group of people. What are they trying to do to us poor little Canadians?'"

As an expert in the marketplace of ideas, he launched a project tailored to correct that perceived tilt: a program of academic exchanges with the United States, adding Canada to the list of 123 countries in the prestigious U.S. Fulbright Fellowship program overseen by the State Department. In Ottawa, the press corps had greeted the announcement with a reaction known as MEGO — My Eyes Glaze Over. But one look at the program's handpicked board might have provoked second thoughts about what Ney considered at stake.

Under a logo designed by Young and Rubicam of Canada, the directors of his Foundation for Educational Exchange included not only himself and Derek Burney, newly installed as ambassador to Washington, but six other prominent figures from each country, all with ties to their government. On the Canadian side were Mulroney's Montreal publisher friend Philippe de Gaspé Beaubien, the chairman of Telemedia, which had acquired the Canadian rights to *TV Guide*; Nancy Jackman, a perennial Conservative candidate in Toronto whose brother Hal had been named Ontario's lieutenant governor; and Halifax lawyer George Cooper, whose law partner, Stewart McInnes, had been in the Tory cabinet. Cooper himself had already carried out a delicate task: authoring a controversial 1986 report that exonerated the government from liability in the CIA-funded brainwashing experiments at McGill University during the 1950s.

For the foundation's American board, Ney had chosen his outspoken predecessor, Paul Robinson; his friend, Chicago advertising executive Richard Christian, once chairman emeritus of Burson-Marsteller Inc; and his former client Richard Munro, who had just stepped down from the chairmanship of Time Inc., but retained a seat on its new board. Considering the demands on a corporate heavyweight such as Munro, it was instructive to note that he had made space on his agenda for an arcane committee on bilateral educational exchanges. But then, both he and Ney understood the pivotal role that academics could play in what their friend Henry Kissinger had dubbed "the age of the expert."

Ney himself sat on the Advisory Board of Washington's Center for Strategic and International Studies, one of the capital's most influential think tanks, where Kissinger and Bill Brock served as counsellors. And no less than Ronald Reagan had paid tribute to the importance of a handful of conservative scholars in paving the way for his presidency. In 1983, on the tenth anniversary of Washington's ultra-conservative Heritage Foundation, Reagan had pilgrimaged to its gleaming new $10 million headquarters to salute its part in changing the nature of the American political debate. "Historians who seek the real meaning of events in the latter part of the twentieth century," he had lyricized, "must look back on gatherings such as this."

As Reagan well knew, the Heritage Foundation and its California counterpart, the Hoover Institute, had relentlessly popularized the free market philosophies of Austrian economist Friedrich Hayek and his American counterpart Milton Friedman, whose monetarism and diatribes against "do-gooder legislation" had provided the twin pillars of Reaganomics. Once ridiculed as fringe fare, by policy makers, their theories had slowly invaded mainstream debate. Through a feisty mix of aggressive marketing and ideological lobbying, they had created a conservative intellectual infrastructure where once only Washington's liberal Brookings Institution held sway.

Packaging New Right ideologues as media stars, they had helped change the cast of what analyst Eric Alterman termed the new "punditocracy," which increasingly ruled the op-ed pages and the talk show circuit. Alterman traced that development in *Sound and Fury: The Washington Punditocracy and the Collapse of American Politics*: "Just as the Reagan crowd came to power, views that had been considered Cro-Magnon just months earlier became sophisticated." As those once outrageous ideas won an airing on call-in radio or *Larry King Live*, they lost their sting — a process of banalization that set the stage for their adoption as public policy. In fact, it seemed no accident that Ed Ney's partner in the Reagan and Bush campaigns had been Roger Ailes, the former Nixon adman who would later bring Rush Limbaugh, the carney barker of right-wing intolerance, to the airwaves only a few years before Newt Gingrich and his Republican footsoldiers commandeered the U.S. Congress.

Fuelling that rightward shift was the generosity of a handful of arch-conservative tycoons and their tax-free charitable foundations: Colorado beer mogul Joseph Coors and the Lilly Endowment, financed by the family foundation behind Indianapolis drug-maker Eli Lilly and Co. In 1990 alone, the John M. Olin Foundation handed out nearly $20 million in grants to think tanks, *Commentary* magazine, and such right-wing campus activists as Dinesh D'Souza, who first promoted the divisive campaign against political correctness when he was a student editor at the *Dartmouth Review*.

But one of the most influential evangelists behind the spread of the conservative gospel was a little-known Second World War Spitfire pilot who had become Britain's broiler chicken king: Sir Antony Fisher. A devotee of Hayek, who had impressed upon him the necessity of changing the way people think, in 1956 Fisher had co-founded London's Institute of Economic Affairs (IEA), which Margaret Thatcher would later credit with shaping her Darwinian policies. As a graduate student in London, Edwin Feulner, who would later become president of the Heritage Foundation, had worked at Fisher's institute. Another Hayek devotee was a Prince Edward Islander doing post-graduate business studies in England at the time, Mulroney's economic policy adviser Charley McMillan. During the two years prior to Mulroney's election, McMillan had hosted a series of weekend seminars for the Conservative caucus, importing Friedman's and Fisher's acolytes to preach the right-wing gospel.

But not content with IEA's influence, Fisher had helped establish more than forty other conservative think tanks around the world. In New York, he had been the moving force behind the Manhattan Institute for Policy Research, begun in 1978 with William Casey. Not only did the institute publish such provocative titles as George Gilder's *Wealth and Poverty* — whose call for unbridled tax cuts became the bible of the Reagan administration — but it later sponsored Charles Murray's *Losing Ground*, which provided the intellectual underpinnings for the ongoing neoconservative attack on the welfare system.

By then Fisher had sold his chicken empire to Galen Weston and planted an ideological beachhead in Canada: in 1975 he became a pivotal figure in the establishment of Vancouver's ultra-conservative Fraser Institute. Set up a year earlier by Michael Walker, an ardent free-marketeer who was fresh from a contract with the federal Finance Department, the institute was also the brainchild of Patrick Boyle, an executive at forestry giant MacMillan-Bloedel. Outraged by Pierre Trudeau and British Columbia's NDP government under Dave Barrett, Boyle rallied fifteen other corporations to establish a think tank that could provide the voice and intellectual where-withal for a counterattack. It was expressly not located in the wishy-washy liberal east, where, as former assistant director Sally Pipes put it, "We were afraid we'd get co-opted." In the process, Boyle persuaded Fisher to come to Vancouver to serve briefly as the Fraser's executive director, helping it tap into many of the same conservative coffers that fed U.S. think tanks. In 1988 the Lilly Endowment granted the institute $100,000 and, three years later, began financing its four-year joint study on the implications of hemispheric free trade. But the Fraser's board could also claim its own homegrown ultra-conservative patrons, including Mulroney's high-flying Edmonton crony Peter Pocklington. One of the most generous, however, had been the late Harold Siebens, the U.S.–born Calgary oil millionaire who was the largest single donor to Mulroney's 1984 election campaign and in whose honour the think tank named a prestigious annual lecture.

Perennially plugging tax cuts and charting liberal bias in the media by counting the number of times interviewers smiled during CBC interviews, Walker and his staff gradually metamorphosed from a libertarian outfit regarded as the Canadian radical fringe to a source of economic studies regularly quoted in the mainstream media. Indeed, if Edward Ney perceived an intellectual conspiracy against free trade, he clearly was not counting the Fraser Institute, one of the agreement's most vocal boosters. By 1991 the Vancouver think tank could banner a testimonial to its new-found respectabil-ity in a form that the U.S. ambassador could only applaud: a thank-you note from none other than Clyde Farnsworth, the Canadian bureau chief of the *New York Times*, reproduced in the institute's annual report, expressing gratitude for "urgently needed statistics on Canadian and American wages."

Nor did Toronto's C. D. Howe Institute appear to qualify for Ney's conspiracy theories. Taken over and resuscitated by Tom Kierans, a longtime Ontario Tory backroom player, "the Howe," as it was known, had already teamed up with Washington's National Planning Association to lobby for the free trade agreement. If the institute reflected a more pronounced corporate bias, it was hardly surprising considering that its $2 million budget was almost entirely funded by its members — two hundred of the country's largest companies.

In 1992, among the new directors the Howe named to its board, was one of Mulroney's closest friends and former law partners, Yves Fortier, who had returned from his stint as UN ambassador to their old firm, Ogilvy Renault. The institute's former president, Wendy Dobson, had graduated to become an assistant deputy minister of finance in Mulroney's government, where her former boss, Michael Wilson, saw fit to praise the Howe for having "influenced my thinking on a number of topics." As if that were not sufficient evidence of its influence, on the cover of its 1992 annual report, CTV's Eric Malling hailed the institute as "my best source for economic information — not just for facts, but perspective." So generously had Malling drawn on that inspiration that in her bestseller, *Shooting the Hippo*, writer Linda McQuaig characterized him as "a voice for the C. D. Howe Institute" — and thus for the corporate elite.

No Liberal think tank of equal stature could offer a rebuttal to either of those conservative world views. But a year after Ney's arrival in Ottawa, Mulroney's government further limited the country's debate. In their 1990 budget, the Conservatives cancelled funding for both the Economic Council of Canada and the Canadian Institute for International Peace and Security, two respected independent voices that might have offered credible counterweights to the government's increasingly continentalist shift. Although the Economic Council had supported free trade, it had been guilty of another neoconservative heresy: after Mulroney's 1984 budget-cutting binge, it had urged him to take any steps, even a tax hike, to safeguard the nation's social safety net. Certainly, no such sentiments would emerge from the C. D. Howe Institute, which would castigate even Liberal Finance Minister Paul Martin for not hacking enthusiastically enough at social programs. Despite its obvious position as the voice of Corporate Canada, the Howe's influence with the media grew — a development not entirely unanticipated by the government. When Don Mazankowski announced the demise of the Economic Council, the finance minister had declared that the Howe would have to fill the void.

But the death blow to the Canadian Institute of Peace and Security came weighted with bitter irony: in 1984, when Trudeau had created it under an act of Parliament, one of those who had fretted most about its freedom from "prevailing political winds" had been Mulroney, then leader of the opposition. Six years later, by eliminating the institute and its pronounced multilateral leanings, he had dispensed with the most authoritative voice likely to contradict his relentless pro-Washington tilt. "It's thought control," the Liberals' foreign affairs critic, Lloyd Axworthy, had protested after the cuts. "It means there's a kind of Newspeak around here — one way of thinking."

But those shifts failed to placate Ney. Scoffing at the critics of free trade as "typewriter and talk show warriors," he accused them of making "a political statement dressed up as an economic argument" — as if he were not doing that very thing himself. After the agreement, as U.S. trade complaints mounted against Canadian industries, Ney was outraged when Derek Burney, the original champion of free trade, urged the country's manufacturers to respond in kind under the agreement's dispute-settlement mechanism, lodging their own complaints against American practices; Burney, he sputtered, was overstepping his bounds. Plants might be closing throughout Ontario's industrial heartland, snuffing out more than 350,000 manufacturing jobs, but Ney waved off that pothole on the road to hemispheric nirvana. "It's a fact of life," he told a crowd of converts at the Canada–U.S. Business Association. "Less efficient manufacturing plants close, sooner rather than later, with tough competition around."

That intolerance for dissent began to infect the free trade conference circuit, where one of the star speakers was Earl Fry, coordinator of Canadian studies at Brigham Young University, Richard Wirthlin's old stamping ground in Provo, Utah. Like most other directors of Canadian studies programs at U.S. universities, Fry displayed a strong empathy for U.S. policy; he had taken his post fresh from serving as a member of Bill Brock's free market shock troops in the U.S. Trade Representative's Office. That experience perhaps helped explain his foresight: in March 1985, scarcely a week after the Shamrock Summit, Fry had convened one of the first conferences on continental free trade at a time when most Canadian officials were still oblivious to its advent.

But whereas the free trade debate had once been boisterous and freewheeling, the new wave of conferences to promote NAFTA, an item higher on the U.S. corporate and national security agenda, became increasingly autocratic. During one gathering of the U.N.

Economic Commission on Latin America, the Canadian pact was hailed as a shining example, a model to demystify the free trade process for nervous Latin nations whose officials filled the auditorium; opinions to the contrary were not welcomed. When one U.S. economist spirited a Canadian critic, Kathleen Canning, onto the program, she was scarcely halfway through her inventory of job losses and plant closings in the deal's wake when mutterings began in the audience of devoted free-marketeers. When Canning declared that the country had been "devastated by the free trade agreement," she found herself being hissed. By the time she had ventured the heresy that free trade was "an outmoded theory," she was being hustled off the dais with a reprimand that she had exceeded her allotted time. As one delegate from the Organization for Economic Cooperation and Development noted later: "We're down to the true believers in this conference."

Similarly, the University of Toronto's Stephen Clarkson protested that neoconservative economics had taken hold on campuses with a ferocity that he christened a new "economic fundamentalism." As Clarkson noted, "A missionary aura hovers over the economics literature on free trade for Canada." Not that Canadian faculties were alone in that ideological shift. Across Latin America, a new political generation was coming to power, bringing with it a free market faith. "It's a kind of intellectual transformation that has taken place in the Latin American elites who've bought neoclassical economics," Clarkson said. "And U.S. graduate schools are the key."

In Mexico, the Harvard credentials of Carlos Salinas de Gortari were incessantly cited as the explanation for his policies, while his technocratic heirs boasted degrees from Princeton and Stanford. In Chile, the next country in line for induction into the hemispheric trading club, the officials leading free market reforms had studied their catechism at the mother church, Milton Friedman's economics department at the University of Chicago. Myer Rashish, one of the self-confessed neoconservatives behind Reagan's original NAFTA vision, termed that intellectual conquest "the most subtle imperial invasion of all. What the Marines couldn't do, Harvard, MIT, and the Chicago School did."

In Canada, where support for state intervention and social programs had remained stubbornly resistant to that neoconservative fashion, Ney had attempted to tackle the problem with his cross-border Fulbright exchange program. Named in honour of their corporate sponsors, the grants ranged over a broad scholarly terrain, from the Chase Manhattan scholarship to survey post-free-trade marketing strategies in Quebec to the Pepsi-Cola Canada scholarship to study the effect of cultural changes on the Inuit. Although the program's academic juries offered no reason to question their selection process, three years into the Fulbright scheme some of Ney's handpicked directors protested that the fellowships had failed to accomplish their unspoken aim. During a November 1993 board meeting of the foundation at the Canadian Embassy in Washington, tempers exploded over the fact that the subjects chosen for study were too, well, too scholarly. According to board member Nancy Jackman, some of her fellow directors objected that the fellowships were not helping to bolster the governments' political line. "Some people said," she confided, "that they weren't doing enough to promote free trade."

A year earlier, with the end of his diplomatic posting, Ney had stepped aside from active duties on the foundation to become an honorary director. But his farewell appearance underlined the cosiness of the program's ties to Corporate America. Both that board meeting and its elegant follow-up lunch were held in the executive penthouse of Amoco's headquarters in Chicago, personally hosted by its chairman, Pat Early, who spent most of the cocktail hour worrying about the effect of Bill Clinton's election on the company's drilling plans for the Arctic National Wildlife Refuge in Alaska.

Earlier that morning, the foundation's directors had been informed that Amoco, Chevron, and the other oil companies that had put up funds for fellowships now wanted their largesse earmarked exclusively for studies on environmental policy. By then, the growing muscle of the green movement had become an obsession in the continent's boardrooms, where environmentalists' legal victories were racking up millions in fines and compliance costs. As Ney delivered his final speech to the board, objections to Mexico's rampant pollution were threatening the survival of NAFTA in Congress.

But that challenge was one which the U.S. and Canadian business communities had no intention of ignoring. Orchestrating their counterattack against the environmental movement was a company that Ney had acquired for Young and Rubicam's corporate stable in 1979: Burson-Marsteller Ltd., whose expertise at cleaning up the image of corporate polluters had helped make it the world's leading public relations agency. Indeed, as Ney bade his farewells to the

Fulbright foundation, he had just taken up his new post-ambassadorial duties as chairman of Burson-Marsteller's Board of Advisors.

"**T**0 Change Perception Is to Change Reality." That simple, one-sentence ad in a 1995 issue of *Marketing* magazine summed up Burson-Marsteller's basic sales pitch — a philosophy that would hardly have displeased Edward Bernays, the godfather of the modern public relations business. In a book disarmingly entitled *Propaganda*, Bernays had spelled out how he saw his profession's role in the world. "The conscious and intelligent manipulation of the organized habits and opinions of the masses is an important element in democratic society," he wrote. "Those who manipulate this unseen mechanism of society constitute an invisible government which is the true ruling power of our country."

Born in Austria, the nephew of Sigmund Freud, Bernays had brought public relations to America in the wake of the First World War along with Enrico Caruso, whom he led on a triumphant national tour. Staying on in New York, in 1919 he had set up one of the country's first PR firms. His accounts included CBS, Procter and Gamble, and the American Tobacco Company, but he never lost sight of the need to mesh their corporate interests with those of government. In 1954 Bernays was working for Boston's United Fruit Company as it helped the CIA bring down the nationalist regime of Jacobo Arbenz in Guatemala. As part of that campaign, he organized jammed fact-finding tours for newsmen, which one United Fruit official described as "a serious attempt to compromise objectivity." By then, Bernays's imitators had turned PR into an American growth industry, but one that would continue to maintain close ties to Washington. A year earlier, a Memphis-born publicist named Harold Burson had teamed up with a New York adman named Bill Marsteller to found an agency which four decades later would have sixty-two offices in twenty-nine countries, including four in Canada.

Burson-Marsteller's specialty was corporate crises, of which there appeared to be no dearth. One of its proudest claims to fame was containing the panic for Johnson and Johnson after a crank's poisoning of its Tylenol gelcaps. The company's booming medical and pharmaceutical unit had finessed the fallout from lawsuits over the Dalkon shield for A. H. Robins, had made a fortune from Dow

Corning over its faulty silicone breast implants, and fended off critics of Eli Lilly and its antidepressant Prozac.

For Burson, crises meant big money — triple billing — and some of its most celebrated paydays had come from environmental mayhem. The company had played spin doctor for Babcock and Wilcox after the Three Mile Island nuclear disaster and for Union Carbide following the catastrophic explosion that left 3,500 dead in Bhopal, India. But neither of those could compare with the agency's windfall in March 1989 when the oiltanker *Exxon Valdez* ran aground in Alaska's Prince William Sound, spilling 11 million gallons of crude into one of the continent's richest fisheries. Exxon would eventually be fined $5 billion — the equivalent of its annual net income. But Burson-Marsteller had persuaded the world's most profitable corporation to dole out another $4 billion in damage claims and clean-up costs for goodwill.

In Canada, Burson's operations had been chaired by one of the corporation's career veterans, Peter Walford, while the managing director of its Toronto office was Ross DeGeer, a former Tory organizer for Ontario premier William Davis. But in 1989, the year Edward Ney arrived in Ottawa, Burson-Marsteller Canada — and its newly purchased capital lobbying firm, Executive Consultants Ltd. — acquired a new high-profile chairman: Ney's frequent Washington host Allan Gotlieb, freshly retired from the diplomatic game himself.

Among Gotlieb's numerous corporate rewards, the Burson-Marsteller post appeared to be one of the most demanding, as he shuttled between its Toronto office and his plush suite at the law firm of Stikeman Elliott, often trailing his secretary in his wake. Underlings were never permitted to know what accounts he was working on, and he reported directly to New York. "It was just incredibly secretive," said one former employee, who, like all Burson staffers, was required to sign a confidentiality agreement. But there was no doubt at the time that the firm was considered the hottest in the business, demanding a signing fee of up to $5,000 just to retain its services. Some of those services involved not merely hyping a client, but tarnishing a competitor. "You'd be astonished at how much of the work is negative," said the former employee, "planting doubts about a company's finances or its sources of materials." Among its targets was Bombardier, a rival of Burson's U.S. client Gulfstream Aerospace.

Mulroney's government proved a boon to Burson-Marsteller, which landed million-dollar accounts for the Royal Mint and the privatization of Air Canada — the latter a delicate process that involved convincing both the business press and employees that the airline could not become competitive unless it freed itself from Ottawa's clutches. Another billing bonanza came from the Canada–U.S. free trade agreement, which brought Burson a brisk business in crises of a different sort — helping multinationals craft their factory shutdowns as they stampeded southward. Thus while Edward Ney was telling business audiences that manufacturing casualties were a fact of life, his old firm was at work in towns like Niagara Falls, collecting a fat fee trying to calm the distraught populace as 240 jobs vanished when Cyanamid Canada Inc., the subsidiary of a New Jersey chemical giant, phased out its local operation. As Ross DeGeer admits, "There was one year when a substantial part of our operations consisted of assisting companies that were closing down."

Nor did Burson-Marsteller Canada lack contentious environmental accounts. Ethyl Canada Inc., the subsidiary of a Virginia-based chemical conglomerate, signed on when Friends of the Earth protested its plans for a $67 million expansion of its Sarnia plant designed to double the production of tetrathyl lead — the component in leaded gasoline that had been banned by both the Canadian and U.S. governments at the time for suspected damage to children's nervous systems. And after the Quebec Cree Grand Council had contracted rival Hill & Knowlton to win public support in New York against the Great Whale hydroelectric project, Burson had snared the potentially more profitable spin control duties for Hydro-Québec — in part attempting to discredit the Cree by planting stories about them as wealthy, whining profiteers.

But increasingly, Burson-Marsteller was promoting a new tack for corporate clashes with ecologists: seizing control of the agenda by clambering on the environmental bandwagon and appearing to out-green the green movement. For the 1992 Earth Summit in Rio, the firm had helped promote a Geneva-based lobby called the Business Council for Sustainable Development, the environmentally friendly face of forty-eight transnationals including the world's worst corporate polluters. Led by a Swiss mogul named Stephan Schmidheiny, who controlled the mining and engineering multinational Asea Brown Boveri, the council had played a pivotal role in shaping the summit's anticlimactic outcome and ensuring its impotence later. As Thomas Bell Jr., Burson's vice-chair and the head of its Washington office, told a gathering of rapt forestry executives in Vancouver: "Business, if it is not a leader in the environmental movement, will be a victim, and that's not a position we can accept."

In 1990, thirteen of British Columbia's leading logging companies bought Bell's argument, hiring Burson to create a new lobby group that called for continuing its clear-cutting practices in the province while presenting a new environmentally friendly public face. The result was the B.C. Forest Alliance, chaired by colourful former labour boss Jack Munro, who was known for zooming through Vancouver on his Harley Davidson. Three-quarters of its $2 million budget came from Munro's woodworkers union and the province's leading forestry firms. Among those firms was Weldwood Canada, a subsidiary of the American forestry giant Champion International — whose board, as it turned out, included Burson-Marsteller's Canadian chairman Allan Gotlieb.

Part of the alliance's campaign was targeted at Europe where the greens had managed to paint Canada as the Brazil of the North because of its forestry practices. But it also mounted an aggressive PR offensive against the environmentalists' most powerful weapon, the dashing lawyer for the New York–based Natural Resources Defence Council, Robert Kennedy Jr., who had made a personal pilgrimage to British Columbia to plead for the Clayoquot Sound rainforest, setting off a massive civil disobedience movement. In fact, it was that $1 million media campaign targeted at the green-minded citizenry of British Columbia that left Burson-Marsteller's own image in tatters.

Alliance ads featured children running through misty, sylvan scenes under the title "The Forest and the People." "A healthy environment AND a healthy economy — you can help," ran another of its clever, inclusive slogans. But as the alliance logo flashed across provincial TV screens, it began provoking questions — some about the history of the image-maker itself. In July 1991 the *Vancouver Sun*'s forestry reporter, Ben Parfitt, recounted an unsavoury chapter in Burson-Marsteller's corporate past: its efforts during the 1970s to put a new face on Argentina's infamous military junta, whose death squads were "disappearing" nearly 9,000 of the generals' least compliant citizens and torturing countless others. The random brutality had been chronicled by one celebrated torture victim, publisher Jacobo Timerman, in his harrowing memoir, *Prisoner with No Name*. But for a fee of $1.5 million a year over four years, Burson-Marsteller had undertaken to downplay those tales and discredit their teller in an effort to lure U.S. investment back to Argentina.

Parfitt reported one internal Burson memo that underlined the need to remind reporters that "terrorism is not the only news from Argentina, nor is it the major news." To assure that message was delivered, the firm had carefully selected only conservative journalists or travel writers for deftly scheduled press tours of the country which offered no time or opportunity for enterprise reporting — a practice Michael Deaver would later dub "manipulation by inundation." Two decades after the Argentinian exercise, Parfitt noted, Burson-Marsteller was running precisely the same sort of dizzying media blitzes through Sweden and Germany for handpicked provincial journalists on behalf of the B.C. Forest Alliance.

The reaction to the *Sun* story was swift and intense. At a meeting with the paper's editors, the alliance's directors vented their fury. Dismissing the Argentinian connection as ancient history, they countered that Parfitt's article itself was unethical. Two weeks later, *Sun* columnist Stephen Hume consulted two business ethics experts and lashed back: "In Argentina, Burson-Marsteller was hired to make the world think better of a government widely known to be butchering its own clients," he concluded. "Thus, what the public relations firm was doing was 'not merely image-making. This is falsification of history.'"

At Burson-Marsteller, where disasters were the company's stock-in-trade, suddenly the tables were turned. "For a company that spends its time dealing with crises," says DeGeer, "it's uncomfortable to have one of your own." The firm summoned its master spin doctor, seventy-year-old chairman emeritus Harold Burson, from semi-retirement to fly to Vancouver in an attempt to repair its tarnished reputation. Bland and bespectacled, the antithesis of New York hustle, Burson insisted that the firm had not worked for Argentina's generals but for its minister of the economy, a banker named José Martinez de Hoz who merely wanted to solicit American business. Whenever he had broached the subject of the death squads' bloody sprees, Burson said, Martinez de Hoz would shrug, "I have no control over them." Nor did Burson pass up an opportunity to take Canadian righteousness down a peg: he pointedly recalled that "one of the great coups of Canada" during that period was to sell Argentina a CANDU nuclear reactor.

But considering that his *Vancouver Sun* interview ran under the headline "Don't Cry for My Argentina," Harold Burson might have conceded that his damage control efforts had been less than an overwhelming success. Burson-Marsteller Canada lost the B.C. Forest Alliance account, as well as that of Ontario Hydro and Hydro-Québec — setting off a haemorrhage of other top clients and, eventually, staff. By early 1995, with Mulroney out of power, Burson's New York head office suddenly decided to merge its Canadian division with Montreal's larger National Public Relations — a marriage that boosted its billings but effectively eliminated Allan Gotlieb's job.

By then, however, the company's biggest bonanzas had already rolled into its Park Avenue headquarters, where Edward Ney had returned to the executive suite. Hired by Mexico's Ministry of Commerce and Industrial Development, known by its Spanish acronym SECOFI, Burson-Marsteller earned at least $18 million over four years promoting the country's prospects as a NAFTA partner during the stormy U.S. congressional debates. Of that sum, $1.3 million came from the Ministry of Fisheries for helping to dispel the threat of an international tuna boycott when environmentalists discovered that Mexican fishermen were netting dolphins. But Burson's principal efforts had been aimed at boosting the notion of Carlos Salinas's new Mexico as a nation of gleaming, modernized factories and Ivy League–educated technocrats who spoke the language of American business. Paradoxically, those efforts proved so successful that, when the peso crashed in late 1994, bringing the Mexican economy clattering down with it, some U.S. investors voiced a sense of betrayal, protesting they had no idea Salinas's vaunted economic miracle had been a construct of massive borrowing — and Burson's deft smoke and mirrors.

In beating the drums for NAFTA, the company had in effect been toiling in the service of George Bush's administration. But with Bill Clinton's arrival in power in January 1993, Burson earned an estimated $81.2 million from the pharmaceutical and insurance industries for working against the U.S. government — fighting Clinton's health care proposals. That unswerving allegiance to the corporate agenda provided grist for reflection on Edward Bernays's argument that those who most adroitly use public relations could effectively form an invisible government. But Burson's new role as the voice of the continental health care industry might also have given Canadians pause: according to British Columbia writer Joyce Nelson, who has made a vocation out of tracking Burson's causes, those same American pharmaceutical and insurance interests now have their sights set on discrediting and dismantling Canada's national health insurance system.

Certainly, when Edward Ney left Ottawa, he did not lose touch with Canada. From his thirteenth-floor Park Avenue office, he tossed off occasional memos to those in Burson's PR trenches in Toronto. And he would return often as a director for a pair of corporations that would soon prove equally solicitous of Washington's friend Brian Mulroney. Less than a year after Peter Munk had named Ney as a director of the Horsham Corporation and its subsidiary American Barrick Resources, he saw fit to award the same honours to Mulroney upon his retirement. Ney had also turned up on the board of Power Financial Corporation, part of the empire controlled by Montreal kingmaker Paul Desmarais, who, after the prime minister's return to Ogilvy Renault, would once again become one of his chief legal clients. Among Power Financial's holdings was Great West Life Insurance, which, through its Colorado subsidiary, had massive interests in the U.S. health care field.

But it was Desmarais who, like his pal the prime minister, most keenly shared Ney's interests in the globalization of the communications industry. In Europe he was already a partner in Radio-Television Luxembourg, the continent's largest broadcasting network, and in the United States he had paired up with DirecTV, a subsidiary of Los Angeles–based Hughes Aircraft Company, in a satellite television consortium. In the final years of Mulroney's term, Desmarais had also quietly begun buying shares in another firm with longstanding connections to Ney: Time Warner Inc., which, in a 1989 merger, had become the world's largest entertainment conglomerate.

I T was a calculated public relations gamble, and one that Brian Mulroney had clearly lost. For an eight-hour summit with George Bush in April 1990, his handlers had agreed on a public outing to Toronto's SkyDome for the home opener between the Blue Jays and the Texas Rangers, owned by the president's eldest son. But no sooner had Mulroney stepped onto the field to toss out the opening pitch than he was pelted with a humiliating volley of boos. Even more remarkable than that ignominious reception was the fact that he continued to run the same risk, meeting Bush in a series of SkyDome summits when his popularity had sunk so precariously low that, during the 1991 All-Star game, aides allowed his image to flash onto the stadium's giant screen only during the final strains of the "Star-Spangled Banner."

For Mulroney, baseball had become both a political minefield and, perhaps not coincidentally, a metaphor for bilateral relations. No matter how often the insults recurred — the anthem booed in New York, the maple leaf flag paraded upside-down onto an Atlanta field by the U.S. Marines — Canadians had become besotted by their newest import, the sport known as America's national pastime. Some saw that love affair as evidence of the country's creeping Americanization, but that verdict did nothing to discourage public affections. And never was the romance more rapturous than in the fall of 1992 when the Blue Jays' Joe Carter made the play at first base for an out against the Atlanta Braves which left the first Canadian team in history carting home the trophy for the World Series.

It was in the wake of that national euphoria that the planners at Time Warner decided to risk their own run at first base. Within weeks, the Toronto office sent out invitations for a reception to announce a new Canadian edition of *Time*'s sister weekly, *Sports Illustrated*. Capitalizing on the series' heart-stopping finale, they announced that, "in keeping with this tradition of 'firsts,'" the magazine was offering Canadian advertisers an opportunity "that will also hit home with Canadian readers of *Sports Illustrated* who currently number well over half a million." A rate card was enclosed and interested parties were directed to place their ads at the Toronto offices of *Time*.

In the Canadian magazine industry, publishers panicked. Only one, James McCoubrey, the president of Telemedia — owned by Mulroney's and Ney's friend Philippe de Gaspé Beaubien — welcomed *Sports Illustrated*'s arrival, declaring the magazine wasn't "eating anyone's lunch." But others shouted him down. The fact that Canada possessed no such weekly of its own was not the point, they argued: *Sports Illustrated* represented only the vanguard — the frontal wedge of the biggest, richest, and most powerful U.S. media empire — which was testing Canadian resolve. If Time Warner succeeded in proving Ottawa's cultural battlements a sham, at least forty other U.S. magazines were waiting just over the horizon to storm the border and overwhelm the country's fragile periodical industry. In an $838 million business where only half the country's 1,440 magazines made a profit — and those averaged a pathetic 2.4 percent margin — the outlook was grim. Already, 60 percent of the magazines sold in Canada were American and, since most Canadian publications reached their readers by subscription, the toll was even higher on the country's newsstands.

But what had caught the country's publishers off guard was Time Warner's strategy. For years as they watched *Time* court Mulroney's favour with lavish cover stories and stellar speaking engagements, they had been expecting the corporation to launch an assault on the Canadian legislative barricades. That prospect had even appeared to provoke Maclean-Hunter, whose flagship weekly had been the principal beneficiary of Bill C-58, to undertake its own efforts to cultivate the Tories' goodwill. Even before the start of the free trade talks, *Maclean's* had enthusiastically editorialized in favour of a U.S. agreement. And the corporation's successive chairmen, Donald Campbell and Ron Osborne, had headed up the private-sector committee from the cultural industries which advised the government's negotiating team. Osborne well knew from confidential briefings that the bill had remained a constant sticking point throughout the trade talks. As Peter Murphy would later acknowledge, "*Time* was all over us."

Indeed, in a confidential parsing of the initial draft text for a Canadian cultural industries' committee, one lawyer had pointed out an ominous clause that left the magazine publishers quaking: a provision to phase out their historic low postal rates. By the time the final text appeared, that clause had disappeared without explanation. Had another under-the-table deal been worked out with Ottawa? The industry suspected the worst when, six months later, the government did an about-face on the promise that Communications Minister Flora MacDonald had made in April 1988, guaranteeing no changes in postal rates for five years. Suddenly, in Michael Wilson's next budget, that allotment, which the Tories had taken to dub postal "subsidies," was cut by $45 million. Publishers were still digesting that betrayal when another $65 million cut landed. Then Mulroney hit magazines with the GST, turning a deaf ear to protests that periodicals had never been subjected to the previous manufacturing tax. The result not only raised newsstand prices by 7 percent but, as an industry study reported, it had eaten into sales by 14 percent.

As the publishers were left reeling, no company felt more vulnerable than Maclean-Hunter, the country's largest magazine empire. Shortly after the free trade agreement, the Canadian Magazine Publishers Association had joined fifteen other cultural industry associations in a brief to the government protesting its long-term effects; the next day, *Maclean's* quit the association in a show of protest (although it would quietly rejoin three months later). That opposition, declared the magazine's publisher, Jim Warrillow, was "not a position I want to adopt."

Throughout the free trade talks, the association's executive director, Catherine Keachie, had braced for *Time* to tackle Bill C-58. What neither she nor others had anticipated was that it would take a run at another legal provision designed to bolster the industry, a two-decade-old regulation with the official tag Tariff Item 9958. Known as the split-run rule, it was designed to prevent U.S. magazines from jamming Canadian ads into an American edition without changing a word of editorial copy — but necessitating a split press run — then shipping it north as a pseudo-Canadian publication, which allowed advertisers to deduct their costs. Under that twenty-five-year-old rule, customs officials had the right to stop such shipments at the border, but technology had made a mockery of enforcement. *Sports Illustrated* was transmitting its copy by satellite across the border and straight into a suburban Toronto printing plant where *Time's* Canadian edition had long been produced. That plant had been bought in 1988, after the free trade deal, by Quebecor, the Montreal-based printing giant owned by Mulroney's sometime crony Pierre Péladeau.

But even before *Sports Illustrated's* defiance, another small Washington-based computer magazine, *Datamation*, had tested the split-run rule four years earlier. In the process, its owners, Reed Publishing, a large U.S. trade house, had established Canada Customs' essential impotence. Receiving a warning letter to "cease and desist," Reed's response, as one industry official paraphrased it, was, "Oh, yeah? F — you." It was a stance that did not fail to catch the attention of those in the executive offices of Time Warner, who, shortly afterward, began negotiations with Investment Canada. But part of that corporate insouciance also came from the lobbyist who had replaced Tom d'Aquino: Ron Atkey, a well-connected Tory who was a senior partner in Toronto's prestigious law firm Osler, Hoskins and Harcourt. Not only had Atkey served as a cabinet minister in Joe Clark's short-lived government, but he was so well trusted by Mulroney that he had been named to head the civilian review committee policing the Canadian Security and Intelligence Service.

Faced with an outcry, the Conservatives announced a task force to study the question. Co-chaired by Roger Tassé, a former federal deputy minister of justice, and Patrick O'Callaghan, the retired publisher of Southam's *Calgary Herald* — an unabashed Mulroney fan — the study managed to drag on, well past the federal election and the Conservatives' ignominious rout. Still, when their report, entitled *A Question of Balance*, finally appeared in April 1994, a full year after *Sports Illustrated*'s first Canadian edition, it appeared to bear out the maxim in a framed cartoon on Atkey's wall: "No matter who is in office, the Tories are always in power." Calling for an 80 percent excise tax to be slapped on the Canadian ad revenues of any future split-run editions, the $350,000 task force ended up exempting *Sports Illustrated* and *Time*.

Later, the Liberals' embattled Heritage Minister Michel Dupuy would privately assure the irate magazine industry that he intended to enforce the excise tax against *Sports Illustrated* anyway. But it would take him nearly a year to even get the proposal on the cabinet agenda. Eight months after his announcement, no legislation had yet materialized. Already the new government of Jean Chrétien seemed spooked by U.S. threats; when a wheat war had heated up shortly after the Liberals assumed power, North Dakota senator Kent Conrad had observed: "We've got 300 Minutemen III's in North Dakota and maybe that will get their attention." No sooner did Dupuy announce his move than Bill Clinton's trade representative, Mickey Kantor, on his way to a Canadian ski holiday, vowed retaliation. In Congress, some senators muttered darkly about invoking the retaliatory provisions of the Free Trade Agreement against the U.S. holdings of Canadian publishers. As it turned out, Clinton was just as well connected to the communications industry as his Republican predecessors.

Given Chrétien's previous capitulations on cultural issues, Canadian magazine publishers were distinctly uneasy about their future. And that insecurity came at a time when their presence had

never seemed more vital to the national fabric. As the commissioners of a 1960 royal commission on the industry under Senator
Grattan O'Leary had once underlined: "Only a truly Canadian printing press, one with the 'feel' of Canada and directly responsible to
Canada, can give us the critical analysis and the informed discourse
and dialogue which are indispensable in a sovereign society." But
increasingly the national interest — and independence — of the
country's media were being called into question.

In a 1990 U.S. study called *The Media Monopoly*, analyst Ben
Bagdikian had shocked Americans with his report that 50 percent of
the nation's newspapers were owned by only fourteen conglomerates. But by the same date, the ownership of the Canadian press had
become even more concentrated: two corporations, Thomson and
Southam, controlled 59 percent of the country's papers. And in both
print and broadcasting, the media bore the stamp of Mulroney's
Tory friends. Two of his chief political backers, Conrad Black and
Paul Desmarais, had teamed up to buy what had become a 40 percent stake in Southam Inc., the largest newspaper chain. Black's
Hollinger Inc. also controlled *Saturday Night*, where he had
installed Allan Gotlieb as co-publisher, and, with the departure of
editor John Fraser, the magazine had come to read like a vehicle for
Black's arch-conservative crusades.

On the airwaves, the Tories' ongoing fiscal assault against the
CBC had turned into a war of psychological attrition as well,
noticeably blunting the public network's willingness to tackle the
government. Bolstering that climate of intimidation had been the
mysterious leak of an unpublished report by a former Queen's
University professor, John Meisel, a onetime Tory appointee to the
CRTC, who had castigated the CBC's English news as biased against
the Conservatives. Although few journalists agreed, Mulroney had
his ultimate revenge, naming right-wing economist John Crispo to
the CBC's board, undeterred by the fact that he had pronounced it
"a lousy left-wing, Liberal–NDP pinko network." While the notion
of public broadcasting was increasingly being questioned, ten firms,
led by Mulroney's supporters — the Bassetts and the Eatons of Baton
Broadcasting and conservative Frank Griffiths of Western
International Communications — were reaping 86 percent of the
country's television revenues.

For Mulroney, who read his press clippings before his briefing
books, that control of the media was no small matter. At all hours of

the day or night, he had taken to phoning *Globe* editor William Thorsell and *Maclean's* Kevin Doyle, offering top-level spin control or blistering tirades. At the *Globe*, journalists learned that cultural nationalism was not a popular topic with their bosses in the Thomson Corp., which had been threatened with U.S. retaliation against its American holdings; reports defending the Canadian publishing industry against U.S. inroads seldom found their way into the paper's otherwise extensive literary coverage.

At *Maclean's*, Doyle displayed a marked reluctance to incur Mulroney's wrath. Never was that more evident than in the magazine's treatment of a June 1990 White House interview with George Bush. Ensconced in the Oval Office behind his desk, his top National Security aides perched on nearby sofas, Bush had accepted a question on Mulroney's friendship with an indulgent smile. But he had batted it back with an unexpected twist. "When we're up there at the baseball club having dinner — and a couple of drinks, I might add," he began, then paused. He glanced at the adjacent sofas, apparently aware what he had said, but also apparently unwilling to take it back. "I hope I don't get the prime minister in trouble with that," he interjected, making clear that he had not merely blundered with a poorly thought-out turn of phrase; when he said "drinks," he was suggesting that Mulroney, a publicly avowed teetotaller, was not sipping Diet Coke. The interview had proceeded without incident, but when Doyle emerged onto Pennsylvania Avenue he worried to colleagues about the furore the president's pointed observation would provoke — not least of all at 24 Sussex Drive. When the interview appeared in the magazine, Bush's telling phrase had been neatly excised.

That incident might have rated a place on the agenda of a 1994 Toronto conference of the Inter-American Press Association, where much of the discussion had turned on intimidation and violence against journalists in the Third World. But one panel centred on another sort of threat to press freedom: "Are newspapers so much part of the business and political establishment they effectively censor themselves?" demanded moderator Roger Parkinson, the *Globe*'s newly appointed publisher. For many of his journalists, that question could not have seemed more ironic: nationalists, including even Mulroney's former mentor Dalton Camp, had howled in protest when Thomson Corp. had appointed Parkinson, an American who had served in Vietnam as a Green Beret, to oversee the country's most influential newspaper. Adding insult to outrage,

Thomson officials proclaimed there had been no suitable Canadian candidates. But after Parkinson's arrival, media scholars noted the *Globe* was running increasing U.S. wire copy, either as a result of a budgetary squeeze, as some editors insisted, or because the publisher's underlings were trying to curry his favour.

University of Western Ontario journalism dean Peter Desbarats blamed that growing confluence of commercial pressures for creating a "eunuch-like, make-no-waves, make-no-enemies style of journalism." And in his 1993 book *Read All About It: The Corporate Takeover of America's Newspapers*, James Squires had charged that the "corporatization" of the press had discouraged the kind of tough reporting that might give advertisers heartburn. In his dissection of that sellout, Squires, a former editor of Colonel McCormick's *Chicago Tribune*, singled out two villains: Gannett chairman Allen Neuharth and the *Globe and Mail's* former publisher Roy Megarry, who had once remarked that newspapers "are primarily in the business of carrying advertising messages."

But in Canada those developments were exacting another long-term toll. Freelance journalists seen as liberals or nationalists complained of the cold shoulder from editors and fewer outlets for their work. Just as in the United States, a new punditocracy was being cultivated, one largely peopled by the champions of Bay Street and such Tory academic favourites as Richard Lipsey and the C.D. Howe's Bill Robson. While the right wing was still railing on about the media's liberal bias, in fact, as the *Globe's* conservative columnist Andrew Coyne would later admit, liberal and left-wing opinions were increasingly rarely heard or read. Slowly but irrevocably, the political debate in Canada was moving to the right. In the process, it was also becoming increasingly continentalist, adopting a corporate vocabulary and mindset that scorned nationalism as yesterday's fashion. Suddenly, the media was giving expression to voices that unashamedly questioned the notion of preserving Canadian institutions — and even the country itself.

That radical shift, which University of Windsor professor James Winter called a "silent revolution," had many roots. But similar erosions of nationalism had a history of taking place in lands whose pesky sense of pride threatened powerful American interests. Indeed, the art of such concerted attempts to alter public opinion had been the subject of a 1981 study on U.S. intelligence methods by General Vernon Walters, who had served as George Bush's deputy at the CIA. An expert on covert operations, Walters had urged the Reagan administration, then arriving in office, to make more efficient use of the subtle spycraft of propaganda and media manipulation to bend troublesome nations to its will.

"The more general form of covert action is to seek to alter in the long term the thinking in the target nation in such a way as to make them perceive that their interest does not lie in hostility to the first nation," he wrote. "If this can be done, then those responsible for the formation of public opinion and the key decisions may be made to see things quite differently from their original views and this can be done at considerably less cost and less loss of life than one day of open warfare. The most successful action of this type takes place without anyone in the target nation being aware of it." As Walters went on to enthuse, U.S. intelligence should not underestimate the power of such tactics: "Covert actions aimed only at moving public opinion can have tremendous effect."

Whatever the forces behind the erosion of Canadian values that occurred on Mulroney's watch, they succeeded in noticeably banking the nationalistic fires that had once turned the free trade debate into a sizzler. By the end of Edward Ney's diplomatic posting, NAFTA was wafting its way through Parliament virtually without protest; some from the previous fight admitted they were resigned to the country's continental fadeout. By 1992, any ambassador who suggested a Canadian media conspiracy against U.S. interests would have been laughed off his soapbox.

Indeed, there was a certain exquisite irony in perhaps the most incongruous of Mulroney's retirement rewards: a seat on the board of the U.S. Freedom Forum Inc., based on the outskirts of Washington, to promote "a free press, free speech and a free spirit across the world for all people." The appointment had resulted when Mulroney once again worked his charms on an older American tycoon: Al Neuharth, the Gannett chairman whom James Squires had blamed for neutering the press. As the founder of *USA Today*, the mass-market daily that had won itself the nickname McPaper for its brief news boil-downs and coloured boxes, Neuharth had revolutionized — and homogenized — the business.

On a whirlwind round-the-world tour in his corporate jet, dropping in on global leaders and whoever else struck his fancy, Neuharth had filed dispatches from farflung outposts for a series he called Jet Capades. During one less farflung stop in Ottawa, he had called on Mulroney, whom he listed as one of the ten heads of state he most admired — along with Margaret Thatcher and Singapore's Lee Kwan Yew — in his memoirs, *Confessions of an SOB.* It had been chemistry at first sight. "In his dress, manner and looks, Mulroney gave the impression of a CEO of a successful company," he reported. "The sort that climbed the ladder with a special knack for promotion and public relations." For Neuharth, a man who had pulled himself up from poverty and lavished money on the Horatio Alger Foundation, the prime minister's Baie Comeau roots proved irresistible: "Mulroney," said a Freedom Forum official, "is Al's kind of guy."

In the fall of 1993, after the prime minister's resignation, Neuharth had asked him to address a Freedom Forum conference in Toronto. Mulroney, who had spent his last two months in office ordering his press secretary to denounce critical journalists for "personal" vendettas, wowed the private gathering. Two months later, he became the first foreign board member of the foundation, which was then being investigated by the New York state Attorney General's Office for its lavish spending. Despite that scrutiny, during his first year his trustee's fees totalled a generous $75,000 — a fixed amount for consultations, unlike other board members' stipends, which depended on the number of meetings they attended.

But that recompense was not the only reward. Having succeeded in subduing the Canadian media — if not the Canadian public — Mulroney now had ample access to the top echelons of the U.S. press, for which he had always harboured more admiration. It was there that the more influential first rough drafts of history would be written, there where he could play master spin controller on a larger stage. No sooner was he out of office than he was complaining, via a column by *Maclean's* Peter Newman, that the Canadian press had treated him with "unremitting hostility . . . the media set itself up as the official opposition." If Canadians had failed to appreciate him, Americans could scarcely help but be more admiring of a man who had made that sometimes obstreperous nation to the north more like them.

14 Going Latin

ON A DESOLATE ISLAND of balding grass at the intersection of three busy Ottawa streets, the swashbuckling bronze figure of Simón Bolívar stood alien and ignored. His sword sheathed at his side, the nineteenth-century Venezuelan soldier-statesman extended one bronzed boot over the ledge of his marble perch as if threatening to stride off in a huff — a reaction that might have been entirely justified considering his reception from Ottawa City Council.

No sooner had Bolívar's statue been offered by five South American ambassadors whose citizenry revered him as a liberator — a visionary who dreamed of forging Peru, Bolivia, Colombia, Ecuador, and Venezuela into a single Latin American state — than the council spurned their gift. Alderman Darrell Kent had led the rebuff, denouncing *El Liberador* as a mass murderer, "inhuman, indifferent to suffering and even to human life." The Bolivian ambassador, whose country was named in Bolívar's honour, declared himself shocked. Even an offer from the mayor of Hull, who hoped that Bolívar might offset the sex shop then across from the Museum of Civilization, failed to console the South Americans. But a month later, conscious of the international uproar they had provoked, the councillors reversed their vote.

In October 1988 Bolívar was finally installed six blocks from Parliament Hill, staring out at the hapless human flotsam washing up across the street at the Union Mission. But the inscription on his pedestal made no mention of his ambitious hemispheric vision — a vision that might have created some awkwardness in the final weeks of an acrid election over free trade with the United States. In the autumn of 1988, Canadians were still largely oblivious of that chaotic continent to the south which seemed to elbow its way into the headlines only when its debts were threatening to cripple the nation's banks or its generals were seeking the perks of the presidential suite.

But in Washington, where others were already taking a longer view, Bolívar's dreams had not passed unnoticed. In November 1988 a newly elected George Bush had not even assumed office when he confided to the Paris daily *Le Figaro* that his heart was set on extending Reagan's free trade pact with Ottawa to Mexico City. Still, Canadians paid little heed. But four years later in the panelled Great Hall of the Organization of American States, Bush presided over the signing of the North American Free Trade Agreement in a rite that he used to spell out his own grand design for the hemisphere.

Hailing NAFTA as merely "the first giant step" towards the creation of a free trade zone from Alaska to the tip of Argentina, he extolled "the dream of a hemisphere united by economic cooperation and free competition." In fact, his pact with Mexico had already proved so controversial at the ballot box that the ceremony was one of the final acts of his defeated presidency; but by then it was a blueprint from which there was no turning back. Among his audience were David Rockefeller and other transnational chiefs who already controlled the global agenda, not mere heads of state. His voice cracking, and often stumbling over his prepared text, Bush unveiled his Latin American scheme by invoking the spirit of the hero whose statue stood outside the OAS door: Bolívar, he said, "spoke about an America united in heart, subject to one law and guided by the torch of liberty."

In his audience, some South Americans winced. For Bolívar's dream had been a Latin dream — one that Washington had actively opposed in the opening decades of the nineteenth century when it had its own designs on the real estate of Spain's crumbling colonial empire. Bush was talking of another, quite different hemispheric agenda — one hatched in Washington by his National Security Council. Unveiled only days after he had announced trade talks with Mexico, it offered other Latin governments the promise of similar access to U.S. markets and relief from their paralysing national debts in return for prodding their economies onto an American-style free market path.

In a post–Cold War landscape where economic muscle had replaced military might as the key to national security, Bush was offering a new manifesto for the Americas where Washington laid out the ground rules. That urgent strategic vision was aimed at building a vast like-minded commercial bloc to fight off the challenge to U.S. supremacy from a united Europe and from Japan's increasing sway over the Pacific. In the still hazy New World Order struggling to be born after the Soviet empire's collapse, the race was on for global influence. And with Japanese and European investment invading Latin America, Washington was reminding both the Latins and their new suitors of its own historic claims in the hemisphere.

In fact, to many, Bush's scheme smacked of an updated economic version of the provocative 1823 declaration by America's fifth president, James Monroe, warning Europe's restive colonial powers that the United States would consider any forays into Latin America "dangerous to our peace and safety." But where once Monroe had backed up his pronouncement with the threat of dispatching U.S. troops, Bush was brandishing a new breed of weapon — trade sanctions and terms of debt relief.

"It's the 1990s' version of the Monroe Doctrine," declared Peter Segall, the former Gray and Company lobbyist who had helped organize Canadian companies to support the free trade agreement. "You exert influence over the hemisphere by setting a series of conditions — without the army and without having to dole out foreign aid. It's a classic carrot-and-stick approach — and America gets to be the Big Daddy of the hemisphere."

If Canadians had never considered that they, too, were pencilled into that strategic master plan, Stephen Clarkson, author of *Canada and the Reagan Challenge*, argued that they had missed the obvious. "American policy has been set in its general form since Monroe articulated his doctrine," he said, "and Canada was part of it, even if we didn't think we were."

Both Reagan and Bush had flexed their hemispheric muscles

early in their terms with sand-in-your-face shows of strength: 5,000 U.S. troops swarming onto the beaches of tiny, benighted Grenada in 1983, and 7,000 Marines descending on Panama six years later to blast Manuel Noriega into submission with loud rock music. But for Canadians who had watched those shenanigans on Washington's southern front with a cynical detachment, the 1985 voyage of the U.S. Coast Guard's icebreaker *Polar Sea* ought to have cut through that smugness. Crunching defiantly through the frozen wastes of the Northwest Passage which Ottawa had historically claimed as its own, the *Polar Sea* had provided a compelling reminder that the Monroe Doctrine could apply north as well as south of the border.

JAMES Kelleher, Mulroney's first minister of international trade, swears he never foresaw the country being drawn into a trade deal with Mexico, let alone with the vast continent to the south. "Our key objective was to get the goddam agreement done with the U.S.," he said. "We never had any interest south of the Rio Grande. The only thing we knew about that was what we saw in John Wayne movies."

Even when a handful of companies like Brascan and Noranda were major players in Brazil, Latin America had traditionally been considered Washington's backyard — a region which, perhaps more than any other, most sharply defined Canada's differences with American foreign policy. Over the years, Canadians had watched with a jaundiced eye as U.S. presidents wielded the Monroe Doctrine in an assortment of guises, cloaking it in such reassuring titles as the Good Neighbor Policy and the Alliance for Progress — or sometimes just sending in the Marines.

In 1904 Theodore Roosevelt had formally pronounced the United States the hemisphere's policeman — a declaration that was to prove handy during the Cold War when Washington peered at the entire land mass south of the Rio Grande through the narrow prism of East-West loyalties. In 1950, at the U.S. Embassy in Brazil, George Kennan, the father of American postwar foreign policy, had spelled out what was at issue for his ambassadors to Latin capitals — "the protection of our raw materials." To that end, Kennan advised overlooking some occasional unpleasantness. "We should not hesitate before police repression by the local government," he said. "It is better to have a strong regime in power than a liberal government if it is indulgent and relaxed and penetrated by communists."

Any vaguely leftist leanings were suspect, and U.S. multinationals like M. A. Hanna proved generous in helping to root out that threat. In 1954 Boston's United Fruit Company had worked with the CIA to topple Guatemala's Jacobo Arbenz, whose land reform schemes had commandeered its plantations. And seven years later the company's banana boats shimmered off Cuba's Playa Giron, where they had just transported the CIA's exile force to its doomed rendezvous at the Bay of Pigs.

Indeed, haunted by the spectre of Fidel Castro across the water in Havana, a succession of U.S. regimes thought of Latin America primarily as a problem in search of a military solution. In 1969 Nelson Rockefeller had returned from a tour of his family's Latin fiefdoms to report to Richard Nixon that the army was "the essential force of constructive social change." And nearly a decade and a half later, Rockefeller's protégé Henry Kissinger served up the same wisdom to Ronald Reagan. To combat the Sandinistas ensconced in Nicaragua and communist guerrillas wreaking havoc in El Salvador, Kissinger recommended more arms sales and military aid, warning that a victory of Soviet expansionism in America's "strategic rear" would be seen by the Latinos as "impotence." At a time when Reagan was so obsessed with the Evil Empire's reach that he was willing to risk impeachment with covert arms sales to the Contras, nobody was ready to talk about the hemisphere as one big happy economic family.

Certainly, no American president was prepared to take a cue from Woodrow Wilson, who had argued in 1913 that trade could accomplish the same ends as sending in U.S. troops — de facto annexation. "I wonder," he had once waxed lyrical to an audience, "if your imaginations have been filled with the significance of the tides of commerce." But with the implosion of the Soviet Union, the hemisphere at last seemed ripe for Wilson's commercial battle plan.

By then, a new, more sinister force threatened the globe's sole remaining superpower: the Latin debt crisis. For nearly a decade, bankers had been scrambling aboard flights to Latin and East Bloc capitals, peddling their recycled petrodollar deposits with the eagerness of Fuller Brush salesmen. But in 1982 the reckoning had come. When Mexico's then finance minister, Carlos Salinas de Gortari, turned up at the annual meeting of the International Monetary Fund (IMF) in Toronto to announce that his country could no longer service its $86 billion in loans, he had sent shock-waves through America's financial system. By 1987 José Sarney of Brazil, the largest Latin debtor, spurned the IMF's draconian pre-scriptions, declaring to apoplectic Western bankers, "We are not going to pay the debt with the hunger of the people."

At the time, Latin nations owed the West $435 billion — $54 billion of that to U.S. banks. Chase Manhattan alone was on the hook for $10 billion, personally authorized by David Rockefeller. Among Canada's big five chartered banks, the most exposed were the two that would later take the lead in pushing the free trade talks: the Royal and the Bank of Montreal. As Brazilian economist Celso Ming had observed, "If I owe a million dollars, then I am lost. But if I owe fifty billion, the bankers are lost."

In the spring of 1989, as that threat hung over the continent's financial institutions, George Bush's treasury secretary, Nicholas Brady, unveiled a relief scheme that discounted some debts to American and Canadian banks by as much as 30 percent. In return, he demanded a package of what IMF officials liked to call "com-pulsory structural adjustments" — stepped-up free market reforms. But despite throwing historic investment and import restrictions to the wind, Salinas was back within a year begging for another $6 billion to service even those discounted debts. The only hope of breaking that vicious borrowing cycle was to increase Mexico's income potential with access to U.S. markets and the selloff of state enterprises to foreign investors. It was out of that escalating debt crisis, not the seductions of free trade, that NAFTA was born — opening up Mexico's highly protected economy at last to American multinationals. Salinas even handed U.S. oil companies with their eyes on the ultimate prize, the state-controlled energy monopoly, a tantalizing wedge: for the first time in half a century he allowed foreign equipment and oil-service companies to bid on contracts with Petróleos Mexicanos, known as Pemex, which controlled Latin America's second largest oil reserves.

Heartened by that example, David Mulford, the smooth, silver-haired undersecretary of the Treasury who had authored the Brady Plan, saw the Latin debt crunch as a window of opportunity to wrest a new economic order from the entire hemisphere. In June 1990, just three weeks after announcing trade talks with Salinas, Bush unveiled Mulford's demanding update on the Brady Plan under the upbeat title, the Enterprise of the Americas Initiative. In addition to debt relief, he held out an invitation to join the exclusive NAFTA club as a reward to those nations that met certain tests — privatizing state enterprises, removing nationalistic barriers that barred foreign investors from controlling key resource industries, and guaranteeing their right to repatriate profits back to the United States. "The countries that do not make themselves attractive will not get investors' attention," Mulford had warned. "This is like a girl trying to get a boyfriend. She has to go out, have her hair done, wear makeup."

Only a minor part of his primping prerequisites involved lowering tariffs. But as Colleen Morton, the former executive director for the Mexico–U.S. Business Committee, the Washington lobbying arm of the Rockefellers' Americas Society, pointed out, "Tariffs aren't the name of the game anymore. It's all these other things." Indeed, trade itself was no longer the name of the game in Washington's new obsession with free trade treaties. "If we were doing trade agreements that made the most economic sense, we wouldn't be doing them with Latin America," Morton admitted. "We'd be focusing on Southeast Asia."

Like the Canadian pact before it, the Mexican deal was aimed at setting an example for other, more problematic nations — a second warning to those governments still balking at a new GATT agreement. But in opening free trade talks with Salinas, Bush also wanted "to reward such a model actor," Morton said, "someone who was actually paying their debts. It was critical in terms of our role in the Third World to be seen to be supporting the economic policies of a government we liked."

Just as Mulroney had dispensed with the thorns of the Foreign Investment Review Agency and the National Energy Program even before he came to the free trade table, Salinas had met most of Washington's conditions before the NAFTA negotiations opened. Four months prior to their start, he had already privatized more than 800 of the country's 1,500 state-controlled corporations. Speaking later to Latin bureaucrats anxious to scramble aboard the NAFTA bandwagon, Donald Abelson, a former aide to Bush's trade representative, Carla Hills, helpfully reminded them of that chronology. "Remember," he warned, "Mexico reformed *before* it initiated free trade agreement negotiations."

Privatization, as Brady would later admit to an assembly of Latin leaders, was the key to Corporate America's goodwill and investment dollars. "This was a central part of the thought process in developing the Enterprise of Americas Initiative," he said. Of course, the process was all for the good of the countries involved, he explained: "Privatization lifts the heavy cost of state-subsidized industries off the backs of the Latin American taxpayer." Soon Carlos Menem, Argentina's dapper Peronista who was agitating for a seat at the NAFTA table, followed Salinas's lead, selling off the state airline, Aerolineas Argentina, the state telephone company, and even offering public shares in the once sacrosanct state oil company, Yacimientos Petroliferos Fiscales S.A., better known as YPF. Venezuela peddled part of its phone company to a consortium headed by GTE Corporation and American Telephone and Telegraph.

Gradually, what Mulford trumpeted as "the unpublicized revolution" swept over Latin economies: multinational investors moved in to take control of pivotal industries that had once been regarded as guarantees of national sovereignty. At the same time, that revolution was sweeping Canada, where Mulroney was also embarking on a privatization binge, briskly auctioning off airlines, rail lines, Petro-Canada, and other crown corporations that had served as connective tissue to bind together the sprawling, underpopulated nation.

Like Mulroney, Salinas was held up as a friend of the United States, a model hemispheric leader who boasted impeccable pro-American credentials. As no White House official or news story failed to note, he had acquired his neoconservative economic principles at three Ivy League colleges; "Harvard-trained economist" became his virtual honorary title. In Washington and Toronto, the Burson-Marsteller publicity mill churned out stirring testimonials to the Mexican economic miracle he had wrought. Inconvenient images of wrenching poverty and toxic cesspools in the border's thriving maquilladora zones were treated to careful damage control: these, it seemed, were the very ills that NAFTA was designed to cure. Again and again, the mantra promising a prospective market of 370 million consumers was repeated to the continent's business communities like a siren song. Critics unkind enough to note that 40 percent of Mexico's prospective shoppers still eked out life at a subsistence level were dismissed as hopeless naysayers — or, as Marjory LeBreton, one of Mulroney's top aides, branded them, "the loony left."

If Canadians were unaware of the hype to which they were being subjected, they might have taken some measure of the exercise in Mexico City, where Trade Minister Michael Wilson was hailed in the state-controlled press as "Sexy Mike!" U.S. and Canadian journalists rushed to report on the new Mexico, with its high-tech assembly lines, its emerging middle class, and its young American-educated technocrats, known as "smurfs," in their tasselled loafers. Old-line politicians of the ruling Institutional Revolutionary Party that had held Mexico in a steely grip for more than six decades were dismissed as "dinosaurs," an endangered species. No matter that they had handpicked Salinas for the country's top job or that a majority of Mexicans believed he had come to power through massive electoral fraud. The colourless technocrat emerged as the media's darling — a visionary who would haul Mexico into the twentieth century by its bootstraps.

What few U.S. officials admitted — at least in public — was that, after Salinas's close call at the ballot box, they were taking no chances with his successor. NAFTA was Washington's insurance policy to lock in Salinas's economic reforms against the whims of any less accommodating president who might follow him. In a classified memo leaked to the newsmagazine Proceso in May 1991, John Negroponte, the U.S. ambassador to Mexico, spelled out that long-term economic strategy. "NAFTA can be seen as an instrument to promote, consolidate and guarantee continued policies of economic reform in Mexico," he wrote, "beyond the Salinas administration."

For Canadians, Negroponte's admission might have had a familiar ring: two years earlier, another leaked briefing memo for Bush had summed up the free trade agreement with Ottawa in precisely those terms. In fact, if NAFTA offered a distant mirror to illustrate the most disturbing implications of the Canadian pact, its full impact would not become obvious until Mulroney left 24 Sussex Drive. As Jean Chrétien failed to renegotiate the energy and environmental provisions of the agreement he had vowed to change during the 1993 election campaign, it became increasingly clear that the government's course had indeed been locked in by the White House. Existing policies were still vulnerable to attacks from U.S. interests, but any attempt by the Liberals to introduce new measures were virtually out of the question; in fact, under the terms of both agreements, any new cultural policies were guaranteed swift U.S. trade retaliation.

Governments could no longer march out of step with Washington's corporate-scripted tune or determine their own fate. As Woodrow Wilson had predicted, the tides of commerce could indeed enforce a kind of Monroe Doctrine Redux without the muss or fuss of mobilizing the Marines. According to Stephen Blank, director of the Canadian Affairs program at the Americas Society and a consultant to U.S. multinationals, that had been the idea behind a continental trading zone all along. "The economic integration of North America has eroded the capacity of central governments to manage national economies," he said, not entirely displeased at the notion. "We see the unbundling of the sovereignty of the state."

FOR the first post–Cold War economic summit of industrialized nations, George Bush had chosen a Tex-Mex theme — a symbol of his new hemispheric passions. In July 1990, just three weeks after he had announced trade talks with Salinas, he welcomed his fellow Group of Seven leaders to Houston's sweltering humidity with ten-gallon-hats and custom-made cowboy boots, which they gamely donned in one of the few shows of unity they would manage. Only weeks earlier, the two Germanies had begun their tortuous road to unification, transforming Helmut Kohl into the summit's star — hailed as the strongman of an emerging new Europe. Already, the old allied strategic consensus was crumbling with the speed of the Berlin Wall. And by the end of the three-day show, with the group's failure to agree on a single major issue from global warming to bailing out Mikhail Gorbachev, pundits were predicting a world fragmenting into three trading blocs.

As the group gathered for the opening ceremonies on the lawn of Rice University — where the White House had thoughtfully sprayed the scorched turf a telegenic green — the tensions were already palpable. For Brian Mulroney, who even in the crispest northern climes felt the need to change his shirt as many as six times a day, the Houston summit was a particular ordeal. Not only did he abhor the sweat-drenching heat, but as the leaders arranged themselves beneath a canvas canopy for the playing of their anthems, he appeared to be the odd man out: a wide, mysterious gap yawned between him and Margaret Thatcher. In the audience, whispers rippled through the VIP rows: was Thatcher avoiding an embarrassing air conditioning vent beneath her skirt? Were the two leaders not speaking? In fact, Mulroney's inner-ear problem had once again demanded surreptitious measures: a small railing, hidden beneath the dais wall, had been installed for him to cling to. But instead of giving him the illusion of assurance, it had left him a solitary awkward figure, sidelined from the rest of the group — a humiliating image that summed up the policy fix in which he found himself.

Never before had Canada been as free to chart its own foreign policy course, independent of the U.S. strategic agenda. But ironically it had never boasted less leverage to strike out alone. At the time of the summit, Mulroney had not yet agreed to be part of the U.S.–Mexican trade talks — a trilateral arrangement that Salinas himself opposed — nor would he give his formal assent for another two months. But that delay was a mere nicety. Having gambled his political fate on forging an exclusive romance with Washington, Mulroney had no choice but to follow Bush's hemispheric tango. No matter how scant the benefits, through the free trade agreement Canadians found themselves locked in as hapless sidekicks in a new Pax Americana.

Throughout the charged NAFTA negotiations in Washington, the country would often rate mention only as an afterthought. Tim Bennett, a former deputy in the U.S. Trade Representative's Office, would observe that, at numerous NAFTA meetings he attended, "the word Canada didn't come up all day." That role was not what Mulroney had led the country to expect in touting the free trade agreement as a ticket to a privileged spot in the U.S. marketplace. But over the next two years, as the Bush administration slapped Ottawa with aggressive trade sanctions, Canadian sentiments would increasingly be greeted with U.S. shrugs and even derision. At the Houston summit, a glimmer of that scorn already seemed apparent as the leaders repaired upstairs to the Rice library to begin their deliberations, only to find Mulroney missing. While TV cameramen waited behind a nearby rope for the group shot, Bush betrayed his exasperation. In his voice was none of the chumminess so often on display whenever he had played administration hand-holder during the free trade talks. "Probably changing his shirt," Bush cracked.

For Mulroney, those slights carried added sting, given the political risks he had taken in aligning himself so closely with Washington. While others in his cabinet were protesting that the government had been caught off guard by the U.S.–Mexican trade initiative, he himself was notably mum. In February 1990, the very month that word of a Bush-Salinas deal leaked out, he had made his first state visit to Mexico, where he sang the reassuring praises of Canada's own pact with the *Yanqui imperialistas*. Quizzed by journalists there about the likelihood of Mexico joining in, Mulroney had replied that he "would not be scandalized" by the prospect.

Four months earlier, his External Affairs Department must also have had some inkling of that possibility. In October 1989 the Canadian Embassy in Washington, under Derek Burney's firm rein, had joined with the Royal Bank to fund a three-day symposium at Baylor University in Waco, Texas, on the potential impact of Mexico's membership in the continental trading club. Called Region North America, the conference featured a compelling pitch by Sidney Weintraub, a former chief of commercial policy for the U.S. State Department, who had been pushing the notion of a trilateral trade zone since Reagan's election in 1981.

Even Burney's own 1983 review of Canadian trade policy had anticipated Mexico's possible admission to any deal with Washington. Under a section listing the economic considerations to bear in mind, it had included a cautionary reminder of "U.S goals . . . and the desirability of including Mexico in any free trade association with the United States." But the clearest signal that something was afoot south of the Rio Grande was the hectic schedule of Peter Murphy, the protagonist of the original U.S. free trade script. Unbeknownst to most Canadians, at the same time that he was confounding Simon Reisman over the negotiating table in Ottawa, he was also commuting to Mexico City and Cancun to hammer out the first 1987 sectoral framework agreement that would pave the way for NAFTA. Later, Murphy would scoff at protests that Ottawa had been ambushed by the Mexican deal. "We notified the Canadians," he said. "We didn't say it was the first stage of NAFTA — but figure it out!"

In fact, any number of familiar faces might have forewarned the Conservatives of Bush's hemispheric designs. For if the Canadian free trade agreement had served as a U.S. dress rehearsal, many from that same cast were back for the full-dress NAFTA passion play unrolling under the top-secret direction of Bush's National Security Council. Not the least among them was Bill Brock, the godfather of the Ottawa negotiations, who had left government to set up his own consulting firm, where he was hired to whisper in the ear of the Salinas government. Between February 1991 and October 1992 alone, his Brock Group Ltd. would receive $630,000 from Mexico's Ministry of Commerce and Industrial Development, known by its Spanish acronym SECOFI, for "strategic counselling on trade, labour and political policy issues." In fact, Brock would enrage former colleagues on the Senate Finance Committee who discovered that, when he had testified on the prospects for multilateral trade talks — slipping in a glowing tribute to "our neighbour Mexico" — he had neglected to mention that he was then on Salinas's payroll.

Back, too, for return engagements were Jim Kelleher's tennis partner Ed Pratt, who led the pharmaceutical lobby to a victory it had never managed to wrest from Ottawa — an intellectual property clause in the NAFTA text — and Ross Johnson's pal Jimmy Robinson, the chairman of American Express, who once again took a leading role as a corporate booster. As early as 1988, with the Canadian pact wrapped up, Robinson had shown a sudden interest in the Latin debt crisis, arguing in a speech to Washington's Overseas Development Council that it ought to be used to strong-arm Third World nations into "market oriented policies." As soon as NAFTA was announced, he commissioned his former lieutenant, Harry Freeman, to organize another lobby based on his efforts for the Canadian free trade agreement, this time called USA*NAFTA and chaired by Robinson's friend Kay Whitmore of Eastman Kodak. Once again American Express would find its enthusiasm for free trade paying dividends. Even before NAFTA was signed, allowing minority foreign ownership of Mexico's recently privatized banking system, Amex snared a foot in the door through a lucrative gold-card partnership with Banamex, the country's largest bank.

Also returning for a reprise of her previous role was Colleen Morton, whose career offered a case study in the evolution of U.S. economic strategy. A former American foreign service officer at the Toronto consulate, she had moved back to Washington to head up the Canadian-American committee of the National Planning Association, a business group that had teamed up with the C. D. Howe Institute to promote the free trade agreement in the U.S. capital. Not that the effort had required much ingenuity, she admitted: "Half of Americans thought Canada was already part of the United States."

No sooner was that deal done than Morton moved on to head the Washington office of the Mexico–U.S. Business Committee, the lobby for multinational corporations that was an arm of David Rockefeller's Americas Society. Chaired by Rodman Rockefeller, Nelson's son and David's nephew, the committee had been prodding the Mexican government towards a free trade agreement since 1985 — "before even the Mexicans themselves felt ready," Morton conceded. She claimed Rodman Rockefeller *really* wrote the bilateral framework agreement" in 1987 — the first of two memos of understanding that set the preconditions for NAFTA. But as congressional controversy heated up, threatening to scuttle the pact, Morton looked back on her previous assignment with nostalgia. "It would have been nice if we could have just slid NAFTA through," she said, "the way we basically slid through the Canadian–U.S. trade agreement."

With so many of the same players back on the scene — not to mention his bimonthly calls from Bush — Mulroney would seem to have had ample advance notice of Washington's courtship of Mexico. Indeed, if he did not foresee NAFTA taking shape on the horizon, he had shown extraordinary foreign policy ESP. For on January 6, 1989 — just as Washington was about to unveil the Brady Plan — a small band at External Affairs launched a policy review that would provide the rationale for a radical shift in Canada's hemispheric relations.

The review was all the more remarkable considering that, for at least two decades, the department had dismissed Latin America as a hopeless case. At the time NAFTA was announced, the ambassador's post in Mexico City had been vacant for thirteen months and External had only one person staffing its Mexican desk. Officials raised on the romance of Europe, NATO, and the great American behemoth to the south showed such a lack of interest in the region that one young diplomat assigned to the Latin beat had concluded grimly, "Well, I guess I screwed up my career."

In 1983, when Trudeau's external affairs minister Allan MacEachen had asked his Latin experts if Ottawa should reconsider its thirty-five-year refusal to join the Organization of American States, Richard Gorham, then Canada's permanent observer at the OAS in Washington, had delivered a resounding no. For nearly half a century, Canada had left its ornately carved mahogany chair at the OAS council table empty, and Gorham argued that it ought to stay that way. Not only did he deem the organization a costly weakling whose Latin members never stood up to the White House, but he feared that Ottawa would be shouted down by Washington, which had already forced the OAS to expel Cuba. At a time when Reagan's macho misadventures in Central America were polarizing the continent, he warned of the risk. "We thought we'd be caught between the Latinos and the Americans," he says, "and each would expect us to support them."

But six years later, in the wake of the U.S. free trade agreement, Gorham and Assistant Deputy Minister Louise Frechette, a former ambassador to Argentina, toiled in a windowless third-floor office of the Lester B. Pearson Building drafting a strategy paper that reversed a half-century of foreign policy doctrine: Canada, it declared, is "a nation of the Americas." Gorham describes the declaration as an attention-getter — a way to add a dash of policy drama to their review — not an argument for prodding Ottawa's priorities into line with those of Washington. When he first coined it, he warned his colleagues of the implications: "Gentlemen," he said, "if we use that phrase, we have just backed into a buzzsaw called the OAS."

But as it turned out, that buzzsaw was already humming. In the summer of 1989, two months before Gorham and Frechette's report went to cabinet recommending that Canada join the OAS, Mulroney confided to the Ottawa press corps that he was on the verge of making that move. When he chose to spill the beans, he happened to be Bush's houseguest on the presidential compound in Kennebunkport.

In January 1990, however, Ottawa's first vote at the OAS promptly confirmed Gorham's worst fears: Canada became the only country in the twenty-two member organization to support Bush's invasion of Panama. "There it was in a nutshell," said Lloyd Axworthy, the Liberals' foreign affairs critic at the time. "We're seen as a little red wagon tying itself to the big U.S. engine."

Later, asked why Mulroney had joined the OAS, his friend L. Ian MacDonald, by then Burney's press counsellor at the Canadian Embassy in Washington, would explain that the organization was "the club of 21. It's the flag cover for NAFTA." But the decision to sign up had been made a full year before the NAFTA talks were announced. In fact, what was most puzzling about the government's new direction was its secrecy. To this day, inexplicably, Gorham and Frechette's strategy review remains a classified document. Once again, Mulroney had reoriented the country's strategic focus without benefit of parliamentary discussion.

One reason for that stealth might have been the fact that Canada stood to gain so little from hitching its fortunes to Washington's hemispheric agenda. In the wake of the free trade agreement when Ontario's manufacturing heartland was just beginning to feel the massive exodus of jobs to come, Mulroney might not have been eager to highlight a more ominous prognosis. In a report to the Congressional Ways and Means Committee, the U.S. International Trade Commission (ITC) had predicted that while NAFTA would likely benefit U.S. industries — which already enjoyed $52 billion in two-way trade with Mexico — it could actually inflict harm on Canadian exports. Whether Mexico made its own deal with Washington or joined a trilateral agreement, it would steal away U.S. markets from Canada. "However," the ITC concluded, "this decrease in U.S. trade with Canada would probably be slightly greater under a trilateral FTA." In February 1991, the same month that Mulroney received that congressional warning, he formally opened trade talks with Bush and Salinas.

But as it turned out, trade was not the only thing the country had to lose from the North American Free Trade Agreement.

ON the third floor of Toronto's downtown Hilton, Halina Ostrovski, the blonde, Brazilian-born president of the Canadian Council for the Americas, shuffled through the papers on her desk in a futile search for statistics. In the council's offices, strung together from former hotel meeting rooms, Ostrovski had been asked by a reporter for the total amount of the country's commerce with Latin America, but she had only glowing growth percentages to repeat, no actual numbers. In fact, despite lavish government publicity that Latin exports were up 7.5 percent, they represented less than 3 percent of the country's markets abroad. A month later, Ostrovski was still unable to produce those figures. "The only thing that's relevant to the people I deal with is the increase," she said. If that seemed an odd response from the head of an organization representing 500 of the country's major corporations, not to mention the Royal Bank, it would not be the only fudging of the facts as Mulroney steered the country on a controversial new hemispheric course.

In the council's *Mexi-Canada Bulletin*, Fred Blaser, the senior manager of international trade services for Ernst & Young, delivered regular broadsides against NAFTA opponents, blasting environmentalists for their "morbid" attacks against Mexico's lax pollution enforcement. In one editorial, apparently oblivious that dysentery was at epidemic levels in some Mexican states — a leading cause of infant mortality — he hailed the quality of the country's tap water. "If a Mexican town's water supply is tainted, its residents would not stand for it," Blaser huffed, "any more than would the residents of a Canadian or American city." In some circles, such proclamations might have been dismissed as ill-informed nonsense. But at a time when NAFTA cheerleading had become a government-funded growth industry, only upbeat news was welcome, no matter how questionable its claims.

In Ottawa, Michael Wilson's trade ministry had spent $3.1 million on radio ads and a slick tabloid promoting NAFTA's glories — complete with falsely inflated Canadian employment figures. At the Canada Export Development Corporation, Latin American lines of credit were being okayed by the dozen and the National Defence College was suddenly offering its top brass courses in Spanish. At a time when Mulroney was closing down the multilateral-minded Canadian Institute for International Peace and Security, External Affairs had no trouble finding funds for a new think tank, the Forum on Canada and Latin America, designed to raise the country's hemispheric consciousness.

As part of that public relations blitz, Ostrovski's Canadian Council for the Americas had been set up to forge Latin business links. Ostensibly founded in 1987 by a handful of Canadian corporations with longtime stakes in Latin America, the council's national chairman was Gary German, a longtime executive with Noranda in Sao Paolo. But, in fact, it was a curious hybrid, born in that increasingly hazy terrain where the corporate agenda met that of Mulroney's regime: as its fact sheet acknowledged, the council's formation had been "assisted and encouraged" by the government. Its honorary co-chairman was Stan Gooch, the assistant deputy minister in charge of Latin America for External Affairs' international trade division. And a substantial part of its funding came from External contracts to host visiting Latin officials at lunches with Toronto's business community.

But if hemispheric projects had become Ottawa's latest fashion,

they were also given a low profile outside corporate boardrooms —
for good reason. Over the years, from the CIA's botched attempts to
knock off Castro to Reagan's mining of Nicaragua's harbours,
Canadians had repeatedly opposed Washington's muscular notions
of Manifest Destiny towards its southern neighbours. No area had
more sharply divided the two nations, and that dissent had
frequently pitted church and aid groups against Canadian corporations. In the 1970s one of the most explosive confrontations had
come when Noranda became the first major international investor
in Chile after the bloody, CIA–backed military coup, lending
General Augusto Pinochet's junta badly needed credibility. In
protest, the ecumenical Task Force on the Church and Corporate
Responsibility had stormed the company's annual meeting, taking
Noranda's irate chairman Alf Powis to task for never speaking out
against Pinochet's assault on human rights. Some members
had even occupied the corporation's Montreal offices, later taking
credit for its decision to close the Andacolla copper project.

As the head of another Montreal mining company at the time —
indeed one whose U.S. parent also controlled South American ore
fields — Mulroney was keenly aware of that outrage. Nor was he
unaware of the potential for a new round of protests as his
hemispheric tilt threatened Canadian jobs and environmental standards. For if Latin America held little allure for many Canadian
businesses, it offered a bonanza for a handful of resource firms
owned by his friends and leading backers in the free trade fight.
Chief among them was the Brascan/Noranda group, whose
loquacious chairman, Trevor Eyton, had not only headed the
government's private sector trade advisory committee but had been
rewarded for his Tory fundraising efforts with a Senate seat. As
NAFTA and the Enterprise of the Americas took shape, Noranda
had joined Vancouver's Placer Dome and two dozen other Canadian
firms in a latter-day copper rush back to Chile.

Another mining mogul who would later enthusiastically follow
the stampede south was Peter Munk, whose American Barrick
Resources Corporation owned major properties in Chile and Peru
and was scouting for more sites in Argentina, Venezuela, and
Bolivia. In fact, Barrick's $2.2 billion acquisition of Lac Minerals in
the summer of 1994 had won it a major Chilean gold mine.

That shift of at least $2 billion in investment to Chile had not
only raised alarming questions about the future of the Canadian

natural resource sector, still the backbone of the country's economy, but had also left British Columbia's mining industry devastated. While Canadian companies were poised to reap record profits in
Latin America, they were doing so at the expense of workers and
mines at home. So serious was the situation that in 1993 the B.C.
government commissioned a strategy report on how to lure the
companies back, even pondering looser environmental and licensing rules. As NAFTA's foes in the green movement had warned,
mining executives were capitalizing on the crisis to pressure the
province into relaxing its regulations at the same time that British
Columbia's beleaguered pulp mills were also being courted by
Santiago with the promise of regulatory laissez-faire. Both developments confirmed fears that NAFTA would bring a downward
pressure on Canadian standards, diluting them in the name of keeping the country competitive with Third World economies. As a
report by the Mexican brokerage firm CBI Casa de Bolsa confirmed,
"The flow of mining investment into Latin America in general is
getting a helping hand from ecological 'hawks' in the U.S. and
Canada."

But NAFTA threatened more than the country's resource industries. Despite optimistic governmental predictions of Canada's
future as a high-tech haven, U.S. and Asian transnationals were
already funnelling their research and development funds into
Mexico, not the decimated factories north of the 49th parallel.
Amid the environmental wasteland of border maquilladora zones,
gleaming new plants such as Sanyo's in Tijuana were rising, their
automated assembly lines requiring only a few computer-trained
workers and a compliant army of robots. In the spring of 1993,
when Michael Wilson detoured from San Diego to visit Sanyo's
facilities, it seemed no surprise that he declined to let any Canadian
reporters accompany him. For those automated manufacturing
palaces, not the sweatshops teeming with Mexico's cheap labour,
were the real daggers aimed at educated and skilled Canadian
workers.

With so few economic benefits in evidence, even some of
Mulroney's staunchest supporters were questioning his hemispheric
commitment. Peter Lougheed, whom he had named to head a bina-
tional panel exploring closer ties with Japan, wrote his old pal arguing that the country's economic future lay in the Pacific, not in
Washington's wake. The former Alberta premier, who had once

trod the corridors of Capitol Hill cheerily making the case for a Canadian free trade pact, now warned Mulroney that "We are vulnerable if we continue to become even more dependent upon the United States and particularly the U.S. Congress."

Meanwhile, Soviet scholars such as Carl McMillan, the U.S.-born director of Carleton University's East-West project, lamented that Mulroney's obsession with the American agenda had cost him a historic opportunity to forge a unique relationship with the emerging Russian republic. Even Tom d'Aquino, the long-faithful president of the Business Council on National Issues, confided during a NAFTA conference: "I don't feel our destiny is in Latin America. The only way Canada can exert itself is really to break out with an aggressive strategy toward Europe and Asia."

But still Mulroney pressed on — enthusiastically showing up at a dizzying series of NAFTA signing rites designed to boost Bush's flagging electoral prospects. Montana Senator Max Baucus had scorned one half-hour Texas photo opportunity in the shadow of the Alamo as "pure political theatre." But Mulroney displayed mock-horror when asked why he had bothered to fly in for the symbolic initialling of an incomplete text. "You would have me stay away," he demanded, "and offend the president of Mexico and the president of the United States, who leads the most important country in the world?"

That apparent compulsion to please the occupant of the Oval Office came to offend even those like Charley McMillan who had once sketched out the broad brushstrokes of hemispheric free trade. McMillan worried that the optics of Mulroney's ardent embrace of Washington were undercutting public support for the policies themselves. Not only was opposition to NAFTA growing, but, after furious External officials leaked a departmental planning memo to the press, the country's activist church and charitable groups were outraged to learn that Mulroney was also contemplating a radical new foreign aid policy that threatened the country's international image.

Drafted by Barry Cairn, then assistant deputy minister for policy and planning under Barbara McDougall, it urged redirecting aid from regions that most needed it, the poorest of the poor, to those where Canada had strategic interests and hot market prospects. That proposal signalled an abrupt departure from longtime policy, articulated in a 1987 report called *Sharing the Burden*, which had declared the driving philosophical force behind Canadian foreign aid to be the disinterested need to alleviate global poverty. To some, it smacked more of Washington's traditional thinking than Ottawa's. Noting that "commitments may have to be broken," Cairn urged a careful spin control campaign.

His memo provoked such an uproar that External quickly announced that the strategy had been shelved. But in fact it reflected a policy realignment already in progress. Within a month of the outcry, the Canadian International Development Agency (CIDA) had quietly — and with no consultation of the governments involved — cancelled major aid programs in six of Africa's impoverished nations — including Rwanda, Ethiopia, and Somalia — most struggling to recover from a tragic cycle of famine and drought. On the day that the Conservatives' budget announced those cuts, CIDA mailed a letter to the Tanzanian high commissioner informing him that his country, which had received $475 million since 1980 — making it the biggest recipient on the continent — was out of luck that year. Ordered to slash 10 percent from its overseas development allotment, the agency had decided to eliminate whole chunks of Africa. As one senior CIDA official explained, those regions were "not going anywhere in the near future." But no such judgment was passed on Latin America, where, Cairn had noted, "NAFTA has significantly enhanced the Canadian interest."

As shock ricocheted through African capitals, others questioned just how that national interest was being defined. Was it purely commercial or were other values at stake, including the country's role on the global stage? In testimony to a Commons subcommittee, Niger's ambassador Aboubacar Abdou reflected the betrayal of ten other African envoys on the benches behind him. "We Africans see Canada as a symbol," he said, "as a pioneer among industrialized nations."

His unspoken subtext was that the Third World had counted on Canadians to take a larger, less self-interested view than Americans. And for years Mulroney had managed to hold that ground with a defiant South African policy that had also pitted him against the iron will of Margaret Thatcher. But as Nelson Mandela strode towards power with the White House's belated blessing, that distinction disappeared. With Mulroney's support for every U.S. military outing from Panama to the Persian Gulf, Ottawa's policies seemed increasingly indistinguishable from Washington's.

At External Affairs, he had Americanized the foreign service with more patronage appointments in nine years than any other prime minister since Confederation. The plum London high commissioner's post became a convenient token of gratitude for free trade boosters like Donald Macdonald and top Tory fundraisers like department store heir Fred Eaton. Diplomats bemoaned the waning internationalist ideals of Lester Pearson that had once inspired them. "They gave us the sense that Canadians could make a difference," one senior official bleated, "that we were different from the Americans." But during the U.S. bombing war against Iraq, he confessed to feeling humiliated by Mulroney's jingoism. "There was no independent role of Canada seeking a negotiated solution," he said. "We were sitting in the back seat cheering the Americans on."

Nor was it clear that there were benefits to reap from that ardent me-tooism. U.S. trade sanctions were making a mockery of Mulroney's claims for free trade. And, having provided a handy pattern for the hemispheric pacts to follow, his government no longer seemed of interest to the White House. "What we have here," said Lawrence Birns of Washington's Council on Hemispheric Affairs, "is that Canada really is becoming an irrelevance."

Privately, some diplomats worried that the process had already begun. When Bush launched his Enterprise of the Americas Initiative, he had neglected to warn Mulroney of one key element — that Ottawa would be expected to contribute to its Multilateral Investment Fund. The prime minister, who put such stock in his role as a presidential phone pal, read the news in the paper, just like everybody else. Britain, too, had been miffed at the White House oversight and had stoutly refused to ante up. But after Bush wrote Mulroney, applying personal pressure, and a senior U.S. Treasury official prepared to follow up with a heavy-handed trip to Ottawa, the prime minister capitulated. Canadians, he finally wrote back in 1991, would be "proud" to contribute $35 million.

Gone, it seemed, was the government's independent course that had once earned it a respected role in the Central American peace process. Even the country's cherished image as a global honest broker seemed to have evaporated amid all the eager White House photo opportunities. In 1992 a survey of foreign perceptions about Canada by Angus Reid revealed that, in eleven of sixteen countries around the world, a majority of those polled believed that, in international affairs, "Canada does pretty much what the U.S. wants it to do." And where was that impression strongest? In the country's newest NAFTA partner, Mexico.

IN the State Department's ground-floor auditorium on Washington's C Street, past elaborate security and a bank of metal detectors, a distinguished cast had gathered in May 1993 to fret about the fate of the hemisphere. Not diplomats or even bureaucrats, most of the pinstriped set filling the upholstered rows were emissaries from multinational executive suites who had been summoned to an extraordinary meeting of David Rockefeller's Americas Society.

The setting left little doubt of the extent to which the White House saw its national security interests bound up with those of Corporate America, and vice versa. After five months in power, Bill Clinton still had not managed to win sufficient Congressional support for NAFTA, and now his top cabinet members were enlisting Wall Street's heavyweights to make their case to legislators. Lobbying instruction kits had been handed out among the crowd for a blitz of Capitol Hill later that afternoon. And over an elegant lunch at the Watergate Hotel, Clinton's treasury secretary, Lloyd Bentsen, would rally the CEOs to act as the administration's proxies. "You fellas get up on the Hill and do your part," he exhorted in his Texas drawl. "If you and your colleagues each make twenty phone calls, you'd do better than we can do."

For David Rockefeller, that exercise was an urgent mission to salvage a family dream. At seventy-seven, he had officially stepped down as chairman of the Americas Society a year earlier. But despite his honorary title and seat at the side of the stage, there seemed no doubt about who wielded the real power in the conference hall. From transnational chairmen to cabinet secretaries, speaker after speaker paid elaborate, even fawning, tribute to the scion of America's most legendary fortune — a man who had played perhaps a greater role than any U.S. leader in promoting Latin America's prospects. Gushed Clifton Wharton Jr., a onetime Rockefeller Foundation retainer who was by then a top State Department official: "No one exemplifies our country's commitment to the region better than you."

But in the course of that commitment, Rockefeller had also been keeping vigil over his family's enormous Latin interests. Touring them as an earnest young banker fresh from a wartime stint in military intelligence, he had found not only huge oil holdings in Venezuela that had later been nationalized, but also vast ranchlands in Peru and substantial slices of Brazil and Argentina's natural riches. With his reverence for stability, Rockefeller had been a staunch disciple of George Kennan's foreign policy rationalizations: he had never brooked a bad word about Washington's Latin dictator friends, no matter how much mayhem they wrought. In 1981, stepping down as chairman of Chase Manhattan Bank, he had held his farewell board meeting in Argentina, then still under the junta's brutal thumb, where he paid tribute to the military government's accomplishments. And during a Princeton debate with Lawrence Birns of the Council on Hemispheric Affairs years later, Rockefeller had dismissed Birns's well-documented litany of atrocities by Argentinian death squads as "Communist slander."

Having learned their lesson in the trust-busting days of the early century, the Rockefellers had bolstered their Latin investments with a calculated effort to leverage U.S. policy: in 1965 they had founded the Americas Society, Inc., to act as a genteel lobby-cum-think-tank for themselves and other top U.S. firms doing business in the hemisphere. Although its chief focus was South America, they were careful not to neglect their interests north of the border. For years, during the Liberal monopoly in Ottawa, the party's corporate Merlin, Maurice Strong, had enjoyed a seat on the Rockefeller Foundation's board — later to be filled by former University of Toronto president John Evans. Conrad Black and the Desmarais family, who in some ways served as the Rockefellers of the North — cultivating prime ministers of every political stripe — also enjoyed a place on the advisory council of the Americas Society. Even the crowd gathered at the State Department to pump for NAFTA included a half-dozen Canadians considered friends: former free trade negotiator Gordon Ritchie, BCNI president Tom d'Aquino, and puckish Toronto arbitrageur Andy Sarlos, a longtime associate of Peter Munk.

In the splendid neo-Federal townhouse on Park Avenue which served as headquarters to both the council and the society, there had been a Canadian Affairs division ever since 1981, a year after Pierre Trudeau brought down his National Energy Policy. Having lost so much of their empire to oil nationalism, the Rockefellers were sensitive about such developments. The Canadian division had been run by a former *Time* correspondent, Lansing Lamont, who had co-authored a book on the two countries' disparities called *Friends So Different* with Duncan Edmonds, a longtime Ottawa continentalist. A defector from Joe Clark's staff, Edmonds had cultivated Mulroney as a continental soulmate when he was still president of Iron Ore in Montreal, and the aspiring prime minister had often relied on his policy papers. Years later, when the Americas Society was orchestrating a flurry of conferences to promote the Canadian free trade talks, Edmonds had been named to its Canadian advisory board.

In 1991, when Lamont retired, the Canadian division had been taken over by Stephen Blank, a former professor of business at New York's Pace University, who also boasted ties to Mulroney's inner circle. As the head of his own consulting company, Multinational Strategies Inc., Blank had once counted Ross Johnson's RJR Nabisco among his clients; in fact, he had reported to Johnson's roving international ambassador, Ken Taylor, the hero of the Canadian Embassy caper in Teheran who had also been given a seat on the Americas Society advisory board. Nabisco had owned plantations in Central America, which Taylor regularly toured, and he himself was close to the prime minister and his cronies — above all to Fred Doucet, for whose lobbying firm he would later perform assorted services.

Given that web of connections, it was no surprise that David Rockefeller looked upon Mulroney as America's man north of the border — the leader who had helped lay the cornerstone for his hemispheric vision. In March 1988 as the beleaguered prime minister headed into an election campaign hinging on the contentious free trade agreement, Rockefeller had hosted a gala dinner in his honour at New York's Plaza Hotel, presenting Mulroney with the Gold Insigne medal of his Pan American Society. Four years later, Rockefeller would award the medal to six other hemispheric favourites — among them President Alberto Fujimoro, who had just seized quasi-dictatorial power in Peru, and Panamanian President Guillermo Endara, installed by the Bush administration after Noriega's rout, who had shown himself inept at stemming his country's transshipments of cocaine.

In 1990, with the Canadian free trade agreement barely in effect, Rockefeller had pilgrimaged to Ottawa and Toronto to promote NAFTA to the country's still-wary business community. For him, the agreement had become an obsession, the penultimate step towards the apotheosis of his family's hemispheric dreams. "Everything is in place after 500 years," he exulted in the *Wall Street Journal*, "to build a true 'new world' in the Western Hemisphere."

He went on to chronicle how protectionism and nationalism, which he regarded as equal sins, were tumbling out of fashion and out of power. Chile had led the way under what he liked to call "special circumstances" — the firm wrenching of the economy onto a neoconservative economic path under Pinochet's military dictatorship. In fact, scholars agreed that Chile's radical economic shift would have been impossible under a democratic government.

By 1992, confident that NAFTA was all but passed, Rockefeller had convened what his publicity machine termed the hemisphere's "highest ranking group of business and government leaders ever assembled" for a Forum of the Americas in the ballroom of the Sheraton Washington hotel. Co-chaired by an elite Latin corporate club and Tom d'Aquino's BCNI, the forum's goal had hardly been a modest one — "to set the agenda for a free trade and investment area in the Western Hemisphere by the year 2000" — nor had its speakers' list. The family's foreign policy retainer, Henry Kissinger, was the star lunch attraction, and dinner had been topped off with an address by George Bush.

The Rockefellers had never lacked for presidential attentions, but they were particularly close to Bush. Even White House protocol chief Joseph Verner Reed had acquired his skills as Rockefeller's personal aide when the Chase Manhattan chairman toured the globe with all the trappings of a head of state — which, in many ways, he was. As the honorary CEO of Corporate America, with the fate of nations hanging on his nod, Rockefeller had once commanded more clout than most elected leaders; with global noblesse oblige, he had assigned Reed to find a new homeland for his friend, the ousted Shah of Iran, and to make hospital arrangements for the ailing king of Saudi Arabia. Through the scholarly smarts at his Council on Foreign Relations, Rockefeller routinely offered presidents and prime ministers foreign policy wisdom.

Thanks to the family's controversial Trilateral Commission gatherings, conspiracy theorists on the far right and left liked to view him as a master schemer plotting to take over the world. But in fact he merely played genial host to those who had already taken over the world and were committed to his agenda — quashing the kind of government meddling that had shattered his grandfather's global empire.

In that quest, political allies might come and go, but David Rockefeller held fast to his goal. When Bush was felled by a fickle American electorate, Rockefeller had transferred his hopes to Bill Clinton, who also happened to be a member of the Trilateral Commission. During the 1992 presidential election campaign, Clinton had finally come out in favour of NAFTA, provided he could secure the side agreements that his union and environmental supporters had demanded. But with the agreement's fate in doubt, Rockefeller's patience was wearing thin. In an uncharacteristic display of pique, he would take to the op-ed pages of the *Wall Street Journal* to pen a call to arms. If Congress rejected NAFTA, he wrote, "I truly don't think 'criminal' would be too strong a word."

By the time Rockefeller assembled his forum at the State Department to help the White House out on Capitol Hill, he also had a price — a clear signal as to where Clinton stood on his larger agenda, extending NAFTA south to Tierra del Fuego. Nor did the president fail to deliver. Standing in for Secretary of State Warren Christopher, Clifton Wharton Jr. had reassured the crowd that Clinton was committed to "forging a true partnership of the Americas" — including "a hemisphere of free trade." In fact, the U.S. administration was split over that question: some of Clinton's closest advisers had argued that if NAFTA opened its membership rolls, it should not be to developing Latin nations but to Singapore and other Asian trade "tigers." Still, by extracting Wharton's declaration during a legislative crunch, Rockefeller had in many ways forced Clinton's foreign policy hand.

While Rockefeller and other Americas Society officials could barely contain their glee, for some Canadians like Tom d'Aquino the declaration held little magic. Obviously reflecting the doubts of his corporate clientele, he cautioned against following Washington's hemispheric drift, unconvinced that it was time, as Joe Clark had counselled in the spring of 1990, for Canadians to make the hemisphere their home. Testifying at parliamentary hearings on NAFTA, d'Aquino had warned that, should other nations sign on to create a hemispheric bloc, those new members could change the rules of the game, not necessarily to Canada's advantage. Still, at the time, d'Aquino had painted the country's course as inevitable. "The choice for Canada is clear," he told the subcommittee.

"Either we adopt an open trade policy towards our own hemisphere, or we will be left outside a future arrangement that may eventually stretch from Alaska to the tip of South America."

That argument — that Canadians had no alternative but to submit to larger forces — had been brandished repeatedly by the apostles of free trade. Different threats had been raised at different times: the sinister spectre of U.S. protectionism, the relentless tides of globalization, and the straitjacket of the deficit that could provoke the International Monetary Fund's accountants to march into Ottawa and take over. But the conclusion was always the same: either Canada bowed to the free market winds pushing it south towards the United States or it would end up some global matchgirl.

Certainly, Brian Mulroney had never questioned that conventional corporate wisdom. Even when NAFTA's future hung in doubt in Congress, he had rammed it through Parliament, celebrating its passage with a televised ceremony before the country's business leaders. For that fealty, David Rockefeller rewarded him with a unique tribute.

In the spring of 1993, a week after the Conservative convention where he had passed the party torch to Kim Campbell — his nine years in power packaged into a slick television extravaganza by the video wizards of rock star David Bowie — few in the parliamentary press corps bothered to note Mulroney's last Ottawa appearance. Already he was yesterday's man, so vilified that even leading Tories were trying to distance themselves from him in the election campaign. But beneath the shimmering glass spires of the National Gallery, le tout Corporate Canada had gathered in black tie and diamonds to pay homage to him at a gala that also happened to be the annual meeting of the International Advisory Council to the Americas Society.

For the occasion, Rockefeller had flown his Latin corporate proconsuls up from New York on his private jet. En route, they had detoured for an aerial glimpse of one of his pet projects, Hydro-Québec's stalled Great Whale dam, and dropped by Paul Desmarais's Power Corporation in Montreal, but the Ottawa testimonial to Mulroney was billed as the capstone of the outing. Although Rockefeller would decline a reporter's request for a transcript of his eulogy, those in attendance recall his praise as lavish. As an assistant later put it, "Mr. Rockefeller wanted to thank Mr. Mulroney for all he had done up there."

In his own speech, Mulroney chose to review his nine years in power as if they flowed in one seamless hemispheric design. Canadian voters might harbour the impression that his government had been dragged willy-nilly into NAFTA and its extension south by the White House. But he recounted each step he had taken towards the creation of a vast trading zone of the Americas as an act of calculated logic: first the OAS seat, which had served as "the foundation for changing the political dynamic of our relationship with the hemisphere," then the NAFTA treaty itself, "the building blocks to give that relationship new meaning and content."

To a listener, it sounded as if Brian Mulroney had known what he was doing all along.

O N New Year's Eve 1994 NAFTA exploded into effect in a burst of automatic rifle fire that shattered Burson-Marsteller's Mexican makeover campaign. As masked indigenous rebels stormed the graceful colonial square of San Cristobal de las Casas, the capital of Mexico's impoverished southernmost province of Chiapas, they exposed the raw poverty and corruption that still festered beneath the surface of Salinas's vaunted economic miracle. While U.S. and Canadian correspondents had chronicled the gleaming office towers rising in Mexico City beneath the neon logos of defence contractors like Unisys, the *campesinos* of Chiapas were living in adobe huts without electricity or water, often doing their laundry in fetid road-side ditches. The windfall of cash from the booming stock market and Salinas's privatization spree appeared to have gone mainly to Mexico's twenty-four new "NAFTA billionaires" — only slightly broadening the oligarchy of eighteen families that had traditionally controlled the country. According to a study by Washington's Development Gap, the assets of the richest man in Mexico outstripped the total annual earnings of seventeen million of the country's poorest citizens. The new Mexico, it seemed, had been but a fragile veneer slapped over the exploitation and inequities of the old.

From his jungle stronghold in the Chiapas mountains, where he spouted sophisticated economic theory behind a black balaclava, the rebels' courtly multilingual leader, Subcomandante Marcos, made clear it was no accident the revolt had coincided with

NAFTA's inauguration. Declaring the pact a "death sentence" on Mexico's peasantry, he pointed out that, in Salinas's fervour to comply with U.S. free market dogma, his government had stripped away the constitution's land reform provisions that had protected small farmers from being driven off their ancestral plots by the government's wealthy rancher friends. Many in the North America media had dismissed Marcos's timing as mere opportunism, a clever stroke of public relations. But in fact, as he predicted, the Chiapas revolt would become the "shot heard around the world" against the perils of globalization. From a ragtag peasant force, some armed only with mock wooden guns, had come the first assault on the new corporate economic order with its slick technological imperatives.

It would take another year for Subcomandante Marcos's message to become clear — a bloody election year of assassinations, twisted coverup plots, and counter-assassinations that would make the Chiapas insurgency look like child's play. During that year, Mulroney had already gone on to his numerous corporate rewards, but he happened to be in Mexico in March 1994 when the next seismic shock struck: as bullets tore through Luis Donaldo Colosio, Salinas's friend and chosen heir, at a Tijuana campaign rally, they laid bare the fact that, beneath all the tasselled loafers and U.S. graduate degrees, the tyranny of corruption and drug cartels still held the ruling party hostage. Mulroney scoffed at such notions, ever faithful to the NAFTA line. "It has nothing to do with Mexico," he said. "It has to do with the psyche."

Chrétien, too, had been in Mexico City at the time, presiding over a trade fair to celebrate the very pact he had once so adamantly opposed. But once in power, he had changed his tune and, after Colosio's assassination, Chrétien and Canadian business leaders had insisted that Mexico remained a stable market of boundless opportunities. In fact, given its political troubles, he argued, the country had all the more need for Canadian investment. And so that investment had continued to pour in.

But by November 1994 when Salinas delivered his last televised address to the nation, Mexico's NAFTA glow was already wearing thin. As he rhymed off optimistic statistics in a self-justification that ran to sixty-five pages, opposition legislators interrupted him with cries of "Falso!" Already, as in Canada after the free trade agreement, the ultimate promise that had seduced the country was proving illusory: although exports were up, not only had no new jobs been created but, in the manufacturing sector, employment was down by 6 percent. Few in Mexican society had benefited from Salinas's free market reforms and, two days before his final *informe*, a poll showed that 66 percent judged the country worse off than a year earlier. Indeed, despite the tons of ticker tape the government dumped along his processional route back to the presidential palace, the capital's streets remained empty. Like Mulroney and so many other foreign leaders who had become Washington's favourites, Salinas left office reviled by his own populace. Within four months, as the country's political and economic crises spun out of control, taking on the bizarre plotlines of a thriller, he had fled to the United States, a haunted tragic figure whose betrayal of the national interest was being spelled out nightly in a theatrical smash hit called *The Trial of Salinas*.

But when his successor, another colourless U.S.–educated technocrat named Ernesto Zedillo Ponce de Léon, took up office at Los Pinos, he had found a missive from Subcomandante Marcos waiting: "Welcome to the nightmare." Within days, its meaning became clear. As the rebels launched a renewed assault in Chiapas, the stock market crashed, sending the peso plummeting by more than 50 percent and setting off a currency and credibility crisis that would virtually bring the country to its knees. As it turned out, Mexico's boom had been built on an illusion — a binge of borrowing and the $30 billion in profits from selling off state enterprises. To counter congressional fears about Mexicans stealing U.S. jobs, Salinas had followed Mulroney's example with the Canadian dollar: he had kept the peso pegged artificially high throughout the NAFTA negotiations and the year-long election campaign afterward, in the process sabotaging his own country's economic prospects. By the time he left office, Mexico's foreign loans stood at $140 billion — greater than when the debt crisis began. In the words of Latin analyst Lawrence Birns, "It was like a giant Ponzi scheme."

Lobbying for a job as head of the new World Trade Organization, apparently with the White House's backing, Salinas also broke with a Mexican tradition that saw outgoing presidents devalue the peso to leave their successors a clean slate. Zedillo's officials at first assured investors they were not contemplating any such move, but when they promptly did an about-face, catching the money markets off guard, the reaction was swift and brutal. With more than $10 billion in Canadian and U.S. investments wiped out overnight, capital fled the country by the millions. As Zedillo all but exhausted Mexican foreign currency reserves, he scrambled for solutions, offering a stepped-up schedule of privatizations at fire-sale prices. But in truth there were not many state treasures left to auction. The only one investors seemed interested in was Pemex, the quasi-mystical symbol of national sovereignty that Salinas had once declared untouchable. But as part of the $52 billion bailout package Clinton negotiated, the state oil company was no longer sacrosanct: to repay the loans, Washington won the right to seize Pemex's revenues, which conveniently passed through New York's Central Reserve bank. Suddenly, Ronald Reagan's notion of continental energy reserves seemed within sight. And, as John Negroponte's leaked memo had predicted, Zedillo had found himself locked into Salinas's free market straightjacket. There was no turning back. Mexico had lost control of its economy.

Ironically, the terms of the rescue package imposed such hardship that they created the very conditions NAFTA had been designed to prevent: lower wages, increased unemployment, and a 42 percent inflation rate virtually guaranteed social unrest on America's southern front and massive emigration to the United States. But then it seemed the money markets had never entirely bought Burson-Marsteller's NAFTA hype: most of the investment pouring into Mexico had been not in the form of manufacturing plants but short-term paper that allowed for a rapid exit when the storm clouds rolled in. In fact, while Mulroney and his government had been touting Mexico's stability, his own superintendent of financial institutions had not removed Mexico from its watch list of high-risk countries until July 1992 — the eleventh hour of the NAFTA negotiations.

But the peso crisis had revealed another feature of the NAFTA negotiations that Mulroney had not cared to publicize: as Canadians discovered with a rude shock, a secretive side agreement had committed the government to come to either of its partners' rescue in a currency meltdown. When that moment of truth arrived, Jean Chrétien, too, found himself locked into a hemispheric two-step he had never agreed to dance: in the very week that he was bracing Canadian taxpayers for draconian budget cuts, especially in social services, he announced an obligatory $1.5 billion rescue package for Mexico.

Bank of Canada officials had taken to the phones in Ottawa, trying to calm outraged MPs, but the peso had continued to fall. "It's a warning to us," Alberta MP Bob Mills, the Reform Party's foreign affairs critic, told *Maclean's*. "The same thing could happen to us." And then it promptly did. The money markets took a run at the Canadian dollar, which plunged to 70 cents, the lowest in a decade. Once again, Mexico's plight provided a disturbing distant mirror. With Chrétien's budget under increasing pressure, even the country's national health insurance scheme — once as sacred as Pemex — seemed in jeopardy: while proclaiming that the system itself was untouchable, the government took its first nibbles around the edges.

As the peso crisis had already demonstrated, the three NAFTA economies were now inextricably linked — not in the hemispheric utopia of so much lofty rhetoric, but in a brutal reckoning that levelled the continent's economic playing field to the lowest common denominator. Barely a year into NAFTA, the costs for hitching the nation's fate to the hemispheric wagon seemed catastrophically high. Chrétien's failure to sacrifice the country's social welfare system to deficit cutting had provided provocation enough for an attack on the country's currency and credit rating. Canada's fate, too, hung on the money market's whims, and their ability to punish any nation that questioned their notion of proper policies.

Only six blocks from Chrétien's office on Parliament Hill, the statue of Simón Bolívar appeared eerily prophetic. For if the inscription on its base told little of his hemispheric vision, it also said nothing of his ignominious end. In the winter of 1830 Bolívar died in wilful exile on the bleak northern Colombian coast, wracked by tuberculosis, devastated by betrayals, and a pariah in many of the countries he had tried to unite. As civil wars raged all around and his glorious Latin dream lay in tatters, his last words, railed against his plight: "Oh, how shall I get out of this labyrinth."

15 | Plus Ça Change

IT WAS A SCENE like so many others before it: a sun-dappled spring day in Washington, the picture-postcard backdrop of the south portico of the White House, and, striding down the walk to meet the press for an obligatory farewell photo op, Brian Mulroney beside America's commander-in-chief. But this time a new twist had been written into the script. George Bush smiled indulgently as Mulroney stepped to the microphones. He knew what was coming. Not only had the scenario been choreographed even before the prime minister's Challenger dropped its wheels at Andrews Air Force Base, but they had just run through it again inside over a ninety-minute Oval Office lunch.

Mulroney's unabashed embrace of Washington was blowing up in his face. His popularity had sunk to 12 percent. A volley of trade sanctions launched by the U.S. administration was making a mockery of his claims for free trade. Once again on the eve of his visit, after twice being ruled guiltless by American tribunals, Canadian softwood lumber producers found themselves accused of subsidizing exports by the U.S. Commerce Department in what had become the trade issue from hell. With little over a year left before the Tories had to call an election, rulings against Ontario-built Hondas and Canadian beer added to his fury. "What are those assholes from

Commerce trying to do?" Mulroney had raged to aides back in Ottawa. Inside the Oval Office, he had waxed only slightly less indignant. "George," he had said over lunch, "I'm taking a goddamn lot of heat about this."

Now, as Mulroney dramatically cleared his throat, Bush looked on like some bemused uncle, prepared to suffer through this orchestrated outburst. "For some time, Canadians have been troubled and angered by the attitude adopted by some people in Washington on major trade issues," the prime minister began. It wasn't exactly a blistering rebuke, but for a man known for his hands-across-the-border panegyrics, they were strong words. Mulroney went on to brand the trade actions "harassment" and "demonstrably unfair." Aides would boast later how he had demanded that James Baker and Carla Hills attend his modest tirade. But in the official line-up behind him, Hills, who had no patience with Canadian complaints, looked at Baker and rolled her eyes. As Mulroney warmed to his subject, the secretary of state glanced at his watch and pulled out a leather pocket memo pad to jot down some reminder. This protest was obviously for political consumption back home. Even the White House reporters on whom the prime minister doted were growing impatient. They had another story on their minds. Finally, ABC's Brit Hume could wait no longer. "What about Murphy Brown?" he shouted.

The night before, in a speech on the Los Angeles riots, Dan Quayle had attacked the CBS sitcom for showing its star, Candice Bergen, as an unwed mother, blithely giving birth to a baby boy. *That* was Washington's story of the day. As Mulroney kept trying to wrest attention back to his trade woes, White House reporters clicked off their tape recorders. He stood there ignored, his fury thinly veiled. Murphy Brown, a fictional TV character, had eclipsed his first attempt to show he was not a White House poodle. "I told you what the issue was," Bush shrugged, chuckling, as they walked off together. "You thought I was kidding."

The next afternoon, after doing the rounds on Capitol Hill, Mulroney tried once again to make his point to the more attentive Canadian media. Standing under a tree on the lawns outside the Capitol, he claimed defiantly that the White House had gotten his message. He hinted knowingly that changes were in the wind, but seemed unable to spell them out. Then a reporter asked him what it would mean if, in fact, nothing changed. "Well, then," he bristled, "I'll have missed the boat."

Within a year, it would seem that he had. Not only did trade harassments continue, but by then his second attempt to write himself into the history books by retailoring the Constitution lay in ashes. Defying his lavish feel-good ad campaign, Canadians had soundly trounced the Charlottetown accord in a vote that was deemed a repudiation not of Quebec but of the prime minister himself. Across the nation, Mulroney found himself reviled. To the party, he had become a liability. Even his once adulatory emissary Allan Gotlieb would soon take his distance, proclaiming in the *Globe and Mail* that, like almost every prime minister before him, Mulroney had failed to "get it right" in dealing with the Yanks. "Though a number of his policies toward the United States advanced Canada's national interests," Gotlieb opined in a striking about-face, "he was perceived by many Canadians as being too subservient to Uncle Sam and as conducting himself in a manner demeaning to our national dignity."

Even Mulroney's onetime backer Conrad Black, now Gotlieb's patron, would dismiss him in print as the Willy Loman of the global stage — "the eager volunteer fixer amassing due bills for the future account." In his memoirs, Black would quick-sketch a politician "not overburdened with convictions, seeking always to conciliate the most persistent lobbyists." In his eyes, Mulroney had never been a real conservative, and, in the end, he left office "an indistinct personality" with "a few sad traces" of *Death of a Salesman*.

As he did so, it seemed unclear what all his closeness with the White House had won — not surcease from trade sanctions or more sovereignty, or even more respect. By the fall of 1992, when Bush lost his own bid for a second term, Bill Clinton was unavailable for Mulroney's congratulatory call; campaign aides reported that the president-elect was taking a nap. At the Canadian Embassy in Washington, Derek Burney, who had worked up a direct channel to Bush's national security advisor, Brent Scowcroft, was glum. Reviewing the election, he suddenly insisted that the personalities in power did not count, only national interests did. Overnight, Mulroney's media handlers were suddenly playing down the prime minister's once-vaunted palsiness with two presidents.

For the second time in two months, Mulroney closeted himself in Palm Beach to lick his wounds and make his arrangements. With so much to ponder, he disappeared behind the pink stucco walls of a seaside villa owned by a Baltimore amusement park king named

Buddy Jenkins, who had proved a generous donor to Maryland governor Donald Schaefer, a longtime chum of George Bush. Power-walking in solitude on the Florida sand, shunning the society rounds, Mulroney hesitated briefly over his fateful decision to resign in dignity, still hoping his fortunes would turn. But Washington had already written him off. At the influential Center for Strategic and International Studies, a report by national security expert Joseph Jockel underlined the depth of public anger against him. "The coming to power of Bill Clinton," Jockel predicted, "can only serve to undermine further Mulroney's fortunes and those of his party."

If the prime minister had any doubts about his reception by the new president, he had only to look at the site that Clinton's aides had chosen for their first joint press conference: placing the podium a football field down the White House lawn, they had deprived Mulroney of a last photo ritual against the treasured backdrop of the rose garden. During the ceremony, Clinton spouted stock briefing-book phrases which betrayed that he had just boned up on Canada 101. But when Mulroney ignored his wrap-up signal, unable to resist one last question, the new president showed he was no neophyte when faced with public one-upmanship. An angry flush rising up his cheeks, Clinton spent their remaining farewells pointedly chatting not with Mulroney but with his deputy, Don Mazankowski. For a prime minister who had staked his political career on his chummi-ness with the White House, the die had been cast. He did, as Conrad Black would slyly characterize it, "the honourable as well as the expedient thing."

Then the farewells began. But as Mulroney jetted about the con-tinent and later Europe, racking up taxpayer air miles and bidding his official adieus, his future still seemed uncertain. Once, he had prevailed upon his former law partner, Yves Fortier, whom he had named U.N. ambassador, to help him snare the secretary general's job, but no one had taken that abortive bid seriously. U.N. insiders knew the post was reserved for an African candidate. Months earlier, after delivering an impassioned defence of his nine-year embrace of Washington during an evening at Harvard organized by his daughter, Caroline, a questioner in the audience had demanded whether James Robinson III would be annointing him his successor at American Express. An Amex appointment might have seemed logical consid-ering the services his government had rendered the corporation and the friends he claimed on its board. But Mulroney had waved off the query with a joke. By the time he stepped down, Robinson had been ousted in a headline-making board coup supported even by his old chums Ross Johnson and David Culver. All Jimmy Three Sticks' hours stumping for free trade might have been very well, but his corporate acquisitions had proved disastrous and profits were down. Amex was not in the market for another international schmoozer. Business, after all, was business, and Jimmy Robinson was sacrificed to the greater corporate good: the bottom line.

Instead, Mulroney would follow Reagan's cue, cashing in on his years in public office with a showiness unprecedented in Canadian history. Just as Reagan had provoked outrage by kicking off his retirement with a $2 million speaking tour in Japan, the nation he had so often depicted as an economic foe, Mulroney would collect his first corporate recompense from a U.S. conglomerate: he joined Ross Johnson and Nelson Rockefeller's widow on the board of Archer Daniels Midland, Dwayne Andreas's Illinois-based agri-giant that had become a symbol of the transnationals' gluttony, swallowing food industries around the globe. Only months earlier, Andreas had been included in the last intimate dinner the prime minister had hosted for Bush at the embassy in Washington, rubbing shoulders with Tory contributor Galen Weston, whose Canadian flour mills he had just snapped up. Indeed, a tiny coterie of transnational tycoons, both Americans and Canadians with substantial U.S. interests, would assure Mulroney a gilded exit from the public stage.

No Canadian prime minister before him had appeared to profit so handsomely once out of office. Even the normally reverential *Globe and Mail* would add up his directorships and stock options to dub him Mulroney, Inc. Like Reagan, the celebration of brisk, sometimes brutal global commerce had been his governing credo — an allegiance to the marketplace enshrined in the litany of multinational donors etched into the marble walls of the Ronald Reagan Presidential Library. For if it was painful for him to leave the spotlight, perhaps nowhere did that seem more poignant than during his lacklustre goodbye on the library terrace high in the dreamlike hills above Simi Valley.

As the Air Force Band of the Golden West played "Hail to the Chief" for an obviously failing Reagan, Mulroney was left to contemplate the somewhat more spartan treatment accorded ex-prime ministers. By then he seemed to have little left to say. At the podium, he told the same joke about his own humiliating poll numbers that he had recounted at his last half-dozen American appearances, and his speech, too, was recycled from his Harvard apologia. Still, in that monument to a president who had helped make the world a more hospitable place for U.S. mass culture, so many skeins from Mulroney's nine years in power seemed to mesh.

Applauding from a front-row seat was Jimmy Pattison, the one-time Vancouver used-car salesman who had become a millionaire transnational in his own right, a favourite of Reagan's Palm Springs crowd who was just preparing to open a Mexico city branch of his Ripley's Believe It or Not! The sole Canadian on the library's donor lists, Pattison had been cultivated by Paramount's Martin Davis to serve on his board at the very moment its Canadian publishing acquisitions were under review by Mulroney's government.

A discreet note at the bottom of the program gave the nod to another library patron, Sam Bamieh, who had footed the bill for the festivities. Mulroney's aides insisted they had never heard of him. But the previous year, as finance chairman of the California Republican Party, the San Mateo trader had been the second most generous contributor to George Bush's presidential campaign. Had he merely been acting in that capacity as he funded Mulroney's swan song? Or was his gesture linked to another cause that had won him headlines? In 1985 Bamieh had testified before a congressional subcommittee that he had been held under virtual house arrest in Saudi Arabia after declining to act as a U.S. conduit for King Fahd's secret financing of Reagan's freedom fighters. But others among his friends had not been so fastidious about serving as royal cutouts in what became known as the Iran-Contra affair — among them Adnan Khashoggi. During Khashoggi's 1990 New York trial, Bamieh had turned up on the benches of Manhattan's grim federal courthouse to lend his support to the controversial royal courtier who had once been his schoolmate.

Was his patronage a signal that, after years of underwriting Reagan's covert foreign adventures, the Saudis were also expressing their gratitude to Mulroney? Although Bamieh denied that link, he admitted that he had never made the prime minister's acquaintance, nor had he visited Canada or done business there. In fact, he had not even shown up to witness the festivities he had bankrolled. He had agreed to pick up the $25,000 tab out of allegiance to Reagan and his neoconservative agenda, he said, and thus to anyone who had carried that banner abroad. "I've never met Prime Minister

Mulroney," Bamieh confessed over a long-distance line from London, "but I have a deep respect for what he's done up there."

To pad out Mulroney's visit, the Canadian consulate in Los Angeles had tried to drum up appointments for him, only to end up with a busier schedule for his wife. Later in the week, his attempts to drop in on Bush's Houston exile would turn into a fiasco, with the ex-president finally cancelling after two no-shows. The prime minister's spokesman would claim that his Challenger had been prevented from landing by the weather. But the *Toronto Star*'s Linda Diebel would report no visibility problems from the Houston airport, prompting an unusual protest to the paper's editor-in-chief. As John Honderich took a call that had been announced from the Prime Minister's Office, he was startled to discover Bush on the line from Texas, blasting Diebel's story, apparently from notes. Even out of office, the Republicans were rushing to the defence of their chosen ally, rerouting their wrath via Parliament Hill.

But that botched stop left the brief, perfunctory Reagan library ceremony as the only U.S. public show of gratitude to a prime minister who had so lavishly made good on his vow to forge a superb relationship with Washington. He had done so at enormous cost to both the country and his own political career. Was this then all the thanks he had reaped? As he strolled through the memorial with the flashbulbs and TV cameras gone, he looked somehow adrift. Then, catching sight of one stray reporter, he brightened. Ruefully, he admitted the sadness he felt. He seemed to want to chat more, to prolong the moment, but a phalanx of Secret Service agents propelled him forward and away. He had, after all, played out his script, another actor who had fulfilled his appointed part. But the show was over. As a limousine whisked him back down the mountainside for his last restive travels, a crew had already dismantled the dais and the elaborate gold-lettered backdrop that had been set up for the ceremony like some Hollywood stage set. A fickle wind swept the empty library terrace, leaving no trace of his passage.

It would be another year before Brian Mulroney was reported back on the California coast, not as a statesman but as an item in a social column. Attending the wedding of TV game show host Alan Thicke, the boy from Baie Comeau had dusted off his past glories and honoured the guests with a few choruses of "When Irish Eyes Are Smiling."

FOR nearly two years, Canadian voters drifted on a tide of wilful euphoria. They had done it — delivered such a stunning rebuke not only to Mulroney's annointed heir, Kim Campbell, but, in the process, to his entire agenda that they had shattered the Conservative Party into a two-seat curiosity washed up on the margins of Parliament. Gone were the summit extravaganzas of pomp and duets, the cross-border cosiness and hyperbolic dinner toasts pledging an affection that never seemed to bring any respect the morning after in the harsh geopolitical light. After nearly a decade decrying Mulroney's "grovelling" to Washington, Jean Chrétien shrewdly avoided a post-election pilgrimage to the White House. In fact, more than a year after his election, *le p'tit gar* from Shawinigan seemed to be having trouble getting any attention from the big guy from Little Rock at all.

Not that he was alone in his plight. Bill Clinton had devoted exactly four minutes of his Democratic convention speech to foreign policy — a foretaste of his presidency. He would be more than two years into his term before he set foot in Ottawa in the winter of 1995. But after Mulroney's obsessive attentions to the White House, Canadians seemed relieved at his successor's canny wariness of Washington. Still, as time went by, some began to wonder whether he had taken merely a symbolic distance, measured in public rituals and public relations. Increasingly, below the chillier surface, nothing fundamental seemed to have altered. The Liberals may have succeeded the Conservatives, but the White House was still having its way with Ottawa. The parties and styles may have changed, but the policies had stayed the same — or worse, they had brought a further erosion of the country's social safety net and cultural sovereignty.

Chrétien's noisy campaign claims about renegotiating NAFTA had faded the instant he took power. Ironically, it was not Canadian voters who took him to task for his retreat; it was Chilean opponents of that country's entry into an extended NAFTA who greeted him with a protest outside Santiago airport. The leader who had once emotively denounced free trade from the opposition benches suddenly seemed to have turned into its most fervent convert, stumping the globe in an attempt to enlarge NAFTA and drum up new pacts with Europe and Asia. Despite the hysteria fanned by

Bush and Mulroney, the world had not, after all, splintered into closed regional fortresses of commerce; an urgently rammed-through GATT agreement had dispatched that threat. But the imperatives of global trade were proceeding at dizzying speed, and, as the Liberals were finally obliged to admit, even the niceties of human rights were no longer sufficient to hinder their frantic quest for business.

Then an announcement sent the arts community scurrying back to Chrétien's little Red Book of campaign vows. In unequivocal type, he had committed himself to defending culture, specifically the Canadian publishing industry. But on a Friday afternoon in the spring of 1994, Industry Minister John Manley and Finance Minister Paul Martin had quietly issued a joint press release announcing a transaction that shook awake the ghosts of cultural wars past: the government's sale of Ginn Canada back to Paramount. After nearly a decade, the last strand of the Prentice Hall takeover package had finally been tied up by Mulroney's political rivals, who brandished a lame explanation that it was all the fault of a secret deal he had made. Paramount, which had so long protested the government's interference with its global acquisitions agenda, at last had a firm monopoly on the country's textbook industry, where three-quarters of Prentice Hall's college titles are now Canadianizations of texts that had originated in the United States. Generations would henceforth receive their introduction to the world pre-screened through Washington's prism.

But as part of their announcement, Manley and Martin had slipped in a second transaction: they had also rubber-stamped Paramount's takeover of another publisher, Maxwell Macmillan Canada, which could hardly be laid at Mulroney's door. A subsidiary of Robert Maxwell's empire, the publishing house had been chaired by André Bisson, a prominent Quebec Liberal who sat on the board of Paul Desmarais's Power Financial Corporation, and its lawyer had been another party luminary, Trudeau's former cabinet minister Marc Lalonde.

As it turned out, the Liberals had their own ties to Paramount and the U.S. entertainment industry leviathan. And some were old family ties that went back more than three decades. In the late 1950s, Paul Nathanson, the reclusive heir of the Famous Players empire, had arranged for the sale of three Vancouver cinemas to his friend and business partner Paul Martin Sr., whose party was temporarily out of power, as an unemployment insurance policy of sorts. Martin, in turn, had passed on the cinemas to his namesake son, Chrétien's minister of finance, who still maintains direct control over them, collecting rents and a percentage of the net box-office take from Famous Players, Paramount's wholly owned Canadian subsidiary. Other studio ties led directly to Chrétien's political backers — Desmarais and the Bronfmans — who happened to have been Mulroney's backers as well. As those links made clear, politics was no longer about parties but interests. Although the parties had changed, the interests had stayed the same — a select and privileged loop that belied public charades of partisanship.

In a flurry of trumped-up crises and apocalyptic sabre-rattling, Mulroney had handed over the public agenda to those corporate interests with their demands for unfettered global trade — for a world without irksome national restrictions or, eventually, even borders. Under the cover of continental competitiveness, he had sacrificed the few measures that had given the country leverage to protect its resources and institutions against international pressures. But then, that had been the impetus behind the rage for globalization all along — an attempt to defang the regulatory powers not just of Ottawa, but of governments everywhere. Free trade pacts were but way stations on the road to a vast homogenized universe of commerce where multinationals could shift capital and assembly lines to new and ever cheaper labour markets, and even the most remote Mexican village marketplace would peddle the wares of Donald Duck and Mickey Mouse.

Not only had Chrétien not attempted to reverse that trend, but he had appeared hellbent on pushing it further in ways Mulroney had not dared — dismantling the policy cornerstones that had once distinguished Canada from the colossus to the south. From medicare to government support for the arts, the pillars of a communal society that had taken decades to raise were suddenly under the shadow of a remorseless budgetary axe. Harmonization had become the new buzzword as the country's standard of living was pushed steadily downward, the better to meld with its continental neighbour. With such discretion that it seemed an act of stealth, Chrétien had introduced an extraordinary piece of legislation to speed up that bulldozer effect. Allowing industries to circumvent inconvenient regulations in exchange for cosy undertakings to ministers, the bill opened the door to the watering down of federal environmental, health, and safety standards.

But as the delegates to a Toronto trade conference agreed in the spring of 1995, those pressures for an even greater integration of the Canadian and American economies were only beginning. They predicted a day when the seductive lure of lower U.S.-style tax rates and minimal social services would translate into an inevitable political and monetary union. Those scenarios were not the ominous forebodings of irate nationalists, but the ponderings of a handful of familiar free-marketeers, from the BCNI's Tom d'Aquino to Allan Gotlieb, who for years had played Pied Piper for a creeping continentalism.

Lest Chrétien or his successors falter in that course, the global markets were on sentry duty — brandishing recurrent threats against the Canadian dollar. Indeed, in the winter of 1995, before the Liberals' timorous corporate-tailored budget came down, some on Bay Street took perverse delight when the editorial high priests of neoconservative dogma on the *Wall Street Journal* cast an eye over the government's debt and blithely pronounced Canada "an honorary member of the Third World." No matter that the country ranked at the top of the U.N.'s standard of living index, five notches above the United States, whose murder and infant mortality rates put it on a par with some of Africa's most unsavoury dictatorships. As the *Journal* made clear, the markets were not interested in a population's well-being, and it was to their tune that the leaders of nations now danced. In the new world order, the great divide was no longer between ideologies but values — about what mattered in life.

In Canada, as elsewhere, the gap between rich and poor was widening; the wealth and assets of the country were increasingly concentrated in the hands of a few. In the wake of the seismic economic upheaval shaking the global landscape, scholars talked with mounting dread of class warfare — of more Chiapas rebellions and LA riots to come. For the new world order emerging bore a striking resemblance to the old — a throwback to the raw appetites of those nineteenth-century industrialists who so ravaged their societies that they provoked the very social and labour policies now being dismantled.

But at the very moment globalization had become the economic gospel, it came under fire from an unlikely source — a stellar capitalist whose name was inscribed in gold on the Reagan

Presidential Library wall. In an interview with a journalist from *Le Figaro*, later published as a book entitled *The Trap*, James Goldsmith, a Franco-British billionaire of impeccable conservative credentials, took exception to the price that the global marketplace was exacting. From his retirement lair on the Mexican coast, where he had become a devoted environmentalist, Goldsmith pointed out that unrestrained trade might be a boon for corporations, but it was proving notoriously noxious for people. As mining and manufacturing magnates were lighting out in search of ever higher profit margins in Vietnam or Chile, they were importing toxic devastation and disease to developing countries desperate for investment at any price. Meanwhile, they were leaving their own societies decimated, permanently stripped of jobs and crippled by a shrunken tax base. In Western nations, GNP might be steadily rising, Goldsmith argued, but so was despair and social unrest. "We seem to have forgotten the purpose of the economy," he raged. "Prosperity with stability." Unless the brakes were put on globalization, he predicted it would "impoverish and destabilize the industrialized world while at the same time cruelly ravaging the Third World."

But as Goldsmith pointed out, what else could be expected from the captains of transnational industry who owed no allegiance to any land? Their fealty was to their shareholders' dividend cheques, not the commonweal. For nearly a century, Canadians, like Americans and Europeans, had looked to government to protect them against that relentless corporate testosterone. But suddenly governments were abandoning the dreams of their communities for a multinational vocabulary and value system — a mindset that, paradoxically, seemed aimed at putting them out of business. At a time when a strong national vision had never been more sorely needed, the very concept of governance had fallen into disrepute. Even the notion of nationhood itself was under siege, and the latest academic fashion trumpeted Canada's virtues as the first "post-national" nation — in effect, no nation at all.

Increasingly, Canadians were being prodded into questioning the meaning of the country — an exercise in existentialism that was unthinkable south of the border. No chest-thumping American patriot would ever be caught pondering whether the United States was merely an outdated commercial convenience. But in Toronto, the business editor of a leading magazine could blithely announce that her constituency considered Canada an irrelevance. Had the nation been reduced to a sentimental accident of geography? A patchwork of fractious regional tribes? Or had it always been something more — a collective will, even a collective dream, no matter how ill-defined? In the summer of 1995, as the fate of the nation had never seemed more uncertain, that, in the end, may have been Brian Mulroney's most damaging legacy: he had left Canadians with a diminished sense of themselves. They might be slowly becoming more Americanized, more uppity and individualistic, quicker to the barricades or the end of a Maritime fishing pier, fists waving at an interloping European trawler. But in the face of global tides, they found themselves impotent to defend those institutions to which they declared themselves most attached from the rampages of their own leaders.

Nothing quite so cruelly summed up that loss of bearings as the musical ambassador Chrétien had chosen in December 1994 for the hemispheric extravaganza in Miami known as the Summit of the Americas. There, on stage alongside Mexico's Ballet Folklorico, dazzling Brazilian dance troupes, and Liza Minelli belting out "New York! New York!" was not Anne Murray or Bryan Adams, not the Crash Test Dummies or even Céline Dion. No, representing Canada was Paul Anka, the aging Ottawa hit-parader who had long ago taken up residence in California and been reluctantly dragged out to croon the tune that Frank Sinatra had made his signature — and an anthem at both of Ronald Reagan's inaugurations: "My Way."

A
Note on
Sources

This book is the product of years of interviews and reading, either in the course of my Washington assignment for *Maclean's* or for my six-part Atkinson Fellowship series, which ran in the *Toronto Star* in October 1993; since many dates were impossible to retrieve, I have omitted them all. In some cases, those who cooperated did so with a request for anonymity in order to protect their current employment, and I have honoured their concerns. My thanks to those many other interviewees who cooperated with the fact-checking process and to librarians at newspapers across the continent who helped dig out clippings that predated the computer age or were not available on-line. A special thanks to the librarians at the National Press Club in Washington. In the cases where I covered the scenes described, I have not indicated a source.

1 HAIL AND FAREWELL
- p. 2, Canadian content: interview with Webster Phillips
  p. 2, John Gavin: *New York Times*, March 14, 1981
- p. 4, Velcro Man: interviews with summit press

2   THE COLONEL'S BOY

- p. 8, Charley McMillan: interview

  p. 8, Polish joke: Roland Perry, *Hidden Power: The Programming of the President* (New York: Beaufort Books, Inc., 1984), 88

  p. 8, State Department briefing notes for Reagan

- p. 10, Stephen Clarkson: interview

- pp. 11–14, Colonel Robert McCormick: Lloyd Wendt, *Chicago Tribune: The Rise of A Great American Newspaper* (New York: Rand McNally & Company, 1979), 581–82, 587

- p. 12, Ben Mulroney: John Sawatsky, *Mulroney: The Politics of Ambition* (Toronto: Mcfarlane, Walter & Ross, 1992), 5

- p. 13, Second World War: Wendt, *Chicago Tribune*, 602

- p. 14, McMillan interview

3   THE CANDIDATE FROM BIG STEEL

- p. 15, Cliche Commission: Sawatsky, *Mulroney*, 252–261

  p. 15, Bourassa: L. Ian MacDonald, *Mulroney: The Making of the Prime Minister* (Toronto: McClelland & Stewart, 1984), 95–96

- p. 16, Ludlow massacre: H.S. Ferns and Bernard Ostry, *The Age of Mackenzie King* (London: William Heinemann Ltd., 1955), 176, 185–214, 243

- p. 17, King's birthday gift: *Ibid*, 215

  p. 17, David Rockefeller visit to King: Peter Collier and David Horowitz, *The Rockefellers: An American Dynasty* (New York: Holt, Rinehart and Winston, 1976), 223

  p. 17, Bourassa to Chase Manhattan: Sean McCutcheon, *Electric Rivers: The Story of the James Bay Project* (Montreal: Black Rose Books, 1991), 20

- p. 18, James Bay hearings: Matthew Fraser, *Quebec Inc.* (Toronto: Key Porter Books, 1987) 174–77

  p. 18, Iron Ore strike: L. Ian MacDonald, *Mulroney: The Making of the Prime Minister*, 114–15

- p. 19, Bennett, Ruby Foo's: *Ibid*, 114

  p. 19, Robert Anderson: interview with author

- pp. 20–25, Marcus Alonzo Hanna and M.A. Hanna Company: Richard Geren and Blake McCullogh, *Cain's Legacy: The Building of the Iron Ore Company of Canada* (Montreal: Iron Ore Co., ND)

- p. 24, Turner, Reisman: *Ibid*, 304–05

- p. 25, leadership bid: Sawatsky, *Mulroney*, 262, 284, 324

  p. 25, Iron Ore contract: L. Ian MacDonald, *Mulroney*, 115–16

- p. 26, Belvedere Road house: Claire Hoy, *Friends in High Places* (Toronto: Key Porter Books, 1987), 72
- p. 27, Iron Ore: interviews with Richard Geren, Robert Anderson
  p. 27, Brazil coup: Kai Bird, *The Chairman: John J. McCloy, The Making of the American Establishment* (New York: Simon & Shuster, 1992), 550–53
- p. 28, Desmarais: interview with L. Ian MacDonald
- p. 29, helicopter contract: interview with former Iron Ore employee
  p. 29, MacAdam, Moores: Sawatsky, *Mulroney: The Politics of Ambition*, 395, 404
- p. 30, profits, Schefferville closing: *Ibid*, 414–20
- p. 31, "jam in the sandwich": Conrad Black, *A Life in Progress* (Toronto: Key Porter, 1993), 299
- p. 32, American Iron and Steel Institute: *Toronto Star*, April 26, 1984

4   TIES THAT BIND
- p. 33, Richard Wirthlin: interview with author
- p. 34, clandestine rendezvous: Perry, *Hidden Power*, 2,6, 12, 13
- p. 36, Tory approach: interview with Wirthlin, Rich Willis
- p. 37, campaign techniques: interview with John Laschinger, Paul Curley
- p. 41, pollster's job: Stevie Cameron, "The Black Arts of Canadian Politics," *Globe and Mail*, October 19, 1992
- p. 41, lampoon: *Globe and Mail*, December 18, 1993
- pp. 43–50, media management operation: interview with Bill Fox
- pp. 43–44, Deaver: Mark Hertsgaard, *On Bended Knee: The Press and the Reagan Presidency* (New York: Farrar Straus Giroux, 1988), 52
- p. 46, manufactured quotes: Larry Speakes, *Speaking Out: The Reagan Presidency from Inside the White House* (New York: Charles Scribner Sons, 1988), 136
- p. 47, coveted space: *Washington Post*, June 22, 1984
  p. 47, Fox: interview with Patrick Gossage; also Gossage's *Close to the Charisma: My Years Between the Press and Pierre Elliott Trudeau* (Toronto: McClelland & Stewart, 1986), 267
- p. 48, Linda Diebel: *Toronto Star*, March 23, 1992
- p. 50, "Tell Carl": interview with Carl Mollins
  p. 50, Paley: Michael K. Deaver, *Behind the Scenes* (New York: William Morrow & Co., 1987), 149

- p. 50, Joe O'Donnell: Hoy, *Friends in High Places*, 211
- p. 51, Hail to the Chief: Michel Gratton, *"So What Are The Boys Saying?": An Inside Look at Brian Mulroney in Power* (Toronto: McGraw Hill Ryerson Ltd., 1987), 65
  p. 51, protestors: *Globe and Mail*, April 6, 1987
- p. 52, leaked memo: Glen Williams, "Symbols, Economic Logic and Political Conflict in the Canada–U.S.A. Free Trade Negotiations," *Queen's Quarterly*, Vol. 92, Winter 1985, 659
- p. 53, NAFTA strategy: "The NAFTA Tapes," *Maclean's*, September 21, 1992
  p. 53, Allan Gregg: *Maclean's*, January 7, 1991

5 CLEARING THE AIR
- p. 55, Russ Wunker: interview
- pp. 55–61, John Gamble: interview
- pp. 57–61, World Anti-Communist League: Jon Lee and Scott Anderson, *Inside The League* (New York: Dodd, Mead & Company, 1986), 52–59, 108
- pp. 57–58, ABN: interview with Orest Steciw
- pp. 58–61, interview with Major General John Singlaub; also his *Hazardous Duty: An American Soldier in the Twentieth Century* (New York: Summit Books, 1991)
- p. 59, Canadian chapter: Lee and Anderson, *Inside the League*, 154
- pp. 61–63, Dump Clark: interviews with John Morrison and Gord Jackson
- p. 62, Siebens: Peter Newman, *The Acquisitors* (Toronto: Seal Books, 1982), 389; also Fraser Institute 1991 Annual Report
- pp. 63–64, Republican: interview with Russ Wunker
- p. 64, Peter Puck: interviews with Peter Pocklington and Michael Adams
- p. 65, Haig/ Pratt and Whitney/ Davis: interview with Woody Goldberg of Worldwide Associates
- p. 66, Amway: interviews with Gamble, Pocklington
- pp. 67–69, Richard Allen: interviews with Allen, Michael Adams, Russ Wunker, Charley McMillan
- pp. 69–70, Ross Johnson/Dwayne Andreas: Bryan Burroughs, *Barbarians at the Gate* (New York: HarperPerennial, 1991), 12–29, 83, 371–72
- p. 72, Pied Piper: *New York Times*, December 11, 1984

- p. 72, love-in: Peter C. Newman, "A Dazzling Debut in New York," *Maclean's*, December 24, 1984, 38

6 GODFATHERS

- p. 74, godfather: interviews with Paul Robinson; *Chicago Tribune*, September 9, 1985
- p. 75, "Shove off"/intentionally: *New York Times*, May 27, 1982
- pp. lid: Christina McCall and Stephen Clarkson, "The Unquiet American," *Saturday Night*, November 1984, 9
- p. 77, Hilton: interview with Robinson
- pp. 78–80, North American Accord: interviews with Richard Allen, Myer Rashish
- pp. 79–80, meeting Mulroney: interview with Robinson
  p. 79, Duncan Edmonds: Lawrence Martin, *Pledge of Allegiance* (Toronto: McClelland & Stewart, 1993), 12, 13, 17
- pp. 80–83, visitor: interviews with Robinson and Tom d'Aquino
- p. 85, teach a lesson/Superbowl: interviews with Bill Merkin
- p. 86, lapdog: McCall and Clarkson, "The Unquiet American," 10
- p. 87, Third Option/review: interview with Derek Burney
- p. 89, vigilant: interview with Robinson
  p. 89, adjective lost: interview with Bill Fox
- p. 90, leap of faith: *Globe and Mail*, November 19, 1984
- p. 91, dread phrase/Brock: interview with Burney
- p. 92, Evil Empire: interview with Fulbright Fellowship trustees in Chicago

7 SINGING IN THE ACID RAIN

- pp. 96–97, Reagan hostile: Lou Cannon, *President Reagan: The Role of a Lifetime* (New York: Simon & Shuster, 1991), 527–34
- p. 96, Larry Speakes: White House briefing
- p. 97, killer trees: Perry, *Hidden Power*, 128
  p. 97, Ruckelshaus/Don: interview with former EPA staffer
- p. 98, artists in politics: Fred Doucet summit briefing
  pp. 98–99, Linda Robinson: John Greenwald, "Power Marriage Has Its Privileges," *Time*, October 21, 1991; Anthony Bianco, "A Powerhouse in Her Own Right," *Business Week*, January 25, 1988; also interviews with former envoy staff
- p. 100, procrastination: Rosemary Speirs, *Out of the Blue: The Fall of the Tory Dynasty in Ontario* (Toronto: Macmillan of Canada, 1986), 5

- pp. 101–9, coalition/John Fraser: interviews with Adèle Hurley and Michael Perley
- p. 102, step-by-step strategy: interview with Moorman, speech
- p. 107, propaganda: Fred Blazer, "Distrust Across the Border," *Maclean's*, March 7, 1983
- p. 109, Rouyn smelter: *Toronto Star*, June 1, 1984
- p. 110, Philippe de Gaspé Beaubien: interview with Jeffrey Shearer
- p. 111, Springfield, Mass.: interview with former Davis aide; *New York Times*, September 14, 1985
- p. 112, report: Joint Report of the Special Envoys on Acid Rain, January 1986; *New York Times*, January 8, 1986
- p. 113, horns-waggled: *Globe and Mail*, January 9, 1986
- pp. 113–14, Davis's $1: *Globe and Mail*, September 13, 1985
- pp. 114–15, hurry: *New York Times*, January 14, 1986
- p. 115, New York Board of Trade: Tom McMillan speech, January 22, 1986
- pp. 115–16, not endorse: *Washington Post*, April 4, 1987; Rep. Gerry Sikorski (D-Minn.), "How Mulroney Should Handle the Summit," *Toronto Star*, March 1987
  pp. 115–16, "a prom": Ian Austen, "A Tough Debate on Acid Rain," *Maclean's*, March 24, 1986
- p. 116, On Golden Pond: interview with L. Ian MacDonald
- pp. 117–18, alcoholism: *Washington Post*, November 17, 1987
- p. 118, Rep. Thomas Luken/David Hawkins: Ian Austen, "The Deaver Connection," *Maclean's*, May 12, 1986
  p. 118, Citizens for Sensible Control: U.S. Justice Department, Foreign Agent Registration
- p. 119, Metropark: *New York Times* and *Washington Post*, September 1, 1988
- p. 120, outcome uncertain: Trip Gabriel, "Greening the White House," *New York Times Magazine*, August 13, 1989
- p. 121, trades: *New York Times*, May 13, 1992, and February 6, 1993; *The Nation*, June 6, 1994
  p. 121, applauding/"over for us": interview with Hurley; she was appointed to the Ontario Hydro board May 1991 for a three-year term and reappointed May 1994
- p. 122, "Who stopped?": Perley to author
  p. 122, Quayle/Waxman: *New York Times*, November 19, 1991; June 26, 1992, and November 26, 1992; also Henry Waxman, "The Environmental Pollution President," *New York Times*, April 29, 1992

8   *STANDING ON GUARD FOR THEE*

- p. 126, White House miffed: Larry Speakes, *Speaking Out*, 79–80
- p. 127, unease over deterrence: interview with Charles Doran
- p. 128, too late: interview with William Arkin

  p. 128, "damn presumptuous": interview with retired Admiral Robert Falls
- p. 128, Arkin: William M. Arkin and Richard W. Fieldhouse, *Nuclear Battlefields: Global Links in the Arms Race* (Cambridge: Ballinger Publishing Company, 1985)
- p. 129, defence against help: interview with Ernie Regehr, Project Ploughshares

  p. 129, ticket to the big-time: interview with Joseph Jockel
- p. 130, General Electric/"so won't be excluded": *Wall Street Journal*, October 5, 1983
- p. 132, pipsqueak: interview with George Bader
- p. 134, Vietnam: Victor Levant, *Quiet Complicity: Canadian Involvment in the Vietnam War* (Toronto: Between the Lines, 1986), 5, 54–60
- p. 135, Pentagon mission: *Globe and Mail*, December 5, 15, 1984; *Maclean's*, December 17, 1984
- pp. 136–38, Mobilization: interview with retired Brigadier General William Yost
- p. 137, FEMA: Ben Bradlee Jr., Guts and Glory: *The Rise and Fall of Oliver North* (New York: Donald I. Fine, Inc., 1988), 129–35

  p. 137, Guiffrida's guest: interview with Yost
- p. 138, remarkable year: *Canadian Defence Review Bulletin*, December 1987
- p. 139, Newman/cruise: interview with former BCNI researcher

  p. 139, "smell a rat": Peter C. Newman, *True North: Not Strong and Free* (Toronto: McClelland and Stewart, 1983), 110, 113
- p. 141, Manson: *Globe and Mail*, September 8, 1992

  p. 141, Edgar Dosman, "The Steady Drummer," *How Ottawa Spends 1988/89*, ed., Katherine A. Graham (Ottawa: Carleton University Press, 1988), 165–94

  p. 141, preliminary report: Beth L. Thomas, "The Environment for Expanding the North American Defence Industrial Base," June 19, 1987
- p. 142, striking similarity: interview with David Langille
- p. 144, U.S. Navy: *Globe and Mail*, January 4, 1990

p. 144, wrong kind of war: interview with Howard Peter Langille; and his *Changing the Guard: Canada's Defence in a World in Transition* (Toronto: University of Toronto Press, 1990)

- p. 145, "hook, line": *Maclean's*, August 27, 1990; Canadian Press, August 29, 1990; *Washington Post*, August 29, 1990

  p. 145, a criminal: *Toronto Star* August 11, 1990

  p. 145, support of U.N.: Southam News Service, January 15, 1991

  p. 145, Bush's family: Seymour M. Hersh, "The Spoils of the Gulf War," *New Yorker*, September 6, 1993, 70

- p. 146, investments: *Globe and Mail*, August 3, 1990

  p. 146, Criminal Code: interviews with Ernie Regehr and Mary Collins

- p. 148, moral authority: *Montreal Gazette*, January 16, 1991

  p. 148, offensive footing: interviews with Mary Collins, General Charles Horner and other U.S. officers

- p. 152, cover story: interview with former NORAD officer, Major-General James O'Blenis

- p. 153, threat: made to author by embassy press official

  p. 153, caution flag: interview with retired Lieut.-General Robert Morton

  p. 153, U.S. eyes only: interview with former embassy military attache

- p. 154, despite $1.1 billion: *Washington Post*, September 16, 1993

  p. 154, hemispheric security: interview with retired Col. Sam Watson

- p. 155, Ballistic Missile Defense: interviews with General Charles Horner, General Timothy Gill

- p. 156, encouraging reply: interview with Lieut.-General Brian Smith

9 SHOWBIZ, INC.

- p. 158, book industry's chief lobbyist: interview with Nicholas Veliotes
- p. 159, in Cairo: *Washington Post*, October 11, 1985, and January 8, 1986
- p. 160, $850,000: *Business Week*, February 13, 1995
- p. 161, Nye, Kristol: American Enterprise Institute Conference, "The New Global Popular Culture: Is It American? Is It Good for America? Is It Good for the World?," March 10, 1992

  p. 161, Jack Lang: *International Herald Tribune*, September 28, 1982

  p. 161, "Tinseltown's Trade War," *National Journal*, February 23, 1991

- p. 162 Baie Comeau: interview with Marcel Masse
- p. 163, bookends: interview with Charley McMillan
- p. 165, *Time*'s Distinguished Speakers Program: *Toronto Star* and *Globe and Mail*, December 5, 1985

- p. 166, Walter Annenberg: Dan Moldea, *Dark Victory: Ronald Reagan, MCA and the Mob* (New York: Viking, 1986), 84–85
- p. 167, Walter Annenberg: "Canada's Unfairness Doctrine," *TV Guide*, November 7, 1981
- pp. 169–71, Hollywood, Inc.: Dan Moldea, *Dark Victory*, 1
- pp. 170–72, Wasserman: Ronald Brownstein, *The Power and the Glitter: The Hollywood-Washington Connection* (New York: Vintage Books, 1992)
- p. 176, Jeremy Kinsman: interview
- p. 177, new wrinkle: Veliotes interview
- p. 181, Donald Oresman: Bryan Burrough, "The Siege of Paramount," *Vanity Fair*, February 1994, 65
  p. 181, hot button: interview with Peter Murphy
- p. 182, Adolf Zukor: Manjunath Pendakur, *Canadian Dreams & American Control: The Political Economy of the Canadian Film Industry* (Toronto: Garamund Press, 1990), 53–63
  p. 182, Chretien squelched: Ibid, 166
- p. 183, did not budge: interview with Harold Greenberg
- p. 185, Canadian lieutenant: interview with Garth Drabinsky
- p. 188, Valenti's clout: interview with Flora MacDonald
  pp. 188–90, Valenti deal: interview with Peter Murphy; *Inside U.S. Trade*, October 9, 1987
- p. 191, abruptly surfaced: External memorandum
- p. 192, Wilson: *Toronto Star*, July 6, 1991
- p. 193, Roy Norton: External memorandum
- p. 194, bargained away: interview with Paul Audley, Marcel Masse
- p. 195, support withered: Masse interview
  pp. 195–96, George Bush: Joe David Bellamy, "On Pens and $words," *The Nation*, November 30, 1992, 668
- p. 197, Segal tours: *Globe and Mail*, February 9, 1985
- p. 199, a trade issue: interview with Jim Robinson
  p. 199, frog: Masse interview

10 *LET'S MAKE A DEAL*
- p. 200, he sat uneasily: Murphy interview
- p. 201, Reisman: Linda McQuaig, *The Quick and the Dead: Brian Mulroney, Big Business and the Seduction of Canada* (Toronto: Penguin Books, 1991), 6

- p. 201, James Baker, "The Geopolitical Implications of the U.S.–Canada Trade Pact," *The International Economy*, January/February 1988
- p. 203, high-profile booster: Rod McQueen, "Canada Warms Up to U.S. Business," *Fortune*, March 4, 1985
- p. 204, Peter's basic premise: Merkin interview
- p. 207, bring in the private sector: interview with Senator James Kelleher
- p. 209, Pratt at White House: *Washington Post*, March 19, 1986
- p. 210, joke: *Montreal Gazette*, September 24, 1991
- p. 211, Bush and Eli Lilly: Alexander Cockburn, "Paradigms of Power: The Case of Eli Lilly," *The Nation*, December 7, 1992, 690; Jim Hogshire, "It's a great day to be a drug manufacturer, *The Bloomington Voice*, September 30, 1992, 8
- p. 212, "barely acceptable:" *Globe and Mail*, August 13, 1987
  p. 212, Yes campaign: Andrew Cohen, "The Politics of Money in the Yes Campaign," *Financial Post*, April 23, 1933
- p. 214, odd day: McQuaig, *The Quick and the Dead*, 207–11
- p. 215, under wraps: interview with Harry Freeman
- p. 217, timing: interview with Myer Rashish
- p. 218, like a rock star: *Journal of Commerce*, October 21, 1994
- p. 219, Fred Jones Hall: interview with author and Ian Austen of Maclean's
- p. 221, Baker and Chemical Bank: *Washington Post*, February 15, 1989
  p. 221, Drew Lewis: Murphy interview
- p. 222, Gotlieb: Ritchie letter to Prof. Bruce Doern, November 2, 1990, provided to author by Gordon Ritchie; interview with Ritchie
- p. 223, Carney files: *Globe and Mail*, November 1, 1991
- p. 225, no exemption: Merkin interview
  p. 225, Ritchie: *Globe and Mail*, December 17, 1991; Reisman: *Vancouver Sun*, January 19, 1992
- p. 227, locked in: State Department briefing memo for President George Bush, 1989

11   PARTYING TO WIN

- p. 229, Slap Flap: *Washington Post*, March 21, 1986
- p. 230, gorgeous sight/Donaldson: *Canada Today/d'aujourd'hui*, Summit '86, Vol. 17, No. 2
  p. 230, another dinner: interview with Connie Connor
- p. 231, Strauss: in the presence of author

p. 231, furious: Michel Gratton, *"So What Are the Boys Saying?,"* 162–66

p. 231, A Big Chill for Canada?: *Washington Post*, May 12, 1986

- p. 232, Nini Pike: Sondra Gotlieb, *First Lady, Last Lady* (Toronto: McClelland & Stewart, 1981), 191

  p. 232, "You pissed . . .": Lawrence Martin, *The Presidents and The Prime Ministers* (Markham: Paperjacks, 1983), 2

  pp. 232–33, Allan Gotlieb, "The United States in Canadian Foreign Policy," O. D. Skelton Memorial Lecture, December 10, 1991

- p. 233, power centres: interview with Elaine Dewar
- p. 235, first slap: interview with Elizabeth Gray
- p. 237, Safire: interview with Rashish
- p. 238, balked: interview with Sondra Gotlieb
- p. 240, gossip is power: *Washingtonian*, December 1988
- p. 242, excess of zeal: interview with Bill Fox
- pp. 244–46, Robert Gray: Susan B. Trento, *The Power House: Robert Keith Gray and the Selling of Access and Influence in Washington* (New York: St. Martin's Press, 1992)
- p. 246, snowbound: interview with Peter Segall
- p. 249, quite so brazen: *Time*, March 3, 1986

  p. 249, Phillips: conversation with author

- p. 253, failed to cooperate: *Executive Branch Lobbying: Report to Congress By Independent Counsel in the Michael Deaver Case*, 28

  p. 253, Baker: *Maclean's*, December 12, 1988

- p. 254, Mulroney thanked: *London Free Press*, November 16, 1988

  p. 254, Margaret Atwood: *Globe and Mail*, November 22, 1988

  p. 254, Timothy Findley: *Globe and Mail*, November 19, 1988

- p. 255, Heather Robertson, *Canadian Forum*, April 1990

  p. 255, June Callwood: *Globe and Mail*, November 28, 1990

12 THE CANADIAN CONNECTION

- p. 258, president weakened: Gotlieb briefing

  p. 258, Robert Gray: Khashoggi's apartment phone logs submitted as evidence during his New York trial with Imelda Marcos

- p. 259, Salt Lake investors: *Wall Street Journal*, December 12, 1986
- p. 260, biographer: Ronald Kessler, *The Richest Man in the World: The Story of Adnan Khashoggi* (New York: Warner Books, 1986)

  p. 260, *Al Shiraa*: a pro-Iranian weekly published in Beirut, November 2, 1986

p. 260, Charles Allen notes: declassified by the CIA and available through the National Security Archives, Washington, D.C.

- pp. 260–63, Oussama Lababedi: Allen notes; interview with his brother-in-law Amin Bohsali in Houston
- p. 262, long cooperation with CIA: James Littleton, *Target Nation: Canada and the Western Intelligence Network* (Toronto: Lester & Orpen Dennys/CBC Enterprises, 1986)

  p. 262, Rauh letter: dated April 8, 1986; released to author April 15, 1986

  p. 262, Furmart/Furbank: author transcript of briefing
- pp. 263–64, John Shaheen: interview with Roy Furmark; *I Chose Canada: The Memoirs of the Honourable Joseph R. "Joey" Smallwood* (Toronto: Macmillan, 1973), 364–514; also U.S. National Archives on Office of Strategic Services
- p. 264, extravagant affair: St. John *Evening Telegram*, October 10–12, 1973
- p. 265, Khashoggi/Shaheen: interview with former Khashoggi aide
- p. 266, The Eagle: Michael A. Ledeen, *Perilous Statecraft: An Insider's Account of the Iran-Contra Affair* (New York: Charles Scribner's Sons, 1988), 105; Samuel Segev, *The Iranian Triangle: The Untold Story of Israel's Role in the Iran-Contra Affair* (New York: The Free Press, 1988), 14

  p. 266, Machiavellian plot: Shaheen affidavit sworn in New York for the Supreme Court of Newfoundland, February 16, 1976
- p. 267, Cyrus Hashemi: memo from William Casey to his Chief, Near East Division, in the CIA operations directorate June 16, 1985
- pp. 267–68, Shaheen/Moores: interview with Bob Fife; PetroCanada archives
- pp. 268–76, Khashoggi's Toronto trip: interviews with Timothy Khan, Bob and Patricia Shaheen, Larry Keach, Frank Miller, Leslie Shimmon, former Lieut.-Governor John Black Aird, Joe Barnicke, Christopher Trump, Leonard Lugsdin; guest lists, telexes, and Ontario government itinerary and video
- pp. 272–74, Munk/Gilmour: author interviews for profile "The Return of Peter Munk," *Financial Post Magazine*, June 1977, 6
- p. 272, Barrick history: John P. Vizard, Trustee for Oasis Petroleum Corporation vs. Finn Moller, Essam Khashoggi, Adnan Khashoggi, Triad International Corp., etc. United States Bankruptcy Court, Central District of California, Chapter 11 Case No. LA 86-01225-BR

- p. 273, Kamal Adham: *Financial Times of Canada*, May 2, 1983
- p. 274, Timothy Khan: Robert Collison, "The Khashoggi Connection," *Toronto*, April 1986, 52
- p. 275, Contra letter: on Akhana letterhead, April 3, 1986; *Washington Times*, March 19, 1987, 1
- p. 276, Chuck Tyson: interview with author
  p. 276, Canadians sell arms too: *Ottawa Citizen*, October 19, 1984
- pp. 277–78, swami: interviews with Steve Martindale, Adnan Khashoggi, and Mervyn Dymally; Dymally's 1981 financial disclosure form
- p. 279, Vertex/Sarsvati: interviews with Emanuel Floor and John Gamble; Triad bankruptcy documents recording loans; Floor deposition to the *Iran-Contra Investigations Appendix B*, Volume 10
- pp. 279–80, Fraser/Gamble: interview with Gamble, Fraser, John Morrison; *Globe and Mail*, December 17, 1986; *New York Times*, December 19, 1986; incorporation papers for Vertex Investments Ltd., begun as Sarsvat Inc., August 13, 1981, Companies Branch, Ontario department of Consumer and Corporate Affairs
- p. 280, Singlaub: interview; also interviews with Witer, Blenkarn; program for Campaign Freedom 20–22, 1986, Holiday Inn, Toronto
- p. 281, Lababedi: interview with Bohsali
  p. 281, Lundrigan: press release from Caribbean Resources, June 12, 1987
  p. 281, Lawrence Walsh: Final Report of the Independent Counsel for Iran/Contra Matters, Vol. I, August 4, 1993, 169
- pp. 281–82, swami: Marci McDonald, "Of Guns and Gurus," *Maclean's*, March 27, 1989, 28
- p. 282, McLean: author summoned to Markham Suites hotel; interview with George D. McLean; guilty plea of Donovan Blakeman and interview; St. John's *Evening Telegram*, January 9, 10, and March 27, April 9, 1973
- p. 283, Munk denied Adnan: Kevin Scanlon, "Tracking the Elusive Partners," *Maclean's*, December 22, 1986
  p. 283, Horsham: Information Circular, United Siscoe Mines, November 26, 1986; Coliton documents
- p. 284, legal bills: James Linn interview; interview with Jerry Dale Allen; Marci McDonald, "A Nose for Opportunities," *Maclean's*, July 26, 1990, 26

- p. 285, Trans World Arms: Marci McDonald with Dan Burke, "The Canada Connection," *Maclean's*, August 3, 1987, 22; *New York Times, December 28, 1994*
  p. 285, Waddell: *Maclean's*, August 3, 1987, 22
- p. 286, Mulroney fees: 1994 annual reports of American Barrick Resources Corporation (now Barrick Gold) and Horsham Corp.

13 SPIN CONTROL

- p. 288, Ross Johnson: Rod McQueen, *Financial Post*, December 20, 1991
- p. 289, Willie Horton: conversation with Ney
- p. 290, brand name: *Marketing*, May 14, 1990, 2
- p. 291, Ney history: Hilary MacKenzie, "Men of Credentials," *Maclean's*, July 3, 1989, 62
- p. 292, Jamaica: *New York Times*, October 6, 1989; February 1990; August 30, 1991
  p. 292, Goodis: *Globe and Mail*, May 11, 1989
- p. 293, Walshe: *Globe and Mail*, June 5, 1993
  p. 293, Bremner: *Globe and Mail*, January 21, 1988
- p. 294, test ban/pretension: *Marketing*, May 14, 1990
  p. 294, mission: Charlotte Gray, "Inside Diplomacy," *Saturday Night*, November 1989, 15
- pp. 294–95, Time/Young and Rubicam: Y&R had been *Time's* agency since 1939
- p. 295, Grunwald: interview with Tom d'Aquino
- p. 296, plot: Lawrence Martin, *Pledge of Allegiance*, 241
- p. 297, think tanks: Eric Alterman, *Sound and Fury: the Washington Punditocracy and the Collapse of American Politics* (New York: HarperPerennial, 1992), 79
- p. 298, Sir Antony Fisher: interviews with Michael Walker and Sally Pipes
- p. 300, Malling: Linda McQuaig, *Shooting the Hippo: Death by Deficit and Other Canadian Myths* (Toronto: Viking, 1995)
- p. 301, thought control: interview with Axworthy
  p. 301, Ney: Lawrence Martin, *Pledge of Allegiance*, 241
  p. 301, fact of life: *Montreal Gazette*, June 29, 1992
- pp. 304–09, *Vancouver Sun*, August 10, 1991; Joyce Nelson, "Green Washing," *Canadian Forum*, July/August 1994; Nelson, "Dr. Rockefeller Will See You Now," *Canadian Forum*, January/February 1995

- p. 304, *Propaganda* and Gautemala: Stephen Kinzer and Stephen Schlesinger, *Bitter Fruit* (New York: Anchor Books, 1982), 80–90
- p. 311, Skydome Summits: Ross Laver, "Ball Park Diplomacy," *Maclean's*, April 23, 1990; Maclean's, July 22, 1991
- p. 311–15, magazine industry: interviews with Catherine Keachie; Warrillow: *Masthead*, September 1988, 5
- p. 315, ownership: James Winter and Amir Hassanpour, "Building Babel," *Canadian Forum*, January/February 1994
- p. 316, Bush interview: *Maclean's*, June 25, 1990, 57
- p. 317, self-censorship: *Toronto Star*, October 20, 1984
  p. 317, Squires: *Globe and Mail*, February 20, 1993
  p. 317, James P. Winter, ed., *The Silent Revolution: Media, Democracy and the Free Trade Debate* (Ottawa: University of Ottawa Press, 1990)
- p. 318, propaganda: Vernon A. Walters, "The Uses of Political and Propaganda Covert Action in the 1980s," *Intelligence Requirements for the 1980s*, ed., Roy Godson, Number Four, National Strategy Information Center, Inc., 1981, 115
  p. 318, Allen Neuharth: *Window on the World Faces, Places and Plain Talk From 32 Countries* (Washington, D.C.: Gannett New Media Services Inc., 1988); Freedom Forum IRS Filings 990-PF, May 31, 1994

14 GOING LATIN

- p. 320, Bolívar statue: *Ottawa Citizen* August 4, 5, 9, 1988; September 8, 1988; October 12, 1988
- p. 321, *Le Figaro: Toronto Star*, November 16, 1988
- p. 323, Kennan: Noam Chomsky, *What Uncle Sam Really Wants*, (Berkeley: Odonian Press, 1986–1992), 10–11
- p. 324, Manifest Destiny/Woodrow Wilson: James Chase, *Endless War* (New York: Vintage Books, 1984), 37
  p. 324, M.A. Hanna: Kai Bird, *The Chairman*, 550–53
- p. 325, Celso Ming: Anthony Sampson, *The Money Lenders* (London: Hodder and Stoughton, 1981), 253
- p. 326, tariffs: interview with Colleen Morton
- p. 327, unpublicized revolution: David Mulford, "Improved Investment Climate in Latin America and the Caribbean", *Washington Report*, Winter 1992, 22
- p. 327, loony left: "The Nafta Tapes, *Maclean's*, September 21, 1992
- p. 329, economic integration: interview with Stephen Blank

- p. 330, Tim Bennett: *The Trading Game: Inside Lobbying for the North American Free Trade Agreement* (Washington: The Centre for Public Integrity, 1993), 95
- p. 331, would not be scandalized: Canadian Press, March 3, 1990
- pp. 331–32, Brock: *The Trading Game*
- p. 332, USA*NAFTA: interview with Harry Freeman
- p. 333, External Review: interview with Richard Gorham
- p. 336, Fred Blaser: *Mexi-Canada Bulletin*, May 1993
  p. 336, falsely inflated: *Globe and Mail*, September 16, 1992; *London Free Press*, September 22, 1992
- p. 337, Noranda in Chile: Bonnie Green, ed., *Canadian Churches and Foreign Policy* (Toronto: James Lorimer & Company, 1990), 109–13
- p. 338, Peter Lougheed: covering letter to Prime Minister Brian Mulroney as chairman of Canada-Japan Forum 2000, Dec. 1, 1992
- p. 339, Alamo: *Toronto Star*, October 8, 1992
- p. 340, Cairn memo/CIDA: Southam News, April 11, 1993; March 31, 1993 hearings on Development and Human Rights by the Standing Committee on External Affairs
- pp. 341–42, poll: *Canada and the World: An International Perspective on Canada and Canadians* (Winnipeg: Angus Reid Group, 1992), 89
- p. 343, Canadian affairs: interview with Stephen Blank
- p. 344, Pan American medal: *Globe and Mail*, March 29, 1988; *Washington Report*, Winter 1992, 29–34
  p. 344, David Rockefeller, *Wall Street Journal*, October 1, 1993
- p. 345, Joseph Verner Reed: *New York Times Magazine*, June 10, 1990
- p. 349, Mulroney: Canadian Press, March 24, 1994
- p. 352, MP Bob Mills: interview with Warren Caragata, *Maclean's*, January 16, 1995
  p. 352, Bolívar: Jerome R. Adams, *Latin American Heroes* (New York: Ballantine Books, 1991), 39

15 PLUS ÇA CHANGE
- p. 355, Willy Loman: Conrad Black, *A Life in Progress*, 506–07,
- p. 356, Jenkins: *Toronto Star*, January 13, 1993; *Baltimore Sun*, August 11, 1992
- p. 358, Paramount board: Jimmy Pattison with Paul Grescoe, *Jimmy: An Autobiography* (Toronto: Seal Books, 1989), 15
  p. 358, Sam Bamieh: interview; Hearing before the Subcommittee on Africa of the House Committee on Foreign Affairs July 1, 1987

- p. 359, Bush blast: interview with John Honderich
  p. 359, Thicke: *In Style*, October 1994; *Toronto Star*, October 9, 1994
- p. 360, Chilean protest: *Toronto Star*, January 25, 1995
- p. 361, human rights: *Globe and Mail*, May 16, 1995
  pp. 361–62, Paul Martin/Paramount: interview with Maurice Strong; Paul Martin Jr.'s financial disclosure statement; Marci McDonald, "The Paramount Connection," *Maclean's*, April 25, 1994, 17
- p. 362, other studio ties: Desmarais owned a stake in Time Warner Inc.; in 1995 the Bronfmans' bought MCA Inc.
- p. 363, economic integration: *Toronto Star, May 31, 1995*
- p. 364, Sir James Goldsmith: *The Trap* (New York: Carroll and Graf Publishers Inc., 1993), 25

Index